HERO-TALES
OF
IRELAND

JEREMIAH CURTIN

DOVER PUBLICATIONS, INC.
Mineola, New York

Published in Canada by General Publishing Company, Ltd., 30 Lesmill Road, Don Mills, Toronto, Ontario.

Bibliographical Note

This Dover edition, first published in 1999, is an unabridged and unaltered republication of the work originally published by Macmillan and Co., London, in 1894.

Library of Congress Cataloging-in-Publication Data

Curtin, Jeremiah, 1835–1906.
  Hero-tales of Ireland / Jeremiah Curtin.
    p. cm.
  Originally published: London : Macmillan, 1894.
  ISBN 0-486-40909-0 (pbk.)
    1. Tales—Ireland. I. Title.

GR153.5 .C8 1999
398.2'09417'02—dc21   99-045379

Manufactured in the United States of America
Dover Publications, Inc., 31 East 2nd Street, Mineola, N.Y. 11501

CONTENTS.

INTRODUCTION.

———•———

THE tales included in this volume, though told in modern speech, relate to heroes and adventures of an ancient time, and contain elements peculiar to early ages of story-telling. The chief actors in most of them are represented as men; but we may be quite sure that these men are substitutes for heroes who were not considered human when the stories were told to Keltic audiences originally. To make the position of these Gaelic tales clear, it is best to explain, first of all, what an ancient tale is; and to do this we must turn to uncivilized men who possess such tales yet in their primitive integrity.

We have now in North America a number of groups of tales obtained from the Indians which, when considered together, illustrate and supplement one another; they constitute, in fact, a whole system. These tales we may describe as forming collectively the Creation myth of the New World. Since the primitive tribes of North America have not emerged yet from the Stone Age of development, their tales are complete and in good preservation. In some cases simple and transparent, it is not difficult to recognize the heroes; they are distinguishable at once either by their names or their actions or both. In other cases these tales are more involved, and the heroes are not so easily known, because they are concealed by names and epithets. Taken as a whole, however, the Indian tales are remarkably clear ; and a comparison of them with the Gaelic throws much light on the latter.

What is the substance and sense of these Indian tales, of what do they treat ? To begin with, they give an account of how the present order of things arose in the world, and are taken up with the exploits, adventures, and struggles of various elements, animals, birds, reptiles, insects, plants, rocks, and other objects before they became what they are. In other words, the Indian tales give an account of what all those individualities accomplished, or suffered, before they fell from their former positions into the state in which they are now. According to the earliest tales of North America, this world was occupied, prior to the appearance of man, by beings called variously " the first people," " the outside people," or simply " people," — the same term in all cases being used for people that is applied to Indians at present.

These people, who were very numerous, lived together for ages in harmony. There were no collisions among them, no disputes during that period ; all were in perfect accord. In some mysterious fashion, however, each individual was changing imperceptibly ; an internal movement was going on. At last, a time came when the differences were sufficient to cause conflict, except in the case of a group to be mentioned hereafter, and struggles began.

These struggles were gigantic, for the "first people" had mighty power; they had also wonderful perception and knowledge. They felt the approach of friends or enemies even at a distance; they knew the thought in another's heart. If one of them expressed a wish, it was accomplished immediately; nay, if he even thought of a thing, it was there before him. Endowed with such powers and qualities, it would seem that their struggles would be endless and indecisive; but such was not the case. Though opponents might be equally dexterous, and have the power of the wish or the word in a similar degree, one of them would conquer in the end through wishing for more effective and better things, and thus become the hero of a higher cause; that is, a cause from which benefit would accrue to mankind, the coming race.

The accounts of these struggles and conflicts form the substance of the first cycle of American tales, which contain the adventures of the various living creatures, plants, elements, objects, and phenomena in this world before they became what they are as we see them. Among living creatures, we are not to reckon man, for man does not appear in any of those myth tales; they relate solely to extra-human existences, and describe the battle and agony of creation, not the adventures of anything in the world since it received its present form and office. According to popular modes of thought and speech, all this would be termed the fall of the gods; for the "first people" of the Indian tales correspond to the earliest gods of other races, including those of the Kelts. We have thus, in America, a remarkable projection of thought, something quite as far-reaching for the world of mind as is the nebular hypothesis for the world of matter. According to the nebular hypothesis, the whole physical universe is evolved by the rotary motion of a primeval, misty substance which fills all space, and which seems homogeneous. From a uniform motion of this attenuated matter, continued through eons of ages, is produced that infinite variety in the material universe which we observe and discover, day by day ; from it we have the countless host of suns and planets whose positions in space correspond to their sizes and densities, that endless choral dance of heavenly bodies with its marvellous figures and complications, that ceaseless movement of each body in its own proper path, and that movement of each group or system with reference to others. From this motion, come climates, succession of seasons, with all the variety in this world of sense which we inhabit. In the theory of spiritual evolution, worked out by the aboriginal mind of America, all kinds of moral quality and character are represented as coming from an internal movement through which the latent, unevolved personality of each individual of these " first people," or gods, is produced. Once that personality is produced, every species of dramatic situation and tragic catastrophe follows as an inevitable sequence. There is no more peace after that ; there are only collisions followed by combats which are continued by the gods till they are turned into all the things, — animal, vegetable, and mineral,—which are either useful or harmful to man, and thus creation is accomplished. During the period of struggles, the gods organize institutions, social and religious, according to which they live. These are bequeathed to man ; and nothing that an Indian has is of human invention, all is divine. An avowed innovation, anything that we call reform, anything invented by man, would be looked on as sacrilege, a terrible, an inexpiable crime. The Indian lives in a world prepared by the gods, and follows in their footsteps, — that is the only morality, the one pure and holy religion.

The struggles in which creation began, and the continuance of which was creation itself, were bequeathed to aboriginal man ; and the play of passions which caused the downfall of the gods has raged ever since, throughout every corner of savage life in America.

This Creation myth of the New World is a work of great value, for by aid of it we can bring order into mythology, and reconstruct, at least in outline, and provisionally, that early system of belief which was common to all races : a system which, though expressed in many languages, and in endlessly varying details, has one meaning, and was, in the fullest sense of the word, one, — a religion truly Catholic and Œcumenical, for it was believed in by all people, wherever resident, and believed in with a vividness of faith, and a sincerity of attachment, which no civilized man can even imagine, unless he has had long experience of primitive races. In the struggle between these " first people," or gods, there were never drawn battles : one side was always victorious, the other always vanquished ; but each could give one command, one fateful utterance, which no power could resist or gainsay. The victor always said to the vanquished : " Henceforth, you 'll be nothing but a ——," and here he named the beast, bird, insect, reptile, fish, or plant, which his opponent was to be. That moment the vanquished retorted, and said : " You 'll be nothing but a ——," mentioning what he was to be. Thereupon each became what his opponent had made him, and went away over the earth. As a rule, there is given with the sentence a characteristic description ; for example : " The people to come hereafter will hunt you, and kill you to eat you ; " or, " will kill you for your skin ; " or, " will kill you because they hate you."

One opponent might be turned into a wolf, the other into a squirrel ; or one into a bear, the other into a fox : there is always a strict correspondence, however, between the former nature of each combatant and the present character of the creature into which he has been transformed, looked at, of course, from the point of view of the original myth-maker.

The war between the gods continued till it produced on land, in the water, and the air, all creatures that move, and all plants that grow. There is not a beast, bird, fish, reptile, insect, or plant which is not a fallen divinity ; and for every one noted there is a story of its previous existence.

This transformation of the former people, or divinities, of America was finished just before the present race of men —that is, the Indians — appeared. This transformation does not take place in every American mythology as a result of single combat. Sometimes a great hero goes about ridding the world of terrible oppressors and monsters: he beats them, turns them into something insignificant; after defeat they have no power over him. We may see in the woods some weak worm or insect which, in the first age, was an awful power, but a bad one. Stories of this kind present some of the finest adventures, and most striking situations, as well as qualities of character in the hero that invite admiration.

In some mythologies a few personages who are left unchanged at the eve of man's coming, transform themselves voluntarily. The details of the change vary from tribe to tribe; but in all it takes place in some described way, and forms part of the general change, or metamorphosis, which is the vital element in the American system. In many, perhaps in all, the mythologies, there is an account of how some of the former people, or gods, instead of fighting and taking part in the struggle of creation, and being transformed, retained their original character, and either went above the sky, or sailed away westward to where the sky comes down, and passed out under it, and beyond, to a pleasant region where they live in delight. This is that contingent to which I have referred, that part of "the first people" in which no passion was developed; they remained in primitive simplicity, undifferentiated, and are happy at present. They correspond to those gods of classic antiquity who enjoyed themselves apart, and took no interest whatever in the sufferings or the joys of mankind.

It is evident, at once, that to the aborigines of America the field for beautiful stories was very extensive.

Everything in nature had a tale of its own, if some one would but tell it; and during the epoch of constructive power in the race, — the epoch when languages were built up, and great stories made, — few things of importance to people of that time were left unconsidered; hence, there was among the Indians of America a volume of tales as immense, one might say, as an ocean river. This statement I make in view of materials which I have gathered myself, and which are still unpublished, — materials which, though voluminous, are comparatively meagre, merely a hint of what in some tribes was lost, and of what in others is still uncollected. What is true of the Indians with reference to the volume of their stories, is true of all races.

From what is known of the mind of antiquity, and from what data we have touching savage life in the present, we may affirm as a theory that primitive beliefs, in all places, are of the same system essentially as the American. In that system, every individual existence beyond man is a divinity, but a divinity under sentence, — a divinity weighed down by fate; a divinity with a history behind it, a history which is tragedy or comedy as the case may be. These histories extend along the whole line of experience, and include every combination conceivable to primitive man.

Of the pre-Christian beliefs of the Kelts, not much is known yet in detail and with certainty. What we may say at present is this, that they form a very interesting variant of that aforementioned Œcumenical religion held in early ages by all men. The peculiarities and value of the variant will be shown when the tales, beliefs, and literary monuments of the race are brought fully into evidence.

Now that some statement has been made touching Indian tales and their contents, we may give, for purposes of comparison, two or three of them, either in part or condensed. These examples may serve to show what Gaelic tales were before they were modified in structure, and before human substitutes were put in place of the primitive heroes.

It should be stated here that these accounts of a former people, and the life of the world before this, as given in the tales, were delivered in one place and another by some of these " former people " who were the last to be transformed, and who found means to give needful instruction to men. On the Klamath River, in Northwestern California, there is a sacred tree, a former divinity, which has been a great source of revelation. On a branch of the Upper Columbia is a rock which has told whole histories of a world before this.

Among the Iroquois, I found a story in possession of a doctor, — that is, a magician, or sorcerer, — who, so far as I could learn, was the only man who knew it, though others knew of it. This story is in substance as follows :

Once there was an orphan boy who had no friends ; a poor, childless widow took the little fellow, and reared him. When the boy had grown up somewhat, he was very fond of bows and arrows, became a wonderful shot. As is usual with orphans, he was wiser than others, and was able to hunt when much smaller than his comrades.

He began to kill birds for his foster-mother ; gradually he went farther from home, and found more game.   The widow had plenty in her house now, and something to give her friends.   The boy and the woman lived on in this fashion a whole year.   He was good, thoughtful, serious, a wise boy, and brought game every day.   The widow was happy with her foster-son.

At last he came late one evening, later than ever before, and had n't half so much game.

" Why so late, my son; and why have you so little game ? " asked the widow.

" Oh, my mother, game is getting scarce around here ; I had to go far to find any, and then it was too late to kill more."

The next day he was late again, a little later than the day before, and had no more game ; he·gave the same excuse.   This conduct continued a week ; the woman grew suspicious, and sent out a boy to follow her foster-son, and see what he was doing.

Now what had happened to the boy ?   He had gone far into the forest on the day when he was belated, farther than ever before.   In a thick and dense place he found a round, grassy opening ; in the middle of this space was a large rock, shaped like a millstone, and lying on one side, the upper part was flat and level.   He placed his birds on the rock, sprang up, and sat on it to rest; the time was just after midday.   While he was sitting there, he heard a voice in the stone, which asked : " Do you want me to tell a story? " He was astonished, said nothing. Again the voice spoke, and he answered : " Yes, tell me a story."

The voice began, and told him a wonderful story, such as he had never heard before. He was delighted ; never had he known such pleasure. About the middle of the afternoon, the story was finished ; and the voice said : " Now, you must give me your birds for the story ; leave them where you put them." He went away toward home, shot what birds he could find, but did not kill many.

He came the next day, with birds, and heard a second story ; and so it went on till the eighth day, when the boy sent by the foster-mother followed secretly. That boy heard the story too, discovered himself, and promised not to tell. Two days later the widow sent a second boy to watch those two, and three days after that a third one. The boys were true to the orphan, however, and would not tell ; the magic of the stories overcame them.

At last the woman went to the chief with her trouble ; he sent a man to watch the boys. This man joined the boys, and would not tell. The chief then sent his most trusty friend, whom nothing could turn aside from his errand. He came on the boys and the man, while they were listening to a story, and threatened them, was very angry. The voice stopped then, and said : " I will tell no more to-day ; but, you boys and you men, listen to me, take a message to the chief and the people, — tell them to come here to-morrow, to come all of them, for I have a great word to say to every person."

The boys and men went home, and delivered the message. On the following day, the whole people went out in a body. They cleared away the thick grass in the open space; and all sat down around the stone, from which the voice came as follows: —

"Now, you chief and you people, there was a world before this, and a people different from the people in the world now, — another kind of people. I am going to tell you of that people. I will tell you all about them, — what they did; how they fixed this world; and what they became themselves. You will come here every day till I have told all the stories of the former people; and each time you will bring a little present of what you have at home."

The stone began, told a story that day, told more the next day. The people came day after day, week after week, till the stone told all it knew. Then it said: "You have heard all the stories of the former world; you will keep them, preserve them as long as you live. In after times some man will remember nearly all of these stories; another will remember a good many; a third, not so many; a fourth man, a few; a fifth, one story; a sixth, parts of some stories, but not all of any story. No man will remember every story; only the whole people can remember all. When one man goes to another who knows stories, and he tells them, the first man will give him some present, — tobacco, a bit of venison, a bird, or whatever he has. He will do as you have done to me. I have finished."

Very interesting and important are these statements touching the origin of stories; they indicate in the Indian system revelation as often as it is needed. In Ireland, the origin of every Fenian tale is explained in a way somewhat similar. All the accounts of Fin Mac Cool and his men were given to Saint Patrick by Ossian, after his return from Tir nan Og, the Land of the Young, where he had lived three hundred years. These Fenian tales were written down at that time, it is stated ; but Saint Patrick gave an order soon after to destroy two-thirds of the number, for they were so entertaining, he said, that the people of Erin would do nothing but listen to them.

In every case the Fenian tales of Ireland, like the tales of America, are made up of the adventures of heroes who are not human. Some writers assert that there have never been such persons on earth as Fin Mac Cool and his men ; others consider them real characters in Irish history. In either case, the substantial character of the tales is not changed. If Fin and his men are historical personages, deeds of myth-heroes, ancient gods of Gaelic mythology, have been attributed to them, or they have been substituted for heroes who were in the tales previously. If Fin and his men are not historical, they are either the original non-human heroes, or a later company of similar character substituted in the tales for the original heroes, or for some successors of those heroes ; at this date it would be difficult to decide how often such substitutions may have been made.

The following tale of Pitis and Klakherrit, though condensed, is complete ; it is given here not because it is the best for illustration, but because it is accessible. The tale is dramatic ; the characters are well known ; it is ancient, and may be used to show how easily the character of stories may be modified without changing their structure, simply by changing the heroes. This tale of Pitis and Klakherrit is not more than third rate, if compared with other Indian tales, perhaps not so high in rank as that, still, it is a good story.

At a place called Memtachnokolton lived the Pitis people ; they were numerous, all children of one father. They lived as they liked for a long time, till one of them who had gone hunting did not return in the evening. Next day two of his brothers went to look for him, and found his headless body four or five miles away, at the side of a deer-trail. They carried the body home, and buried it.

On the following day, another went to hunt, and spent the night out in like manner. Next day his headless body was found, brought home, and buried. Each day a Pitis went to hunt till the last one was killed ; and the way they died was this : —

Not very far south of the deer-trail were the Klak people, at Klakkewilton. They lived together in one great house, and were all blind except one Klakherrit, who was young and strong, bad, a great liar, and very fond of gambling. This Klakherrit hated the Pitis people, and wanted to kill them all ; he used to go out and watch for them. When a Pitis went hunting, and was following the deer, Klakherrit sat down at the trail, some distance ahead ; and, as the Pitis came up, he would groan, and call out,

"Oh, I have a big splinter in my foot; I cannot take it out alone, help me!"

The Pitis pitied him always, and said : "I will pull it out for you;" then he sat down, took the foot in his hand, looked at it, and pulled at the splinter.

"Oh, you cannot pull it out with your fingers; you must take it between your teeth." The Pitis took the end of the splinter between his teeth, and began to pull; that moment Klakherrit cut his head off, and carried it to Klakkewilton, leaving the body by the roadside.

When Klakherrit killed the last Pitis, he took his skin, put it on and became just like Pitis. He went then to Memtachnokolton, and said to the Pitis women and children, "I killed a deer to-day; but Klakherrit ran off with it, so I come home with nothing."

"We have enough to eat; never mind," said the women, who thought he was their man.

About dark that evening, Klakherrit, the counterfeit Pitis, killed all the women and children except one little child, a boy, who escaped by some wonderful fortune, and hid under the weeds. Klakherrit burned the village then, and went home, thinking : "I have killed every Pitis."

Next morning little Pitis came out of his hiding-place, and wandered around the burnt village, crying. Soon an old woman, Tsosokpokaila, heard the child, found him, took him home, called him grandson, and reared him; she gave him seeds to eat which she took from her own people, — a great many of them lived in her village. She was a small person, but active.

In a few days, little Pitis began to talk ; and soon he was able to run around, and play with bows and arrows. The old woman said to him then : " My grandson, you must never go to the south nor to the east. Go always to the north or west, and don't go far ; you need n't think to meet any of your people, they are dead, every one of them."

All this time Klakherrit went out every morning, and listened long and carefully ; hearing no sound of a Pitis, he went in one day, and said to his blind relatives : " I hear nothing, I see nothing of the Pitis people ; they are all dead."

There was one old man in the house, an uncle of Klakherrit, and he answered : " My nephew, I can't see anything ; but some day you may see a Pitis. I don't think all the Pitis people are dead yet ; I think some are living in this world somewhere."

Klakherrit said nothing, but went out every morning as before ; at last he saw far away in the west a little smoke rising, a slender streak of it. " Some people are living off there," thought he ; " who can they be, I must know." He hurried to the house for his choicest clothes, and weapons, and made ready. He took his best bow, and a large quiver of black fox-skin, this he filled with arrows ; then he put beads of waterbone on his neck, and a girdle of shining shells around his waist. When dressed to his wish, he started, and went straight toward the fire. As he came near it, he walked slowly, to see who was there ; for a time he saw no one, but he heard pounding at the other side of a big pine-tree. He went around slowly to the other side, and saw a man pounding something. He would pound a while, and then pick up nuts, crack the shells with his teeth, and eat the kernels. This person was Kaisusherrit; and he was so busy that he did not see Klakherrit, who stood looking on a good while. "Hallo, my friend!" said Klakherrit, at last, "why are you alone; does no one else live around here?"

Kaisusherrit said nothing; he went on pounding pine cones, getting nuts out of them, did n't look at the stranger. Around his neck he had a net bag filled with pine nuts. After a while he stopped pounding, cracked some nuts, put the kernels in his mouth, and then pounded pine cones again.

"My friend, you are alone in this place. I came here by myself; there are only two of us. I saw your smoke this morning; and I said, before I started, 'I will go and see a good man to-day.' I thought that you were here, and I found you."

Kaisusherrit said nothing, but pounded away.

"My friend, why not talk to me; why not say something? Let us gamble: there is plenty of shade under the trees here; we might as well play."

Kaisusherrit was silent, did n't take his eyes off the pine cones.

"Why not talk to me, my friend? If you don't talk to me, who will; there are only two of us in this place. I came to see you this morning, to have a talk with you. I thought you would tell me what is going on around here

where you live ; and I would tell you what I know. Stop
eating ; let's gamble, and have a good talk."

Klakherrit talked, and teased, and begged, all the fore-
noon. He did n't sit down once ; he was on his feet all the
time. At last, a little after noon, Kaisusherrit looked up,
and said : " Why do you make all this fuss? That is not
the way for one grown person to talk to another. You
act like some little boy, teasing, and talking, and hanging
around. Why don't you sit down quietly, and tell me
who you are, what you know, and where you live? Then
I can tell you what I like, and talk to you."

Klakherrit sat down, and told who he was. Then he
began again : " Well, my friend, let us play ; the shade is
good here under the trees."

" Why do you want to play?" asked Kaisusherrit ; " do
you see anything here that you like? I have nothing to bet
against your things."

" Oh, you have," said Klakherrit, — " you have your
pounding stone, your net full of nuts, your pine cones."

" Very well," said Kaisusherrit ; " I will bet my things
against yours ; " and he placed them in one pile. Klakherrit took off his weapons and ornaments, and tied them
up with Kaisusherrit's things in one bundle, so that the
winner might have them all ready to carry away. Kaisusherrit brought sticks to play with, and grass to use with
the sticks. He sat down then with his back to the tree, and
motioned to the other to sit down in front. The bundle
was near the tree, and each had a pile of grass behind him.

" Let us go away from this tree to the shade out there ;
I don't like to be near a tree," said Klakherrit.

"Oh, I can't go there; I must have my back against a tree when I play," said Kaisusherrit. "Oh, come, I like that place; let us go out there." "No, my back aches unless I lean against a tree; I must stay here." "Never mind this time; come on, I want to play out there," urged Klakherrit. "I won't go," said Kaisusherrit; "I must play here."

They talked and disputed about the place till the middle of the afternoon: but Kaisusherrit would n't stir; and Klakherrit, who was dying to play, agreed at last to let Kaisusherrit put his back to the tree, and to sit opposite himself. They began, and were playing about two hours, when Klakherrit was getting the advantage; he was winning. Both were playing their best now, and watching each other. Kaisusherrit said then in his mind, "You, Klakherrit's grass, be all gone, be grass no more, be dust." The grass in Klakherrit's hand turned to dust. He reached behind to get more grass, but found none; then he looked to see where it was. That moment Kaisusherrit snatched the bundle, and ran up the tree. Klakherrit sprang to his feet, looked through the branches; and there he saw Kaisusherrit with the bundle on his back.

"Oh, my friend," cried he, "what is the matter; what are you doing?" Kaisusherrit said nothing, sat on a limb, and looked at the stranger. "Oh, my friend, why go up in the tree? Come, let us finish the game; maybe you 'll win all my things. Come down."

Klakherrit talked and talked. Kaisusherrit began to

come down slowly, stopping every little while ; he reached the lower limbs. Klakherrit thought he was coming surely ; all at once he turned, and hurried up again, went to the very top, and sat there. Klakherrit walked around the tree, persuading and begging. Kaisusherrit slipped down a second time, was near the ground, seemed to be getting off the tree ; Klakherrit was glad. Kaisusherrit did n't get off, though ; he went up to the next limb, smiled, and looked at Klakherrit, who was getting terribly angry. Kaisusherrit went higher. Klakherrit could hold in no longer ; he was raging. He ran, picked up sharp rocks, and hurled them at Kaisusherrit. The first one hit the limb on which he was sitting, and cut it right off ; but he was very quick and sprang on to another. Klakherrit hurled stone after stone at the tree, with such force and venom that a limb fell whenever a stone struck it. At dusk there was n't a limb left on the tree ; but Kaisusherrit was there yet. He was very quick and resolute, and dodged every stone. Klakherrit drew breath a moment, and began again to hurl stones at Kaisusherrit ; wherever one struck the tree, it took the bark off. At dark the tree was all naked and battered, not a branch nor a bit of bark left. Kaisusherrit was on it yet ; but Klakherrit could n't see him. Klakherrit had to go home ; when he went into the house, he said, " Well, I 've met a man to-day who is lucky ; he won all my things in play."

" My son," said Klakherrit's father, who was very old, " you have been telling us that you are a great player ; but I thought all the time that you would meet a person some day who would beat you. You have travelled much to find such a one; you have found him."

Next morning Klakherrit went out, and saw a smoke in the west. "That is my friend," said he; "I must see him." He took his best dress and weapons, and soon reached the fire. "Hallo, my friend," said Klakherrit, "I 've come to play with you to-day." "Very well," answered Kaisusherrit, who was wearing Klakherrit's clothes that he had carried up the tree. "But, my friend, you won't do as you did yesterday?" "Oh, no; I 'll play nicely to-day, I 'll play to please you." They tied the stakes in one bundle, brought sticks and grass. Kaisusherrit put his back to a tree much larger than the first one. Klakherrit wished to play in the open; Kaisusherrit would n't go there. They disputed and quarrelled till Klakherrit had to yield; but he made up his mind not to let Kaisusherrit go up the tree this time.

They played as before till the middle of the afternoon, when Klakherrit was winning. Kaisusherrit turned the grass into dust, and was up the tree before Klakherrit could stop him. The deeds of the day before were repeated with greater force. Kaisusherrit was more cynical in his conduct. Klakherrit was more enraged; he cut all the limbs, and stripped all the bark from this tree with stone-throwing. At dark he had to go home, leaving Kaisusherrit unhurt.

On the third morning, Klakherrit was watching for smoke; he wanted to win back what he had lost in the west. Soon he saw a herd of deer pass, followed by a Pitis.

It was the end of summer; little Pitis had grown very fast, was a young man now. While Klakherrit was gambling, Pitis told his grandmother that he wanted to hunt. "Oh, my grandson," said she, "you must never go hunting; all your people were killed while out hunting. I don't want you to hunt; I don't want you to be killed."

"I don't want to be killed, my grandmother; but I don't like to stay around the house here all the time. I want to find food and bring it home; I want, besides, to see where my people were killed. I want to see the place where they died; I want to look at the person who killed them."

"My grandson, I don't like to hear you talk in that way; I don't want you to go far from this house. There is a very bad person south of us: he is the one who killed all your people; he is Klakherrit."

"My grandmother, I can't help going, — I must go; I must see the place where my people were killed. If I can find him, I must look at Klakherrit, who killed all my relatives."

Next morning, young Pitis rose, and dressed himself beautifully. He took a good bow, and a quiver of black fox-skin; his arrows were pointed with white flint; in his hair he had Winishuyat[1] to warn him of danger. "My grandmother," said he, at parting, "do the best you can while I am gone." The old woman began to cry, and said,

---

[1] This Winishuyat is represented as no larger than a man's thumb, and confined under the hair on the top of the head, the hair being tied over him. He is foresight itself. *Winis* means "he sees," what *huyat* means I have not discovered yet.

" Oh, my grandson, be on the watch, and guard yourself well ; take good care, my grandson."

Pitis started off ; and, when out of sight, Winishuyat said, " My brother, a little ahead of us are deer. All your relatives were killed by Klakherrit for the sake of these deer. The deer obeyed your people, and went wherever they told them." Pitis saw twenty deer, and, a few moments later, twenty more. He shouted ; they ran around, stopped, and looked at him. " I want you, deer," said Pitis, " to go toward the south, and go past Klakherrit's house, so that he can see you and I can see him."

Pitis shouted three times ; and Klakherrit, who was watching for Kaisusherrit's smoke, heard him. The forty deer went on one after another in a line, Pitis following. When Klakherrit saw them, he ran into the house, and called to his relatives : " Deer are coming ; and a Pitis is with them ! "

" Oh, my nephew," cried the blind uncle, " you kept saying all the time that there was not another Pitis in this world ; but I knew there were some left somewhere. Did n't I say that you would see Pitis people ; did n't I tell you that you had n't killed all that people, my nephew ? You will meet a Pitis to-day."

Klakherrit made no answer ; he took his bow and quiver quickly, and hurried out. The deer had passed the house and Pitis was just passing. Klakherrit saw him well ; and Pitis had a good look at Klakherrit. Klakherrit went away on one side of the trail, got ahead of the deer, and sat down at the side of the trail near a rock. When they came up, the deer passed him ; but Winishuyat said to

Pitis, " My brother, Klakherrit is near that rock right there ; when you pass, don't stop, don't speak to him. It is he who killed our people ; he wants to kill you."

When Pitis came to the rock; Klakherrit jumped up on one leg, and cried, " Oh, my friend, I can't travel farther. I was going to help you, but I have this great splinter in my foot ; draw it out for me."   Pitis did n't look at him, went straight past. A little later, Winishuyat said, " My brother, on the other side of that clump of bushes your enemy is sitting : go by ; don't speak to him."   When Pitis came, Klakherrit begged him again to pull the splinter out of his foot ; but Pitis did n't stop, did n't speak to him.   Five times that day did Klakherrit run ahead by side-paths, and beg Pitis to pull a splinter out of his foot ; but Pitis never stopped, never answered him.   In the evening, Pitis said to the deer, " You, deer, meet me in the morning where you met me to-day."   That night, Pitis said to his grandmother, " I saw Klakherrit ; he bothered me all day.   Five times he was ahead of me with a sore foot ; but if his foot is sore, how can he travel so ?   There must be a great many of his people just like him."

" My grandson, Klakherrit has many relatives ; but he is the only one of that people who can travel.   All the rest are blind ; he is the one who was ahead of you all day."

" Well, grandmother, I have seen Klakherrit ; I know all about him.   I know what I can do to him ; I shall follow the deer to-morrow."   (Pitis did n't hunt deer ; he just followed them.)   Next morning, Pitis rose very early, bathed in the creek, ate his breakfast, and dressed for the

road ; then he brought two flat stones, a blue and a white
one, each about a foot wide, put them down before the
old woman, and said, " My grandmother, watch these
two stones all day.   If you see thick black spots of blood
on the blue stone, you may know that I am killed ; but if
you see light red blood on the white stone, you may know
that I am safe."   The old woman began to cry ; but he
went to the place where he met the deer the day before.
He sent them by the same road ; and, after a while, he met
Klakherrit, who begged him to pull the splinter out of
his foot.   Pitis passed in silence ; when out of sight, he
stopped the deer, and said, " Now, my deer, let the
strongest of you go ahead ; and if Klakherrit is by the
trail again, run at him, and stamp him into the ground
with your fore-feet ; jump on him, every one of you."

Some distance farther on, they saw Klakherrit sitting
at the side of the trail.   The first deer ran and thrust his
hoofs into his body ; the second and the third did the
same, and so did the whole forty.   He was all cut to
pieces, one lump of dirt and blood.   The deer went on ;
Pitis followed.   Soon Pitis called to the deer, " We 'll go
back again ; " and he walked ahead till they returned to
where they had trampled his enemy.   Klakherrit was up
again, begging, " Oh, my friend, pull this great splinter
out of my foot ; I cannot do it alone, help me ! "   Pitis
sent the deer at him again ; they trampled him into the
ground, and went on.   When they had gone perhaps two
miles, Klakherrit was sitting at the roadside as before, and
begged Pitis to pull the splinter out of his foot.   Pitis

was terribly angry now ; he stopped in front of Klakherrit, and walked up to him. " My friend," said he, " what are you talking about ; what do you want ? Are you one person, or are there many like you ? You bothered me all yesterday ; what do you want to-day ? "

" I am only one person," said Klakherrit ; " but, my friend, pull this splinter out ; my foot pains me terribly."

"But how do you run so fast, and go ahead of me every time, if your foot is hurt ; how do you pull the splinter out ? "

" I get it out at last, and run ahead ; but by that time there is another splinter in my foot."

" Why do you follow me ; what do you want ; why don't you let me alone ? " inquired Pitis, sitting down.

" Oh, my friend, pull this splinter out ; my foot is so sore I cannot talk. Pull the splinter, and I will tell you."

Pitis took hold of the splinter and pulled, but no use, he could not draw it out. " Take it between your teeth, that is the only way," said Klakherrit.

" My brother," said Winishuyat, " look out for your life now ; that is the way in which Klakherrit killed all your people. Do what he says ; but dodge when I tell you."

Pitis took the splinter between his teeth, and began to pull. That moment Klakherrit drew his knife, and struck ; but before the knife came down, Winishuyat cried, " Dodge to the left ! " Pitis dodged, and just escaped. Pitis struck now with his white-flint knife. Every blow he gave hit Klakherrit ; he dodged every blow himself so that it struck only his clothes. Klakherrit was very strong, and fought fiercely. Pitis was quick, and hit all the time. The fight was a hard one. In the middle of the afternoon, Pitis was very tired, and had all his clothes cut to pieces; and Klakherrit's head was cut off. But the head would not die; it fought on, and Pitis cut at it with his knife.

Now Winishuyat called out, " My brother, you can't kill Klakherrit in that way; you can't kill him with any weapon on this earth. Klakherrit's life is in the sky; Klakherrit's heart is up there on the right side of the place where the sun is at midday."

Pitis looked up, and saw the heart. He stretched out his right hand then, pulled down the heart, and squeezed it; that moment Klakherrit died.

Pitis took the skin off Klakherrit's body, put it on himself, and became just like him. He cut up his enemy's flesh, then carried it to Klakkewilton, went into the house, and said, " I have some venison to-day; I will roast it." He roasted Klakherrit's flesh, and gave it to his relatives. All ate except the old uncle, who grumbled, and said, " This meat does n't seem right to me; it has the smell of our people." Pitis walked out, pulled off Klakherrit's skin, threw it into the house, and was himself again; then he set fire to the house, and stopped the door. He listened; there was a great noise inside and an uproar. If any broke through, he threw them back again. At last one woman burst out, and rushed away; she escaped, and from her were born all the Klaks in the world. But she and they were a people no longer; they had become rattlesnakes. The Pitis people became quails, and Kaisusherrit's people, gray squirrels.

The old woman, Tsosokpokaila, who reared Pitis, became a weed about a foot high, which produces many seeds; the quails are fond of these seeds.

The following summary shows in outline the main parts of a tale which could not be so easily modified as the preceding, and one which is much more important as to contents.

Before thunder and lightning were in this world, Sulapokaila (trout old woman) had a house on the river Winimem, near Mount Shasta. One evening, a maiden called Wimaloimis (grisly bear maiden) came, and asked a night's lodging of the old woman; she gave it. Next morning, Wimaloimis wanted to eat Sulapokaila, and had almost caught her, when the old woman turned into water, and escaped. Wimaloimis went her way then, but remained in the neighborhood. She built a house, lay down near the door, and gazed at the sun for a long time; at last she grew pregnant from gazing. In time she had twins. When the first one was born, she tried to swallow it; but the infant gave out a great flash of light and frightened her. When the second child was born, she tried to eat that; but it roared terribly, and she was so frightened that she rushed out of the house, and ran off. The old woman, Sulapokaila, came and took the children home, washed them, cared for them, named the first-born Walokit (Lightning), and the second Tumukit (Thunder).

The boys grew very fast, and were soon young men. One day, Walokit asked, " Brother, do you know who our mother is, who our father is ? "

" I do not know," answered Tumukit ; " let us ask our grandmother."

They went and asked the old woman. " I know your father and mother," replied the old woman. "Your mother is very bad ; she came to my house, and tried to eat me. She wanted to eat trees, bushes, everything she saw. When you were born, she tried to eat you ; but somehow you little boys frightened her. She ran away, and is living on that mountain yonder. Your father is good ; he is living up there in the sky."

A couple of days later, Walokit said to his brother, " Let us go and find our mother." They went off, and found her half-way up on the slope of a mountain, sitting in front of her house, and weaving a basket. Her head was down ; she did not see them even when near. They stood awhile in silence, and then walked right up to her.

" Oh, my children ! " cried she, putting the basket aside, " come into the house, and sit down." She went in ; the boys followed. She sat down.

" Come here, and I 'll comb your hair ; come both of you, my children." They sat down in front of her, and bent their heads. She stroked their hair, took her comb, and began to comb ; next, she opened her mouth wide, and was going to swallow both at one gulp. That moment some voice said, " Look out, boys ; she is going to eat you." They saw no one, but heard the voice. Next

instant, Walokit flashed, and Tumukit roared. The
mother, dazzled, deafened, rushed out of the house in
great terror.

"I don't believe she is our mother," said Tumukit.

"I don't believe she is either," answered Walokit.
They were both very angry, and said, "She is a bad
woman anyhow. She may be our mother; but she is a
bad woman."

They went home, and later Walokit found his mother,
and killed her. Tumukit merely stood by, and roared.
The woman's body was torn to pieces, and scattered.
The brothers wept, and went to their grandmother, who
sent them to various sacred springs to purify themselves,
and wash away the blood of their mother. When they
had done that, after many pilgrimages, they said, "We
will go to our father, if we can."

Next day they said, "Grandmother, we will stay with
you to-morrow, and leave you the next day." On the second morning, they said, "We are going, and you, our
grandmother, must do the the best you can without us."

"To what place are you going, my grandsons?"

"We are going to our father, if we can."

When the old woman heard this, she went into the
house, and brought out a basket cup full of trout blood
(water), and gave it to Walokit, "Rub this over your
whole body; use it always; it will give you strength.
No matter how much you use the blood, the basket will
never be empty."

They took farewell of the old woman, and went to the

upper side of the sky, but did not go to their father. They live up there now, and go over the whole world, sometimes to find their father, sometimes for other purposes. When they move, we see one, and hear the other.

This tale has a few of the disagreeable features peculiar to some of the early myth-tales of all races, — tales which, if not forgotten, are misunderstood as the race advances, and then become tragedies of horror. Still, such tales are among the most precious for science, if analyzed thoroughly.

In another tale, told me by the same man who related this one, the sun, after his road had been marked out, finally, was warned against his own children, the grisly bears, who would beset his path through the sky, and do their best to devour him.

The grisly bear maiden, Wimaloimis, is a terrible criminal; she piles horror upon horror. She tries to eat up the hospitable trout woman who gives her lodging; she has twins from her own father; she tries to eat her own children; she brings them to commit matricide under cruel conditions. The house of Pelops and Lot's daughters, combined, barely match her. If the tale of Wimaloimis had belonged to early Greece, and had survived till the time of the Attic tragedians, the real nature of the actors in it would have been lost, in all likelihood, and then it might have served as a striking example of sin and its punishment. Instead of discovering who the *dramatis personæ* were really, the people of that time would have made them all human. In our day, we try to discover the point of view of the old myth-maker, to learn what it really was that he dealt with. In case we succeed, we are able to see that many of the repulsive features of ancient myths were not only natural and' explicable, but absolutely unavoidable. The cloud, a grisly bear, is a true daughter of the sun. The sun and the cloud are undoubtedly the parents of the twin brothers, Thunder and Lightning ; there are no other parents possible for them. That the cloud, according to myth description, tried to devour her own children, and was destroyed at last, and torn to pieces by them, is quite true. When we know the real elements of the tale, we find it perfectly accurate and truthful. If the personages in it were represented as human, it would become at once, what many a tale like it is made to be, repulsive and horrible.

Among Gaelic tales there are few in which the heroes are of the earliest period, though there are many in which primitive elements are prominent, and some in which they predominate. In a time sufficiently remote, Gaelic tales were made up altogether of the adventures of non-human heroes similar to those in the tales of America, — that is, heroes in the character of beasts, birds, and other living creatures, as well as the phenomena and elements of nature.

Beasts and birds are frequent in Gaelic tales yet ; but they never fill the chief rôle in any tale. At most they are friends of the hero, and help him ; not infrequently he could not gain victory without them. If on the bad side, the rôle is more prominent, a monster, or terrible beast, may be the leading opponent, or be one in a series of powerful enemies.

In a few Gaelic tales, phenomena or processes of nature appear still as chief actors ; but they appear in human guise. The two tales in which this position is most evident, are those of Mor and Glas Gainach, — not the tale of Mor as given in this volume, but an older tale, and one which, so far as I know, exists only in fragments and sayings. This tale of Mor, which I gathered bit by bit in one place and another through West Kerry, is, in substance, as follows :

Mor (big), a very large woman, came by sea to Dunmore Head, with her husband, Lear, who could not live with Mor, and went around by sea to the extreme north, where he stayed, thus putting, as the phrase runs, " All Ireland between himself and the wife." Mor had sons, and lived at Dun Quin (the ruins of her house Tivorye [Mor's house], are shown yet) at the foot of Mount Eagle. She lived on pleasantly ; much came to her from the sea. She was very proud of her sons, and cared for no one in the world except them. The woman increased greatly in substance, was rich and happy till her sons were enticed away, and went to sea.

One day, she climbed to the top of Mount Eagle, and, for the first time, saw Dingle Bay with the highlands of Iveragh and Killarney. " Oh, but is n't Erin the big country ; is n't it widely spread out ! " cried she. Mor was enormously bulky, and exerted herself to the utmost in climbing the mountain. At the top, certain necessities of nature came on her ; as a result of relieving these, a number of deep gullies were made in Mount Eagle, in various directions. These serve to this day as water-courses ; and torrents go through them to the ocean during rainfalls.

News was brought to Mor on the mountain that her sons had been enticed away to sea by magic and deceit. Left alone, all her power and property vanished ; she withered, lost her strength, went mad, and then disappeared, no man knew whither. " All that she had came by the sea," as people say, " and went with the sea." She who had been disagreeable and proud to such a degree that her own husband had to leave her ; the woman whose delight was in her children and her wealth, — became the most desolate person in Erin, childless, destitute, a famishing maniac that disappeared without a trace.

There is an interesting variant to this story, referring to Lear, Mor's husband. This represents him not as going to the other end of Erin, but as stopping where he touched land first ; there he died, and was buried. This is the version confirmed by the grave mound at Dunmore Head.

From the artistic point of view, it is to be regretted that the tale of Mor has not come down to us complete with its variants ; but we may be thankful for what we have. The fragments extant, and the sayings, establish the character of the tale, especially in view of a most interesting bit of testimony preserved in a book published in 1757.

After I had collected all the discoverable scraps and remnants of the tale, I came upon the statement in Smith's " History of Kerry," page 182, that Dunmore Head was called by the people thereabout, " Mary Geerane's house." The author adds the name in Gaelic (which he did not know), in the following incorrect form : " Ty-Vorney Geerane." Now this sentence does not mean Mary Geerane's house at all, but the house of Mor, daughter of the sun, Tigh Mhoire ni Greine, pronounced, " Thee Vorye nyee Grainye." Here is the final fact needed, — a fact preserved with an ignorance of its nature and value that is absolutely trustworthy.

What does the story mean now? Mor, daughter of the sun, leaves her husband, Lear, and comes to land herself. The husband cannot follow ; for Lear is the plain of the sea, — the sea itself in its outward aspect. Lear is the Neptune of the Gaels. One version represents Lear as coming to his end at Dunmore Head ; the other, as going around the island to Donaghedee, to live separated from a proud and disagreeable wife by the land of all Ireland. Each of these variants is equally consonant with the character of the couple. Let us pursue the tale further. Mor, the cloud woman, — for this she is, — has issue at Dun Quin, has sons (the rain-drops), and is prosperous, is proud of her sons, cares only for them; but her sons cannot stay with her, they are drawn to the sea irresistibly. She climbs Mount Eagle, is amazed at the view from the summit, sits down there and performs her last act on earth, the result of which is those tortuous and remarkably deep channels on the sides of Mount Eagle. After that she hears on the mountain that her sons are gone, she vanishes from human ken, is borne out of sight from the top of Mount Eagle.

Such is the myth of the cloud woman, Mor (the big one), a thing of wonder for the people.

In "Glas Gainach," with which this volume opens, we have, perhaps, the best tale preserved by memory in Ireland. The tale itself is perfect, apparently, and its elements are ancient.

The prize for exertion, the motive for action, in this tale, is a present from King Under the Wave to his friend the King of Spain. This King of Spain is, of course, supposititious. Who the former friend was whose place he usurped, we have no means of knowing ; but we shall not be far out of the way, I think, if we consider him to be the monarch of a cloud-land, — a realm as intangible as the Nephelokokkygia of Aristophanes, but real.

In Elin Gow, the swordsmith, we have a character quite as primitive as the cow or her owners. Elin Gow is found in Scotland as well as in Ireland. Ellin Gowan's Height, in Guy Mannering, is simply Elin Gow's Height, *Gowan* (*Gobhan* in Gaelic) being merely the genitive case of *Gow* (*Gobha*). Elin Gow means simply Elin the smith. Under whatever name, or wherever he may be, Elin Gow occupies a position in Gaelic similar to that of Hephæstos in Greek, or Vulcan in Latin mythology ; he is the maker of weapons, the forger of the bolt.

In a short tale of Glas Gavlen, which I obtained near Carrick, County Donegal, it is stated that the cow came down from the sky. According to the tale, she gives milk in unlimited quantities to all people without exception. Time after time the rich or powerful try to keep her for their own use exclusively, but she escapes. Appearing first at Dun Kinealy, she goes finally to Glen Columkil near the ocean, where a strong man tries to confine her ; but she rises in the air, and, clearing the high ridge on the northern side of the glen, disappears. Since then, there is no free milk in Erin, and none but that which common cows give.

The cow, Glas Gainach or Gaunach or Gavlen, for all three refer to the same beast, betrays at once her relationship with those cows of India so famous in the Rig Veda, those cloud cows whose milk was rain, cows which the demon Vritra used to steal and hide away, thus causing drought and suffering. Indra brought death to this demon with a lightning bolt ; for this deed he received the name Vritrahan (slayer of Vritra). The cows were freed then from confinement ; and the world was refreshed by their milk, which came to all, rich and poor, in like manner. So far the main characters of the tale are quite recognizable. Cian and Cormac are simply names current in Irish history, and are substituted for names of original heroes, who were characters as far from human and as mythologic as King Under the Wave or Glas Gainach.

A comparison of Gaelic tales with the Indian tales of America shows that the Gaelic contain materials some of which is as ancient as the Indian, while the tales themselves are less primitive.

There are many Indian tales which we can analyze, genuine myths, — a myth, in its earliest form, being a tale the substance of which is an account of some process in nature, or some collision between forces in nature, the whole account being given as a narrative of personal adventure.

Among the Irish tales there are very few ancient myths pure and simple, though there are many made up of myth materials altogether. The tale of Mor, reconstructed from fragments, is a myth from beginning to end ; the history of a cloud in the guise of a woman, as Glas Gainach is the history of a cloud in the guise of a cow.

Tales like Glas Gainach and Mor are not frequent in Gaelic at present; but tales of modified structure, composite tales to which something has been added, and from which something has been taken away, are met with oftener than any. The elements added or taken away are not modern, however ; they are, if we except certain heroes, quite ancient.

In course of time, and through change of religion, ancient heroes were forgotten in some cases, rejected in others, and new ones substituted ; when the argument of a tale, or part of it, grew less distinct, it was strength ened from the general stock, made more complete and vivid. In this way came adventure tales, constructed of materials purely mythic and ancient. Parts were transferred from one tale to another, the same incidents and heroes being found in tales quite different in other respects.

The results to be obtained from a comparison of systems of thought like the Indian and the Gaelic would be great, if made thoroughly. If extended to all races, such a comparison would render possible a history of the human mind in a form such as few men at present even dream of, — a history with a basis as firm as that which lies under geology. If this work is to be accomplished, we must make large additions indeed to our knowledge of primitive peoples. We must complete the work begun in America. We must collect the great tales of Africa, Asia, and the islands of the Pacific, — tales which embody the philosophy of the races that made them. The undertaking is arduous, and there is need to engage in it promptly. The forces of civilized society, at present, are destroying on all sides, not saving that which is precious in primitive people. Civilized society supposes that man, in an early degree of development, should be stripped of all that he owns, both material and mental, and then be refashioned to serve the society that stripped him. If he will not yield to the stripping and training, then slay him.

In view of this state of things, there is no time for delay; primitive man is changing, and the work is extensive.

Of Chinese thought we know very little, especially of Taoism, the most ancient system of the country, — the one which has grown up from Chinese myth-tales. Of African tales, only few have been collected, and those of small value mainly.

In Asia and Eastern Europe, the Russians have done the best work by far; besides many good volumes of Slav tales, they have given us much from the Tartars and Mongols of exceptional value and ancient.   In the United States, little was accomplished till recent years ; of late, however, public interest has been roused somewhat, and, since Major Powell entered the field, and became Director of the Bureau of Ethnology, more has been done in studying the native races of America than had been done from the discovery of the country up to that time.

To sum up, we may say, that the Indian tales reveal to us a whole system of religion, philosophy, and social polity.   They take us back to the beginning of things ; they describe Creation and the establishment of the present order in the world.

Those tales form a complete series.   The whole mental and social life of the race to which they belong is evident in them.   The Gaelic tales are a fragment of a former system.   The earliest tales in that system are lost ; those which formed the Creation myth, and related directly to the ancient faith and religious practices of the Gaels, were set aside and prohibited at the introduction of Christianity.   In many of those that remained, leading heroes were changed by design, or forgotten, and others put in their places.   In general, they were modified consciously and unconsciously, — some greatly, others to a less degree, and a few very little.

We find various resemblances in the two systems, some of which are very striking in details, and others in general features ; the question, therefore, rises readily enough : Can we not use the complete system to aid us in explaining and reconstructing, in some degree, the imperfect one? We can undoubtedly ; and if to materials preserved by oral tradition, like those in this volume, be added manuscript tales, and those scattered through chronicles ecclesiastical and secular, we may hope to give some idea of what the ancient system of Gaelic thought was, and discover whether the Gaelic gods had a similar origin with the Indian. What is true of the Gaelic is true also of other ancient systems in Europe, such as the Slav and Teutonic. These have much less literary material than the Gaelic ; but the Slav has vastly greater stores of oral tradition, and tales which contain much precious thought from pre-Christian ages.

During eight years of investigation among Indian tribes in North America, I obtained the various parts of that Creation myth mentioned in this introduction, from tribes that were remote from one another, and in different degrees of development. Such tales I found in the east, in the central regions, and finally in California and Oregon. Over this space, the extreme points of which are three thousand miles apart, each tribe has the Creation myth, — one portion being brought out with special emphasis in one tribe, and another portion in a different one. In tribes least developed, the earliest tales are very distinct, and specially valuable on some points relating to the origin and fall of the gods. Materials from the extreme west are more archaic and simple than those of the east. In fact the two regions present the two extremes, in North America, of least developed and most developed aboriginal thought. In this is their interest. They form one complete system, a single conception richly illustrated.

Shall we find among tribes of Africa, Australia, and the Pacific Islands, tales which are component parts of great Creation myths like that of North America? We shall find them no doubt, if we spend time and skilled labor sufficient.

The discovery and collection of these materials, and the proper use of them afterward, constitute, for scientific zeal and activity, a task as important as self-knowledge is important to man.

In 1887, I made a journey to Ireland ; when I collected tales from which were selected the twenty forming the " Myths and Folk-lore of Ireland," Boston, Little, Brown, and Company, 1889. While in Ireland, during that first visit, and this one, I have met with much good will and kindness which are pleasant to remember.

I must mention, to begin with, my indebtedness to Rev. P. A. Walsh, of the St. Vincent Fathers, Cork, a widely known Gaelic scholar, and a man whose acquaintance with the South of Ireland is extensive and intimate. Father Walsh gave me much information concerning the people, and letters to priests. I am greatly obliged to J. J. MacSweeny, Esq., of the Royal Irish Academy, for help in many ways, and for letters to people in Donegal. To Rev. Eugene O'Growney, Professor of Gaelic at Maynooth, I am grateful for letters and advice.

If I were to mention all who have done me deeds of kindness, the list would be long indeed. I must name, however, in Dingle, the venerable Canon O'Sullivan and Father Scollard, in Bally Ferriter, Rev. John O'Leary. To Mr. Patrick Ferriter, of Dingle, a man of keen intelligence and an excellent Gaelic scholar, I am deeply indebted for assistance in Gaelic. Canon Brosnan, of Cahirciveen, placed all his knowledge of the region where he lives at my service, and on one occasion led in an unwilling story-teller. Father MacDevitt, of Carrick, County Donegal, assisted me much in his neighborhood. Rev. James MacFadden, of Glena, County Donegal, and his curate, Rev. John Boyle, of Falcarra, helped me effectively, and showed the most courteous hospitality. I should return special thanks to Prof. Brian O'Looney, of Dublin, whose knowledge of ancient Gaelic lore is unmatched, and who at all times was as willing as he was able to aid me.

In America, the list of my obligations is short ; there is only one man on that continent to whom thanks are due in connection with this volume, but that man, like the hero in Gaelic tales, was worth more than the thousands on all four sides of him. The contents of this book would not have been collected without the co-operation of Hon. Charles A. Dana, who published fifty of these Gaelic tales in the Sunday edition of " The Sun." At that time no other editor was willing to join in the enterprise ; and I did not feel able to endure both the financial burden and the labor of finding and collecting Gaelic tales, as I had done in 1887. Mr. Dana, with his keen eye for literary character, noted at once in the " Myths and Folk-lore " the originality of Gaelic tales and their heroes. When I told him that relics like the Cuculin and Gilla na Grakin of my first book were on the verge of extinction, he joined hands with me to save them, and I set out on my second journey to Ireland.

JEREMIAH CURTIN.

LONDON, ENGLAND, August, 1894.

HERO-TALES OF IRELAND.

ELIN GOW, THE SWORDSMITH FROM ERIN, AND THE COW GLAS GAINACH.

ONCE King Under the Wave went on a visit to the King of Spain, for the two were great friends. The King of Spain was complaining, and very sorry that he had not butter enough. He had a great herd of cows; but for all that, he had not what butter he wanted. He said that he 'd be the richest man in the world if he had butter in plenty for himself and his people.

"Do not trouble your mind," said King Under the Wave. "I will give you Glas Gainach, — a cow that is better than a thousand cows,. and her milk is nearly all butter."

The King of Spain thanked his guest for the promise, and was very glad. King Under the Wave kept his word; he sent Glas Gainach, and a messenger with instructions how to care for the cow, and said that if she was angered in any way she would not stay out at pasture. So the king took great care of her; and the report went through all nations that the King of Spain had the cow called Glas Gainach.

The King of Spain had an only daughter, and he was to give the cow with the daughter; and the cow was a great fortune, the best dower in the world at that time. The king said that the man who would do what he put on him would get the daughter and the cow.

Champions came from every part of the world, each man to try his fortune. In a short time hundreds and thousands of men lost their heads in combat. The king agreed then that any man who would serve seven years, and bring the cow safe and sound every day of that time to the castle, would have her.

In minding the cow, the man had to follow her always, never go before her, or stop her, or hold her. If he did, she would run home to the castle. The man must stop with her when she wanted to get a bite or a drink   She never travelled less than sixty miles a day, eating a good bite here and a good bite there, and going hither and over.

The King of Spain never told men how to

mind the cow; he wanted them to lose their heads, for then he got their work without wages.

One man would mind her for a day; another would follow her to the castle for two days; a third might go with her for a week, and sometimes a man could not come home with her the first day. The man should be loose and swift to keep up with Glas Gainach. The day she walked least she walked sixty miles; some days she walked much more.

It was known in Erin that there was such a cow, and there was a smith in Cluainte above here, three miles north of Fintra, and his name was Elin Gow. He was the best man in Erin to make a sword or any weapon of combat. From all parts of Erin, and from other lands also, young princes who were going to seek their fortunes came to him to have him make swords for them. Now what should happen but this? It came to him in a dream three nights in succession that he was to go for Glas Gainach, the wonderful cow. At last he said, "I will go and knock a trial out of her; I will go toward her."

He went to Tramor, where there were some vessels. It was to the King of Munster that he went, and asked would he lend him a vessel. Elin Gow had made many swords for the king. The king said that he would lend the vessel with willingness, and that if he could do more for him he would do it. Elin Gow got the vessel, and put stores in it for a day and a year. He turned its prow then to sea and its stern to land, and was ploughing the main ocean till he steered into the kingdom of Spain as well as if he had had three pilots, and there was no one but himself in it. He let the wind guide the ship, and she came into the very harbor of the province where the king's castle was.

When Elin Gow came in, he cast two anchors at the ocean side and one at the shore side, and settled the ship in such a way that there was not a wave to strike her, nor a wind to rock her, nor a crow to drop on her; and he left her so that nothing would disturb her, and a fine, smooth strand before her : he left her fixed for a day and a year, though he might not be absent an hour.

He left the vessel about midday, and went his way walking, not knowing where was he or in what kingdom. He met no man or beast in the place. Late in the evening he saw, on a broad green field at a distance, a beautiful castle, the grandest he had ever set eyes on.

When he drew near the castle, the first house he found was a cottage at the wayside; and when he was passing, who should see him but a very old man inside in the cottage. The old man rose up, and putting his two hands on the jambs of the door, reached out his head and hailed him. Elin Gow turned on his heel; then the old man beckoned to him to enter.

There were four men in front of the castle, champions of valor, practising feats of arms. Flashes of light came from their swords. These men were so trained that they would not let a sword-stroke touch any part of their bodies.

"Come in," said the old man; "maybe you would like to have dinner. You have eaten nothing on the way."

"That was a mistake of my own," said Elin Gow; "for in my ship are provisions of all kinds in plenty."

"Never mind," said the old man; "you will not need them in this place;" and going to a chest, he took out a cloth which he spread on a table, and that moment there came on it food for a king or a champion. Elin Gow had never seen a better dinner in Erin.

"What is your name and from what place are you?" asked the old man of his guest.

"From Erin," said he, "and my name is Elin Gow. What country is this, and what castle .is that out before us?"

"Have you ever heard talk of the kingdom of Spain?" asked the old man.

"I have, and 't is to find it that I left home."

"Well, this is the kingdom of Spain, and that building beyond is the castle of the king."

"And is it here that Glas Gainach is?"

"It is," said the old man. "And is it for her that you left Erin?"

"It is then," said Elin Gow.

"I pity you," said the old man; "it would be fitter for you to stop at home and mind something else than to come hither for that cow. 'T is not hundreds but thousands of men that have lost their heads for her, and I am in dread that you 'll meet the same luck."

"Well, I will try my fortune," said Elin Gow. "'T is through dreams that I came."

"I pity you," said the old man, "and moreover because you are from Erin. I am half of your country, for my mother was from Erin. Do you know now how this cow will be got?"

"I do not," said Elin Gow; "I know nothing in the world about it."

"You will not be long," said the old man, "without knowledge. I 'll tell you about her, and what conditions will be put on you by the king. He will bind you for the term of seven years to bring the cow home safe and sound to his castle every evening. If you fail to bring her, your head will be cut off that same evening.

That is one way by which many kings' sons and champions that came from every part of the world were destroyed. There are spikes all around behind the castle, and a head on each spike of them. You will see for yourself to-morrow when you go to the castle, and a dreadful sight it is, for you will not be able to count the heads that are there on the spikes. I will give you now an advice that I have never given any man before this, but I have heard of you from my mother. You would be a loss to the country you came from. You are a great man to make swords and all kinds of weapons for champions.

"The king will not tell you what to do, but I 'll tell you: you 'll be as swift as you can when you go with the cow; keep up with her always. The day she moves least she will travel thirty miles going and thirty miles coming, and you will have rest only while she 'll be feeding, and she will take only a few minutes here and a few minutes there; wherever she sees the best place she'll take a bite; and do not disturb her wherever she turns or walks, and do not go before her or drive her. If you do what I say, there will be no fear of you, if you can be so swift as to keep up with the cow."

"I am not in dread of falling back," said Elin Gow.

"Then there will be no fear of you at all," said the old man.

Elin Gow remained in the cottage that night. In the morning the old man spread his cloth on the table; food and drink for a king or a champion were on it that moment. Elin Gow ate and drank heartily, left good health with the old man, and went to the castle. The king had a man called the Tongue-speaker, who met and announced every stranger. "Who are you or why do you come to the castle?" asked this man of Elin Gow.

"I wish to speak to the king about Glas Gainach."

"Oh," said the speaker, "you are badly wanted, for it is three days since the last man that was after her lost his head. Come, and I will show it to you on the spike, and I am in dread your own head will be in a like place."

"Never mind," said Elin Gow; "misfortune cannot be avoided. We will do our bést."

The Tongue-speaker went to the king then, and said, "There is a man outside who has come for Glas Gainach."

The king went out, and asked Elin Gow what he wanted or what brought him. He told him, as he told the speaker, that it was for the cow he had come.

"And is it in combat or in peace that you want to get her?"

"'T is in peace," said Elin Gow.

"You can try with swords or with herding, whichever you wish."

"We will choose the herding," said Elin Gow.

"Well," said the king, "this is how we will bind ourselves. You are to bring Glas Gainach here to me every evening safe and sound during seven years, and, if you fail, 't is your head that you will lose. Do you see those heads on the spikes there behind? 'T is on account of Glas Gainach they are there. If you come home with the cow every night, she will be yours when seven years are spent, — I bind myself to that," said the king.

"Well," said Elin Gow, "I am satisfied with the conditions."

Next morning Glas Gainach was let out, and both went together all day, she and Elin Gow. She went so swiftly that he threw his cap from him; he could not carry it half the day. All the rest he had was while she was feeding in any place. He was after her then till she came home, and he brought her back as safe and sound as in the morning. The king came out and welcomed him, saying, "You've taken good care of her; many a man went after her that did not bring her home the first day."

"Life is sweet," said Elin Gow; "I did the best hand I could. I know what I have to get if I fail to bring her."

The king gave Elin Gow good food and drink, so that he was more improving than failing in strength, and made his way and brought the cow every day till he had the seven years spent; then he said to the king, "My time is up; will I get the cow?"

"Oh, why not?" said the king. "You will: you have earned her well; you have done more than any man who walked the way before. See now how many have lost their heads; count them. You are better than any of them. I would not deny or break my word or agreement. You were bound to bring her, and I am bound to give her. Now she is yours and not mine, but if she comes back here again, don't have any eye after her; you'll not get her."

"That will do," said Elin Gow. "I will take good care not to let her come to you. I minded her the last seven years."

"Well," said the king, "I don't doubt you."

They gave the cow food that morning inside; did not let her out at all. Elin Gow bound the cow in every way he wished, to bring her to the vessel. He used all his strength, raised the two anchors on the ocean side, pulled in the vessel to put the cow on board. When Elin Gow was on board, he turned the stem of the ship toward the sea, and the stern toward land. He was sailing across the wide ocean till he came to Tramor, the port in Erin from which he had started when going to Spain. Elin Gow brought Glas Gainach on shore, took her to Cluainte, and was minding her as carefully as when he was with the King of Spain.

Elin Gow was the best man in Erin to make swords and all weapons for champions; his name was in all lands. The King of Munster had four sons, and the third from the oldest was Cian. He was neither dreaming nor thinking of anything night or day but feats of valor; his grandfather, Art Mac Cuin, had been a great champion, and was very fond of Cian. He used to say, "Kind father and grandfather for him; he is not like his three brothers."

When twenty years old, Cian said, "I will go to try my fortune. My father has heirs enough. I would try other kingdoms if I had a sword."

"You may have my sword," said the father.

Cian gave the sword a trial, and at the first turn he broke it. "No sword will please me," said Cian, "unless, while grasping the hilt with the blade pointed forward, I can bend the blade till its point touches my elbow on the upper side, then let it spring back and bend it again till the point touches my elbow on the under side."

"There is not a man in Erin who could make a sword like that," said the father, "but Elin Gow, and I am full sure that he will not make it at this time, for he is minding Glas Gainach. He earned her well, and he will guard her; seven years did he travel bareheaded without hat or cap, — a thing which no man could do before him. It would be useless to go to him, for he has never worked a stroke in the forge since he brought Glas Gainach to Erin, and he would not let her go. He would make the sword but for that. It's many a sword he made for me."

"Well, I will try him," said Cian. "I will ask him to make the sword."

Cian started, and never stopped till he stood before Elin Gow at Cluainte, and told him who he was.

Elin Gow welcomed the son of the king, and said, "Your father and I were good friends in our young years. It was often I made swords and other weapons for him. And what is it that brought you to day?"

"It is a sword I want. I wish to go and seek my fortune in some foreign land. I want a good sword, and my father says you are the best man in Erin to make one."

"I was," said Elin Gow; "and I am sorry that I cannot make you one now. I am engaged in minding Glas Gainach; and I would not trust any one after her but myself, and I have enough to do to mind her."

Cian told how the sword was to be made.

"Oh," said Elin Gow, "I would make it in any way you like but for the cow, and I would not wish to let your father's son go away without a sword. I will direct you to five or six smiths that are making swords now, in place of me since I went for Glas Gainach."

He gave the names, and the king's son went away.

None of them could make the sword in the way Cian wanted. He came back to Elin Gow.

"You have your round made?" said Elin Gow.

"I have," said Cian, "but in vain; for none of them would make the sword in the way asked of him."

"Well, I do not wish to let you go. I will take the risk."

"Very well," said Cian; "I will go after Glas Gainach to-morrow, while you are making the sword, and if I don't bring her, you may have my head in the evening."

"Well," said Elin Gow, "I am afraid to trust

you, for many a champion lost his head on account of her before; but I 'll run the risk. I
must make the sword for you."

The king's son stopped that night with Elin
Gow, who gave him the best food and drink he
had, and let out Glas Gainach before him next
morning, and told him not to come in front of her
in any place where she might want to feed or
drink. He advised him in every way how to
take care of her. Away went Cian with the cow,
and he was doing the right thing all day. She
moved on always, and went as far as Caorha,
southwest of Tralee, the best spot of land in
Kerry for grass. When she had eaten enough,
she turned toward home, and Cian was at her tail
all the day. When he and Glas Gainach were
five miles this side of Tralee, near the water at
Derrymor, where she used to drink, Cian saw
her going close to deep water; he came before
her, and turned her back; and what did she do
but jump through the air like a bird, and then
she went out through the sea and left him. He
walked home sad and mournful, and came to Elin
Gow's house. The smith asked him had he the
cow, and he said, "I have not. I was doing
well till I came to Derrymor, and she went so
near deep water that I was afraid she would go
from me. I stopped her, and what did she do

but fly away like a bird, and go out through the sea."

"God help us," said Elin Gow, "but the misfortune cannot be helped."

"I am the cause," said Cian; "you may have my head."

"What is done, is done. I would never take the head off you, but she is a great loss to me."

"I am willing and satisfied to give you my head," said Cian. "Have you the sword made?"

"I have," said Elin Gow.

Cian took the blade, tested it in every way, and found that he had the sword he wanted.

He swore an oath then to Elin Gow that he would not delay day or night, nor rest anywhere, till he had lost his head or brought back Glas Gainach.

"I am afraid your labor will be useless," said Elin Gow, "and that you will never be able to bring her back. I could not have brought her myself but for the advice of an old man that I met before I saw the King of Spain."

Cian went home to his father's castle. The king saw him coming with the sword. "I see that Elin Gow did not refuse you."

"He did not," said Cian. "He made the sword, and it is a sore piece of work for him. He has parted with Glas Gainach. I promised to give my head if I did not bring her home to him in safety while he was making the sword. I minded her well all day till she came to a place where she used to drink water. I did not know that; but it was my duty to know it, for he directed me in every way needful how to mind her. I was bringing her home in safety till I brought her to Derrymor River; and I went before her to turn her back, — and that was foolish, for he told me not to turn her while I was with her, — and she did nothing but spring like a bird and out to sea and away. I promised Elin Gow in the morning if I did not bring the cow to give him my head; and I offered it when I came, as I had not the cow, but he said, 'I will never take the head off a son of your father, even for a greater loss.' And for this reason I will never rest nor delay till I go for Glas Gainach and bring her back to Elin Gow, or lose my head; so make ready your best ship."

"The best ship," said the king, "is the one that Elin Gow took."

The king's son put provisions for a day and a year in the vessel. He set sail alone and away with him through the main ocean, and he never stopped till he reached the same place to which Elin Gow had sailed before. He cast two anchors on the ocean side, and one next the

shore, and left the ship where there was no wind
to blow on her, no waves of the ocean to touch
her, no crows of the air to drop on her. He
went his way then, and was walking always till
evening, when he saw at a distance the finest
castle he had ever set eyes on. He went toward
it; and when he was near, he saw four champions
at exercise near the castle. He was going on
the very same road that Elin Gow had taken,
and was passing the same cottage, when the old
man saw him and hailed him. He turned toward
the cottage.

"Come to my house and rest," said the old
man. "From what country are you, and what
brought you?"

"I am a son of the King of Munster in Erin;
and now will you tell me what place is
this?"

"You are in Spain, and the building beyond
there is the king's castle."

"Very well and good. It was to see the king
that I left Erin," said Cian.

"It is for Glas Gainach that you are here, I suppose," said the old man. "It is useless for you to
try; you never can bring her from the king. It
was a hundred times easier when Elin Gow
brought her; it is not that way now, but by force
and bravery she is to be taken. It is a pity to

have you lose your head, like so many kings and champions."

"I must try," said Cian; "for it was through me that Elin Gow lost Glas Gainach. I wanted a sword to try my fortune, and there was not a smith in Erin who could make it as I wanted except Elin Gow; he refused. I told him that I would give my head if I did not bring the cow home to him in safety. I followed her well till, on the way home, she went to drink near the sea, and I went before her; that moment she sprang away like a bird, and went out through the water."

"I am afraid," said the old man, "that to get her is more than you can do. You see those four men? You must fight and conquer them before you get Glas Gainach."

The old man spread out the table-cloth, and they ate.

"I care not," said the king's son, "what comes. I am willing to lose my head unless I can bring back the cow."

"Well," said the old man, "you can try."

Next morning breakfast was ready for Cian; he rose, washed his hands and face, prayed for mercy and strength, ate, and going to the pole of combat gave the greatest blow ever given before on it.

"Run out," said the king to the Tongue-speaker; "see who is abroad."

"What do you want?" asked the Tongue-speaker of Cian.

"The king's daughter and Glas Gainach," said Cian.

The speaker hurried in and told the king. The king went out and asked, "Are you the man who wants my daughter and Glas Gainach?"

"I am," answered Cian.

"You will get them if you earn them," said the king.

"If I do not earn them, I want neither the daughter nor the cow," replied Cian.

The king ordered out then the four knights of valor to kill Cian. He was as well trained as they, for he had been practising from his twelfth year, and he was more active. They were at him all day, and he at them: he did not let one blow from them touch his body; and if a man were to go from the Eastern to the Western World to see champions, 't is at them he would have to look. At last, when Cian was hungry, and late evening near, he sprang with the strength of his limbs out of the joints of his bones, and rose above them, and swept the heads of the four before he touched ground.

The young champion was tired after the day,

and went to the old man. The old man asked, "What have you done?"

"I have knocked the heads off the four champions of valor."

The old man was delighted that the first day had thriven in that way with Cian. He looked at the sword. "Oh, there is no danger," cried he; "you have the best sword I have ever seen, and you'll need it, for you'll have more forces against you to-morrow."

The old man and Cian spent the night in three parts, — the first part in eating and drinking, the second in telling tales and singing songs, the third in sound sleep.

The old man told how he had been the champion of Spain, and at last when he grew old the king gave him that house.

Next morning Cian washed his face and hands, prayed for help and mercy, ate breakfast with the old man, went to the pole of combat, and gave a greater blow still than before.

"What do you want this day?" asked the Tongue-speaker.

"I want three hundred men on my right hand, three hundred on my left, three hundred after my poll, three hundred out in front of me." The king sent the men out four deep through four gates. Cian went at them, and as they came he struck the heads off them; and though they fought bravely, in the evening he had the heads off the twelve hundred. Cian then left the field, and went to the old man.

"What have you done after the day?" asked the old man.

"I have stretched the king's forces."

"You'll do well," said the old man.

The old champion put the cloth on the table, and there was food for a king or a champion. They made three parts of that night, — the first for eating and drinking, the second for telling tales and singing songs, the third for sleep and sound rest.

Next morning, Cian gave such a blow on the pole of combat that the king in his chamber was frightened.

"What do you want this time?" asked the Tongue-speaker.

"I want the same number of men as yesterday."

The king sent the men out; and the same fate befell them as the other twelve hundred, and Cian went home to the old man untouched. Next morning Cian made small bits of the king's pole of combat.

"Well, what do you want?" asked the Tongue-speaker.

"Whatever I want, I don't want to be losing time. Let out all your forces against me at once."

The king sent out all the forces he wished that morning. The battle was more terrible than all the others put together; but Cian went through the king's forces, and at sunset not a man of them was living, and he let no one nearer than the point of his sword.

"How did the day thrive with you?" asked the old man when Cian came in.

"I have killed all the king's champions."

"I think," said the old man, "that you have the last of his forces down now; but what you have done is nothing to what is before you. The king will come out and say to-morrow that you will not get the daughter with Glas Gainach till you eat on one biscuit what butter there is in his storehouses, and they are all full; you are to do this in the space of four hours. He will give you the biscuit. Take this biscuit from me, and do you hide the one that he will give you, — never mind it; put as much as you will eat on this, and there'll be no tidings of what butter there is in the king's stores within one hour, — it will vanish and disappear."

Cian was very glad when the old man told him what to do. They spent that night as they had the nights before. Next morning Cian breakfasted, and went to the castle. The king saw him coming, and was out before him.

"What do you want this morning?" asked the king.

"I want your daughter and Glas Gainach," said Cian.

"Well," said the king, "you will not get my daughter and Glas Gainach unless within four hours you eat on this biscuit what butter there is in all my storehouses in Spain; and if you do not eat the butter, your head will be on a spike this evening."

The king gave him the biscuit. Cian went to the first storehouse, dropped the king's biscuit into his pocket, took out the one the old man had given him, buttered it, and began to eat. He went his way then, and in one hour there was neither sign nor trace of butter in any storehouse the king had.

That night Cian and the old man passed the time in three parts as usual. "You will have hard work to-morrow," said the old man, "but I will tell you how to do it. The king will say that you cannot have his daughter and Glas Gainach unless within four hours you tan all the hides in Spain, dry and green, and tan them as well as a hand's breadth of leather that he will give you. Here is a piece of leather like the piece the king will give. Clap this on the first hide you come to; and all the hides in Spain will be tanned in one hour, and be as soft and smooth as the king's piece."

Next morning the king saw Cian coming, and was out before him. "What do you want now?" asked the king.

"Your daughter and Glas Gainach," said Cian.

"You are not to get my daughter and Glas Gainach unless within four hours you tan all the dry and green hides in Spain to be as soft and smooth as this piece; and if you do not tan them, your head will be on one of the spikes there behind my castle this evening."

Cian took the leather, dropped it into his pocket, and, taking the old man's piece, placed it on the first hide that he touched. In one hour all the hides in Spain were tanned, and they were as soft and fine as the piece which the king gave to Cian.

The old man and Cian spent this night as they had the others.

"You will have the hardest task of all to-morrow," said the old man.

"What is that?" asked the young champion.

"The king's daughter will come to a window in the highest chamber of the castle with a ball in her hand: she will throw the ball through the window, and you must catch it on your hurley, and keep it up during two hours and a half;

never let it touch the ground. There will be a hundred champions striving to take the ball from you, but follow my advice. The champions, not knowing where the ball will come down when the king's daughter throws it, will gather near the front of the castle; and if either of them should get the ball, he might keep it and spoil you. Do you stand far outside; you will have the best chance. I don't know, though, what you are to do, as you have no hurley, but wait. In my youth I was great to play at hurley, and I never met a man that could match me. The hurley I had then must be in this house somewhere."

The old man searched the house through, and where did he find the hurley but up in the loft, and it full of dust; he brought it down. Cian swung it, knocked the dust from the hurley, and it was as clean as when made.

"It is glad I am to find this, for any other hurley in the kingdom would not do you, but only this very one. This hurley has the virtue in it, and only for that it would not do."

Both were very glad, and made three parts of that night, as they had of the nights before. Next morning Cian rose, washed his hands and face, and begged mercy and help of God for that day.

After breakfast he went to the king's castle, and soon many champions came around him.

The king was outside before him, and asked what he wanted that day.

"I want your daughter and Glas Gainach."

"You will not get my daughter and Glas Gainach till you do the work I'll give, and I'll give you the toughest task ever put before you. At midday, my daughter will throw out a ball through the window, and you must keep that ball in the air for two hours and a half: it must never touch ground in that time, and when the two hours and a half are spent, you must drive it in through the same window through which it went out; if not, I will have your head on a spike this evening."

"God help us!" said Cian.

All the champions were together to see which man would get the ball first; but Cian, thinking of the old man's advice, stood outside them all. At midday the king's daughter sent out the ball through the highest window; and to whom should it go but to Cian, and he had the luck of getting it first. He drove the ball with his hurley, and for two hours and a half he kept it in the air, and did not let another man touch it. Then he gave it a directing blow, and sent it in through the window to the king's daughter.

The king watched the ball closely; and when it went in, he ran to Cian, shook his hand warmly, and never stopped till he took him to his daughter's high chamber. She kissed him with joy and great gladness. He had done a thing that no other had ever done.

"I have won the daughter and Glas Gainach from you now," said Cian.

"You have," said the king; "and they are both yours. I give them with all my heart. You have earned them well, and done what no other man could do. I will give you one-half of the kingdom till my death, and all of it from that out."

Cian and the king's daughter were married. A great feast was made, and a command given out that all people of the kingdom must come to the wedding. Every one came; and the wedding lasted seven days and nights, to the pleasure of all, and the greatest delight of the king. Cian remained with the king; and after a time his wife had a son, the finest and fairest child ever born in Spain, and he was increasing so that what of him did n't grow in the day grew in the night, and what did not grow in the night grew in the day, and if the sun shone on any child, it shone on that one. The boy was called Cormac after Cian's father, Cormac Mac Art.

Cian remained with the King of Spain till Cormac's age was a year and a half. Then he remembered his promise to Elin Gow to bring back Glas Gainach.

Cian put stores in the vessel in which he had come, and placed Glas Gainach inside, firmly fettered. He gave then the stem of his ship to the ocean, the stern to land, raised the limber sails; and there was the work of a hundred men on each side, though Cian did the work all alone. He sailed through the main ocean with safety till he came to Tramor, — the best landing-place in Erin at that time. Glas Gainach was brought to shore carefully, and Cian went on his way with her to go to Elin Gow's house at Cluainte.

There was no highway from Tramor but the one; and on that one were three brothers, three robbers, the worst at that time in Erin. These men knew all kinds of magic, and had a rod of enchantment. Cian had brought much gold with him on the way, coming as a present to his father.

The three brothers stopped Cian, saluted him, and asked would he play a game. He said that he would. They played, and toward evening the robbers had the gold won; then they said to Cian, "Now bet the cow against the gold you have lost, and we will put twice as much with it." He laid the cow as a wager, and lost her.

One of the three robber brothers struck Cian with the rod of enchantment, and made a stone pillar of him, and made an earth mound of Glas Gainach with another blow. The two remained there, the man and the cow, by the roadside.

Cian's son Cormac was growing to manhood in Spain, and heard his mother and grandfather talk of his father, and he thought to himself, " There was no man on earth that could fight with my father; and I promise now to travel and be walking always till I find out the place where he is, living or dead."

As Cormac had heard that his father was from Erin, to Erin he faced, first of all. The mother was grieved, and advised him not to go wandering. " Your father must be dead, or on the promise he made me he 'd be here long ago."

" There is no use in talking; the world will not stop me till I know what has happened to my father," said Cormac.

The mother could not stop him; she gave her consent. He turned then to his grandfather. " Make ready for me the best vessel you have," said he. The vessel was soon ready with provisions for a day and a year, and gold two thousand pieces. He embarked, and went through the main ocean faster than his father had gone till he sailed into Tramor. He was on his way walking till he came to the robbers about midday.

They saluted him kindly, thinking he had gold, and asked, " Will you play a game with us? "

"I will," said Cormac; "I have never refused."

They played. The robbers gained, and let him gain; they were at him the best of the day, till they won the last piece of gold of his two thousand pieces.

When he had lost what he had, he was like a wild man, and knew not what to do for a while. At last Cormac said to himself, "It is an old saying never contradicted that strength will get the upper hand of enchantment." He jumped then, and caught two of the three robbers, one in each hand, and set them under his two knees. The third was coming to help the two; but Cormac caught that one with his hand and held the three, kept them there, and said, "I will knock the heads off every man of you."

"Do not do that," begged the three. "Who are you? We will do what you ask of us."

"I am seeking my father, Cian Mac Cormac, who left Spain eighteen years ago with Glas Gainach."

"Spare us," said the three brothers; "we will give back your gold and raise up your father with Glas Gainach."

"How can ye do that," asked Cormac, "or where is my father?"

"He is that pillar there opposite "

"And where is Glas Gainach?"

They showed him the earth mound.

"How can ye bring them back to their own shapes?" asked Cormac.

"We have a rod of enchantment," said the brothers; and they told where the rod was. When Cormac had a true account of the rod, what he did was to draw out his sword and cut the heads off the three brothers, saying, "Ye will never again rob any man who walks this way." Cormac then found the rod of enchantment, went to the pillar, gave it a blow, and his father came forth as well and healthy as ever.

"Who are you?" asked Cian of Cormac.

"I am your son Cormac."

"Oh, my dear son, how old are you?"

"I'm in my twentieth year," said Cormac. "I heard my mother and grandfather talk of your bravery, and I made up my mind to go in search of you, and be walking always till I found you. I said I'd face Erin first, for 't was there you went with Glas Gainach. I landed this morning, met these three robbers; they won all my gold. I was like a wild man. I caught them, and swore I would kill them. They asked who was I; I told them. They said you were the stone pillar; that they had a rod that would raise you up with Glas Gainach. They told where the rod was. I took the heads off them, and raised you with the rod."

Now Cormac struck the earth mound, and Glas Gainach rose up as well as before. Everything was now in its own place, and they were glad. Cian would not stop till he brought Glas Gainach to Elin Gow, so he was walking night and day till he came here behind to Cluainte, where Elin Gow was living. He screeched out Elin Gow's name, told him to come. He came out; and when he saw Cian and Glas Gainach he came near fainting from joy. Cian put Glas Gainach's horn in his hand, and said, "I wished to keep the promise I made when you spared my head; and it was gentle of you to spare it, for great was the loss that I caused you;" and he told all that had happened, — how he had won and lost Glas Gainach, and lost her through the robbers.

"Who is this brave youthful champion with you?" asked Elin Gow.

"This is my son, and but for him I'd be forever where the three robbers put me. I was eighteen years where they left me; but for that, the cow would have been with you long ago. What were you doing all this time?" asked Cian of Elin Gow.

"Making swords and weapons, but I could not have lived without the support of your father."

"He promised me that," said Cian, "before I left Erin. I knew that he would help you."

"Oh, he did!" said Elin Gow.

The father and son left good health with Elin Gow, and never stopped nor stayed till they reached the castle of Cian's father. The old king had thought that Cian was dead, as he had received no account of him for so many years. Great was his joy and gladness, and great was the feast that he made.

Cian remained for a month, and then went to the house of the robbers, took out all its treasures, locked up the place in the way that no man could open it; then he gave one-half his wealth to his father. He took the rest to Spain with his son, and lived there.

Elin Gow had grown old, and he was in dread that he had not the strength to follow Glas Gainach, and sent a message to Caol na Crua, the fleetest champion in Kerry. Caol came. Elin Gow agreed to pay him his price for minding the cow, and was glad to get him. He told Caol carefully how to herd the cow. She travelled as before, and was always at home before nightfall.

Glas Gainach had milk for all; and when any one came to milk her she would stop, and there never was a vessel that she did not fill. One

woman heard this; and once when Glas Gainach
was near a river, the woman brought a sieve
and began to milk. She milked a long time.
At last the cow saw the river white with milk;
then she raised her leg, gave the woman a kick
on the forehead, and killed her.

Caol na Crua was doing well, minding the
cow all the time, till one evening Glas Gainach
walked between the two pillars where she used
to scratch herself; when she was full, her sides
would touch both pillars. This evening she
bellowed, and Elin Gow heard her. Instead of
going home then, she went down to a place
northwest of Cluainte, near a ruin; she used to
drink there at times, but not often. Caol na
Crua did not know this. He thought she was
going into the sea, and caught her tail to hold
her back. With that, instead of drinking, she
went straight toward the water. Caol tried to
hold her. She swept him along and went
through the ocean, he keeping the grip he had,
and she going with such swiftness that he was
lying flat on the sea behind her; and she took
him with her to Spain and went to the king, and
very joyful was the king, for they were in great
distress for butter while Glas Gainach was gone.

MOR'S SONS AND THE HERDER FROM UNDER THE SEA.

IN old times, there was a great woman in the southwest of Erin, and she was called Mor. This woman lived at Dun Quin; and when she came to that place the first time with her husband Lear, she was very poor. People say that it was by the water she came to Dun Quin. Whatever road she took, all she had came by the sea, and went the same way.

She built a small house, and their property was increasing little by little. After a while she had three sons, and these grew to be very fine boys and then strong young men.

The two elder sons set out to try their fortunes; they got a vessel, sailed away on the sea, and never stopped nor halted till they came to the Kingdom of the White Strand, in the eastern world. There they stayed for seven years, goaling and sporting with the people.

The king of that country wished to keep them forever, because they were strong men, and had risen to be great champions.

The youngest son remained at home all the time, growing to be as good a man as his brothers. One day he went out to look at a large field of wheat which his mother had, and found it much injured.

"Well, mother," said he when he came in, "all our field is destroyed by something. I don't know for the world what is it. Something comes in, tramples the grain and eats it."

"Watch the field to-night, my son, and see what is devouring our grain."

"Well, mother, boil something for me to eat to give me strength and good luck for the night."

Mor baked a loaf, and boiled some meat for her son, and told him to watch well till the hour of night, when perhaps the cattle would be before him.

He was watching and looking there, till all at once, a little after midnight, he saw the field full of cattle of different colors, — beautiful colors, blue, and red, and white. He was looking at them for a long time, they were so beautiful. The young man wanted to drive the beasts home with him, to show his mother the cattle that were spoiling the grain. He had them out of the field on the road when a herder stood before him, and said, "Leave the cattle behind you."

"I will not," said Mor's son; "I will drive them home to my mother."

"I will not let them with you," said the herder.

"I'll carry them in spite of you," replied Mor's son.

He had a good strong green stick, and so had the herder; the two faced each other, and began to fight. The herder was too strong for Mor's son, and he drove off the cattle into the sea.

"Oh," said the herder, as he was going, "your mother did not boil your meat or bake your loaf rightly last night; she gave too much fire to the loaf and the meat, took the strength out of them. You might do something if your mother knew how to cook."

When Mor's son went home, his mother asked, "Did you see any cattle, my son?"

"I did, mother; the field was full of them. And when I was bringing the herd home with me to show you, a man stood there on the road to take the beasts from me; we fought, and when he beat me and was driving the cattle into the sea, what did he say but that you boiled the meat and baked the loaf too much last night. To-night, when you boil my meat, do not give it half the fire; leave all the strength in the meat and the loaf."

"I will," said the mother.

When night came, the dinner was ready. The young man ate twice as much of the meat and the loaf as the evening before. About the same hour, just after midnight, he went to the field, for he knew now what time the cattle would be in it. The field was full of the same cattle of beautiful colors.

Mor's son drove the beasts out, and was going to drive them home, when the herder, who was not visible hitherto, came before him and said, "I will not let the cattle with you."

"I will take them in spite of you," replied Mor's son.

The two began to fight, and Mor's son was stronger this time.

"Why do you not keep your cattle out of my wheat?" asked he of the herder.

"Because I know very well that you are not able to take them with you."

"If I am not able to take the cattle, you may have them and the wheat as well," said Mor's son.

The herder was driving the cattle one way, and Mor's son was driving them the opposite way; and after they had done that for a while, they faced each other and began to fight again.

Mor's son was doubly angry at the herder this

night for the short answers that he gave. They fought two hours; then the herder got the upper hand. Mor's son was sorry; and the herder, as he drove the cattle to the sea, called out, "Your mother gave too much fire to the meat and the loaf; still you are stronger to night than you were last night."

Mor's son went home.

"Well, my son," asked the mother, "have you any news of the cattle and the herder?"

"I have seen them, mother."

"And what did the herder do?"

"He was too strong for me a second time, and drove the cattle into the sea."

"What are we to do now?" asked the mother. "If he keeps on in this way, we'll soon be poor, and must leave the country altogether."

"The herder said, as he drove the cattle away, 'Your mother gave too much fire to the meat and the loaf; still you are stronger to-night than you were last night.' Well, mother, if you gave too much fire to my dinner last night, give but little to-night, and I will leave my life outside or have the cattle home with me this time. If I do not beat him, he may have the wheat as well as the cattle after to-night."

Mor prepared the dinner; and this time she barely let the water on the meat begin to bubble, and to the bread she gave but one roast.

He ate and drank twice as much as the day before. The dinner gave him such strength that he said, "I'll bring the cattle to-night."

He went to the field, and soon after midnight it was full of cattle of the same beautiful colors; the grain was spoiled altogether. He drove the cattle to the road, and thought he had them. He got no sight of the herder till every beast was outside the field, and he ready to drive them home to his mother. Then the herder stood before him, and began to drive the cattle toward the sea.

"You'll not take them this time," said Mor's son.

"I will," said the herder.

They began to fight, caught each other, dragged, and struggled long, and in the heel of the battle Mor's son was getting the better of the herder.

"I think that you'll have the upper hand of me this time," said the herder; "and 't is my own advice I blame for it. You'll take the cattle to-night in spite of me. Let me go now, and take them away with you."

"I will," said Mor's son. "I will take them to the house, and please my mother."

He drove the cattle home, and said to his mother, "I have the cattle here now for you, and do whatever you wish with them."

The herder followed Mor's son to the house.

"Why did you destroy all my grain with your cattle?" asked Mor.

"Let the cattle go with me now, and I promise that after to-night your field of wheat will be the best in the country."

"What are we to do?" asked Mor of the son. "Is it to let the cattle go with him for the promise he gives?"

"I will do what you say, mother."

"We will give him the cattle," said Mor.

"Well," said the son to the herder, "my mother is going to give you the cattle for the promise that our grain will be the best in the country when 't is reaped. We ought to be friends after the fighting; and now take your cattle home with you, though you vexed and hurt me badly."

"I am very grateful to you," said the herder to Mor's son, "and for your kindness you will have plenty of cattle and plenty of wheat before you die, and seeing that you are such a good man I will give you a chance before I leave you. The King of Mayo has an only daughter; the fairies will take her from him to-morrow. They will bring her through Daingean, on the shoulders of four men, to the fairy fort at Cnoc na Hown. Be at the cross-roads about two o'clock to-morrow night. Jump up quickly, put your shoulder under the coffin, the four men will disappear and leave the coffin on the road; do you bring what's in the coffin home with you."

Mor's son followed the herder's directions. He went toward Daingean in the night, for he knew the road very well. After midnight, he was at the cross-roads, waiting and hidden. Soon he saw the coffin coming out against him, and the four men carrying it on their shoulders.

The young man put his shoulder under the coffin; the four dropped it that minute, and disappeared. Mor's son took the lid off the coffin; and what did he find lying inside but a beautiful woman, warm and ruddy, sleeping as if at home in her bed. He took out the young woman, knowing well that she was alive, and placing her on his back, left the coffin behind at the wayside.

The woman could neither walk nor speak, and he brought her home to his mother. Mor opened the door, and he put the young woman down in the corner.

"What's this you brought me? What do I want with the like of her in the house?"

"Never mind, mother; it may be our luck that will come with her."

They gave her every kind of drink and nourishing food, for she was very weak; when daylight came, she was growing stronger, and could speak. The first words she said were, " I am no good to you in the way that I am now; but if you are a brave man, you will meet with your luck to-morrow night. All the fairies will be gathered at a feast in the fort at Cnoc na Hown; there will be a horn of drink on the table. If you bring that horn, and I get three sips from it (if you have the heart of a brave man you will go to the fort, seize the horn, and bring it here), I shall be as well and strong as ever, and you will be as rich yourself as any king in Erin."

"I have stood in great danger before from the like of them," replied Mor's son. " I will make a trial of this work, too."

"Between one and two o'clock in the night you must go to the fort," said the young woman, "and you must carry a stick of green rowan wood in your hand."

The young man went to the fairy fort, keeping the stick carefully and firmly in his hand. At parting, the young woman warned him, saying, " They can do you no harm in the world while you have the stick, but without the stick there is no telling what they might do."

When Mor's son came to Cnoc na Hown, and went in through the gate of the fairy fort, he saw a house and saw many lights flashing in different places. In the kitchen was a great table with all sorts of food and drink, and around it a crowd of small men. When he was making toward the table, he heard one of the men say, —

"Very little good will the girl be to Mor's son. He may keep her in the corner by his mother. There will be neither health nor strength in her; but if she had three drinks out of this horn on the table here, she would be as well as ever."

He faced them then, and, catching the horn, said, "She will not be long without the drink!"

All the little men looked at one another as he hurried through the door and disappeared. He had the stick, and they could not help themselves; but all began to scold one another for not having the courage to seize him and take the horn from him.

Mor's son reached home with the horn. "Well, mother," said he, "we have the cure now;" and he did n't put the horn down till the young woman had taken three drinks out of it, and then she said, —

"You are the best champion ever born in Erin, and now take the horn back to Cnoc na Hown; I am as well and hearty as ever."

He took the horn back to the fairy fort, placed

it on the table, and hurried home. The fairies looked at one another, but not a thing could they do, for the stick was in his hand yet.

"The woman is as well as ever now," said one of the fairies when Mor's son had gone, "and we have lost her;" and they began to scold one another for letting the horn go with him. But that was all the good it did them; the young woman was cured.

Next day the young woman said to Mor's son, "I am well now, and I will give you a token to take to my father and mother in Mayo."

"I will not take the token," said he; "I will go and seek out your father, and bring back some token to you first."

He went away, searched and inquired till he made out the king's castle; and when he was there, he went around all the cattle and went away home to his mother at Tivorye with every four-footed beast that belonged to the king.

"Well, mother," said he, "it is the luck we have now; and we'll have the whole parish under stock from this out."

The young woman was not satisfied yet, and said, "You must go and carry a token to my father and mother."

"Wait awhile, and be quiet," answered Mor's son. "Your father will send herders to hunt for the stock, and these men will have token enough when they come."

Well, sure enough, the king's men hunted over hills and valleys, found that the cattle had been one day in such a place and another day in another place; and they followed on till at length and at last they came near Mor's house, and there they saw the cattle grazing above on the mountain.

There was no house in Dun Quin at that time but Mor's house, and there was not another in it for many a year after.

"We will send a man down to that house," said the herders, "to know can we get any account of what great champion it was that brought the cattle all this distance."

What did the man see when he came near the house but his own king's daughter. He knew the young woman, and was struck dumb when he saw her, and she buried two months before at her father's castle in Mayo. He had no power to say a word, he forgot where he was, or why he was sent. At last he turned, ran up to the men above on the mountain, and said, "The king's daughter is living below in that house."

The herders would not believe a word he said, but at last three other men went down to see for themselves. They knew the king's daughter, and were frightened; but they had more courage, and after a while asked, "Where is the man that brought the cattle?"

"He is sleeping," said the king's daughter. "He is tired after the long journey; if you wish, I will wake him."

She woke Mor's son, and he came out.

"What brought you here?" asked he of the men.

"We came looking for our master's cattle; they are above on the mountain, driven to this place by you, as it seems. We have travelled hither and over till we found them."

"Go and tell your master," said Mor's son, "that I brought the cattle; that Lear is my father, and Mor is my mother, and that I have his daughter here with me."

"There is no use in sending them with that message," said the young woman; "my father would not believe them."

"Tell your master," said Mor's son, "that it is I who brought the cattle, and that I have his daughter here in good health, and 't is by my bravery that I saved her."

"If they go to my father with that message, he will kill them. I will give them a token for him."

"What token will you give?"

"I will give them this ring with my name and my father's name and my mother's name written inside on it. Do not give the ring," said she to the men, "till ye tell my father all ye have seen; if he will not believe you, then give the ring."

Away went the men, and not a foot of the cattle did they take; and if all the men in Mayo had come, Mor's son would not have let the cattle go with them, for he had risen to be the best champion in Erin. The men went home by the straightest roads; and they were not half the time going to the king's castle that they were in finding the cattle.

On the way home, one man said to the others, "It is a great story we have and good news to tell; the king will make rich men of us for the tidings we are taking him."

When they reached the king's castle, there was a welcome before them.

"Have ye any news for me after the long journey?" asked the king.

"We found your daughter with a man in Tivorye in the southwest of Erin, and all your cattle are with the same man."

"Ye may have found my cattle, but ye could not get a sight of my daughter."

"If you do not believe us in this way, you will in another. We may as well tell you all."

"Ye may as well keep silent. I'll not believe a word of what ye say about my daughter."

"I will give you a token from your daughter,"
said one of the men, pulling out a purse. He
had the purse rolled carefully in linen. (And he
did well, for the fairies cannot touch linen, and
it is the best guard in the world against them.
Linen thread, too, is strong against the fairies.
A man might travel all the fairy forts of the
world if he had a skein of flax thread around his
neck, and a steel knife with a black handle in
his pocket.) He took out the ring, and gave it
to the king. The king sent for the queen. She
came. He put the ring in her hand and said,
"Look at this, and see do you know it."

"I do indeed," said she; "and how did you
come by this ring?"

The king told the whole story that the men
had brought.

"This is our daughter's ring. It was on her
finger when we buried her," said the queen.

"It was," said the king, "and what the men
say must be true." He would have killed them
but for the ring.

On the following morning, the king and queen
set out with horses, and never stopped till they
came to Tivorye (Mor's house). The king knew
the cattle the moment he saw them above on the

mountain, and then he was sure of the rest. They were sorry to find the daughter in such a small cabin, but glad that she was alive. The guide was sent to the house to say the king and queen were coming.

"Your father and mother are coming," said he to the king's daughter.

She made ready, and was standing in the door before them. The father and mother felt weak and faint when they looked at her; but she ran out, took them by the hands, and said, "Have courage; I am alive and well, no ghost, and ye ought to thank the man who brought me away from my enemies."

"Bring him to us," said they; "we wish to see him."

"He is asleep, but I will wake him."

"Wake him," said the father, "for he is the man we wish to see now."

The king's daughter roused Mor's son, and said, "My father and mother are above in the kitchen. Go quickly, and welcome them."

He welcomed them heartily, and he was ten times gladder to see them than they were to see him. They inquired then how he got the daughter, and she buried at home two months before. And he told the whole story from first to last : How the herder from the sea had told

him, and how he had saved her at Cnoc na Hown.
They had a joyful night in the cabin after the
long journey, and anything that would be in any
king's castle they had in Mor's house that night,
for the king had plenty of everything with him
from the castle.   Next morning the king and
queen were for taking the daughter home with
them; but she refused firmly, and said, —

"I will never leave the man who saved me
from such straits.   I 'll never marry any man but
him, for I 'm sure that he is the best hero ever
reared in Erin, after the courage that he has
shown."

"We will never carry you away, since you like
him so well; and we will send him twice as many
cattle, and money besides."

They brought in the priest of whatever religion
was in it at the time (to be sure, it was not
Catholic priests were in Erin in those days), and
Mor's son and the king's daughter were married.
The father and mother left her behind in Tivorye,
and enjoyed themselves on the way home, they
were that glad after finding the daughter alive.

When Mor's son was strong and rich, he could
not be satisfied till he found his two brothers,
who had left home years before, and were in the
kingdom of the White Strand, though he did not
know it.   He made up a fine ship then, and got

provisions for a day and a year, went into it, set sail, and went on over the wide ocean till he came to the chief port of the King of the White Strand. He was seven days on the water; and when he came in on the strand, the king saw him, and thought that he must be a brave man to come alone on a ship to that kingdom.

"That must be a great hero," said he to his men. "Let some of the best of you go down and knock a trial out of him before he comes to the castle."

The king was so in dread of the stranger that out of all the men he selected Mor's two elder sons. They were the best and strongest men he had, and he sent them to know what activity was in the new-comer. They took two hurleys for themselves and one for the stranger, and a ball.

The second brother challenged the stranger to play. When the day was closing, the stranger was getting the upper hand. They invited him to the king's castle for the night, and the elder brother challenged him to play a game on the following day.

"How did the trial turn out?" asked the king of the elder brother.

"I sent my brother to try him, and it was the strange champion that got the upper hand."

Mor's son remained at the castle that night,

and found good welcome and cheer. He ate breakfast next morning, and a good breakfast it was. They took three hurleys then and a ball, and went to the strand. Said the eldest brother to the second, "Stop here and look at us, and see what the trial will be between us."

They gave the stranger a choice of the hurleys, and the game began. It couldn't be told who was the better of the two brothers. The king was in dread that the stranger would injure himself and his men. In the middle of the day, when it could not be determined who was the better man, the elder brother said, "We will try wrestling now, to know which of us can win that way."

"I'm well satisfied," said Mor's son.

They began to wrestle. The elder brother gave Mor's son several knocks, and he made several turns on the elder.

"Well, if I live," said the elder, "you are my brother; for when we used to wrestle at home, I had the knocks, and you had the turns. You are my younger brother, for no man was able to wrestle with me when I was at Tivorye but you."

They knew each other then, and embraced. Each told his story.

"Come home with me now," said the youngest

brother, "and see our mother. I am as rich as any king, and can give you good entertainment."

The three went to the King of the White Strand, and told him everything. The eldest and second brother asked leave of him to go home to see their father and mother. The king gave them leave, and filled their vessel with every kind of good food, and the two promised to come back.

The three brothers set sail then, and after seven days came in on the strand near Tivorye. The two found their brother richer than any king in any country. They were enjoying themselves at home for a long time, having everything that their hearts could wish, when one day above another they saw a vessel passing Dun Quin, and it drew up at the quay in Daingean harbor. Next day people went to the ship; but if they did, not a man went on board, for no man was allowed to go.

There was a green cat on deck. The cat was master of the vessel, and would not let a soul come near it. A report went out through the town that the green cat would allow no one to go near the ship, and for three weeks this report was spreading. No one was seen on the vessel but the cat, and he the size of a big man.

Mor's sons heard of the ship and the green cat

at Daingean, and they said, "Let us have a day's pleasure, and go to the ship and see the cat."

Mor bade them stay at home. "Don't mind the ship or the cat," said she, "and follow my advice." But the sons would not follow her advice, nor be said by her, and away they went, in spite of all she could do.

When the cat saw them coming, he knew very well who were in it. He jumped out on the shore, stood on two legs, and shook hands with the three brothers. He was as tall himself as the largest man, and as friendly as he could be. The three brothers were glad to receive an honor which no one else could get.

"Come down now to the cabin and have a trial of my cooking," said the cat.

He brought them to the cabin, and the finest dinner was on the table before them, — meat and drink as good as ever they tasted either in Tivorye or the kingdom of the White Strand.

When the cat had them below in the cabin, and they eating and drinking with great pleasure and delight, he went on deck, screwed down the hatches, raised the sails, and away went the vessel sailing out of the harbor; and before the three.brothers knew where they were, the ship was miles out on the ocean, and they thought they were eating dinner at the side of the quay in Daingean.

"We'll go up now," said they when their dinner was eaten, "thank the cat, and go on shore for ourselves."

When on deck, they saw water on all sides, and did not know in the world where they were. The cat never stopped till he sailed to his own kingdom, which was the kingdom of the White Strand, for who should the cat be but the King of the White Strand. He had come for the two brothers himself, for he knew that they would never come of their own will, and he could not trust another to go for them. The king needed them, for they were the best men he had. In getting back the two, he took the third, and Mor was left without any son.

Mor heard in the evening that the ship was gone, and her own three sons inside in it.

"This is my misfortune," cried she. "After rearing my three sons, they are gone from me in this way." She began to cry and lament then, and to screech wonderfully.

Mor never knew who the cat was, or what became of her sons. The wife of Mor's youngest son went away to her father in Mayo, and everything she had went with her. Mor's husband, Lear, had died long before, and was buried at

Dunmore Head.   His grave is there to this day. Mor became half demented, and died soon after.

If women are scolding at the present time, it happens often that one says to another, "May your children go from you as Mor's sons went with the enchanted cat!"

SAUDAN OG AND THE DAUGHTER OF THE KING OF SPAIN; YOUNG CONAL AND THE YELLOW KING'S DAUGHTER.

R I NA DURKACH (the King of the Turks) lived many years in Erin, where he had one son, Saudan Og. When this son grew up to be twenty years old, he was a prince whose equal was hard to be found.

The old king was anxious to find a king's daughter as wife for his son, and began to inquire of all wayfarers, rich and poor, high and low, where was there a king's daughter fit for his son, but no one could tell him.

At last the king called his old druid. "Do you know," asked he, "where to find a king's daughter for Saudan Og?"

"I do not," said the druid; "but do you order your guards to stop all people passing your castle, and inquire of them where such a woman may be."

As the druid advised, the king commanded; but no man made him a bit the wiser.

A year later, an old ship captain walked the way, and the guards brought him to the king.

"Do you know where a fitting wife for my son might be found?" asked the king.

"I do," said the captain; "but my advice to you, and it may be a good one, is to seek a wife for your son in the land where he was born, and not go abroad for her. You can find plenty of good women in Erin."

"Well," said the king, "tell me first who is the woman you have in mind."

"If you must know," said the old captain, "the daughter of the King of Spain is the woman."

Straightway the king had a notice put up on the high-road to bring no more tidings to the castle, as he had no need of them.

When Saudan Og saw this notice, he knew that his father had the tidings, but would not give them. Next morning he went to the father and begged him to tell. "I know," said he, "that the old captain told you."

The king would say nothing, for he feared that his son might fall into trouble.

"I will start to-morrow," said Saudan Og at last, "in search of the woman; and if I do not find her, I will never come back to you, so it is better to tell me at once."

"The daughter of the King of Spain is the

woman," said the father; "but if you take my advice, you'll stay at home."

On the following day, Saudan Og dressed himself splendidly, mounted a white steed, and rode away, overtaking the wind before him; but the wind behind could not overtake him. He travelled all that was dry of Erin, and came to the seashore; so he had nowhere else to travel on land, unless he went back to his father. He turned toward a wood then, and saw a great ash-tree: he grasped the tree, and tore it out with its roots; and, stripping the earth from the roots, he threw the great ash into the sea. Leaving the steed behind him, he sat on the tree, and never stopped nor stayed till he came to Spain. When he landed, he sent word to the king that Saudan Og wished to see him.

The answer that Saudan got was not to come till the king had his castle prepared to receive such a great champion.

When the castle was ready, the King of Spain sent a bellman to give notice that every man, woman, or child found asleep within seven days and nights would lose their heads, for all must sing, dance, and enjoy themselves in honor of the high guest.

The king feasted Saudan Og for seven days and nights, and never asked him where was he going or what was his business. On the evening of the seventh day, Saudan said to the king, "You do not ask me what brought me this way, or what is my business."

"Were you to stay twenty years I would not ask. I'm not surprised that a prince of your blood and in full youthful beauty should travel the world to see what is in it."

"It was not to see the world that I came," said Saudan Og, "but hearing that you have a beautiful daughter, I wished her for wife; and if I do not get her with your consent, I will take her in spite of you."

"You would get my daughter with a hundred thousand welcomes," said the king; "but as you have boasted, you must show action."

The king then sent a messenger to three kings — to Ri Fohin, Ri Laian, and Conal Gulban — to help him. "If you will not come," said he, "I am destroyed, for Saudan Og will take my daughter in spite of me."

The kings made ready to sail for Spain. When Conal Gulban was going, he called up his three sons and said, "Stay here and care for the kingdom while I am gone."

"I will not stay," said the eldest son. "You are old and feeble: I am young and strong; let me go in place of you."

The second son gave a like answer. The youngest had his father's name, Conal, and the king said to him, "Stay here at home and care for the kingdom while I am gone, since your brothers will not obey me."

"I will do what you bid me," said Conal.

"Now I am going," said the old king; "and if I and your brothers never return, be not bribed by the rich to injure the poor. Do justice to all, so that rich and poor may love you as they loved your father before you."

He left young Conal twelve advisers, and said, "If we do not return in a day and a year, be sure that we are killed; you may then do as you like in the kingdom. If your twelve advisers tell you to marry a king's daughter of wealth and high rank, it will be of help to you in defending the kingdom. You will be two powers instead of one."

The day and the year passed, and no tidings came of Conal's two brothers and father. At the end of the day and the year, the twelve told him they had chosen a king's daughter for him, a very beautiful maiden. When the twelve spoke of marriage, Conal let three screeches out of him, that drove stones from the walls of old buildings for miles around the castle.

Now an old druid that his father had twenty

years before heard the three screeches, and said,
"Young Conal is in great trouble. I will go
to him to know can I help him."

The druid cleared a mountain at a leap, a
valley at a hop, twelve miles at a running leap,
so that he passed hills, dales, and valleys; and in
the evening of the same day, he struck his back
against the kitchen door of Conal's castle just as
the sun was setting.

When the druid came to the castle, young
Conal was out in the garden thinking to himself,
"My father and brothers are in Spain; perhaps
they are killed." The dew was beginning to fall,
so he turned to go, and saw the old man at the
door. The druid was the first to speak; but not
knowing Conal, he said, —

"Who are you coming here to trouble the
child? It would be fitter for you to stay in your
own place than to be trying to wake young Conal
with your screeches."

"Are you," asked Conal, "the druid that my
father had here years ago?"

"I am that old druid; but are you little
Conal?."

"I am," said Conal, and he gave the druid a
hundred thousand welcomes.

"I was in the north of Erin," said the druid,
"when I heard the three screeches, and I knew

that some one was troubling you, and your father in a foreign land. My heart was grieved, and I came hither in haste. I hear that your twelve advisers have chosen a princess, and that you are to marry to-morrow. Put out of your head the thought of that princess; she is not your equal in rank or power. Be advised by me, as your father was. The right wife for you is the daughter of the Yellow King, Haughty and Strong. If the king will not give her, take her by force, as your fathers before you took their queens."

Conal was roused on the following morning by his advisers, who said, "Make ready and go with us to the king's daughter we have chosen."

He mounted his steed, and rode away with the twelve till they came to a cross-road. The twelve wished to turn to one side; and when Conal saw this, he put spurs to his horse, took the straight road, and never stopped till he put seven miles between himself and the twelve. Then he turned, hurried back to the cross-road, came up to the adviser whom he liked best, and, giving him the keys of the castle, said, —

"Go back and rule till I or my father or brothers return. I give you the advice that I myself got: Never let the poor blame you for taking bribes from the rich; live justly, and do good to the poor, that the rich and the poor may like you. If you twelve had not advised me to marry, I might be going around with a ball and a hurley, as befits my age; but now I will go out in the world and seek my own fortune."

He took farewell of them then, and set his face toward the Yellow King's castle. A long time before it was prophesied that young Conal, son of Gulban, would cut the head off the Yellow King, so seven great walls had been built around the castle, and a gate to each wall. At the first gate, there were seven hundred blind men to obstruct the entrance; at the second, seven hundred deaf men; at the third, seven hundred cripples; at the fourth, seven hundred sensible women; at the fifth, seven hundred idiots; at the sixth, seven hundred people of small account; at the seventh, the seven hundred best champions that the Yellow King had in his service.

All these walls and defenders were there to prevent any man from taking the Yellow King's daughter; for it had been predicted that the man who would marry the daughter would take the king's head, and that this man would be Conal, son of Conal Gulban.

The only sleep that the guards at the seven gates had was half an hour before sunrise and half an hour after sunset. During these two half hours, a plover stood on the top of each gate; and if any one came, the bird would scream, and wake all the people in one instant.

The Yellow King's daughter was in the highest story of the castle, and twelve waiting-maids serving her. She was so closely confined that she looked on herself as a prisoner; so one morning early she said to the twelve maids, "I am confined here as a criminal, — I am never free even to walk in the garden; and I wish in my heart that some powerful young king's son would come the way to me. I would fly off with him, and no blood would be shed for me."

It was about this time that young Conal came, and, seeing all asleep, put spurs to his steed, and cleared the walls at a bound. If the birds called out, he had the gates cleared and was in before the champions were roused; and when he was inside, they did not attack him.

He let his horse out to graze near the castle, where he saw three poles, and on each one of two of them a skull.

"These are the heads of two king's sons who came to win the Yellow King's daughter," thought Conal, "and I suppose mine will be the third head; but if I die, I shall have company."

At this time the twelve waiting-maids cast lots to know who was to walk in the yard, and see if a champion had come who was worthy of the princess. The maid on whom the lot fell came back in a hurry, saying, "I have seen the finest man that I ever laid eyes on. He is beautiful, but slender and young yet. If there is a man born for you, it is that one."

"Go again," said the Yellow King's daughter, "and face him. Do not speak to him for your life till he speaks to you; say then that I sent you, and that he is to come under my window."

The maid went and crossed Conal's path three times, but he spoke not; she crossed a fourth time, and he said, "I suppose it is not for good that you cross my path so early?"

(It is thought unlucky to meet a woman first in the morning.)

"My mistress wishes you to go under her window."

Conal went under the window; and the king's daughter, looking down, fell deeply in love with him. "I am too high, and you are too low," said the Yellow King's daughter. "If we speak, people will hear us all over the castle; but I 'll take some golden cord, and try can I draw you up to me, that we may speak a few words to each other."

"It would be a poor case for me," said young Conal, "to wait till you could tie strings together to raise me." He stuck his sword in the earth then, and, making one bound, went in at the window. The princess embraced him and kissed him; she knew not what to give him to eat or to drink, or what would please him most.

"Have you seen the people at the seven gates?" asked the Yellow King's daughter.

"I have," answered Conal.

"They are all awake now, and I will go down and walk through the gates with you; seeing me, the guards will not stop us."

"I will not do that. It will never be said of young Conal of Erin that he stole his wife from her father. I will win you with strength, or not have you."

"I'm afraid there is too much against you," said the Yellow King's daughter.

These words enraged Conal, and, making one bound through the window, he went to the pole of combat, and struck a blow that roused the old hag in the eastern world, and shook the castle with all the land around it. The Yellow King was sleeping at the time; the shake that he got threw him out of his bed. He fell to the floor with such force that a great lump came out on his forehead; he was so frightened that he said to the old druid who ran in to help him, "Many a year have I lived without hearing the like of that blow. There must be a great champion outside the castle."

The guard was sent to see if any one was left alive near the castle. "For," said the king, "such a champion must have killed all the people at the gates." The guard went, saw no one dead, but every one living, and a champion walking around, sword in hand.

The guard hurried back, and said to the king, "There is a champion in front of the castle, handsome, but slender and young."

"Go to him," said the king, "and ask how many men does he want for the combat." The guard went out and asked.

"I want seven hundred at my right hand, seven hundred at my left, seven hundred behind me, and as many as all these out in front of me. Let them come four deep through the gates: do you take no part in this battle; if I am victorious, I will see you rewarded."

The guard told the king how many men the champion demanded. Before the king opened the gates for his men, he said to the chief of them, "This youth must be mad, or a very great champion. Before I let my men out, I must see him."

The king walked out to young Conal, and saluted him. Conal returned the salute. "Are you the champion who ordered out all these men of mine?" asked the king.

"I am," said young Conal.

"There is not one among them who would not kill a dozen like you," said the king. "Your bones are soft and young. It is better for you to go out as you came in."

"You need not mind what will happen me," answered Conal. "Let out the men; the more the men, the quicker the work. If one man would kill me in a short time, many will do it in less time."

The men were let out, and Conal went through them as a hawk goes through a flock of birds; and when one man fell before him, he knocked the next man, and had his head off. At sunset every head was cut from its body. Next he made a heap of the bodies, a heap of the heads, and a heap of the weapons. Young Conal then stretched himself on the grass, cut and bruised, his clothes in small pieces from the blows that had struck him.

"It is a hard thing," said Conal, "for me to have fought such a battle, and to lie here dying without one glimpse of the woman I love; could I see her even once, I would be satisfied."

Crawling on his hands and knees, he dragged himself to the window to tell her it was for her he was dying. The princess saw him, and told him to lie there till she could draw him up to her and care for him.

"It is a hard thing if I have to wait here till strings and cords are fastened together to raise me," said he, and, making one bound from where he was lying on the flat of his back, he went up to her window; she snatched at him, and pulled him into the chamber.

There was a magic well in the castle; the Yellow King's daughter bathed him in the water of it, and he was made whole and sound as before he went to battle. "Now," said she, "you must fly with me from this castle."

"I will not go while there is anything that may be cast on my honor in time to come," answered Conal.

Next day he struck the pole of combat with double the force of the first time, so that the king got a staggering fit from the shock that it gave him.

The Yellow King had no forces now but the deaf, the blind, the cripples, the sensible women, the idiots, and the people of small account. So out went the king in his own person. He and young Conal made the hills, dales, and valleys tremble, and clear spring wells to rise out of hard, gravelly places. Thus they fought for three days and two nights. On the evening of the third day, the king asked Conal for a time to rest and take food and drink.

"I have never begun any work," said Conal, "without finishing it. Fight to the end, then you can rest as long as you like."

So they went at it again, and fought seven days and seven nights without food, drink, or rest, and each trying to get the advantage of the other. On the seventh evening, Conal swept the head off the king with one blow.

"'T is your own skull that will be on the pole in place of mine, and I 'll have the daughter," said Conal.

The Yellow King's daughter came down and asked, "Will you go with me now, or will you take the kingdom?"

"I will go," answered Conal.

"You did not go to the battle?" asked Conal of the guard.

"I did not."

"Well for you that you did not. Now," said Conal to the princess, "whomever of the maids you like best, the guard may marry, and they will care for this kingdom till we return."

The guard and maid were married, and put in charge of the kingdom. The following morning young Conal got his steed ready and set out for

home with the princess. As they were riding
along near the foot of a mountain, Conal grew
very sleepy, and said to the princess, "I'll go
down now and take a sleep."

The place was lonely, — hardly two houses in
twenty miles. The Yellow King's daughter
advised Conal: "Take me to some habitation
and sleep there; this place is too wild."

"I cannot wait, — I'm too drowsy and weary
after the long battle; but if I might sleep a little,
I could fight for seven days and seven nights
again." He dismounted, and she sat on a green
mossy bank. Putting his head on her lap, he
fell asleep, and his steed went away on the mountain side grazing.

Conal had slept for three days and two nights
with his head in the lap of the Yellow King's
daughter, when on the evening of the third day
the princess saw the largest man she had ever
set eyes on, walking toward her through the sea
and a basket on his back. The sea did not
reach to his knees; a shield could not pass between his head and the sky. This was the High
King of the World. This big man faced up to
where Conal and his bride were; and, taking the
tips of her fingers, he kissed her three times.
"Bad luck to me," said the King of the World,
"if the young woman I am going for were beyond

the ditch there I would not go to her. You are fairer and better than she."

"Where were you going?" asked the princess. "Don't mind me, but go on."

"I was going for the Yellow King's daughter, but will not go a step further now that I see you."

"Go your way to her, for she is the finest princess on earth; I am a simple woman, and another man's wife."

"Well, pain and torments to me if I go beyond this without taking you with me!"

"If this man here were awake," said the Yellow King's daughter, "he would put a stop to you." She was trying all this time to rouse Conal.

"It is better for him to be as he is," said the High King; "if he were awake, it's harm he'd get from me, and that would vex you."

When she saw that he would take her surely, she bound him not to make her his wife for a day and a year.

"This is the worst promise that ever I have made," said the High King, "but I will keep it."

"If this man here were awake, he would stop you," said the princess.

The High King of the World thrust the tip of his forefinger under the sword-belt of Conal, and hurled him up five miles in the air. When Conal came down, he let out three waves of blood from his mouth.

"Do you think that is enough?" asked the king of the princess.

"Throw him a second time," said the Yellow King's daughter.

He threw him still higher, and Conal put out three greater waves. "Is that enough?"

"Try him a third time." He threw him still higher this time. Conal put out three greater waves, but waked not.

While the High King was throwing up Conal, the princess was writing a letter telling all,—that she knew not whither she was going, that she had bound the High King of the World not to make her his wife for a day and a year, "and," said she, "I'm sure that you will find me in that time."

The king took her in his arms, and away he went walking in the sea, throwing fish into his basket as he travelled through the water.

Conal slept a hero's sleep of seven days and nights, and woke four days after his bride had been stolen. He rubbed his eyes, and, glancing toward the mountain side, saw neither steed nor wife, and said, "No wonder that I cannot see wife nor horse when I'm so sleepy; what am I to do?"

Not far away were some small boys, and they herding cows. The boys began to make sport of Conal for sleeping seven days and nights. "I do not blame you for laughing," said Conal (ever since, when there is a great sleeper, people say that he sleeps like Conal on the side of Beann Edain), "but have you tidings of my wife and my steed; where are they, or has any man taken them?"

A boy older and wiser than the others said, "Your horse is on the mountain side feeding; and every day he came hither and sniffed you, and you sleeping, and then went away grazing for himself. Four days ago the greatest giant ever seen by the eye of man walked in through the ocean; he tossed you three times in the air. Every time we thought you'd be broken to dust; and the lady you had, wrote something and put it under your belt."

Conal read the letter, and knew that, in spite of her, the Yellow King's daughter had been carried away. He then preferred battle to peace, and asked the boys was there a ship that could take him to sea.

"There is no right ship in the place, but there is an old vessel wrecked in a cove there beyond," said the oldest boy.

The boys went with Conal, and showed him the vessel.

"Put your backs to her now, and help me," said Conal.

The boys laughed, thinking that two hundred men could not move such a vessel. Conal scowled, and then they were in dread of him, and with one shove they and Conal put the ship in the sea; but the water was going in and out through her. Conal knew not at first what to do, as there was no timber near by, but he killed seven cows, fastened the hides on the ship, and made it proof against water. When the boys saw the cows slaughtered, they began to cry, saying, "How can we go home now, and our cows killed?"

"There is not a cow killed," said Conal, "but you will get two cows in place of her." He gave two prices for each cow of the seven, and said to the boys, "Go home now, and tell what has happened."

Conal sailed away for himself; and when his ship was in the ocean, he let her go with the wind. On the third afternoon, he saw three islands, and on the middle island a fine open strand, with a great crowd of people. He threw out three anchors, two at the ocean side and one at the shore side, so that the ship would not stir, no matter what wind blew, and, planting his sword in the deck, he gave one bound and went

out on the strand seven miles distant. He
saluted a good-looking man, and asked, "Why are
so many people here?   What is their business?"

"Where do you live?   Of what nation are you
that you ask such a question?"

"I am a stranger," said Conal, "just come to
this island."

The islander showed Conal a man sitting on
the beach as large as twelve of the big men of
the island.   "Do you see him?"

"I do," said Conal.

"There are three brothers of us on these three
islands; that man is our youngest brother, and
he has grown so strong and terrible that we are
in dread he will drive us from our share of the
islands, and that is why we are here to-day.   My
eldest brother and I have come with what men
we have to this middle island, which belongs to
our youngest brother.   We are to play ball
against all his forces; if we beat them, we shall
think ourselves safe.   Now, which side will you
take, young champion?"

"If I go on your side, some may say that I fear
your men; and if I go with your younger brother,
you and your elder brother may say that I fear
your strong brother's forces.   Bring all the men
of the three islands.   I will play against them."

"Well," asked the stranger, "what wager will
you lay?"

"I'll wager," said Conal, "those two islands out there on the ocean side."

"They are ours already," said the man.

"Bad luck to you! Why claim everything?" said Conal. "Well, I'll lay another wager. If I lose, I'll stand in the middle of the strand, and every man of the three islands may give me a blow of the hurley; and if I win, I am to have a blow on every man who played against me. But first, I must have my choice of the hurleys; all must be thrown in a heap. I will take the one I like best."

This was done, and Conal took the largest and strongest hurley he could find. The ball was struck about the middle of the strand; and there was a goal at each end of it, and these goals were fourteen miles apart. Conal took the ball with hurley, hand and foot, and never let it touch ground till he put it through the goal. "Is that a fair inning?" asked he of the other side.

Some said it was foul, for he kept the ball in the air all the time.

"Well, I'll make a second trial; I will put it through the opposite goal." He struck the ball in the middle of the strand, and sent it toward the other goal with such force that whoever tipped it never drew breath again, and every man whom it passed was driven sixty feet to one side or the

other. Conal was always within a few yards of
the ball, and he put it through the goal seven
miles distant from the middle of the strand with
two blows.

"Is that a fair inning?" asked Conal.

"It would be hard to say that it is not," said
one man, and no man gainsaid him.

"Let all stand now in ranks two deep, till I
get my blow on each man of you."

All the men were arranged two deep; and when
Conal came up, the foremost man sprang behind
the one in the rear of him, and that one behind
the man at his side, and so on throughout. None
would stand to receive Conal's blow.

Away rushed every man, woman, and child,
and never stopped till they were inside in their
houses. First of all, ran the brothers of the
islands.

When they reached the castle, they began to
lament because they had insulted the champion,
and knew not who he was or whence he had come.

The three brothers had one sister; and when
she saw them lamenting and grieving, she asked:
"What trouble is on you?"

"We fled from the champion, and the people
followed us."

"None of you invited the champion to the
castle," said the sister; "now he will fall into

such a rage on the strand that in one hour he will not leave a person alive on the islands. If I had some one to go with me, I would invite him, and the people would be spared."

"I will go with you," said her chief maid.

Away they went, walking toward the strand; and when they had come near, they threw themselves on their knees before Conal. He asked who they were and what brought them.

"My brothers sent me to beg pardon for them, and invite you to the castle."

"I will go," said Conal; "and if you had not come, I would not have left a man alive on the three islands." Conal went with the princess, and saw at the castle a very old and large man; and the old man rose up before him and said, "A hundred thousand welcomes to you, young Conal from Erin."

"Who are you who know me, and I never before on this island?" asked Conal.

"My name is Donach the Druid, from Erin. I was often in your father's house, and it was a good place for rich or poor to visit, for they were alike there; and now I hope you will take me home to be buried among my own people. It was God who drove you hither to this island to take me home."

"And I will do that," said Conal, "if I go

there myself.   Tell me now how you came to
this place."

"I was taken," said Donach, "out on the wild
arm of the wind, and was thrown in on this island.
I am here ever since.   I am old now, and I wish
to be home in my own place in Erin."

Now young Conal, the sister, and three
brothers sat down to dinner.   When dinner was
over, and they had eaten and drunk, they were
as happy as if they had lived a thousand years
together.   The three brothers asked Conal where
was he going, and what was his business.   Conal
did not say that he was in search of his wife, but
he said that he was going to his own castle and
kingdom.   The old druid, two of the brothers,
and the sister said, "We will go with you, and
serve you till you come to your kingdom."

They got a boat and took him to the ship.   He
weighed anchor, and sailed away.   For two or
three days they saw nothing wonderful.   The
fourth day they came to a great island; and as
they neared it, they saw three champions inside,
and the three fighting with swords and spears.
Young Conal was surprised to see three fighting
at the same time.

"Well," said he, "it is nothing to see two
champions in combat, but 't is strange to see
three.   I will go in and see why they are fight-

ing." He threw out his chains, and made his ship fast; then he made a rush from the stern of the vessel to the bow, and as he ran, he caught Donach the Druid and carried him, and with one leap was in on the strand, seven miles from the ship.

Young Conal faced the champions, and, saluting the one he ·thought best, asked the cause of their battle. The champion sat down, and began. "I will tell you the reason," said he. "Seven miles from this place there stands a castle; in that castle is the most beautiful woman that the eye of man has ever seen, and the three of us are in love with her. She says she will take only the best man; and we are striving to know who is best, but no man of us three can get the upper hand of another. We can kill every man who comes to the island, but no man of us can kill another of the three."

When Conal heard this he sprang up, and told the champions to face him and he would see what they could do. The three faced him, and went at him. Soon he swept the heads off two of them, but the third man was pressing hard on Conal. His name was the Short Dun Champion; but in the end Conal knocked him with a blow, and no sooner had he him knocked than Donach the Druid had him tied with strong cords and strings of enchantment. Then young Conal spoke to Donach the Druid and said, "Come to this champion's breastbone and split it, take out his heart and his liver, and give them to my young hound to eat;" and turning to the Short Dun Champion, he asked, "Have you ever been so near a fearful death as you are at this moment?"

"'T is hard for me to answer you," said he, "for 't is firmly I am bound by your Druid, bad luck to him."

"Unbind the champion," said Conal, "till he tells us at his ease was he ever nearer a fearful death than he is at this moment."

"I was," said the champion to Conal. "Sit down there on that stool. I will sit here and tell you. I did not think much of your torture, for I knew that when my heart and liver were taken, I should be gone in that moment. Once I had a longer torture to suffer. Not many months ago, I was sailing on my ship in mid-ocean when I saw the biggest man ever seen on earth, and he with a beautiful woman in his hand. The moment I saw that woman I was in love with her, and I sailed toward the High King of the World, for it was he that was in it; but if I did, he let my ship go out in full sail between his two legs, and travelled on in another direction. I turned the ship again, and went after him. I climbed to the topmast, and stood there. I came up to the King of the World, for wind and wave were with me, and, being almost as high as the woman in his hand, I made a grasp at her; he let my ship out between his legs, but if he did, I took the woman with me and kissed her three times. This enraged the High King. He came to my ship, bound and tied me with strong hempen cords, then, putting a finger under me, he tossed me out on the sea and let my ship drift with the wind. I had some enchantment of my own, and the sea did not drown me. When little fish came my way, I swallowed them, and thus I got food. I was in this state for many days, and the hempen cords began to rot and weaken. Through good luck or ill, I was thrown in on this island. I pulled the cords, and struggled with them till one hand was free; then I unbound myself. I came to shore where the island is wildest. A bird called Nails of Daring had a nest in a high, rugged cliff. This bird came down, and, seizing me, rose in the air. Then she dropped me. I fell like a ball, and struck the sea close to land. I feigned death well, and was up and down with the waves that she might not seize me a second time, but soon she swooped down and placed her ear near me to know was I living. I held my breath, and she, thinking me dead, flew away.   I rose up, and ran with all speed to the first house I found.   Now, was I not nearer a worse death than the one to which you condemned me?   Nails of Daring would have given me a frightful and slow death, and you wished to give me a quick one."

"Short Dun Champion," said Conal, "the woman you saw with the High King was my wife.   It was luck that brought me in your way, and it was luck that Donach the Druid tied you in such a fashion.   Now you must guide me to the castle of the High King."

"Come, now, druid, bind my hands and feet, take my heart and liver and give them to young Conal's hound whelp, rather than take me to that king.   I got dread enough before from him."

"Believe me, all I want of you now is to guide my ship; you will come back in safety and health," said young Conal.

"I will go with you and guide you, if you put me beneath your ship's ballast when you see him nearing us, for fear he will get a glimpse of me."

"I will do that," said Conal.

Now they went out to the ship, and steered away, with the Short Dun Champion as pilot. They were the fifth day at sea when he steered the ship toward the castle of the High King.

"That," said the Short Dun Champion, pointing to a great building on an island, "is the castle of the High King of the World; but as good a champion as you are, you cannot free your wife from it. That castle revolves; and as it goes around it throws out poison, and if one drop of that poison were to fall on you the flesh would melt from your bones. But the King of the World is not at home now, for to-morrow the day and the year will be up since he stole the wife from you. I have some power of enchantment and I will bring the woman to you in the ship."

The Short Dun Champion went with one leap from the deck of the ship to the strand, and, caring for no man, walked straight to the castle where the Yellow King's daughter was held. The castle had an opening underneath, and the Short Dun Champion, keeping the poison away by his power, passed in, found the princess, and wrapping her in the skirt of an enchanted cloak that he had, took her out, and running to the strand was in on the deck of the ship with one bound.

The moment the princess set eyes on Conal, she gave such a scream that the High King heard her, and he off in the Western World inviting all the great people to his wedding. He started that minute for the castle, and did not wait to throw fish in his basket as he went through the sea. When he came home, the princess was not there before him. "Where has my bride gone, or has some one stolen her?" asked he.

"A man who has a ship in the harbor came and stole the lady."

"A thousand deaths! What shall I do, and all the high people on the way to the wedding?"

He seized a great club and killed half his servants, then rushed to the strand, and seeing the ship still at anchor, shouted for battle.

When the Short Dun Champion heard the king's voice, he screamed to be put under the ballast. He was put there and hidden from sight. "If I whistle with my fingers," asked young Conal, "will you come to me?"

"I will, if I were to die the next moment," said the Short Dun Champion.

Conal told Donach the Druid to stand at the bows of the ship, then, walking to the stern, he was so glad at having his wife on the vessel, and he going to fight with the High King, that he made a run, seized the druid, and carried him with one leap to the strand, eleven miles distant.

The High King demanded his wife.

"She is not your wife, but mine," said young Conal. "I won her with my sword, and you stole her away like a thief, and I sleeping. Though she is mine, I did not flee when I took her away from you."

"It is time for battle," said the king, and the two closed in combat. The king, being so tall, had the advantage. "I might as well make him shorter," thought Conal, and with one blow he cut the two legs off the king at the knee joints. The king fell. No sooner was he down than the druid had him tied with hard cords of enchantment. Conal whistled through his finger. The Short Dun Champion, hearing the whistle, screamed to be freed from the ballast. The men took him out. He went in on the strand with one bound, and when he came up to where the High King was lying, Conal said, "Cut this man at the breast-bone, take out his heart with his liver, and give them as food to my hound whelp."

"He is well bound by your druid; but firmly as he is bound, I am in dread to go near him to do this."

Conal then drew his own sword, and with a blow swept the head off the High King. Then Conal, Donach the Druid, and the Short Dun Champion went to the ship and sailed homeward. On their way, where should they sail but along the coast of Spain? While they were sailing, Conal espied three great castles, and not far from them a herd of cattle grazing.

"Will one of you go and inquire why these three castles are built near together?" asked Conal of the two island brothers.

"I will go," said the elder.

He went on shore to the herdsman and asked, "Why are those three castles so near one another?"

"I will tell you," said the herdsman; "but you must come first and touch my finger-tips."

No sooner had the champion done this, than the man drew a rod of enchantment, struck him a blow, and turned him to stone.

Conal saw this from the ship, and asked, "Who will go in now?"

"I will go," said the second brother. "I have the best right." He went and met the same fate as his brother.

"I will go this time," said Conal.

The Yellow King's daughter, Donach the Druid, and the Short Dun Champion seized Conal to keep him from going.

"If I do not live but a moment, I must go and knock satisfaction out of the herdsman for what he has done to my men," cried out Conal. So he went, and walking up to the herdsman, asked the same questions as the two brothers.

"Come here and touch my finger tips."

Conal walked up to the herdsman, caught his

fingers, then ran under the rod and seized the herdsman; but if he did, the herdsman had him that moment on the flat of his back. But Conal was up, and had the herdsman down, and, drawing his sword, said, "I'll have your head now unless you tell me why these three castles are here close together."

"I will tell you, but do you remember, young Conal, when in our father's castle how I used to get the first blow on you?"

"Are you my brother?" asked Conal.

"I am," said the herdsman.

"Why did you kill my men?"

"If I killed them, I can raise them;" and going to the two brothers, he struck each a blow, and they rose up as well and strong as ever.

"Well," said the brother to Conal, "Saudan Og arrived in Spain the day before we did, and he had one-third of the kingdom taken before us. We went against him the following day, and kept him inside that third, and we have neither gained nor lost since. The King of Spain had a castle here; my father and the King of Leinster built a second castle near that; Saudan Og built the third near the two, for himself and his men, and that is why the three castles are here. We are ever since in battle; Saudan has the one-third, and we the rest of Spain."

Conal arrayed himself as a champion next morning, and went to Saudan's castle. He struck a blow on the pole of combat that shook the whole kingdom, and that day he killed Saudan and every man of his forces.

Conal's eldest brother married the daughter of the King of Spain. He took the second brother with him, married him to the sister of the two island brothers, and gave him the three islands. He went home then, gave the kingdom of the Yellow King to the Short Dun Champion, and had the two island brothers well married to king's daughters in Erin. All lived happily and well; if they did not, may we!

THE BLACK THIEF AND KING CONAL'S
THREE HORSES.

THERE was a king once in Erin who had a beautiful queen, and the queen's heart was as good as her looks. Every one loved her, but, above all, the poor people. There wasn't a needy man or woman within a day's journey of the castle who was not blessing the beautiful queen. On a time this queen fell ill suddenly, and said to the king, "If I die and you marry a second wife, leave not my three sons to a strange woman's rule. Send them away to be reared till they come to age and maturity."

The queen died soon after. The king mourned for her one year and a second; then his chief men and counsellors urged him to seek out a new queen.

The king built a castle in a distant part of his kingdom, and put his three sons there with teachers and servants to care for them. He married a second wife then; and the two lived on happily till the new wife had a son. The young queen never knew that the king had other children than her son, or that there was a queen in the king-dom before her.

On a day when the king was out hunting in the mountains, the queen went to walk near the castle, and as she was passing the cottage of a greedy old henwife, she stumbled and fell.

"May the like of that meet you always!" said the henwife.

"Why do you say that?" asked the queen, who overheard her.

"It is all one to you what I say. It is little you care for me or the like of me. It was n't the same with the queen that was here before you. There was n't a week that she did not give support to poor people, and she showed kind-ness to every one always."

"Had the king a wife before me?" asked the queen.

"He had, indeed; and I could tell enough to keep you thinking for a day and a year, if you would pay me."

"I will pay you well if you tell all about the queen that was in it before me."

"If you give me one hundred speckled goats, one hundred sheep, and one hundred cows I will tell you."

"I will give you all those," said the queen, "if you tell everything."

"The queen that was here at first had three sons; and before the king married you, he prepared a great castle, and the sons are in that castle now with teachers and men taking care of them. When the three are of age, your son will be without a place for his head."

"What am I to do to keep my son in the kingdom?" asked the queen.

"Persuade the king to bring his three sons to the castle, then play chess with them. I will give you a board with which you can win. When you have won of the three young men, put them under bonds to go for the three steeds of King Conal for you to ride three times around all the boundaries of the kingdom. Many and many is the champion and hero who went for King Conal's horses; but not a man of them was seen again, and so it will be with these three. Your son will be safe at home, and will be king himself when his time comes."

The queen went home to the castle, and if ever she had a head full of plans it was that time. She began the same night with the king.

"Isn't it a shame for you to keep your children away from me, and I waiting this long time for you to bring them home to us?"

"How am I keeping my children from you?" asked the king. "Haven't you your own son and mine with you always?"

"You have three sons of your own. You were married before you saw me. Bring your children home. I will be as fond of them as you are."

No matter what the king said, the queen kept up her complaining with sweet words and promises, and never stopped till the king brought his sons to the castle.

The king gave a great feast in honor of the young men. After the feast the queen played chess for a sentence with the eldest. She played twice; won a game and lost one. Next day she played one game with the second son. On the third day, she played with the youngest; won one game and lost one.

On the fourth day, the three were in the queen's company.

"What sentence do you put on me and my brothers?" asked the eldest.

"I put you and your brothers under sentence not to sleep two nights in the same house, nor to eat twice off the same table, till you bring me the three steeds of King Conal, so that I may ride three times around the kingdom."

"Will you tell me," asked the eldest son, "where to find King Conal?"

"There are four quarters in the world; I am sure it is in one of these that he lives," said the queen.

"I might as well give you sentence now," said the eldest brother. "I put you under bonds of enchantment to stand on the top of the castle and stay there without coming down, and watch for us till we come back with the horses."

"Remove from me your sentence; I will remove mine," said the queen.

"If a young man is relieved of the first sentence put on him, he will never do anything good," said the king's son. "We will go for the horses."

Next day the three brothers set out for the castle of King Conal. They travelled one day after another, stopping one night in one place and the next in another, and they were that way walking till one evening, when whom should they meet but a limping man in a black cap. The man saluted them, and they returned the salute.

"What brought you this road, and where are you going?" asked the stranger.

"We are going to the castle of King Conal to know can we bring his three horses home with us."

"Well," said the man, "my house is near by, and the dark night is coming; stay with me till morning, and perhaps I can help you."

The young men went with the stranger, and

soon came to his house. After supper the man said, "It is the most difficult feat in the world to steal King Conal's three horses. Many a good man went for them, and never came back. Why do you go for those horses?"

"Our father is a king in Erin, and he married a second time. Our stepmother bound us to bring the three horses, so she may ride three times around our father's kingdom."

"I will go with you," said the man. "Without me, you would lose your lives; together, we may bring the horses."

Next morning the four set out, and went their way, walking one day after another, till at long last they reached the castle of King Conal at nightfall.

On that night, whatever the reason was, the guards fell asleep at the stables. The stranger and the three young men made their way to the horses; but if they did, the moment they touched them the horses let three screeches out of them that shook the whole castle and woke every man in the country around it.

The guards seized the young men with the stranger, and took the four to King Conal.

The king was in a great room on the ground-floor of his castle. In front of him was an awfully big pot full of oil, and it boiling.

"Well," said the king when he saw the stranger before him, "only that the Black Thief is dead, I'd say you were that man."

"I am the Black Thief," said the stranger.

"We will know that in time," said the king; "and who are these three young men?"

"Three sons of a king in Erin."

"We'll begin with the youngest. But stir up the fire there, one of you," said King Conal to the attendants; "the oil is not hot enough." And turning to the Black Thief, he asked, "Isn't that young man very near his death at this moment?"

"I was nearer death than he is, and I escaped," said the Black Thief.

"Tell me the story," said the king. "If you were nearer death than he is, I will give his life to that young man."

"When I was young," said the Black Thief, "I lived on my land with ease and plenty, till three witches came the way, and destroyed all my property. I took to the roads and deep forests then, and became the most famous thief that ever lived in Erin. This is the story of the witches who robbed and tried to kill me: —

"There was a king not long ago in Erin, and he had three beautiful daughters. When they grew up to be old enough for marriage, they were enchanted in the way that the three became

brazen-faced, old-looking, venomous hags every
night, and were three beautiful, harmless young
women every day, as before.

"I was living for myself on my land, and
had laid in turf enough for seven years, and I
thought it the size of a mountain. I went out at
midnight, and what did I see but the hags at
my reek; and they never stopped till they put
every sod of the turf into three creels on their
backs, and made off with it.

"The following season I brought turf for
another seven years, and the next midnight the
witches stole it all from me; but this time I
followed them. They went about five miles, and
disappeared in a broad hole twenty fathoms deep.
I waited, then looked down, and saw a great fire
under a pot with a whole bullock in it. There
was a round stone at the mouth of the hole. I
used all my strength, rolled it down, broke the
pot, and spoiled the broth on the witches.

"Away I ran then, but was not long on the
road when I saw the three racing after me. I
climbed a tree to escape from them. The
witches came in a rage, stopped under the tree,
and looked up at me. The eldest rested awhile,
then made a sharp axe of the second, and a
venomous hound of the third, to destroy me.
She took the axe herself then, gave one blow

of it, and cut one-third of the tree; she gave a second blow, and cut another third; she had the axe raised a third time when a cock crowed, and there before my eyes the axe turned into a beautiful woman, the hag who had raised it into a second, and the venomous hound into a third. The three walked away then, harmless and innocent as any young women in Erin. Was n't I nearer death that time than this young man?"

"Oh, you were," said the king; "I give him his life, and it 's his brother that 's near death now. He has but ten minutes to live."

"Well, I was nearer death than that young man," said the Black Thief.

"Tell how it was. If you convince me, I 'll give him his life, too."

"After I broke their pot, the witches destroyed my property night after night, and I had to leave that place and find my support on the roads and in forests. I was faring well enough till a year of hunger and want came. I went out once into a great wood, walked up and down to know could I find any food to take home to my wife and my children.

"I found an old white horse and a cow without horns. I tied the tails of the two to each other, and was driving them home for myself with great labor; for when the white horse pulled backward, the cow would pull forward, and when the horse tried to go on, the cow would n't go with him. They were that way in disagreement till they drew the night on themselves and on me. I had a bit of flint in my pocket, and put down a fire. I could not make my way out of the wood in the night-time, and sat down by the fire. I was not long sitting when thirteen cats, wild and enormous, stood out before me. Of these, twelve were each the bulk of a man; the thirteenth, a red one, the master of the twelve, was much larger. They began to purr on the opposite side of the fire, and make a noise like the rumbling of thunder. At last the big red cat lifted his head, opened his wide eyes, and said to me, 'I 'll be this way no longer; give me something to eat.' "

" I have nothing to give you," said I, "unless you take that white horse below there and kill him."

"He went down then, and made two halves of the horse, left half to the twelve, and ate the other half himself. They picked every bone, and were not long at it.

"The thirteen came up again, sat opposite me at the fire, and were purring. The big red cat soon spoke a second time, 'I 'll not be long this way. Give me more food to satisfy my hunger.'

"'I have nothing to give unless you take the cow without horns,' replied I.

"He made two halves of the cow, ate one-half himself, and left the other to the twelve. While they were eating the cow, I took off my coat, for I knew what was coming, wrapped it around a block which I made like myself, and then climbed a tree quickly. The red cat came up to the fire a third time, opened his great eyes, looked toward my coat, and said, 'I'll not be long this way; give me more food.'

"My coat gave no answer. The big cat sprang at it, struck the block with his tail, and found it was wood.

"'Ah,' said he, 'you are gone; but whether above ground or under ground, we will find you.'

"He put six cats above and six under ground to find me. The twelve cats were gone in a breath. The big red cat sat there waiting; and when the other twelve had run through all Erin, above ground and under ground, and come back to the fire, he looked up, saw me, and cried, 'Ah, there you are, you deceiver. You thought to escape, but you will not. Come, now,' said he to the cats, 'and gnaw down this tree.'

"The twelve sprang at the tree under me, and they were not long cutting it through. Before it fell, I escaped to another tree near by, and they attacked that, gnawing it down. I sprang to a third. We were that way, I escaping and they cutting, till near daybreak, when I was on the last tree next the open country. When the tree was half cut, what should come the way but thirteen terrible wolves, — twelve, and a thirteenth above them, their master. They fell upon the cats, and fought desperately a good while. At length the twelve on each side were stretched, but the two chiefs were fighting each other yet. At last the wolf nearly took the head off the cat with one snap; the cat whirled in falling, struck the wolf with the sharp hook in his tail, made two halves of his skull, and the two fell dead, side by side.

"I slipped down then, but the tree shook in the way that I was in dread it would tumble beneath me, but it did n't. Now, was n't I nearer death that time than this young man?"

"Oh, you were," said King Conal. "He 's not near death at all, for I give his life to him; but if the two have escaped, we 'll put the third man in the pot; and have you ever seen any one nearer death than he is?"

"I was nearer myself," said the Black Thief.

"If you were, I will give his life to this young man as well as his brothers."

"I had apprentices in my time," said the Black

Thief. "Among them was one, a young man of great wit, and he pleased me. I gave no real learning to any but this one; and in the heel of the story he was a greater man than myself, — in his own mind. There was a giant in the other end of the kingdom; he lived in a mountain den, and had great wealth gathered in there. I made up my mind to go with the apprentice, and take that giant's treasures. We travelled many days till we reached the mountain den. We hid, and watched the ways of the giant. He went out every day, brought back many things, but often men's bodies. At last we went to the place in his absence. There was only one entrance, from the top. I was lowering the young man with a rope, but when halfway to the bottom he called out as if in pain. I drew him up. ' I am in dread,' said he, ' to go down in that place. Go yourself. I will do the work here for you.'

"I went down, found gold and precious things in plenty, and sent up what one man could carry. ' I will go out of this now,' thought I, ' before the giant comes on me.' I called to the apprentice; no answer. I called again; not a word from him. At last he looked down and said, —

"' You gave me good learning, and I am grateful; I will gain my own living from this out. I hope you 'll spend a pleasant night with the giant.'

"With that, he made off with himself, and carried the treasure. Oh, but I was in trouble then! How was I to bring my life home with me? How was I to escape from the giant? I looked, but found no way of escape. In one corner of the giant's kitchen were bodies brought in from time to time. I lay down with these, and seemed dead. I was watching. After a while I heard a great noise at the entrance, and soon the giant came in carrying three bodies; these he threw aside with the others. He put down a great fire then, and placed a pot on it: he brought a basket to the bodies, and began to fill it; me he threw in first, and put six bodies on the top of me. He turned the basket bottom upward over the pot, and six bodies fell in. I held firmly to my place. The giant put the basket aside in a corner bottom upward, — I was saved that time. When the supper was ready, the giant ate the six bodies, and then lay down and slept soundly. I crept from under the basket, went to the entrance; a tree trunk, standing upright in the wall at one end of it, was turned around. There were steps in its side from bottom to top; this was the giant's ladder. Whenever the giant wished to go up, he turned the tree till the steps came outside; and when on top, he turned it till the smooth side was out in the way no one could

go down in his absence. When he wished to
go down, he turned the steps out; and when at
the bottom, he turned them in again in the way
no one could follow him. This time he forgot
to turn the tree, and that gave me the ladder.
I went up without trouble; and, by my hand, I
was glad, for I was much nearer death at the giant's
pot than this man at yours."

"You were, indeed, very near death," said
King Conal, "and I give his life to the third
man. The turn is on you now; the three young
men are safe, and it's you that will go into the
pot."

"Must I die?" asked the Black Thief.

"You must, indeed," said King Conal, "and
you are very near death."

"Near as I am," said the Black Thief, "I was
nearer."

"Tell me the story; and if you were ever
nearer death than you are at this minute, I will
give your life to you."

"I set out another day," said the Black Thief,
"and travelled far. I came at last to a house,
and went into it. Inside was a woman with a
child on her knee, a knife in her hand, and she
crying. Twice she made an offer of the knife
at the child to kill it. The beautiful child
laughed, and held out its hands to her.

"'Why do you raise the knife on the child,' asked I, 'and why are you crying?'

"'I was at a fair,' said the woman, 'last year with my father and mother; and while the people were busy each with his own work, three giants came in on a sudden. The man who had a bite of bread in his hand did not put the bread to his mouth, and the man who had a bite in his mouth did not swallow it. The giants robbed this one and that, took me from my father and mother, and brought me to this place. I bound them, and they promised that none of the three would marry me before I was eighteen years of age. I 'll be that in a few days, and there is no escape for me now unless I raise hands on myself.

"'Yesterday the giants brought this child; they said it was the son of some king, and told me to have it cooked and prepared in a pie for their supper this evening.'

"'Spare the child,' said I. 'I have a young pig that I brought to roast for myself on the road; take that, and prepare it instead of the child.'

"'The giants would know the pig, and kill me,' said the woman.

"'They would not,' said I; 'there is only a small difference between the flesh of a young pig and a child. We will cut off the first joint of the left little finger. If they make a remark, show them that.'

"She cooked the pie, and I watched outside for the giants. At last I saw the three coming. She hid the child in a safe place aside; and I went to the cellar, where I found many dead bodies. I lay down among them, and waited. When the giants came home, the eldest ate the pie, and called to the woman, 'That would be very good if we had enough of it.' Then he turned to his second brother, and sent him down to the cellar to bring a slice from one of the bodies. The brother came down, took hold of one body, then another, and, catching me, cut a slice from the end of my back, and went up with it. He was not long gone when he came down again, raised me on his back, and turned to take me with him. He had not gone many steps when I sent my knife to his heart, and there he fell on his face under me. I went back, and lay in my old place.

"The chief giant, who had tasted my flesh and was anxious for more of it, now sent the youngest brother. He came, saw the middle brother lying there, and cried out, —

"'Oh, but you are the lazy messenger, to be sleeping when sent on an errand!'

"With that, he raised me on his back, and was

going, when I stabbed him and stretched him on the ground not far from his brother.

"The big giant waited and waited, grew angry, took his great iron club with nine lumps and nine hooks on it.　He hurried down to the cellar, saw his two brothers, shook them, found them dead.　I had no chance of life but to fight for it; I rose and stood a fair distance in front of the giant.　He ran toward me, raised the club, and brought it down with what strength there was in him.　I stepped aside quickly; the club sank in the earth to the depth of a common man's knee. While the giant was drawing the club with both hands, I stabbed him three times in the stomach, and sprang away to some distance.　He ran forward a second time, and came very near hitting me; again the club sank in the ground, and I stabbed him four times, for he was weaker from blood loss, and was a longer time freeing the club.　The third time the club grazed me, and tore my whole side with a sharp iron hook.　The giant fell to his knees, but could neither rise nor make a cast of the club at me; soon he was on his elbow, gnashing his teeth and raging.　I was growing weaker, and knew that I was lost unless some one assisted me.　The young woman had come down, and was present at the struggle. 'Run now,' said I to her, 'for the giant's sword, and take the head off him.' She ran quickly, brought the sword, and as brave as a man took the head off the giant.

"'Death is not far from me now,' said I.

"'I will carry you quickly to the giant's caldron of cure, and give you life,' said the woman.

"With that, she raised me on her back, and hurried out of the cellar. When she had me on the edge of the caldron, the death faint was on me, I was dying; but I was not long in the pot when I revived, and soon was as well as ever.

"We searched the whole house of the giants, found all their treasures. I gave some to the woman, kept some myself, and hid the remainder. I took the woman home to her father and mother. She kept the child, which was well but for the tip of its little finger. Now wasn't I nearer death that time than I was when I began this story?"

"You were, indeed," said King Conal; "and even if you were not, I would not put you in the pot, for if you had not been in the house of the three giants that day there would be no sign of me now in this castle. I was that child. Look here at my left little finger. My father searched for you, and so did I when I grew up, but we could not find you. We made out only one thing, that it was the Black Thief who saved me.   Men told me that the Black Thief was dead, and I never hoped to see you.   A hundred thousand welcomes!   Now we 'll have a feast.   The three young men will get the three horses for your sake, and take them home after we have feasted together.   You will stay with me now for the rest of your life."

"I must go with the young men as far as my own house," said the Black Thief; "then I 'll come back to you."

King Conal made a feast the like of which had never been in his kingdom.   When the feast was over, he gave the three horses to the young men, and said at parting, "When you have done the work with the horses, let them go, and they will run home to me; no man could stop them."

"We will do that," said the brothers.

They set out then with them, stopped one night with the Black Thief at his house, and after that travelled home to their father, and stood in front of the castle.   The stepmother was above, watching for them.   She was glad when she saw them, and said, "Ye brought the horses, and I am to have them."

"If we were bound to bring the horses," said the elder brother, "we were not bound to give them to you."

With that, he turned the horses' heads from the castle, and let them go. They ran home to King Conal.

"I will go down now," said the queen, "and it is time for me."

"You will not go yet," said the youngest; "I have a sentence which I had no time to give when we were going. I put you under sentence to stay where you are till you find three sons of a king to go again to King Conal for the horses."

When she heard that sentence, she dropped dead from the castle.

THE KING'S SON FROM ERIN, THE SPRISAWN, AND THE DARK KING.

THERE was a king in Erin long ago who was called King of Lochlinn, and his wife died. He had two sons. The elder of the two was Miach Lay; the second was Manus. Miach Lay was a fine champion, and trained in every art that befitted a king's son.

One day the father called Miach Lay to his presence, and said, "It is time for you to marry, and I have chosen for you a maiden of great beauty and high birth."

"I am willing to marry," said Miach Lay.

The king and his son then left the castle, and went to the house of the young woman's father, and there they spent seven days and seven nights. On their way home, the king said to his son, "How do you like the young lady?"

"I like her well, but I'll not marry her."

"Oh, my shame!" said the father. "How can I ever face those people a second time?"

"I cannot help that," said Miach Lay.

The king was greatly confused. After another while he said to his son, "I have another maiden chosen for you, and it is well for us to go to her father's, and settle the match."

"I am willing," said Miach Lay.

They went away together, and never stopped nor stayed till they reached the house of the young lady's father. They were welcomed there warmly, and spent seven days and seven nights, and were better attended each day than the day before.

"Well, my son," asked the father, "how do you like this match?"

"Well, and very well," said Miach Lay; "but I will not marry this lady either. She is ten times better than the first; and if I had married the first, I could not marry this one, and so I will not marry the second any more than the first lady."

"Oh, my shame!" said the father. "I can never show my face to these people again."

After another while the king told Miach Lay that he had a better lady than ever selected, and asked him to go with him to arrange the marriage.

"I am willing," answered the son.

The two went to the father of the maiden; they spent seven days and seven nights at his house, and were fully satisfied with everything. They were on the way home a third time. "Well," said the king, "you have no reason to refuse this time."

"Well, and very well, do I like the match," said Miach Lay; "but I will not marry this lady. If I had married the first lady, I should have had no chance of getting the second, and the second is ten times better than the first; if I had married the second lady, I should have had no chance of this one, and she is twenty times better than the second."

"I have lost all patience with you," said the king, "and I turn the back of my hand to you from this out."

"I 'm fully satisfied," said Miach Lay, so they came home, and passed that night without conversation. The following morning, when Miach Lay rose, he said to his father, "I am for leaving the house now; will you prepare for me the best ship that you have, and put in it a good store of provisions for a long voyage?"

The vessel was prepared, and fully provisioned for a day and a year. The king's son went on board, sailed out of the harbor, and off to sea. He never stopped sailing till he entered a harbor in the kingdom of Greece. There was a guard there on watch at the harbor with a keen eye on all ships that were passing or coming. The King of Greece was at war in that time with the King of Spain, and knew not what moment his kingdom would be invaded.

The guard saw the vessel coming when she was so small to the eye that he could not tell was it a bird or a vessel that he was looking at. He took quick tidings to the castle; and the king ordered him to go a second time and bring tidings. When he reached the sea, the ship was inside, in the harbor.

"Oh," said the king, when the guard ran to him a second time, "that is a wonderful vessel that was so far away a few minutes ago as not to be told from a bird, and is now sailing into harbor."

"There is but one man to be seen on board," said the guard.

In front of the king's castle was the landing-place, the only one of the harbor; and even there no one went beyond the shore without passing through a gate where every man had to give an account of himself. There was a chosen cham·pion guarding the gate, who spoke to Miach Lay, and asked, "Who are you, and from what country?"

"It is not the custom for a man of my people to answer a question like that till he is told first what country he is in, and who asks the question."

"It was I asked the question," said the champion; "and you must tell me who you are, first of all."

"I will not tell you," said Miach Lay. With that, he drew his ship nearer land till it grounded; then, taking an oar, he put the blade end in the sand, and sprang to shore. He asked then the champion at the gate to let him pass, but the champion refused. Miach Lay raised his hand, gave him a blow on the ear, and sent him backward spinning like a top, till he struck the pillar of the gate and broke his skull. As Miach Lay had no thought to kill the man, he was grieved, and, delaying a short time, went to the castle of the king, not knowing what country he was in or what city.

When he came to the castle, he knelt down in front of it. The people in the castle saw a young champion with bared head outside; the king came out, and asked what trouble was on him. Miach Lay told of all that had happened at the harbor, and how he had killed the champion at the gate without wishing it.

"Never mind that," said the king.

"I did not intend to kill or harm him at all," said Miach Lay; "he wanted to know who I was, and from what country. By the custom of my land, I cannot tell that till I know where I am, and who are the people among whom I am travelling."

"Do you know now where you are?"

"I do not," answered Miach Lay.

"You are in front of the castle of the King of Greece, and I am that king."

"I am the son of the King of Lochlinn from Erin," said Miach Lay, "and have come this way to seek my fortune."

The King of Greece welcomed him then, took the young champion by the hand, and did not stop till he brought him to where all the princes and nobles were assembled; he was rejoiced at his coming, for, being at war, he expected aid from this champion.

"Will you remain with me for a day and a year," asked the king, "and perform what service I ask of you?"

"I will," said Miach Lay.

Manus, the second son of the King of Lochlinn, stopped going to school when Miach Lay, his elder brother, left home, and, after a time, the father wished him to marry. As the elder son had acted, so did the second; he refused to marry each of the three maidens whom the king had chosen, and left his father at last.

Manus was watching when his brother sailed away, and noticed the course of the vessel, so now he sailed the same way.

Miach Lay was gaining favor continually; and just as the day and the year of his service were out to a month, the king's guard saw a vessel sailing in swiftly. He ran with tidings to the king, and added, "There is only one man on board."

The king and the nobles said it was best not to let him land till he gave an account of himself. Miach Lay was sent to the landing-place to get account of him.

He was not long at the landing-place when the vessel came within hailing, and Miach Lay asked the one man on board who was he and from what land he came. The man would not tell, as it was not the custom in his country. "But," said he, "I want something to eat."

"There is plenty here," said Miach Lay; "but if there is, you will get none of it, — you would better be sailing away."

"I have enough of the sea; I 'll come in."

He put down the blade of his oar, and sprang ashore. No sooner had he touched land than he was grappled by Miach Lay. As neither man knew the other, they were in hand grips all day. They were nearly equal in strength, but at last Miach Lay was getting the worst of it. He asked Manus for a truce.

"I will grant you that," said Manus; "but you do not deserve it, for you began the battle."

They sat apart then, and Miach Lay asked, "How long can you hold out?"

"It is getting stronger and braver I am," replied Manus.

"Not so with me. I could not hold out five minutes longer," said Miach Lay. "My bones were all falling asunder, and I thought the earth was trembling beneath me. Till this day I thought to myself, 'There is no champion I cannot conquer.' Now tell me your name and your country."

"I am from Erin and a son of the King of Lochlinn," said Manus.

"Oh," said Miach Lay, "you are my brother."

"Are you Miach Lay?" inquired Manus.

"I am."

They embraced each other, and sat down then to eat. Miach Lay was so tired that he could taste nothing, but Manus ate his fill. Then they went arm in arm to the castle. The king and all the nobles of Greece had seen the combat from the castle, and were surprised to see the men coming toward them in such friendliness, and all went out to know the reason. The king asked Miach Lay, "How is all this?"

"This man is my brother," said Miach Lay. "I left him at home in Erin, and did not know him at the harbor till after the combat."

The king was well pleased that he had another champion. The following day Manus saw the king's daughter, and fell in love with her and she with him. Then the daughter told the king if she did not get Manus as husband, the life would leave her.

The king called Miach Lay to his presence, and asked, "Will you let your brother marry my daughter?"

"If Manus wishes to marry her, I am willing and satisfied," answered Miach Lay. He asked his brother, and Manus said he would marry the king's daughter.

The marriage was celebrated without delay, and there was a wedding feast for three days and three nights; and the third night, when they were going to their own chamber, the king said, "This is the third husband married to my daughter, and after the first night no tidings could be had of the other two, and from that time to this no one knows where they are."

Miach Lay was greatly enraged that the king had permitted the marriage without mentioning this matter first.

"I will do to-night," said the king, "what has never been done hitherto; I will place sentries all around the grounds, and my daughter and Manus will not lodge in the castle at all, but in one of the houses apart from it."

"I 'll watch myself," said Miach Lay; "and if it is the devil that is taking the husbands, I 'll not let him take my brother."

Sentries were stationed in all parts; a house was prepared in the courtyard. Miach Lay stood on guard at the entrance all the time. Soon after midnight a gust of wind blew through the yard; it blew Miach Lay to the ground, and he fainted. When he recovered, he rushed to search for his brother, but he was not in his chamber. He then roused the king's daughter, and asked, "Where is my brother?"

"I cannot tell where he is," said she: "it is you who were on guard; it is you who should know where to find him."

"I will have your head, wicked woman, unless you give tidings of my brother."

"Do not take my head; it would not serve you. I have no account of what happened to your brother."

Miach Lay then refrained from touching her, and waited till morning. The king came in the morning to see was Manus well; and when Miach Lay saw him, he ran at him to destroy him, but the king fled away. After a while, when the household was roused, the king's daughter was brought in and asked where was her husband, or could she give any account of him.

"I cannot tell," replied she; "but one day before I was married the first time, something came to my chamber window in the form of a black bee, and asked would I let it in. I said that I would not. The bee remained outside all the day, watching to see could it enter my chamber. I did not let it come in; before going away in the evening, the black bee said, 'Well, I will worry the heart in you yet.'"

The king's old druid, who was present, slapped his knee with his hand, and said, "I know the story now; that was Ri Doracha (the Dark King). He is a mighty magician, and it is he who has taken the husbands."

"I will travel the world till I find my lost brother," said Miach Lay.

"I will go with you, and take all my forces," said Red Bow, the son of the King of Greece.

"I need no assistance," said Miach Lay. "If I myself cannot find him, I think that no man can; but if you wish to come, you are welcome."

Miach Lay went to his vessel; and Red Bow chose the best ship from all that his father had, and went on board of it. The two ships sailed away together. In time they neared land; and on reaching the mouth of the harbor, they saw a third ship sailing toward them as swiftly as the wind blew, and it was not long till it came alongside. There was only one man on board; he hailed Miach Lay, and asked, "Where are you going?"

"It would not be the custom of my country for me to tell you what you ask till you tell me who you are yourself, and where your own journey lies."

"I know myself," said the warrior, "where you are going; you are in search of the Dark King, and I myself would like to see him."

With that, he took a bundle of branches he had on deck, and blew them overboard. Then every rod and twig of the bundle became an enormous log of wood, so that the harbor was covered with one raft of timber, and then he sailed away without waiting.

After much struggling with the logs, shoving them hither and over, Miach Lay was able by pushing with oars to make room for his vessel, and at last came to land. Red Bow and his men were cast into deep sleep by the man on the vessel that had sailed away.

After Miach Lay landed, he passed through a great stretch of wild country, and, drawing near a large forest, saw rising up a small, slender smoke far in among trees. He made for the place where the smoke was, and there he discovered a large, splendid castle in the depth of the forest, but could find no sign of an entrance.

When Miach Lay had stood outside some time, a young woman looked through the window, hailed him, and said, "You are a stranger, and will find no lodgings in these parts; but if I could at all, I would let you come in here."

"Open the window if you are able," said Miach Lay.

The window had hinges, and she opened it in the middle; he stepped backward nine yards, and went in at one bound to the chamber.

"You are welcome," said she, and soon she had dinner prepared for him. When he had eaten, she inquired who was he, from what place had he come, and what brought him that way.

He told her all that had happened to him from the first; and when he had finished, he said, "I know not where to find my brother."

"You are not far from him now," said she; "'t is in this country he is living, and the land he is in bounds our land."

When they had talked long, she said, "You are tired and need rest, so sleep in this chamber." She went then to her own place. The following morning his breakfast was ready before him; and after he had eaten, the young woman said, "I suppose you will be thankful if I tell you where to find the castle of the Dark King."

"I shall, indeed," said he. Then she gave him full directions how to go. He took his sword then, and sprang out as he had sprung in, in the evening, and went in the direction which she told him to take. About midday he met a man, who hailed him, and asked, "Who are you, and from what country?"

"'T is not the custom for a man of my country to answer that question till told where he is, and to whom he is speaking."

"I know who you are and whither you are going. You are going to the castle of the Dark King, and here he is before you; now show your daring."

They made at each other; and if they did, they made soft ground hard and hard ground soft, they made high places low and low places high, they brought cold spring water through dry, gravelly places, and if any one were to come from the Eastern to the Western World, it is to look at these two he should come.

They were this way till evening, and neither had the better of the other. Miach Lay was equal to the Dark King; but the Dark King, having magic, blew a gust of wind at Miach Lay which knocked him flat on the earth, and left him half dead.   Then the Dark King took Miach Lay's sword, and went away.   When he recovered, Miach Lay regretted his sword more than all else, and went back to the castle where he had spent the night before.   He was barely able to go in at the window.

"How have you fared this day?" asked the young woman.

He told her of all that had happened.

"Be not grieved; you will meet him another time," said the young woman.

"What is the use?   I have no sword now."

"If 't is a sword you need, I will bring you a blade far better than the one which the Dark King took from you."

After breakfast next morning she brought him her father's sword, which he grasped in his hand, and shook.   Miach Lay bade farewell to the young woman, and sprang out through the window. Knowing the way better this time, he hastened forward, and met the Dark King just where he met him before.

"Did not yesterday tire you?" asked the king.

"No," said Miach Lay.

"Your journey is useless," said the king.

"We shall see," answered Miach Lay, and they made at each other; and terrible as the battle was on the first day, it was more terrible on the second; but when the Dark King thought it time to go home, he blew a gust of wind which threw Miach Lay to the earth, and left him sense-less. The Dark King did not take the sword this time.

After the Dark King had gone, another man came the way, who was called Sprisawn Wooden Leg.[1]

"Well, my good man, you are nearly dead," said the Sprisawn.

"I am," said Miach Lay, rousing up.

"You are his equal but for the magic. I watched the combat these two days, and you would have overcome him but for his magic; he will finish you to-night if he finds you. He has three magic tricksters who are leaving his house at this moment. They have a spear which the rear man of the three hurls forward, the trickster in front catches the spear in the heel of his foot, and in turn hurls it with all his force forward; those behind rush ahead of the front man, and in turn catch the spear in their heels. No matter how far nor how often the spear is thrown for-ward, there is always a man there before it to catch it. They are rushing hither a long distance apart."

---

[1] *Sprisawn*, in Gaelic *spriosan*, a small twig, and, figuratively, a poor little creature, a sorry little fellow.

The Sprisawn saw the tricksters approach, and told Miach Lay that they were coming. When they came within a spear-cast, one of them hurled the spear at Miach Lay; it went through his heart, passed out through his body, and killed him.

When the Sprisawn saw Miach Lay lying dead, he fell to weeping and wailing; and so loud was his wail that every one heard it throughout the whole kingdom. Red Bow was sleeping yet in the harbor; but so loud was the wail of the mourning Sprisawn that it roused him from the slumber which the Dark King had put on him. He landed at once with his forces, and made on toward the wailing. When they came to the place, and saw Miach Lay lying dead, they themselves began to wail; they asked the Sprisawn then, "Are there any means by which we might raise him to life?"

"There are," replied the Sprisawn. "The Dark King is rejoicing now in his castle with the King of Mangling, and the Gruagach of Shields. They are drinking each other's health from a horn, and the Dark King is telling the other two that Miach Lay was the best man that ever stood in front of him; and if he could drink from that horn, he would rise up as well as he ever was."

"I with my men will go for that horn," said Red Bow.

"Not you nor all the men like you living on earth could bring that horn from the castle of the Dark King," replied the Sprisawn. "That castle is surrounded by three walls. Each wall is four feet in thickness and twenty feet high. Each wall has a gate as high and as thick as the wall is itself. How could you pass through those walls? Remain here and watch over this body; I will bring the horn hither myself."

Off went the Sprisawn, and he had more control over magic than even the Dark King. When he arrived at the castle, he struck the gate with the heel of his wooden foot and it opened before him; the second and third gate opened too, in like manner, when he struck them. In he went to the room where the king and his two friends were drinking. There he found them raising toasts to each other. He was himself invisible. As soon as they rested the horn on the table, he snatched it and made off for the place where Miach Lay was lying dead. Then Red Bow and his men raised up the dead man, and poured down his throat some of the wine or whatever liquor was held in the horn.

After a time Miach Lay opened his eyes, and yawned. They were all so delighted that they raised three shouts of joy.

"Come on with me now," said the Sprisawn, "to the castle of the Dark King. We will have a trial of strength with him. I will take the Dark King in hand myself. Do you, Miach Lay, take the King of Mangling, and you, Red Bow, take the Gruagach of Shields."

"This will be very good for us to keep," said Red Bow, when he saw the virtue of the horn.

"No," said the Sprisawn; "it is good for the man who owns it, and I will return it."

The Sprisawn, who could travel as swiftly as his own thought, vanished with the horn, placed it on the table from which he had snatched it, and came back to the others. No one had missed the horn; when they turned to use it, it was there on the table before them, in the chamber of the Dark King. Miach Lay and his friends went on together, and never stopped till they stood in the chamber where the Dark King was sitting with his friends. The gates had remained open since the Sprisawn opened them. When the Dark King saw the dead man alive, standing in his chamber before him, he said, "Never a welcome to you, you miserable creature with the wooden foot. What brought you hither, or how did you come?"

"I have come to you with combat," said the Sprisawn; "and now do you choose the manner of fighting."

In the castle were three chambers, in each chamber a cross-beam as high from the floor as a man's throat; in the middle of each cross-beam was a hole, through this hole passed a chain, at each end of the chain was an iron loop; above the hole and lengthwise with the beam was a sword with a keen edge on it. Each pair of champions was to take one room of the three, and each man of them was to place a loop on his own neck; each then was to pull the other to the hole if he could, and then pull till the sword cut his head off.

The Sprisawn and the Dark King took one room, Miach Lay and the King of Mangling another, Red Bow and the Gruagach of Shields took the third.

The first pair were not long at each other, as the Sprisawn was greatly anxious for the other two, and with the second pull that he gave he had the head off the Dark King. He ran then to see how it fared with Miach Lay. Miach Lay was tired and nearly beaten.

"Come out of that for me," said the Sprisawn. "What playing is it you have with him?"

"Fully satisfied am I to give this place to you," said Miach Lay, raising the loop; and the Sprisawn put it quickly on his own neck.

With the first pull the Sprisawn gave he had

the head off the King of Mangling. They ran then to Red Bow, whose head was within two feet of the sword.

"Go on out of this," said the Sprisawn, putting the loop on his own neck. The Gruagach, by reason of having Red Bow so near the beam, was himself at a distance, but at the first pull which the Sprisawn gave he drew the Gruagach within a foot of the beam. Fearing that if he killed the third man there would be no one to give an account of those carried off by the Dark King, the Sprisawn offered the Gruagach his life if he told him where Manus and the other two husbands of the king's daughter were.

"If I tell you that," said the Gruagach, "the Dark King will knock the head off me."

"If you saw the head of the Dark King would you tell me?"

"I would."

The Sprisawn sent Miach Lay for the head of the Dark King; he brought it.

"Is that his head?" asked the Sprisawn.

"It is," said the Gruagach.

"Well, tell me now."

"Were I to tell you," said the Gruagach, "the King of Mangling would knock the head off me."

"If you saw his head would you tell me?"

"I would."

The head of the King of Mangling was brought.

"Is this the head?"

"It is."

"Well, tell me, or you'll lose your own head."

"Near this castle is a lake," said the Gruagach, "and under its water is an enchanted steel tower, with high walls three feet in thickness; around that tower on the outside a long serpent has wound herself closely from the bottom to the top. This serpent is called the Worm of Nine Eyes. Inside in the tower are the three men."

"And how can we come at them?" asked the Sprisawn.

"Whoever wants to free them," said the Gruagach, "must stand on the shore of the lake and shout to the serpent, calling her the Worm of Nine Eyes. Hearing this, the serpent will unwind, and with lashing will drive all the water of the lake in showers through the country and flood the whole land. The basin of the lake will be dry then, and the serpent will rush at the man who uttered the insult and try to devour him. The serpent must be killed, and the champion must run to the tower; if he can break in, he will rescue the three men."

"Is that all?" asked the Sprisawn.

"It is," said the Gruagach. "I have no further account of the matter; that is all I know."

"Then you 'll lose your head, too," said the Sprisawn; and with one pull of the chain he swept the head off the Gruagach. The three champions went to the lake then. Miach Lay and Red Bow wished to help the Sprisawn, but he forced them to remain behind, saying that they would be swept away by the waters if they went.

The Sprisawn, coming to the bank of the lake, shouted: "Worm of Nine Eyes!" No sooner did the serpent hear the name than she uncoiled from the tower, lashed the lake, and sent the water over the country. When the lake bed was dry the serpent rushed toward the Sprisawn with open mouth. When the Sprisawn saw the serpent he took his sword in both hands and held it crosswise in front of his face, and when the serpent was coming to swallow him so great was the force with which she rushed forward and sucked the air to draw him in, that the Sprisawn split her in two from the mouth to the tail, dividing the back from the belly, and the two pieces fell apart like the two halves of a split log of timber.

Miach Lay and Red Bow came then to the Sprisawn and went to the tower, but if they did, they could not go in.

"Oh," said the Sprisawn, "if you had all the arms in the world you could not break through that tower." He went himself to the door then, and striking it slightly with his wooden foot, for fear of killing the men inside by too hard a blow, he burst in the door. The three men inside came out, and Miach Lay embraced his own brother. All were glad, and all started for home, but had not gone far when the other two men began to dispute whose would the king's daughter be. The first husband said his claim was strongest; the second said his was. The Sprisawn tried to settle the quarrel, but could not. "I would advise you," said he, "to leave the matter to the first man you meet."

All agreed to do this.

The Sprisawn now left them and vanished as if he had never been with them. They had not gone far when they met a man. "Well met," said they; "we are glad to see you."

"What is the trouble that is on you?" asked the man.

"So and so," said they, telling him the whole story; "and now you are to be our judge."

"I will do my best," said the man, "if each one will be satisfied with my decision."

"We will," said they.

"Now let each man tell his story."

Each man told his story to the end.

"Who rescued you?" asked he.

"Miach Lay and his forces," said they.

"Had not this man and his forces come, you would have been there till this time?"

"We should," said the three.

"If so," said the man, "my decision is that the first and second husband should each be thankful, go to his own people, and get another wife for himself; and that the daughter of the King of Greece belongs to the brother of the man who rescued all three."

The two princes went away toward their own homes, and the man remained, and who was he when he took his own form again but the Sprisawn. They went then to the castle where the young lady had entertained Miach Lay, and whose castle was it but the Sprisawn's; the young woman was his daughter. After resting there for some days, the Sprisawn asked Miach Lay would he marry his daughter. Miach Lay was willing and glad, and remained there.

Manus and Red Bow returned to the King of Greece. Manus lived in Greece happily, and so did his children.

The two brothers did well not to marry any

woman their father found for them, for they would not have had the grand ladies that they had in the end, and Miach Lay had the dominions of the Dark King, as well as those of the Sprisawn, and they were very rich kingdoms.

THE AMADAN MOR AND THE GRUA-GACH OF THE CASTLE OF GOLD.

ON a time in Erin the King of Leinster resolved to make war on the King of Munster, and sent him a message to be ready for battle on a day mentioned. They raised flags for combat when the day came, and stood face to face. The forces closed in battle, and were at one another then till the King of Leinster and his men killed all the warriors of the King of Munster and the king himself.

After the King of Munster and all his champions were slain, the King of Leinster thought it better to live in Munster than in his own kingdom, so he took possession of Munster and went to live in the king's castle.

The wife of the King of Munster fled in haste to a forest, a thing easily done, for all Erin was under forests in that time. The queen had a son in the forest, and after a time she had no clothes for herself or the child. Hair came out on them as on wild beasts of the wilderness. The child was thriving and growing; what of him did not grow in the day grew threefold at night, till at last there was no knowing what size was he.

The queen was seven years without leaving the place around her hut in the forest. In the eighth year she went forth from the forest and saw her husband's castle and open kingdom, and began to weep and lament. There was a great crowd of people around the castle where she had herself lived in past years. She went to see what was happening. It was a summer of great want, and the king was giving out doles of meal to people daily, and the man who was giving the meal gave her a dole also. He was greatly surprised when he saw her, and in the evening he was telling the king that he had never seen such a sight in his life; she was all covered with hair like a beast of the forest.

"She will come again to-morrow," said the king; "then do you inquire what sort is she, and where is her place of abode."

She went next day to the castle; the man in charge gave her meal. After she had gone he followed her, and when he was coming near she sat down at the roadside from shame.

"Fear me not," said the man. "I wish to know if you are of the dead or the living, and what sort are you."

"I am a living person, though I may seem like one from the dead."

"Where do you live?"

"I have no house or home save a small hut in the forest, and I have the look of a beast because I eat fruits and leaves of trees and grass of the earth."

The man told the king, and the king said, "Tell the woman to-morrow that I will give her a house of some kind to live in."

The king gave the strange woman a house, and she went to live with her son in it. The son was seven years old at that time, and not able to walk or speak, although he was larger than any giant. His mother had called him Micky, and soon he was known as Micky Mor (Big Micky).

She was there for awhile in the house with her son, and she taking doles of food like any poor person. One fine summer day she was sitting at the doorstep, and she began to weep and lament.

"What is the cause of your crying?" asked the boy, who had never spoken before till that moment.

"God's help be with us," said the mother. "It is time for you to get speech. Thank God you are able to talk now."

"It is never too late, mother."

"That is right, my child," said she, "it is better late than never."

"Tell me, mother, why do you cry in this way and lament?"

"It is no use for me to tell you, my child; three men have just gone back to the strand, and once I was able to give the like of them a good warm dinner."

"Well, mother, you must go and invite them to dinner this time."

"What have I to give them to eat, my poor child?"

"If you have nothing to give them but only to be talking till morning, you will have to go and invite them."

When she was ready he said: "Mother, before you go tie my two hands to the beam that is here in the house above the hearth, that I may not fall in the fire while you are absent."

Before the mother went out she passed a rope under his arms, tied him to the cross-beam, and put a stool under his feet. He kicked the stool away; he had to pull and drag himself to swing, the fire was catching his feet, the beam was cracking from his weight and the swinging. The sinews of his legs stretched, he got his footing then, and walked to the door.

"Thanks be to God," said the mother, when she came back. "It is curious how your talk and your walk came to you on the one day."

"It is nearly always the case that 't is together talk and walk come to a child; but now it is time for us to be providing something for the friends that are coming to-night."

He went away then and asked the man who brought turf out of the reeks to the king's castle to give him as much as would make fire for himself and his mother for the night.

"Go away," said the man; "I will not give you a sod of turf. Go to the king and get an order; then I will give you turf in plenty."

"I would not be tiring myself going for an order, but I will have plenty in spite of you."

Micky took away then a great basket of turf and no thanks to the man.

"Well, mother," said he, "here is turf enough for you, and make down a good fire."

He went to the mill and said to the miller: "My mother sent me for flour. There will be three at the house to-night, and what will not be used will be brought to you in the morning."

"You stump of a fool, why should I give you flour? Go to my master, the king; if he gives an order, I will give you flour in plenty."

Micky caught the miller. "I will put you,"

said he, "in one of the hoppers of the mill unless you make away with yourself out of this."

The miller ran away in dread that Micky would kill him. Micky laid hold of a strong, weighty chain, and tied a great sack of flour and put it on his back. When the sack was across his back he could not pass through the doorway, and knew not what to do.

"It would be a shame for me to say of the first load I put on my back that I left that same after me." He stepped backward some paces and made such a rush that he carried out the frame of the door with him.

"Well, mother," said he, "we have fire and flour enough now, and let you be making loaves for the visitors."

He went next to the woman in charge of the milk-house. "It is hither my mother sent me for a firkin of butter. There are three strangers above in our house. What will be left of the butter I will bring back in the morning, and all my own help and assistance to you for a week to come."

"Be out of my milk-house, you stump of a fool," said the woman. "What assistance can you give to pay for my milk and butter?"

"Let you be out of this, my good woman,"

said Micky, "or I will not leave much life in you from this day out."

She went away in a hurry, and he carried a firkin of butter home on his shoulder.

"Now, mother," said he, "you have bread, fire, butter, and all things you need. If we had a bit of meat, that would be all that we care for."

He went away then and never stopped nor stayed till he reached the place where all the king's fine fat sheep were. He caught up one and brought it home on his shoulder.

Next day the turf-keeper, the miller, the dairy-woman, and the shepherd went to complain to the king of what Micky had done.

"It is not luck we asked for the first day we drew him on us," said the king.

The king started and never stopped nor stayed till he went to his old druid. "Such a man as we have brought on us," said the king. "Tell me now how to put an end to him."

"There is," said the druid, "a black mad hound in a wood beyond the mountain. Tell Micky that you lost that hound one day in the hunt, and to bring her and he will be well paid for his trouble."

The king sent for Micky, and told him all as the druid advised.

"Will you send any man with me to show me the road?"

"I will," said the king.

Micky and the man were soon travelling along the road toward the mountain. When Micky thought it too slow the man was walking, he asked, "Have you any walk better than that?"

"Why, then, I have not," said the man, "and I am tired, and it is because I have such a good walk that I was sent with you."

Micky took up his guide, put him under his arm, with the man's head near his own breast, and they began to talk as Micky moved forward. When they came near the wood, the man said, "Put me down, and beware of the hound. Be not rash with her, or she may harm you."

"If she is a hound belonging to a king or a man of high degree, it must be that she has training and will come with me quietly. If she will not come gently, I will make her come in spite of her."

When he went into the wood the hound smelt him and rushed at his throat to tear him to pieces. He hurled her off quickly, and then she made a second drive at him, and a fierce one.

"Indeed," said Micky, "you are an impudent hound to belong to a king;" and, taking a long, strong tree branch, he gave her a blow on the flank that raised her high in the air.

After that blow the hound ran away as fast as her legs could carry her, and Micky made after her with all the speed of his own legs to catch her. On account of the blow she was losing breath fast, and he was coming nearer and nearer, till at length he ran before her and drove her in against the ditch. When she tried to go one way he shook the branch before her, and when she tried to rush off in another direction, he shook it there too, till he forced her into the road, and then she was mild and quiet and came with him as gently as any dog.

When he was near home some one saw Micky and the mad hound with him. A messenger ran and told the king he was coming and the mad hound walking with him. The king gave orders to close every door in the castle. He was in dread that the hound would devour every one living.

When the hound was brought before the closed door of the castle the king put his head out the window and said, "That hound has been so long astray that she is of no use to me now; take her to your mother, and she will mind the house for her."

Micky took the hound home, and she was that tame and watchful that not a hen, nor a duck, nor a goose belonging to the king's castle could come near the house.

The king went to the druid a second time, and asked, "What can I do to kill Micky Mor?"

"There is a raging wild boar in the woods there beyond that will tear him to pieces," said the druid. "Tell Micky Mor that one of the servants, when coming from the town, lost a young pig, that the pig is in that wood, and to bring him."

The king sent for the boy, and said, "One of my men lost a young pig while coming from the town; it is in that wood there beyond. If you 'll go to the wood and bring the pig hither, I 'll pay you well when you come."

"I will go," said the boy, "if you will send some one to show me the wood where the pig is."

The king sent a man, but not the man who went the first time with Micky Mor, for that man said, "I am tired, and have n't the strength to go." They went on then, walking toward the wood. This guide grew tired like the first man, for the wood was far distant from the castle of the king. When he was tired, the boy put him under his arm, and the two began to chat away as they journeyed. When near the wood, the man begged and said, "Micky Mor, put me down now: it is a mad boar that is in the wood; and if you are not careful, he will tear you to pieces."

"God help you!" said Micky; "'t is the innocent man you are to let such a small thing put
dread on you."

"I will leave you," said the guide: "I cannot
help you; you are able to fight the battle
yourself."

Away went the man; and when Micky Mor
entered the wood, the wild boar was facing him,
and the beast foaming from both sides of the
mouth. As the guide had warned him to be on
his guard, Micky gave one spring out of his body,
and came to the boar with such a kick that his
leg went right into the mouth of the beast, and
split his jaw back to the breast. The wild boar
dropped lifeless, and the boy was going home,
leaving the great beast behind him. He stopped
then, and said to himself, "If I go back without the boar, the king will not believe that I
met him at all." He turned back, caught the
wild boar by the hind legs, and threw him across
his shoulders.

The king thought, "As he brought the mad
hound the first day, he may bring the wild boar
to me this time." He placed guards on all roads
leading to the castle.

The guards saw Micky coming with the boar
on his back. Thinking the boar alive, they ran
hither and over, closed every door, window, hole,

or place that a mouse might pass through, for fear the wild boar would tear them to pieces.

The youth went up to the castle, and struck the door; the king put his head out the window, and asked, "Can it be that you have the wild boar?"

"I have him; but if I have, he is dead."

"As he is dead, you might take him home to your mother; and, believe me, he will keep you in meat for a long while."

The king went to the druid again.

"I have no advice for you this time," said the druid, "but one: he is of as good blood as yourself; and the best thing you can do is to give him your daughter to marry."

This daughter was the king's only child, and her name was Eilin Og. The king sent for the youth then, and said, "I will give you my daughter to marry."

"It is well," said Micky Mor; "if you give her in friendship, I will take her."

Micky Mor made himself ready; they gave him fine clothes, and he seemed fit to marry any king's daughter. After the marriage he was a full week without going to see his own mother.

When he went to her at the end of the week, she cried out, "What is keeping you away from me a whole week?"

"Dear mother," said he, "it is I that have

met with the luck. I got the king's daughter
to marry."

"Go away out of my sight, and never come
near me again!"

"Why so, mother, what ails you? Could I get
a better wife than a king's daughter?"

"My dear son, if she is a king's daughter, you
are a king's son, so you are as high as she."

"If I am a king's son, why have you and I
been so poor?"

She told him then that the king had killed his
father and all his forces, and that the whole
castle and kingdom had belonged to his father.

"Why did you not tell me that long ago?"

"I would never have told you," said she, "but
that you have married the murderer's daughter."

Away went the son when he heard what his
mother said, and the eyes going out of his head
with wild rage, and he saying that he would kill
every one living about the king's castle. The
people in the castle saw him coming, and thought
from his looks that his mother had said some
strong words to him, and they closed every door
and window against him. The young man put
his shoulder to the door of the castle, and it flew
in before him. He never stopped nor stayed till
he went to the highest chamber of the castle to
the king and queen, killing every one that came

in his way. "Pardon me! Spare me!" cried the king.

"I will never kill you between my own two hands; but I'll give you the chance that you gave my own father while the spear was going from the hand to his breast." With that, he caught the king, and threw him out through the window. When he had all killed who did not flee before him, he could find no sight of his own wife, though he looked for her everywhere.

"Well, mother," said he when he went home, "I have all killed before me, but I cannot find my own wife."

The mother went with him to search for the wife, and they found her in a box. When they opened the box, she screamed wildly.

"Sure, you know well that I did not marry you to kill you; have no fear."

She was glad to have her life. Micky Mor then moved into the castle, and had his father's kingdom and property back again. After awhile he went to walk one day with his wife, Eilin Og. While he was walking for himself, the sky grew so dark that it seemed like night, and he knew not where to go; but he went on till he came at last to a roomy dark glen. When he was inside in the glen, the greatest drowsiness that ever came over a man came over him.

"Eilin Og," said he, "come quickly under my head, for sleep is coming on me."

"It is not sleep that is troubling you, but something in this great gloomy glen, where you were never before in your life."

"Oh, Eilin Og, come quickly under my head."

She came under his head, and he got a short nap of sleep. When he woke, hunger and thirst came on him greater than ever came upon any man ever born. Then a vessel came to him filled with food, and one with drink.

"Taste not the drink, take not a bite of the food, in this dark glen, till you know what kind of a place is it."

"Eilin Og, I must take one drink. I'll drink it whomsoever it vexes."

He took a draught hard and strong from the vessel; and that moment the two legs dropped off Micky Mor from the knees down.

When Eilin Og saw this, she fell to wailing and weeping.

"Hold, hold, Eilin Og! silence your grief; a head or a leg will not be in the country unless I get my two legs again."

The fog now dispersed, and the sky became clear. When he saw the sky clear, he knew where to go; and he put his knife and spear and wife on the point of his shoulder. Then his strength and activity were greater, and he was swifter on his two knees than nine times nine other men that had the use of their whole legs.

While he was going on, he saw huntsmen coming toward him. A deer passed him. He threw the spear that he had in his hand; it went through the deer, in one side and out through the other. A white dog rushed straightway after the deer. Micky Mor caught the deer and the dog, and kept them.

Now a young Gruagach, light and loose, was the first of the huntsmen to follow the white dog. "Micky Mor," said he, "give me the white dog and the deer."

"I will not," said Micky. "For it is myself that did the slaughter, strong and fierce, that threw the spear out of my right hand and put it through the two sides of the deer; and whoever it be, you or I, who has the strongest hand, let him have the white dog and the deer."

"Micky Mor," said Eilin Og, "yield up the white dog and the deer."

"I will," said he, "and more if you ask; for had I obeyed you in the glen, the two legs from the knees down would not have gone from me."

The hunter, who was the Gruagach of Dun an Oir, was so glad to get his white dog and deer that he said, "Come with me, Micky Mor, to my castle to dinner."

The three were then passing along by the
strand of Ard na Conye to the Gruagach's castle,
when whom should they meet but a champion who
began to talk with the men; but, seeing Eilin
Og, he stopped on a sudden and asked Micky
Mor, "Who is this woman with you? I think
there is not another of such beauty in all the
great world."

"That is my wife, Eilin Og," said Micky Mor.

"It is to find her that I am here, and to take
her in spite of herself or her father," said the
champion.

"If you take her, you will take her in spite of
me," said Micky Mor; "but what champion are
you with such words?"

"I am Maragach of the Green Gloves from
Great Island. I have travelled the world twice,
and have met no man to match me. No weapons
have hurt my skin yet or my body. Where are
your arms of defence in this great world, Micky
Mor?"

"I have never wished for a weapon but my own
two fists that were born with me."

"I name you now and forever," said Maragach,
"the Big Fool (Amadan Mor)."

"Not talk of the mouth performs deeds of
valor, but active, strong bones. Let us draw
back now, and close with each other. We shall

know then who is the best man; and if there is valor in you, as you say, you dirty little Maragach, I will give you a blow with strength that will open your mouth to the bone."

They went toward each other then threateningly, and closed like two striking Balors or two wild boars in the days of the Fenians, or two hawks of Cold Cliff, or two otters of Blue Pool. They met in close, mighty struggle, with more screeching than comes from a thousand. They made high places low, and low places high. The clods that were shot away by them, as they wrestled, struck out the eye of the hag in the Eastern World, and she spinning thread at her wheel.

Now Maragach drew his sword strong, keen-edged, and flawless; this sword always took with the second blow what it did not cut with the first; but there was no blow of it that time which the Big Fool did not dodge, and when the sun was yellow at setting, the sword was in small bits, save what remained in the hand of the champion. That moment the Fool struck the champion a blow 'twixt neck and skull, and took the head off his body.

The three went on then to the castle of Dun an Oir (Castle of Gold), and had a fine dinner. During the dinner they were discoursing and telling tales; and the Gruagach's wife took greatly to heart the looks that her husband was giving Eilin Og, and asked, "Which is it that you will have, Negil Og's daughter or the wife of the Big Fool?"

Said Eilin Og to the Gruagach's wife, "This man's name is not the Big Fool in truth or in justice, for he is a hero strong and active; he is master of all alive and of every place. All the world is under his command, and I with the rest."

"If he is all this, why did he let the legs go from him?" asked the Gruagach's wife.

Eilin Og answered, "I have said that he has high virtues and powers; and only for the drink that was brought him in the dark lonely glen, he would not have let the legs go from him."

The Gruagach was in dread that the Big Fool might grow angry over their talks, and that enchantment would not get the upper hand of strength, and said, "Give no heed to woman's talk, Micky Mor, but guard my castle, my property, and my wife, while I go to the Dun of the Hunt and return."

"If any man comes in in spite of me," said Micky Mor, "while you are absent, believe me, he will not go out in spite of me till you return."

The Gruagach went off then, and with the

power of his enchantment put a heavy sleep on Micky Mor.

"Eilin Og," said he, "come quickly under my head, for over-strong sleep has come on me."

Eilin Og came under his head, and he got a short nap of sleep. The Gruagach returned soon in a different form altogether, and he took a kiss from his own wife.

"Oh," said Eilin Og to her husband, "you are in your sleep, and it is to my grief that you are in it, and not at the right time."

Micky Mor heard her, and he, between sleeping and waking, gave one leap from his body when he heard Eilin Og's words, and stopped at the door. It would have been a greater task to break any anvil or block made by blacksmith or wood-worker, than to force the Big Fool from the door.

"Micky Mor," said the Gruagach, disguised, "let me out."

"I will not let you out till the Gruagach of Dun an Oir comes home, and then you will pay for the kiss that you took from his wife."

"I will give you a leg swift and strong as your own was; it is a leg I took from the Knight of the Cross when he was entering his ship."

"If you give me one of my legs swift and strong as ever, perhaps I may let you go out."

That moment the Fool got the leg. He jumped up then, and said, "This is my own leg, as strong and as active as ever.

"The other leg now, or your head!" said Micky Mor.

The Gruagach gave him the other leg, blew it under him with power of enchantment. Micky Mor jumped up. "These are my own legs in strength and activity. You'll not go out of this now till the Gruagach comes, and you pay for the kiss you took from his wife."

"I have no wish to knock a trial out of you," said the Gruagach, and he changed himself into his own form again. "You see who I am; and I am the huntsman who took your legs with the drink that you got from the cup, and I am your own brother born and bred."

"Where were you," asked the Big Fool, "when my father was killed with all his men?"

"I was in the Eastern World at that time, learning enchantment and magic."

"If you are my brother," said the Big Fool, "we will go with each other forevermore. Come with me now to such a wood. We will fight there four giants who are doing great harm to our people these many years."

"Dear brother," said the Gruagach, "there is no use for us to go against the four giants; they are too powerful and strong for us, they will kill us."

"Let me fight with three of them," said Micky Mor, "and I'll not leave a foot or a hand of them living on earth; you can settle one."

The Gruagach had his great stallion of the road brought from the stable for himself and his brother to ride. When they led him out, the stallion gave three neighs, — a neigh of lamentation, a neigh of loyalty, and a neigh of gladness.

This stallion had the three qualities of Fin Mac Cool's slim bay steed, — a keen rush against a hill, a swift run on the level, a high running leap; three qualities of the fox, — the gait of a fox gay and proud, a look straight ahead taking in both sides and turning to no side, neat in his tread on the road; three qualities of a bull, — a full eye, a thick neck, a bold forehead.

They rode to the forest of the giants; and the moment they entered, the giants sniffed them, and one of them cried out, "I find the smell of men from Erin, their livers and lights for my supper of nights, their blood for my morning dram, their jawbones for stepping-stones, and their shins for hurleys. We think you are too big for one bite and too small for two bites, and sooner or later we'll have you out of the way."

The Big Fool and three of the giants made at

one another then; and he did n't leave a hand nor a foot of the three alive. He stood looking then at his brother and the other giant. The young Gruagach was getting too much from the giant; and he called out, "Dear born brother, give me some aid, or the giant will put me out of the world."

"I will give him," said the Big Fool, "a blow of my fist that will drive his head through the air."

He ran to him then, gave the giant one blow under the jawbone, and sent his head through the air. It is not known to man, woman, or child to this day where the head stopped, or did it stop in any place.

THE KING'S SON AND THE WHITE-
BEARDED SCOLOG.

NOT in our time, nor the time of our fathers, but long ago, there lived an old king in Erin. This king had but the one son, and the son had risen up to be a fine strong hero; no man in the kingdom could stand before him in combat.

The queen was dead, and the king was gloomy and bitter in himself because old age was on him. The strength had gone from his limbs, and gladness from his heart. No matter what people said, they could not drive sorrow from him.

One day the king called up his son, and this is what he said to him, "You are of age to marry. We cannot tell how long I'll be here, and it would cheer and delight me to see your wife; she might be a daughter to me in my last days."

"I am willing to obey you," said the son; "but I know no woman that I care for. I have never seen any one that I would marry."

With that, the old king sent for a druid, and said, "You must tell where my son can find the right bride for himself. You must tell us what woman he should marry."

"There is but one woman," said the druid, "who can be the right wife for your son, and she is the youngest daughter of the white-bearded scolog; she is the wisest young woman in the world, and has the most power."

"Where does her father live, and how are we to settle it?" asked the king of the druid.

"I have no knowledge of the place where that scolog lives," said the druid, "and there is no one here who knows. Your son must go himself, and walk the world till he finds the young woman. If he finds her and gets her, he 'll have the best bride that ever came to a king's son."

"I am willing to go in search of the scolog's daughter," said the young man, "and I 'll never stop till I find her."

With that, he left his father and the druid, and never stopped till he went to his foster-mother and told her the whole story, — told her the wish of his father, and the advice the old druid had given him.

"My three brothers live on the road you must travel," said the foster-mother; "and the eldest one knows how to find that scolog, but without the friendship of all of them, you 'll not be able to make the journey. I 'll give you something that will gain their good-will for you."

With that, she went to an inner room, and made three cakes of flour and baked them. When the three were ready, she brought them out, and gave them to the young man.

"When you come to my youngest brother's castle," said she, "he will rush at you to kill you, but do you strike him on the breast with one of the cakes; that minute he 'll be friendly, and give you good entertainment. The second brother and the eldest will meet you like the youngest."

On the following morning, the king's son left a blessing with his foster-mother, took one for the road from her, and went away carrying the three cakes with him. He travelled that day with great swiftness over hills and through valleys, past great towns and small villages, and never stopped nor stayed till he came in the evening to a very large castle. In he went, and inside was a woman before him.

"God save you!" said he to the woman.

"God save yourself!" said she; "and will you tell me what brought you the way, and where are you going?"

"I came here," said the king's son, "to see the giant of this castle, and to speak with him."

"Be said by me," replied the woman, "and go away out of this without waiting for the giant."

"I will not go without seeing him," said the king's son. "I have never set eyes on a giant, and I'll see this one."

"I pity you," said the woman; "your time is short in this life. You'll not be long without seeing the giant, and it's not much you'll see in this world after setting eyes on him; and it would be better for you to take a drink of wine to give you strength before he comes."

The king's son had barely swallowed the wine when he heard a great noise beyond the castle.

"Fee, faw, foh!" roared some one, in a thundering voice.

The king's son looked out; and what should he see but the giant with a shaggy goat going out in front of him and another coming on behind, a dead hag above on his shoulder, a great hog of a wild boar under his left arm, and a yellow flea on the club which he held in his right hand before him.

" I don't know will I blow you into the air or put my foot on you," said the giant, when he set eyes on the king's son. With that, he threw his load to the ground, and was making at his visitor to kill him when the young man struck the giant on the breast with one of the three cakes which he had from the foster-mother.

That minute the giant knew who was before him, and called out, "Isn't it the fine welcome I was giving my sister's son from Erin?"

With that, he changed entirely, and was so glad to see the king's son that he didn't know what to do for him or where to put him. He made a great feast that evening; the two ate and drank with contentment and delight. The giant was so pleased with the king's son that he took him to his own bed. He wasn't three minutes in the bed when he was sound asleep and snoring. With every breath that the giant took in, he drew the king's son into his mouth and as far as the butt of his tongue; with every breath that he sent out, he drove him to the rafters of the castle, and the king's son was that way going up and down between the bed and the roof until daybreak, when the giant let a breath out of him, and closed his mouth; next moment the king's son was down on his lips.

"What are you doing to me?" cried the giant.

"Nothing," said the king's son; "but you didn't let me close an eye all the night. With every breath you let out of you, you drove me up to the rafters; and with every breath you took in, you drew me into your mouth and as far as the butt of your tongue."

"Why didn't you wake me?"

"How could I wake you when time failed me to do it?"

"Oh, then, sister's son from Erin," said the giant, "it's the poor night's rest I gave you; but if you had a bad bed, you must have a good breakfast."

With that, the giant rose, and the two ate the best breakfast that could be had out of Erin.

After breakfast, the king's son took the giant's blessing with him, and left his own behind. He travelled all that day with great speed and without halt or rest, till he came in the evening to the castle of the second giant. In front of the door was a pavement of sharp razors, edges upward, a pavement which no man could walk on. Long, poisonous needles, set as thickly as bristles in a brush, were fixed, points downward, under the lintel of the door, and the door was low.

The king's son went in with one start over the razors and under the needles, without grazing his head or cutting his feet. When inside, he saw a woman before him.

"God save you!" said the king's son.

"God save yourself!" said the woman.

The same conversation passed between them then as passed between himself and the woman in the first castle.

"God help you!" said the woman, when she

heard his story. "'T is not long you'll be alive after the giant comes. Here's a drink of wine to strengthen you."

Barely had he the wine swallowed when there was a great noise behind the castle, and the next moment the giant came in with a thundering and rattling.

"Who is this that I see?" asked he, and with that, he sprang at the stranger to put the life out of him; but the king's son struck him on the breast with the second cake which he got from his foster-mother. That moment the giant knew him, and called out, "A strange welcome I had for you, sister's son from Erin, but you'll get good treatment from me now."

The giant and the king's son made three parts of that night. One part they spent in telling tales, the second in eating and drinking, and the third in sound, sweet slumber.

Next morning the young man went away after breakfast, and never stopped till he came to the castle of the third giant; and a beautiful castle it was, thatched with the down of cotton grass, the roof was as white as milk, beautiful to look at from afar or near by. The third giant was as angry at meeting him as the other two; but when he was struck in the breast with the third cake, he was as kind as the best man could be.

When they had taken supper together, the
giant said to his sister's son, "Will you tell me
what journey you are on?"

"I will, indeed," said the king's son; and he
told his whole story from beginning to end.

"It is well that you told me," said the giant,
"for I can help you; and if you do what I tell,
you'll finish your journey in safety. At midday
to-morrow you'll come to a lake; hide in the
rushes that are growing at one side of the water.
You'll not be long there when twelve swans will
alight near the rushes and take the crests from
their heads; with that, the swan skins will fall
from them, and they will rise up the most beautiful women that you have ever set eyes on.
When they go in to bathe, take the crest of the
youngest, put it in your bosom next the skin,
take the eleven others and hold them in your
hand. When the young women come out, give
the eleven crests to their owners; but when the
twelfth comes, you'll not give her the crest
unless she carries you to her father's castle in
Ardilawn Dreeachta (High Island of Enchantment). She will refuse, and say that strength
fails her to carry you, and she will beg for the
crest. Be firm, and keep it in your bosom; never
give it up till she promises to take you. She will
do that when she sees there is no help for it."

Next morning the king's son set out after breakfast, and at midday he was hidden in the rushes. He was barely there when the swans came. Everything happened as the giant had said, and the king's son followed his counsels.

When the twelve swans came out of the lake, he gave the eleven crests to the older ones, but kept the twelfth, the crest of the youngest, and gave it only when she promised to carry him to her father's. The moment she put the crest on her head, she was in love with the king's son. When she came in sight of the island, however much she loved him when they started from the lakeside, she loved him twice as much now. She came to the ground at some distance from the castle, and said to the young man at parting, —

"Thousands of kings' sons and champions have come to give greeting to my father at the door of his castle, but every man of them perished. You will be saved if you obey me. Stand with your right foot inside the threshold and your left foot outside; put your head under the lintel. If your head is inside, my father will cut it from your shoulders; if it is outside, he will cut it off also. If it is under the lintel when you cry 'God save you!' he'll let you go in safety."

They parted there; she went to her own place and he went to the scolog's castle, put his right foot inside the threshold, his left foot outside, and his head under the lintel. "God save you!" called he to the scolog.

"A blessing on you!" cried the scolog, "but my curse on your teacher. I'll give you lodgings to-night, and I'll come to you myself in the morning;" and with that he sent a servant with the king's son to a building outside. The servant took a bundle of straw with some turf and potatoes, and, putting these down inside the door, said, "Here are bed, supper, and fire for you."

The king's son made no use of food or bed, and he had no need of them, for the scolog's daughter came soon after, spread a cloth, took a small bundle from her pocket, and opened it. That moment the finest food and drink were there before them.

The king's son ate and drank with relish, and good reason he had after the long journey. When supper was over, the young woman whittled a small shaving from a staff which she brought with her; and that moment the finest bed that any man could have was there in the room.

"I will leave you now," said she; "my father will come early in the morning to give you a task. Before he comes, turn the bed over; 't will be a shaving again, and then you can throw it into the fire. I will make you a new bed to-morrow."

With that, she went away, and the young man slept till daybreak. Up he sprang, then turned the bed over, made a shaving of it, and burned it. It was not long till the scolog came, and this is what he said to the king's son, " I have a task for you to-day, and I hope you will be able to do it. There is a lake on my land not far from this, and a swamp at one side of it. You are to drain that lake and dry the swamp for me, and have the work finished this evening; if not, I will take the head from you at sunset. To drain the lake, you are to dig through a neck of land two miles in width; here is a good spade, and I 'll show you the place where you 're to use it."

The king's son went with the scolog, who showed the ground, and then left him.

"What am I to do?" said the king's son. "Sure, a thousand men could n't dig that land out in ten years, and they working night and day; how am I to do it between this and sunset?"

However it was, he began to dig; but if he did, for every sod he threw out, seven sods came in, and soon he saw that, in place of mending his trouble, 't was making it worse he was. He cast aside the spade then, sat down on the sod heap, and began to lament. He was n't long there when the scolog's daughter came with a cloth in her hand and the small bundle in her pocket.

"Why are you lamenting there like a child?" asked she of the king's son.

"Why should n't I lament when the head will be taken from me at sunset?"

"'T is a long time from this to sunset. Eat your breakfast first of all; see what will happen then," said she. Taking out the little bundle, she put down before him the best breakfast a man could have. While he was eating, she took the spade, cut out one sod, and threw it away. When she did that, every spadeful of earth in the neck of land followed the first spadeful; the whole neck of land was gone, and before midday there was n't a spoonful of water in the lake or the swamp, — the whole place was dry.

"You have your head saved to-day, whatever you 'll do to-morrow," said she, and she left him.

Toward evening the scolog came, and, meeting the king's son, cried out, "You are the best man that ever came the way, or that ever I expected to look at."

The king's son went to his lodging. In the evening the scolog's daughter came with supper, and made a bed for him as good as the first one. Next morning the king's son rose at daybreak, destroyed his bed, and waited to see what would happen.

The scolog came early, and said, "I have a field outside, a mile long and a mile wide, with a very tall tree in the middle of it. Here are two wedges, a sharp axe, and a fine new drawing knife. You are to cut down the tree, and make from it barrels to cover the whole field. You are to make the barrels and fill them with water before sunset, or the head will be taken from you."

The king's son went to the field, faced the tree, and gave it a blow with his axe; but if he did, the axe bounded back from the trunk, struck him on the forehead, stretched him on the flat of his back, and raised a lump on the place where it hit him. He gave three blows, was served each time in the same way, and had three lumps on his forehead. He was rising from the third blow, the life almost gone from him, and he crying bitterly, when the scolog's daughter came with his breakfast. While he was eating the breakfast, she struck one little chip from the tree; that chip became a barrel, and then the whole tree turned into barrels, which took their places in rows, and covered the field. Between the rows there was just room for a man to walk. Not a barrel but was filled with water. From a chip she had in her hand, the young woman made a wooden dipper, from another chip she made a pail, and said to the king's son, —

"You'll have these in your two hands, and be walking up and down between the rows of barrels, putting a little water into this and a little into that barrel. When my father comes, he will see you at the work and invite you to the castle to-night, but you are not to go with him. You will say that you are content to lodge to-night where you lodged the other nights." With that, she went away, and the king's son was going around among the barrels pouring a little water into one and another of them, when the scolog came.

"You have the work done," said he, "and you must come to the castle for the night."

"I am well satisfied to lodge where I am, and to sleep as I slept since I came here," said the young man, and the scolog left him.

The young woman brought the supper, and gave a fresh bed. Next morning the scolog came the third time, and said, "Come with me now; I have a third task for you." With that, the two went to a quarry.

"Here are tools," said the scolog, pointing to a crowbar, a pickaxe, a trowel, and every implement used in quarrying and building. "You are to quarry stones to-day, and build between this and sunset the finest and largest castle in the world, with outhouses and stables, with cellars and kitchens. There must be cooks, with men and women to serve; there must be dishes and utensils of every kind and furniture of every description; not a thing is to be lacking, or the head will go from you this evening at sunset."

The scolog went home; and the king's son began to quarry with crowbar and pickaxe, and though he worked hard, the morning was far gone when he had three small pieces of stone quarried. He sat down to lament.

"Why are you lamenting this morning?" asked the scolog's daughter, who came now with his breakfast.

"Why should n't I lament when the head will be gone from me this evening? I am to quarry stones, and build the finest castle in the world before sunset. Ten thousand men could n't do the work in ten years."

"Take your breakfast," said the young woman; "you 'll see what to do after that."

While he was eating, she quarried one stone; and the next moment every stone in the quarry that was needed took its place in the finest and largest castle ever built, with outhouses and cellars and kitchens. A moment later, all the people were there, men and women, with utensils of all kinds. Everything was finished but a small spot at the principal fireplace.

"The castle is ready," said the scolog's daughter; "your head will stay with you to-day, and there are no more tasks before you at present. Here is a trowel and mortar; you will be finishing this small spot at the fire when my father comes. He will invite you to his castle to-night, and you are to go with him this time. After dinner, he will seat you at a table, and throw red wheat on it from his pocket. I have two sisters older than I am; they and I will fly in and alight on the table in the form of three pigeons, and we'll be eating the wheat; my father will tell you to choose one of his three daughters to marry. You'll know me by this: there will be a black quill in one of my wings. I'll show it; choose me."

All happened as the scolog's daughter said; and when the king's son was told to make his choice in the evening, he chose the pigeon that he wanted. The three sprang from the table, and when they touched the floor, they were three beautiful women. A dish priest and a wooden clerk were brought to the castle, and the two were married that evening.

A month passed in peace and enjoyment; but the king's son wished to go back now to Erin to his father. He told the wife what he wanted; and this is what she said to him, "My father will refuse you nothing. He will tell you to go, though he does n't wish to part with you. He will give you his blessing; but this is all pretence, for he will follow us to kill us. You must have a horse for the journey, and the right horse. He will send a man with you to three fields. In the first field are the finest horses that you have ever laid eyes on; take none of them. In the second field are splendid horses, but not so fine as in the first field; take none of these either. In the third field, in the farthest corner, near the river, is a long-haired, shaggy, poor little old mare; take that one. The old mare is my mother. She has great power, but not so much as my father, who made her what she is, because she opposed him. I will meet you beyond the hill, and we shall not be seen from the castle."

The king's son brought the mare; and when they mounted her, wings came from her sides, and she was the grandest steed ever seen. Away she flew over mountains, hills, and valleys, till they came to the seashore, and then they flew over the sea.

When the servant man went home, and the scolog knew what horse they had chosen, he turned himself and his two daughters into red fire, and shot after the couple. No matter how swiftly the mare moved, the scolog travelled faster, and was coming up. When the three reached the opposite shore of the sea, the daughter saw her father coming, and turned the mare into a small boat, the king's son into a fisherman, and made a fishing-rod of herself. Soon the scolog came, and his two daughters with him.

"Have you seen a man and a woman passing the way riding on a mare?" asked he of the fisherman.

"I have," said the fisherman. "You 'll soon overtake them."

On went the scolog; and he never stopped till he raced around the whole world, and came back to his own castle.

"Oh, then, we were the fools," said the scolog to his daughters. "Sure, they were the fisherman, the boat, and the rod."

Off they went a second time in three balls of red fire; and they were coming near again when the scolog's youngest daughter made a spinning-wheel of her mother, a bundle of flax of herself, and an old woman of her husband. Up rushed the scolog, and spoke to the spinner, "Have you seen a mare pass the way and two on her back?" asked he.

"I have, indeed," said the old woman; "and she is not far ahead of you."

Away rushed the scolog; and he never stopped till he raced around the whole world, and came back to his own castle a second time.

"Oh, but we were the fools!" said the scolog. "Sure, they were the old woman with the spinning-wheel and the flax, and they are gone from us now; for they are in Erin, and we cannot take our power over the border, nor work against them unless they are outside of Erin. There is no use in our following them; we might as well stay where we are."

The scolog and his daughters remained in the castle at Ardilawn of Enchantment; but the king's son rode home on the winged mare, with his wife on a pillion behind him.

When near the castle of the old king in Erin, the couple dismounted, and the mare took her own form of a woman. She could do that in Erin. The three never stopped till they went to the old king. Great was the welcome before them; and if ever there was joy in a castle, there was joy then in that one.

DYEERMUD ULTA AND THE KING IN SOUTH ERIN.

THERE was a king in South Erin once, and he had an only daughter of great beauty. The daughter said that she would marry no man but the man who would sail to her father's castle in a three-masted ship, and the castle was twenty miles from deep water. The father said that even if the daughter was willing, he'd never give her to any man but the man who would come in a ship.

Dyeermud Ulta was the grandson of a great man from Spain who had settled in Erin, and he lived near Kilcar. Dyeermud heard of the daughter of the king in South Erin, and fixed in his mind to provide such a ship and go to the castle of the king.

Dyeermud left home one day, and was walking toward Killybegs, thinking how to find such a ship, or the man who would make it. When he had gone as far as Buttermilk Cliff, he saw a red champion coming against him in a ship that was sailing along over the country like any ship on the sea.

"What journey are you on?" asked the red champion of Dyeermud; "and where are you going?"

"I am going," answered Dyeermud, "to the castle of a king in South Erin to know will he give me his daughter in marriage, and to know if the daughter herself is willing to marry me. The daughter will have no husband unless a man who brings a ship to her father's castle, and the king will give her to no other."

"Come with me," said the red man. "Take me as comrade, and what will you give me."

"I will give you what is right," said Dyeermud.

"What will you give me?"

"I will give you the worth of your trouble."

Dyeermud went in the ship, and they sailed on till they came to Conlun, a mile above Killybegs. There they saw twelve men cutting sods, and a thirteenth eating every sod that they cut.

"You must be a strange man to eat what sods twelve others can cut for you," said Dyeermud; "what is your name?"

"Sod-eater."

"We are going," said the red man, "to the castle of a king in South Erin. Will you come with us?"

"What wages will you give me?"

"Five gold-pieces," said the red man.

"I will go with you."

The three sailed on till they came to the river Kinvara, one mile below Killybegs, and saw a man with one foot on each bank, with his back toward the sea and his face to the current. The man did not let one drop of water in the river pass him, but drank every drop of it.

"Oh," said the red man, "what a thirst there is on you to drink a whole river! How are you so thirsty?"

"When I was a boy, my mother used to send me to school, and I did not wish to go there. She flogged and beat me every day, and I cried and lamented so much that a black spot rose on my heart from the beating; that is why there is such thirst on me now."

"What is your name, and will you go with us?"

"My name is Gulping-a-River. I will go with you if you give me wages."

"I will give you five gold-pieces," said the red man.

"I will go with you," said Gulping-a-River.

They sailed on then to Howling River, within one mile of Dun Kinealy. There they saw a man blowing up stream with one nostril, and the other stopped with a plug.

"Why blow with one nostril?" asked the red man.

"If I were to blow with the two," replied the stranger, "I would send you with your ship and all that are in it up into the sky and so far away that you would never come back again."

"Who are you, and will you take service with me?"

"My name is Greedy-of-Blowing, and I will go with you for wages."

"You will have five gold-pieces."

"I am your man," said Greedy-of-Blowing.

They sailed away after that to Bunlaky, a place one mile beyond Dun Kinealy; and there they found a man crushing stones with the end of his back, by sitting down on them suddenly.

"What are you doing there?" asked the red man.

"My name is Ironback," answered the stranger. "I am breaking stones with the end of my back to make a mill, a bridge, and a road."

"Will you come with us?" asked the red man.

"I will for just wages," said Ironback.

"You will get five gold-pieces."

"I will go in your company," said Ironback.

They went on sailing, and were a half a mile below Mount Charles when they saw a man running up against them faster than any wind, and one leg tied to his shoulder.

"Where are you going, and what is your hurry? Why are you travelling on one leg?" asked the red man.

"I am running to find a master," said the other. "If I were to go on my two legs, no man could see me or set eyes on me."

"What can you do? I may take you in service."

"I am a very good messenger. My name is Foot-on-Shoulder."

"I will give you five gold pieces."

"I will go with you," said the other.

The ship moved on now, and never stopped till within one mile of Donegal they saw, at a place called Kilemard, a man lying in a grass field with his cheek to the earth.

"What are you doing there?" asked the red man.

"Holding my ear to the ground, and hearing the grass grow."

"You must have good ears. What is your name; and will you take service with me?"

"My name is Hearing Ear. I will go with you for good wages."

"You will have five gold-pieces."

"I am your man," said Hearing Ear.

They went next to Laihy, where they found a man named Fis Wacfis (Wise man, Son of Knowledge), and he sitting at the roadside chewing his thumb.

"What are you doing there?" asked the red man.

"I am learning whatever I wish to know by chewing my thumb."

"Take service with me, and come on the ship."

He went on the same terms as the others, and they never stopped nor halted till they came to the castle of the king. They were outside the walls three days and three nights before any man spoke a word to them. At last the king sent a messenger to ask who were they and what brought them.

"I have come in a ship for your daughter, and my name is Dyeermud Ulta," was the answer the king got.

The king was frightened at the answer, though he knew himself well enough that it was for the daughter Dyeermud had come in the ship, and was greatly in dread that she would be taken from him. He went then to an old henwife that lived near the castle to know could he save the daughter, and how could he save her.

"If you'll be said by me," said the henwife, "you'll bid them all come to a feast in the castle.   Before they come, let your men put sharp poisoned spikes under the cushions of the seats set apart for the company.   They will sit on the spikes, swell up to the size of a horse, and die before the day is out, every man of them."

Hearing Ear was listening, heard all the talk between the king and the henwife, and told it.

"Now," said Fis Wacfis to Dyeermud, "the king will invite us all to a feast to morrow, and you will go there and take us.   It is better to send Ironback to try our seats, and sit on them, for under the cushion of each one will be poisoned spikes to kill us."

That day the king sent a message to Dyeermud.   "Will you come," said he, "with your men, to a feast in my castle to-morrow?   I am glad to have such guests, and you are welcome."

"Very thankful am I," said Dyeermud.   We will come to the feast."

Before the company came, Ironback went into the hall of feasting, looked at everything, sat down on each place, and made splinters of the seats.

"Those seats are of no use," said Ironback; "they are no better than so many cabbage stalks."

The king had iron seats brought in, strong

ones. There was no harm to Dyeermud and his company from that feast.

Away went the king to the henwife, and told how the seats had been broken. "What am I to do now?" asked he.

"Say that to get your daughter they must eat what food is in your castle at one meal."

Next day Dyeermud went to the castle, and asked, "Am I to have your daughter now?"

"You are not," said the king, "unless your company will eat what food is in my castle at one meal."

"Very well," said Dyeermud; "have the meal ready."

The king gave command to bring out the hundred and fifty tons of provisions in the castle all prepared and ready for eating.

Dyeermud came with his men, and Sod-eater began; and it was as much as all the king's servants could do to bring food as fast as he ate it, and he never stopped till there was n't a pound of the hundred and fifty tons left.

"Is this all you have to give me?" asked Sod-eater. "I could eat three times as much."

"Oh, we have no more," said the servants.

"Where is our dinner?" asked Dyeermud.

The king had nothing for the others, and he had nothing for himself. All had to go away hungry, and there was great dissatisfaction in the castle, and complaining.

The king had nothing to do now but to go to the henwife a third time for advice in his trouble.

"You have," said she, "three hundred and fifty pipes of wine. If his company cannot drink every drop of the wine, don't give him the daughter."

Next day Dyeermud went to the castle. "Am I to have the daughter now?" asked he of the king.

"I will not give my daughter," said the king, "unless you and your company will drink the three hundred and fifty pipes of wine that are in my castle."

"Bring out the wine," said Dyeermud; "we'll come to-morrow, and do the best we can to drink it."

Dyeermud and his men went next day to where the wine was. Gulping-a-River was the man for drinking, and they let him at it. After he got a taste, he was that anxious that he broke in the head of one pipe after another, and drank till there wasn't a drop left in the three hundred and fifty pipes. All the wine did was to put thirst on Gulping-a-River; and he was that mad with thirst that he drank up the spring well at the castle, and all the springs in the neighborhood, and a loch three miles distant, so that in the evening there was n't a drop of water for man or beast in the whole place.

What did the king do but go to the henwife the fourth time.

"Oh," said she, "there is no use in trying to get rid of him this way; you can make no hand of Dyeermud by eating or drinking. Do you send him now to the Eastern World to get the bottle of cure from the three sons of Sean [pronounced Shawn, — John] Mac Glinn, and to have it at the castle before noon to-morrow."

"Am I to get the daughter now?" asked Dyeermud of the king.

"You 'll not get my daughter," said the king, "unless you have for me here to-morrow the bottle of cure which the three sons of Sean Mac Glinn have in the Eastern World."

Dyeermud went to his ship with the king's answer.

"Let me go," said Foot-on-Shoulder. "I will bring you the bottle in season."

"You may go," said Dyeermud.

Away went Foot-on-Shoulder, and was at the sea in a minute. He made a ship of his cap, a mast of his stick, a sail of his shirt, and away with him sailing over the sea, never stopping nor halting till he reached the Eastern World.

In five hours, he came to a castle where the walls of defence were sixty-six feet high and fifty-five feet thick. Sean Mac Glinn's three sons were playing football on the top of the wall.

"Send down the bottle of cure to me," said Foot-on-Shoulder, "or I 'll have your lives."

"We will not give you the bottle of cure; and if you come up, it will be as hard to find your brains five minutes after as to find the clay of a cabin broken down a hundred years ago."

Foot-on-Shoulder made one spring, and rose six feet above the wall. They were so frightened at the sight of what he did, and were so in dread of him that they cried, "You 'll get what you want, only spare us, — leave us our lives. You are the best man that we have ever seen coming from any part; you have done what no man could ever do before this. You 'll get the bottle of cure; but will you send it back again?"

"I will not promise that," said Foot-on-Shoulder; "I may send it, and I may not."

They gave him the bottle, he went his way to his ship, and sailed home to Erin. Next morning the henwife dressed herself up as a piper, and, taking a rod of enchantment with her, went away, piping on a hill which Foot-on-Shoulder had to cross in coming to the castle. She thought he would stop to listen to the music she was making, and then she would strike him with the rod, and make a stone of him. She was piping away for herself on the hill like any poor piper making his living. Hearing Ear heard the music, and told Dyeermud. Fis Wacfis chewed his thumb at Dyeermud's command, and found out that the piper was the king's henwife, and discovered her plans.

"Oh," said Fis Wacfis to Dyeermud, "unless you take her out of that, she will make trouble for us."

"Greedy of-Blowing, can you make away with that old woman on the hill?" asked Dyeermud.

"I can indeed," said Greedy-of-Blowing.

With that, he ran to the foot of the hill; and with one blast from both nostrils, he sent the old hag up into the sky, and away she went sail ing so that neither tale nor word of her ever came back.

Foot-on-Shoulder was at the ship outside the castle walls half an hour before noon, and gave the bottle of cure to Dyeermud. Dyeermud went that minute to the castle, and stood before the king.

"Here is the bottle of cure which I got from the three sons of Sean Mac Glinn in the Eastern World. Am I to get the daughter now?"

"I'll send you my answer to the ship," said the king.

Where should the king go now in his trouble but to find the henwife. She was not at home. He sent men to look for the old woman; no tidings of her that day. They waited till the next day; not a sight of her. The following morning the king sent servants and messengers to look for the henwife. They searched the whole neighborhood; could not find her. He sent all his warriors and forces. They looked up and down, searched the whole kingdom, searched for nine days and nights, but found no trace of the henwife.

The king consented at last to give the daughter to Dyeermud, and he had to consent, and no thanks to him, for he could n't help himself. The daughter was glad and willing; she loved Dyeermud from the first, but the father would not part with her.

The wedding lasted a day and a year, and when that time was over, Dyeermud went home on the ship to Kilcar, and there he paid all his men their wages, and they went each to his own place.

The red man stayed some time in the neighborhood, and what should he do one day but seize Dyeermud's wife, put her in the ship, and sail away with her. When going, she put him under injunction not to marry her for a day and a year.

Now Dyeermud, who was hunting when the red man stole his wife, was in great grief and misery, for he knew not where the red man lived nor where he should travel to find him. At last he sent a message of inquiry to the King of Spain; and the king's answer was, "Only two persons in the whole world know where that man lives, Great Limper, King of Light, and Black Thorn of Darkness. I have written to these two, and told them to go to you."

The two men came in their own ship through the air to Kilcar, to Dyeermud, and talked and took counsel.

"I do not know where the red man can be," said Black Thorn, "unless in Kilchroti; let us go to that place."

They sailed away in their ship, and it went straight to the place they wanted. They had more power than the red man, and could send their ship anywhere.

In five days and nights they were at Kilchroti. They went straight to the house, and no one in the world could see the red man's house there but these two. Black Thorn struck the door, and it flew open. The red man, who was inside, took their hands, welcomed them heartily, and said, "I hope it is not to do me harm that ye are here."

"It is not to harm you or any one that we are here," replied they. "We are here only to get what is right and just, but without that, we will not go from this."

"What is the right and just that ye are here for?" asked the red man.

"Dyeermud's wife," replied Black Thorn, "and it was wrong in you to take her; you must give her up."

"I will fight rather than give her," said the red man.

"Fighting will not serve you," said Black Thorn, "it is better for you to give her to us."

"Ye will not get her without seven tons of gold," said the red man. "If ye bring me the gold, I will give her to you. If ye come without it, ye'll get fight from me."

"We will give you the gold," said Great Limper, "within seven days."

"Agreed," said the red man.

"Come to the ship," said Great Limper to Black Thorn.

They went on board, and sailed away.

"I was once on a ship which was wrecked on the coast of Spain with forty-five tons of gold. I know where that gold is; we will get it," said Great Limper.

The two sailed to where the gold was, took seven tons of it, and on the sixth day they had it in Kilchroti, in front of the red man's house. They weighed out the gold to him. They went then to find Dyeermud's wife. She was behind nine doors; each door was nine planks in thickness, and bolted with nine bars of iron. The red man opened the doors; all went in, and looked at the chamber. The woman went out first, next the red man; and, seizing the door, he thought to close it on Great Limper and Black Thorn, but Black Thorn was too quick for him, and before the red man could close the door he shot him, first with a gold and then with a silver bullet.

The red man fell dead on the threshold.

"I knew he was preparing some treachery," said Black Thorn. "When we weighed the gold to him, he let such a loud laugh of delight out of him."

They took the woman and the gold to Dyeermud; they stayed nine days and nights with him in Kilcar, eating, drinking, and making merry. They drank to the King of Spain, to all Erin, to themselves, and to their well-wishers. You see, I had great work to keep up with them these nine days and nights. I hope they will do well hereafter.

CUD, CAD, AND MICAD, THREE SONS OF THE KING OF URHU.

THERE was a king once in Urhu, and he had three sons. The eldest was three, the second two, the youngest one year old. Their names were Cud, Cad, and Micad. The three brothers were playing one day near the castle, which was hard by the seashore; and Cud ran in to his father, and said, "I hope you will give me what I ask."

"Anything you ask that I can give you will get," said the father.

"'T is all I ask," said Cud, "that you will give me and my brothers one of your ships to sail in till evening."

"I will give you that and welcome, but I think you and they are too weak to go on a ship."

"Let us be as we are; we 'll never go younger," said Cud.

The king gave the ship. Cud hurried out, and, catching Cad and Micad, one under each of his arms, went with one spring to the best ship in the roadstead. They raised the sails then, and

the three brothers did as good work as the best
and largest crew. They left the harbor with the
fairest wind a ship ever had. The wind blew in
a way that not a cable was left without stretching, an oar without breaking, nor a helm without
cracking with all the speed the ship had. The
water rose in three terrible ridges, so that the
rough gravel of the bottom was brought to the top,
and the froth of the top was driven down to the
bottom of the sea. The sight of the kingdom
of the world soon sank from the eyes of the
brothers; and when they saw nothing but blue
sea around them, a calm fell on the water.

Cud was going back and forth on the deck,
sorry for what was done; and a good right he had
to be sorry, but he was not sorry long. He saw
a small currachan (boat) a mile away, and went
with one spring from his ship to the currachan.
The finest woman in the world was sleeping in
the bottom of the boat. He put a finger under
her girdle, and went back with a spring to the
ship. When he touched his own deck, she woke.

"I put you under bonds and the misfortune of
the world," cried she, "to leave me where you
saw me first, and to be going ever and always till
you find me again."

"What name am I to call you when I go in
search of you?"

"The Cat of Fermalye, or the Swan of Endless Tales," said the woman.

He took her with one spring to the little boat, and with another spring went back to his own ship. Whatever good wind they had coming, they had it twice better going home. In the evening the ship was anchored among the others again. The brothers went ashore in a boat. When Cud came in, his father put out a chair for him, and gave him great welcome. Cud sat down; but as he did, he broke three rungs in the chair, two ribs in himself, and a rafter in the roof of the castle.

"You were put under bonds to-day," said the father.

"I was," said Cud.

"What bonds?"

"To be going ever and always till I find the Cat of Fermalye, or the Swan of Endless Tales."

Himself and his father spent that night together, and they were very sad and down-hearted. As early as the dawn came, Cud rose and ate his breakfast.

"Stay with me; I 'll give you half my kingdom now, and all when I die," said the father.

"I cannot stay under bonds; I must go," replied Cud.

Cud took the ship he liked best, and put supplies for a day and seven years in her.

"Now," said the father, "ask for something else; anything in the world I can give, I will give you."

"I want nothing but my two brothers to go with me."

"I care not where they go if yourself leaves me," said the king.

The three brothers went aboard the ship; and if the wind was good the first day, it was better this time. They never stopped nor rested till they sailed to Fermalye. The three went on shore, and were walking the kingdom. They had walked only a short piece of it when they saw a grand castle. They went to the gate; Cud was just opening it when a cat came out. The cat looked at Cud, bowed to him, and went her way. They saw neither beast nor man in the castle, or near it; only a woman at the highest window, and she sewing.

"We'll not stop till we go as far as the woman," said Cud.

The woman welcomed them when they came to her, put out a gold chair to Cud and a wooden chair to each of his brothers.

"'T is strange," said Micad, "to show so much greater respect to one than the other two."

"No cause for wonder in that," said the

woman. "I show respect to this one, for he is my brother-in-law."

"We do not wonder now, but where is his wife?"

"She went out a cat when ye came in."

"Oh, was that she?" cried Cud.

They spent the night with good cheer and plenty of food, the taste of honey in every bit they ate, and no bit dry. As early as the day dawned, the three rose, and the sister-in-law had their breakfast before them.

"Grief and sorrow, I'm in dread 't is bad cooking ye have on the ship. Take me with you; you'll have better food."

"Welcome," said Cud. "Come with us."

Each of the others welcomed her more than Cud. The four went on board; the brothers raised sails, and were five days going when they saw a ship shining like gold and coming from Western waters.

"That ship has no good appearance," said Cud. "We must keep out of danger;" and he took another course. Whatever course he took, the other ship was before him always, and crossing him.

"Isn't it narrow the ocean is, that you must be crossing me always?" shouted Cud.

"Do not wonder," cried a man from the other ship; "we heard that the three sons of the King of Urhu were sailing on the sea, and if we find them, it's not long they'll be before us."

The three strangers were the three sons of the King of Hadone.

"If it is for these you are looking," said Cud, "you need go no farther."

"It is to find you that we are here," said the man on the shining ship, "to take you on a visit to our own kingdom for a day and seven years. After that, we will go for the same length of time to your kingdom."

"You will get that and welcome," said Cud.

"Come on board my ship," said the eldest son of the King of Hadone: "we'll make one company; your ship is not much to look at."

"Of the food that our father gave us," said Cud, "there is no bit dry, and we have plenty on board. If it is dry food that you have in that big ship, leave it and come to us."

The sons of the King of Hadone went to the small ship, and let the big one go with the wind. When Cud saw that they let their own ship go, he made great friends of them.

"Have you been on sea ever before?" asked he of the eldest of the strangers.

"I am on sea since I was of an age to walk by myself," replied he.

"This is my first voyage," said Cud. "Now

as we are brothers and friends, and as you are
taking us to visit your kingdom, I 'll give you
command of my ship."

The king's son took this from Cud willingly,
and steered home in a straight course.

When the sons of the King of Hadone were
leaving home, they commanded all in the kingdom, big and little, small and great, weak and
strong, to be at the port before them when they
came back with the sons of the King of Urhu.
"These," said they, "must never be let out alive
on the shore."

In the first harbor the ship entered, the shore
was black and white with people.

"Why are all those people assembled?" asked
Cud.

"I have no knowledge of that," said the king's
son; "but if you 'll let your two brothers go with
me and my brothers, we 'll find out the reason."

They anchored the ship, put down a long-boat,
and Cad and Micad went into it with the three
sons of the King of Hadone.   Cud and his sister-
in-law stayed behind on the ship.   Cud never
took his eyes off his brothers as they sat in the
boat.   He watched them when near the shore,
and saw them both killed.   With one bound he
sprang from the bowsprit to land, and went
through all there as a hawk through small birds.
Two hours had not passed when the head was off

every man in the kingdom. Whatever trouble
he had in taking the heads, he had twice as
much in finding his brothers. When he had the
brothers found, it failed him to know how to bury
them. At last he saw on the beach an old ship
with three masts. He pulled out the masts, drew
the ship further on land, and said to himself, "I
will have my brothers under this ship turned
bottom upward, and come back to take them
whenever I can."

He put the bodies on the ground, turned the
ship over them, and went his way.

The woman saw all the slaughter. "Never
am I to see Cud alive," thought she, and fell
dead from sorrow.

Cud took the woman to shore, and put her
under the ship with his brothers. He went to
his ship then, sailed away alone, and never
stopped till he came to the kingdom where lived
Mucan Mor Mac Ri na Sorach. Cud went
ashore, and while walking and looking for himself, he came to a castle. He was wondering at
the pole of combat, such a terribly big one, and
he gave a small blow to it. The messenger
came out, and looked up and down to know could
he find the man who gave the blow. Not a
soul could he see but a white-haired young child
standing near the pole. He went into the castle
again.

"Who struck the pole?" asked Mucan Mor.

"I saw no one but a small child with white hair; there is no danger from him."

Cud gave a harder blow.

"That blow is harder," said Mucan Mor, "than any child can give. Go and see who is in it."

The man searched high and low, and it failed him to find any one but the child.

"It would be a wonder if you are the one, you little child, that struck the blow."

"What harm," said the little child, "if I gave the pole a touch?"

"Mucan Mor is going to dinner soon," said the messenger; "and if you vex him again, 't is yourself that he'll eat in place of the dinner."

"Is dinner ready?" asked Cud.

"It is going to be left down," was the answer he got.

When the man went in, Cud gave the pole a hard blow, and did n't leave calf, foal, lamb, kid, or child awaiting its birth, or a bag of poor oats or rye, that did n't turn five times to the left, and five to the right with the fright that it got. He made such a noise and crash that dishes were broken, knives hurled around, and the castle shaken to its bottom stone. Mucan Mor himself was turned five times to the left and five to the right before he could put the soles of his feet under him. When he went out, and saw the small child, he asked, "Was it you that struck the pole?"

"I gave it a little tip," said Cud.

"You are a child of no sense to be lying so, and it is yourself that I'll eat for my supper."

He thought he had only to take Cud into the castle, and roast him on the spit. He went to catch the child; but if he did, the child faced him, and soon they were fighting like two bulls in high grass. When it was very late in the day, Mucan Mor rose up in a lump of fog, and Cud didn't know where he had gone.

All Cud had to do was to go to the forest, and gather twigs for a fire to keep himself warm until morning. It wasn't many twigs he had gathered when twelve swans came near him.

"Love me!" said he. "I believe ye are the blessed birds that came from my father's kingdom to be food to relieve me in need."

"Sorry am I that I have ever looked on you or you on me," said one of the swans; and the twelve rose and flew away.

Cud gathered the twigs for the fire, and dried the blood in his wounds. In the morning, Mucan Mor struck his own pole of combat. He and Cud faced each other, and fought till late in the day, when Mucan Mor rose as a lump of fog in the air. Cud went to the forest as before to gather twigs. It was few he had gathered when the twelve swans came again.

"Are ye the blessed birds from my own kingdom?" asked he.

"No," said one of the swans; "but I put you under bonds not to turn me away as you did last night."

"As you put me under bonds," said Cud, "I will not turn you away."

The twelve began to gather twigs, and it wasn't long till they had a great fire made. One of the twelve sat at the fire then with Cud, and said, "There is nothing in the world to kill Mucan Mor but a certain apple. For the last three days I have been looking for that apple. I found it to-day, and have it here for you. To-morrow you'll be getting the upper hand of Mucan Mor earlier than other days. He has no power to rise as a fog until a given hour. When the time comes, he'll raise his two hands and be striving to go in the air. If you strike him then in the right side in the ribs with the apple, you'll make a green stone of him. If you do not, he'll come down and make a green stone of you."

Cud took the apple, and had great thanks for the swan. She left down the best food then before him. She had the food with her always.

Glad was he, for he was greatly in want of it after the fast of two days. She put her own wing and head over his head and sheltered him till day·break. There was n't a wound on him next morning that was n't cured. As early as the day dawned she roused him.

"Be up now," said she, "and have the soles of your feet under you."

He went first to the pole and struck a blow that took three turns out of the stomach of Mucan Mor and three more out of his brain, before he could stand on the soles of his feet, so great was the dread that came on him.

They fought the third day, and it was n't very late when Cud was getting the upper hand. Mucan Mor raised his two arms toward the sky, striving to escape in a fog from his enemy. Cud struck him then with the apple, and made a green stone of him. Hardly had he Mucan Mor killed when he saw an old hag racing up; she took one hill at a step and two at a leap.

"Your face and your health to you," said the hag, when she stood before Cud. "I am looking at you for three days, fighting without food or drink. I hope that you 'll come with me now."

"It 's long that you were thinking of asking me," said he.

"I hope you 'll not refuse me," said the hag.

"I will not," replied Cud.

"Give me your hand," said the hag, "and I'll help you to walk."

He took the hag's hand. There wasn't a jump that she gave while she had a grip of his hand but he thought she was dragging the arm from him.

"Curses on you for an old hag! Is it little I have gone through that you treat me in this way?"

"I have a cloth about my shoulders. Go into that, and I will carry you," said the hag.

There wasn't a joint in the hag's back that wasn't three inches long When she had him on her back there wasn't a leap that she gave that the joints of her backbone were not going into Cud's body.

"Hard luck to you for a hag, after all I have gone through to have me killed at last."

"You have not far to go now," said she; and after a few leaps she was at the end of her journey. She took him into a grand castle. The best table of food that he had ever set eyes on was left down there before him.

"Sit there, now, son of the King of Urhu; eat and drink."

"I have never taken food without company," said Cud, "and I will not take it this time."

"Will you eat with me?"

"Bad luck to you for a hag, I will not."

She opened a door and let in twelve pigs, and one pig, the thirteenth, without a head.

"Will you take food with these, son of the King of Urhu?"

"Indeed, then, old hag, bad as you are yourself, I 'd rather eat with you than with these, and I 'll not eat with you."

She put them back, opened another door and let out twelve of the rustiest, foulest, ugliest old hags that man could set eyes on.

"Will you take food with these?" asked she.

"Indeed, then, I will not."

She hurried them back, opened a door, and brought out twelve beautiful young women.

"Will you take food with these?"

"These are fit to take food with any one," said Cud.

They sat down and ate with good-will and pleasure. When they had the dinner eaten the hag opened the door, and the twelve went back to their own chamber.

"I 'll get great blame," said the old hag, "for all the delay I 've had. I 'll be going now."

"What trouble is on you that you 'll be blamed for your delay?"

"Those twelve pigs that you saw," said the hag,

"are twelve sons of mine, and the pig without a head is my husband. Those twelve foul, yellow hags that you saw are my twelve daughters. The twelve beautiful women who ate with you are my daughters' attendants."

"Why are your twelve sons and your husband pigs, and your twelve daughters yellow old hags?"

"The Awus in that house there beyond has them enchanted and held in subjection. There isn't a night but I must go with a gold apple to him."

"I will go with you to-night," said Cud.

"There is no use in going," said the hag.

They were talking a long time before she would let him go. She went first, and he followed. She knocked, and they opened the door. Cud was in with her that instant. One Awus rose and put seven bolts and seven locks on the door. Cud rose and put on seven locks and seven bolts more. All began to laugh when they saw Cud doing this. The old chief, who was standing at the hearth, let such a roar out of him that Cud saw the heart inside in his body.

"Why are you laughing?" asked Cud.

"We think you a nice bit of meat to roast on the spit. Rise up," said he to a small attendant, "and tie that fellow."

The attendant rose and tried to tie Cud, but soon Cud had him down and tied.

"Bad luck to you, 't is sorry I am that I ever lost food on the like of you," said the old chief to the small attendant. "Rise up," said he to a big attendant, "and tie him."

The big one rose up, and whatever time the small one lasted, the big one did n't last half that length. Cud drew strings from his pocket and began tying the Awuses. He caught the old Awus by the shins, dragged him down, and put his knee on him.

"You are the best champion ever I have seen," said the old Awus. "Give me quarter for my soul; there is never a place where you need it but my help will attend you with bravery. I'll give you also my sword of light that shines in the dark, my pot of cure that makes the dead alive, and the rod of enchantment to help the pot of cure."

"Where can I find them?" asked Cud.

"In a hole in the floor under the post of my bed. You cannot get them without help."

"It cannot be but I can do anything that has been done ever in your house," said Cud.

With that he went to the bed, and whatever work he had in his life he never found a harder task than to move the post of the bed; but he found the sword of light, the pot of cure, and the rod of enchantment. He came to the Awus with the sword in one hand, and the two other things in the other hand.

"The head off you now if you don't take this hag and her family from under enchantment. Make men and women of her sons and daughters, a king of her husband, and a queen of herself in this kingdom, while water is running, and grass is growing, and you are to go to them with a gold apple every evening and morning as long as you live or any one lives who comes after you to the end of all ages."

"I will do that," said the Awus.

He gave the word, and the hag was as fine a queen as she was before. She and Cud went back to the castle. The twelve pigs were twelve young men, and the thirteenth without a head was the king. She opened the chamber of the twelve yellow hags, and they were as beautiful as ever. All were very grateful to Cud for the good turn he had done them.

"I had one son," said the queen; "while he was here he gave the old Awus enough to do."

"Where is he now?" inquired Cud.

"In the Eastern World, in a field seven miles in length, and seven in width, and there isn't a yard of that field in which a spike is not standing taller than a man. There is not a spike, except one, without a king's son or a champion on it, impaled through his chin."

"What name had your son?"

"Gold Boot."

"I promise to bring Gold Boot here to you, or leave my own head on the spike."

As early as the day rose Cud was ready, and away he went walking, and very little food had he with him. About mid-day he was at the enchanted field, in the Eastern World. He was walking till he came to Gold Boot. When he touched the body, the foot gave him a kick that sent him seven acres and seven ridges away, and put three bunches of the blood of his heart out of him.

"I believe what your mother said, that when you were living you were strong, and the strength you have now to be in you."

"Don't think we are dead," said Gold Boot; "we are not. It is how we are enchanted and unable to rise out of this."

"What put you in it?" asked Cud.

"A man will come out by and by with pipes, making music, and he'll bring so much sleep on you that he'll put you on that empty spike, and the field will be full. If you take my advice you will not wait for him."

"My·grief and my sorrow! I will never stir till I see all that is here," replied Cud.

It was n't long he was waiting when the piper came out, and the very first sound that he heard Cud ran and caught the pipes; whatever music the man was making, Cud played seven times better.

When Cud took the pipes, the piper ran crying into the castle where the wizard was.

"What is on you?" asked the wizard.

"A man caught my pipes, and he is a twice better player than what I am."

"Never mind that, take these with you; these are the pipes that won't be long in putting sleep on him."

When Cud heard the first note of these pipes, he struck the old ones against a stone, and ran and caught the new pipes. The piper rushed to the wizard; the old man went out, threw himself on his knees, and begged mercy.

"Never give him mercy," said Gold Boot, "till he burns the hill that is standing out opposite him."

"You have no pardon to get till you set that hill there on fire," answered Cud.

"That is as bad for me as to lose my head," said the wizard.

"That same is not far from you unless you do what I bid," replied Cud.

Sooner than lose his head he lighted the hill. When the hill began to burn, all the men except Gold Boot came from under enchantment as sound as ever, and rose off the spikes. Every one was making away, and no one asking who let him out. The hill was on fire except one spot in the middle of it. Gold Boot was not stirring. "Why did you not make him set all the hill on fire?" asked he.

"Why did you not set the whole hill on fire?" demanded Cud of the wizard.

"Is it not all on fire?"

"Do you see the centre is not burning yet?"

"To see that bit on fire," said the wizard, "is as bad for me as to lose the head itself."

"That same is not far from you," said Cud.

"Sooner than lose the head I will light it."

That moment he lighted the hill, and Cud saw the very woman he saw the first day sleeping in the little boat come toward him from the hill. He forgot that he had seen Gold Boot or the enchanted hag and her sons. The wizard, seeing this, stopped the centre fire, and Gold Boot was left on the spike. Cud and the woman embraced till they smothered each other with kisses and drowned each other with tears. After that they neither stopped nor stayed till they reached his little ship and sailed away on it; they never delayed till they came to where his two brothers and sister-in-law were under the boat. Cud took out the three bodies, put a drop of the cure on each one, and gave each a blow of the rod. They rose up in good health and sound vigor. All entered the ship and sailed toward Urhu.

They had only the sailing of one day before them, when Cud recollected his promise to bring Gold Boot to his mother.

"Take the wife to Fermalye," said he to his brothers. "I must go for Gold Boot; the king will give you food till I come. If you were to go to our own father he'd think that it is dead I am."

Cud drew out his knife, cut a slip from a stick; this he threw into the sea. It became a ship, and away he sailed in that ship, and never stopped till he entered the harbor next the enchanted field. When he came to Gold Boot he gave him a drop of cure and a blow of the rod. He rose from the spike, well and strong. The two embraced then, went to the ship, and sailed away. They had not gone far when such a calm came that they cast anchor near shore, and Gold Boot began to get dinner. It wasn't long he was at it when they saw food at the foot of a tree on the shore.

"Who would be getting trouble with cooking,

and such food as that on the shore?" said Gold Boot.

"Don't mind that food," replied Cud.

"Whatever I think of I do," said Gold Boot.

He went to shore with one jump, caught the food, sprang back, and laid it down for himself and Cud. When this was done there was food seven times better on the land again.

"Who would taste of this, and that table over there?" cried Gold Boot.

"Never mind it," said Cud. "If the man who owns this table was sleeping when you took it, he is not sleeping now."

"Whatever I think of I must do," replied Gold Boot.

"If you did that before, I will do it now," said Cud, and he sprang to land. He looked up in the tree, and there he saw a man ready to take the life from him.

"Grief and sorrow!" said the man. "I thought it was Gold Boot again. Take this table, with welcome, but I hope you'll invite me to dinner."

"I will, indeed," said Cud; "and what name am I to give you?"

"The Wet Mantle Champion."

Cud took one end of the table and the champion the other. Out they went to the ship with one bound. They sat down then together with Gold

Boot at the table. When dinner was over, the wind rose, and they sailed on, never delaying till they came to the castle of Gold Boot's father, where there was a great welcome before them, and thanks beyond estimate.

"I will give you half my kingdom while I live and all of it when I die," said the king, "and the choice of my twelve daughters."

"Many thanks to you," replied Cud; "the promise of marriage is on me already, but perhaps Wet Mantle is not married or promised."

"I am not," said Wet Mantle.

"You must have my chance," said Cud.

Wet Mantle took Cud's place, and the king sent for a big dish priest, and a great wooden clerk. They came, and the couple were married. When the three days' wedding was over, Cud went away alone. While sailing near land he saw a castle by the sea, and as he drew near he wondered more and more. A raven was going in and out at the uppermost window, and each time bringing out something white. Cud landed, walked up from the strand, and went to the top of the castle. He saw a woman there, and the whole room full of white pigeons. She was throwing them one by one from a loft to the raven.

"Why do you throw those to the raven?" asked Cud of the woman.

"The raven is an enchanted brother of mine, who comes to this castle once in seven years. I can see him only while I am throwing him pigeons. I get as many pigeons as possible, to keep him with me while I can."

"Keep him for a while yet," said Cud.

He rushed to the ship, took his rod, and ran to the loft where the woman was. "Entice him in further," said Cud.

Cud struck the raven a blow, and he rose up as fine a champion as ever was seen.

"Your blow on me was good," said the champion, "and 't is work you have now before you. Your two brothers are killed and under seven feet of earth in Fermalye. Your wife and her sister are to their knees in foul water and filth in the stable, and are getting two mouthfuls of water, and two of bread in the day till they die."

Cud did not wait to hear more of the story. Away he went, and never stopped till he came to Fermalye. When he was coming to the castle all the children he met he was throwing at each other, he was so vexed. He took the wife and sister out of the stable, then dug up the brothers and brought them to life with the rod. The five made no delay after that, but went to the ship and sailed to Urhu. When near land he raised white flags on every mast.

"A ship is coming!" cried a messenger, running to the king. "I am thinking it is Cud that is in it."

"That's what I will never believe," said the king, "till he puts his hand into my hand."

Since Cud left home, the father and mother had never risen from the fireside, but were sitting there always and crying. When the ship was three miles from land, Cud ran from the stern to the stem, sprang to land, ran into the castle, gave one hand to his mother, and the other to his father.

It wasn't one boat, but boats, that went out to the ship for the brothers and the women. When they came, all spent the night with great pleasure in the castle. Next day the king sent seven score of ships and one ship to sea to bring supplies for the wedding. When the ships came back laden from foreign parts, he sent messengers to invite all the people in the kingdom. They were coming till they blackened the hills and spotted the valleys. I was there myself, and we spent nine nights and nine days in great glee and pleasure.

CAHAL, SON OF KING CONOR, IN ERIN, AND BLOOM OF YOUTH, DAUGHTER OF THE KING OF HATHONY.

THERE was a king in Hathony long ago who had an old castle by the sea. This king went out walking one day along the clean, smooth strand, and, while walking, the thought rose in him to take a sail near the shore. He stepped into his boat with attendants and men, and was sailing about in enjoyment and pleasure, when a wind came with a mist of enchantment, and drove the boat away through the sea with the king and his men.

They were going before the wind, without a sight of sky or sea; no man in the boat could see the man who sat next to him. They were that way moving in the mist without knowledge of where they were, or where they were going, and the boat never stopped till it sailed into a narrow harbor in a lonely place without house or habitation.

The king left the boat well fastened at the shore, and went his way, walking till he came to a castle, and what castle should it be but the castle of King Conor, in Erin.

King Conor received the King of Hathony with great hospitality and welcome.

When the two had spent some days in company, they became great friends, and made a match between their two children. The King of Hathony had a daughter called Bloom of Youth, who was nine years of age, and King Conor had a son ten years old, named Cahal.

When the King of Hathony wished to go back to his own land, King Conor of Erin gave a ship to him, and the king sailed away with good wishes and with supplies for a day and a year.

Bloom of Youth grew up in such beauty that she had not her equal in Hathony or in other lands, and Cahal, King Conor's son, became such a hero that no man knew was the like of him in any place.

On a day Cahal said to his father, "Make up some treasure for me and stores for my ship. I must leave home now and be travelling through the world till I know is there a better man than myself in it."

"It is, indeed, time for you to be going," said King Conor, "for in three years you are to marry Bloom of Youth, the daughter of the King of Hathony, and you should be making out the place now where her father lives."

Next morning Cahal took what treasures his

father gave him, and provisions, went to his ship and raised sails. Away he went on his voyage, sailing over the sea in one way and another, in this direction and that. He sailed one year and three-quarters of a second year, but found no man to give tale or tidings of the King of Hathony.

Once on a gloomy day he was sailing along through the waves, when a strong north wind rose, and blew with such force that he let his ship go with it.

Three days and nights the ship went before the north wind, and on the fourth day, in the morning, it was thrown in on a rocky coast.

Cahal saved his life and his sword, and went away walking through the country. On the evening of the fifth day he came to an old castle near the seashore, and said to himself, "I will not go in here to ask for lodgings like any poor traveller." With that he walked up and put a blow on the pole of combat that made the whole castle tremble.

Out rushed the messenger. "What brought you here, and what do you want?" asked he of King Conor's son.

"I want men to meet me in combat, seven hundred champions on my right hand, seven hundred on my left, seven hundred behind me, and the same number in front of me."

The man ran in and gave the message to the king.

"Oh," said the King of Hathony, "that is my son-in-law from Erin;" and out he went.

"Are you the son of King Conor?" asked the king.

"I am," said Cahal.

"A hundred thousand welcomes to you," said the king.

"Thankful am I for the welcomes, and glad to receive them," said Cahal. "I had great trouble in coming; it is not easy to find you."

"It is not easy to find any man unless you know the road to his house," said the king.

There was great feasting that night and entertainment for Cahal. Next day the king said, "Your bride, my daughter, is gone these two months. Striker, son of the King of Tricks, came to my castle and stole her away from me."

"My word for it, he will not keep her unless he is a better man than I am," said Cahal.

"I am sure of that," said the king, "and I said so."

"My own ship was wrecked on your coast, and now you must give me another in place of it," said Cahal.

"I will," said the king, "and a good one; but you can do nothing on sea against Striker."

"I am more used to the sea now than to land, I am so long on it," answered Cahal.

"If you were born on the water and had lived every day of your life on it, you could do nothing at sea against Striker. There is not a man living who can face him at sea."

Nothing would satisfy Cahal but to go against Striker by sea; so he took the ship which the king gave and sailed away, sailed week after week till he was within a day's journey of Striker's castle. Striker thrust his head up through the top of the castle then, and let a blast out through his mouth that sent Cahal's ship back twice the distance it had come.

King Conor's son sailed forward again, and again Striker blew him back as far as he had the first time.

Cahal sailed now to the castle of the King of Hathony.

"I said that you could do nothing against Striker on sea. If you wish to get the upper hand of him I will tell you what to do. Take this bridle and shake it behind the castle; whatever beast comes to you take that one, and ride away against Striker."

When Cahal shook the bridle, out came the smallest and ugliest beast in the stables, a lean, shaggy mare.

"Oh, then, bad luck to you for coming," said the king's son, "and so many fine steeds in the stables."

"That is the pony my daughter used to ride, that is the best horse in the stables; take her. She is not easy to ride though, for she is full of tricks and enchantment, but if you are the right man she'll not throw you. She goes on water as well as land, and you will be at your enemy's castle to-day."

Cahal mounted, and away went the mare. She crossed one hill at the first leap, three at the second, then twelve hills and valleys at the third leap; went over land and sea, and never stopped till she was in front of Striker's castle, two hours before sunset.

Cahal sprang from the mare, and struck the pole of combat.

"What do you want?" asked the attendant, running out.

"I want seven hundred champions in combat at my right side, seven hundred at my left, seven hundred behind me, and seven hundred out before my face."

The attendant went in, and out came the twenty-eight hundred against Cahal.

He went at the champions, and before sunset he had them in three heaps, a heap of their bodies, a heap of their heads, and a heap of their weapons.

Next morning Cahal struck the pole again.

"What do you want this time?" asked the attendant.

"Seven thousand champions against me for every hundred that I had yesterday."

Out came the champions in thousands. As they were coming Cahal was going through them, and before the day was ended he had them in three heaps without leaving a man, a heap of their heads, a heap of their bodies, and a heap of their weapons.

He struck the pole on the third morning, and before the attendant had time to open his mouth, Cahal shouted, "Send out every man in the place. I may as well spend one day on them all as to be calling for champions occasionally."

The forces of Striker, son of the King of Tricks, were coming as fast as ever they could make their way through the gates. They were rushing at Cahal like showers of hail on a stormy day, but they could neither kill him nor get the upper hand. They could neither defend themselves nor hurt him, and Cahal never stopped till he had them all in a heap at one side.

Cahal struck the pole on the fourth day.

"What do you want now?" asked the attendant.

"Striker, son of the King of Tricks, in combat before me."

Out came Striker, and fell upon Cahal. The two fought seven days and six nights without stopping or resting, then Striker called for a truce and got it. He went into his castle, healed himself in his caldron of cure, ate enough, slept, and was as fresh as ever next morning. They spent three days and two nights in combat after that without rest.

Striker called for cessation a second time and got it. On the eleventh morning a goldfinch perched opposite Cahal and said, "Bad luck to you for a foolish young man to be giving your enemy rest, time to eat, drink, and cure himself, and you lying outside at the foot of the wall in hunger and cold. Keep him working till he yields. Give him no rest till you snatch from his breast the pin which he has in the left side of it."

They were struggling four days and nights without rest or cessation till the fifth morning, when Cahal snatched the pin from the bosom of Striker.

"Oh, spare my life!" cried Striker. "I 'll be your servant in every place, only spare me."

"I want nothing of you," said Cahal, "but this: Send out my bride to me; you took her from her father, the King of Hathony, and she was to be my wife soon when you took her. Send her to me, and put no fog or enchantment on us while we are on the way home."

"You ask more than I can give," said Striker, "for Wet Mantle, the hero, took that maiden from me two months ago. When going, she put him under bonds not to molest her for two days and two years."

"Where can I find Wet Mantle?"

"That is more than I can tell; but put your nose before you and follow it."

"That's a short answer, and I would take your life for three straws on account of it; but I'll let some other man have his chance to take the head off you."

Cahal mounted his mare then, and was travelling over seas and dry land, — travelling a long time till he came at last to Wet Mantle's castle. He struck the pole of combat, and out came the messenger.

"Who are you, and what do you want?"

"Seven hundred at my right hand, seven hundred at my left, seven hundred behind me, and seven hundred before my face."

"That's more men than you can find in this

place," said the messenger. "Wet Mantle lives here in his own way, without forces or company; he keeps no man but me, and is very well satisfied."

"Go then," said Cahal, "and tell him to come out himself to me."

Wet Mantle came out, and the two fought seven days and six nights. Wet Mantle called for a truce then and got it. The hero went to his castle, cured himself, and was as fresh the eighth morning as the first. They began to fight, and the struggle continued three days and two nights. Wet Mantle called for a truce, and received it the second time. On the eleventh morning he was well again, and ready for the struggle.

"Oh, then, it is foolish and simple you are, and small good in your travelling the world," cried a goldfinch to Cahal. "Why are you out here in hunger and cold, and he cured and fresh in his castle? Give him no rest the next time, but fight till you tire him and take the mantle from him. He'll be as weak as a common man then, for it is in the mantle his strength is."

On the eleventh morning they began for the third time and fought fiercely all day. In the evening Wet Mantle called for a rest.

"No," said Cahal, "you'll get no rest. There is no rest for either of us. You must fight till you or I yield."

They fought on till the following evening. Wet Mantle called for rest a second time.

"No rest till this battle is ended," cried Cahal.

They held on all that night venomously, and were fighting at noon of the following day. Then Cahal closed on his enemy, and tore the mantle from his body.

The hero without his mantle had no more strength than a common man.

"You are the best champion that ever I have met," said he to Cahal. "I will give you all that you ask, but don't kill me."

"I have no wish to kill or to hurt you, though good treatment is not what you deserve from me. You caused me great trouble and hardship searching and travelling, not knowing where to find you. I want nothing of you but my bride, and your promise not to put fog or magic on us or harm us until we reach Erin in safety."

"That is more than I can promise," said Wet Mantle.

"Why so?" asked Cahal.

"The gruagach, Long Sweeper, took that maiden from me, and she put him under bonds not to molest her, or come near her for three days and three years."

"Where can I find Long Sweeper?"

"That is more than I can tell," said Wet Mantle. "The world is wide, you have free passage through it, and you can be going this way and that till you find him; he lives in a very high castle, and he is a tall man himself; he has a very long broom, and when he likes he sweeps the sky with that broom three times in the morning, and the day that he sweeps, there is no man in the world that can contradict him or conquer him."

Cahal went riding his pony from the north to the south, from the east to the west, and west to east, three years and two days. At daylight of the third day he saw a tall castle in the ocean before him. So tall was the castle that he could not tell the height of it, and a man on the summit twice as tall as the castle itself, and he with a broom sweeping the sky.

"Ah," said Cahal to himself, "I have you at last."

He rode forward then to the castle, and struck the pole of combat.

"What do you want?" asked the messenger.

"I want men to meet me in combat."

"Well, that is what you'll not get in this place. There is no man living on this island but Long Sweeper and myself. The Black Horseman came from the Western World three months ago, and killed every man, gave Long Sweeper great hardship and trouble, and after terrible fighting got the upper hand of him."

"Well, if he has no men, let him come out himself, for I'll never leave the spot till I knock satisfaction out of Long Sweeper for the trouble he gave me before I could find him."

Long Sweeper came out, and they began to fight; they fought for seven days and six nights. Toward evening of the seventh day Long Sweeper called for rest and got it. He went into his high castle, ate, drank, healed himself in his caldron of cure, and slept well and soundly, while Cahal had to rest as best he was able on the ground beyond the wall. The eighth morning Long Sweeper went up on his castle and swept the sky back and forth three times, and got such strength that no man on earth could overcome him that day.

They fought three days and two nights, and fought all the time without rest. Long Sweeper called for rest then and got it, and was cured and refreshed as before. Next morning he mounted the castle, swept the sky three times with his broom, and was ready for combat.

Before Long Sweeper came, the goldfinch perched in front of Cahal and said, "Misfortune to you, son of King Conor in Erin; 't is to a bad

place you came with your life to lose it, and
is n't it foolish of you to give your enemy rest,
while yourself has nothing to lie on but the
earth, and nothing to put in your mouth but cold
air? Give neither rest nor truce to your enemy.
He will be losing strength till three days from
now. If he gets no chance to sweep the sky,
he 'll be no better than a common man."

That evening Long Sweeper called for rest.

"No," said Cahal, "you 'll get no rest from
me. We must fight till either one or the other
yields."

"That 's not fair fighting."

"It is not, indeed. I am ten days and nights
without food, drink, or rest, while you have had
them twice. We have not fought fairly so far,
but we will hereafter. You must remain as you
are now till one of us is conquered."

They were fighting till noon, the thirteenth
day. "I am beaten," said Long Sweeper.
"Whatever I have I am willing to give you, but
spare my life, for if there is a good hero in the
world you are he."

"I want nothing of you," said Cahal, "but to
send out to me my bride, Bloom of Youth,
daughter of the King of Hathony, the maiden
you took from Wet Mantle. You have caused
me great hardship and trouble, but I 'll let some

one else take your life, or may you live as you are."

"I cannot send out your bride," said Long Sweeper, "for she is not in my castle. The Black Horseman took her from me three months ago."

"Where am I to find that man?"

"I might tell you to put your nose before you and walk after it, but I will not; I will give you a guide. Here is a rod; whichever way the rod turns, follow it till you come to the Western World, where the Black Horseman lives."

Cahal mounted his mare, made off with the rod in his hand, and rode straight to the Black Horseman's castle. The messenger was in front of the castle before him.

"Tell your master to send out champions against me, or to come himself," said Cahal.

That moment the Black Horseman himself was on the threshold. "I am here all alone," said he to Cahal. "I have lost all my wealth, all my men, all my magic. I am now in a poor state, though I was living pleasantly and in greatness after the conflict in which I got the better of Long Sweeper. It's rich and strong I was after parting with that man, and I was waiting here to marry when White Beard from the Western World came, made war on me, and continued it for a day and a year; then he left me poor and lonely, as I am at this moment."

"Well," said Cahal, "you have caused me great labor and hardship; but I ask nothing of you except to send out my bride, Bloom of Youth, to me, and not to bring fog or magic on her or on me till we reach home in safety."

"White Beard took your bride from me, and he cannot marry her for four days and four years, for she put him under bond not to do so. I will tell you now how to find her. Do you see that broad river in front of us? It flows from the Northern to the Southern World, and there is no way to cross it unless a good hero does so by springing from one bank to the other. When White Beard took the maiden from me, they walked to the brink of the river; he placed the woman then on his shoulder and sprang over the river to the west. ' Let me down, now,' said the woman. ' I will not,' replied White Beard, ' I have such regard for you that I will show you every place on the road.' He did not let her down till he showed her everything between the river and the castle. ' You may come down,' said he, when they entered the castle (she could see everything from his shoulder, but nothing from the ground). When coming down she thrust a sleeping pin that she had in the head of the old man, and he fell fast asleep standing there. She has whatever she wishes to eat or to drink in the castle. All is in a mist of enchantment. She can see nothing outside the castle, but everything within. That was my home at one time. I was born and reared in that castle, and lived in it till White Beard drove me away with magic and violence. I came to this place and lived here a time without trouble, till I took Bloom of Youth from Long Sweeper. I was waiting to marry her, when White Beard came, destroyed all my forces, took away my enchantment, carried off Bloom of Youth, and left me here without strength or defence. But one thing is left me, and that I will give you. Here is a torch. When you cross the river, light it. You 'll find the road, and no one has found it since I was there. When you light the torch follow the road to an old cottage, at one side from the castle. In this cottage is a henwife, who has lived there since my childhood. She will show the way to the castle and back to her cottage. From there you may journey homeward in safety, by lighting the torch a second. time, and keeping it till you ride out of the castle's enchantment. This is all I have to tell you."

Cahal rode briskly to the river, rode across, lighted his torch on the other side, saw a narrow bright road, but nothing on either side. The road was a long one, but he came to the end of it at the door of the henwife's old cottage. Cahal greeted the henwife.

"A hundred thousand welcomes," said the old woman. "You are here from my master, the Black Horseman, or you could not be in it. Can I help you in any way?"

"I want nothing of you but to show me the way to the castle of White Beard, where my bride is, and then bring me back to this place."

"Follow me," said the henwife, "and leave your horse here."

She took Cahal by the hand and went forward till she came to the castle and entered it. There Cahal saw the finest woman that ever he had met in the world. "Well," said he to himself, "I am not sorry, after all my troubles and hardships, if you are the woman I am to marry."

"A greeting to you, young hero," said the woman. "Who are you who have been able to come to this castle, and why are you here?"

"My name is Cahal, son of King Conor, in Erin. I am long travelling and fighting to find and to rescue my bride, Bloom of Youth, daughter of the King of Hathony. Who are you, fair lady?" asked Cahal.

"I am the daughter of the King of Hathony.

The day before I was taken by Striker, son of the King of Tricks, my father told me that the son of King Conor, in Erin, was betrothed to me. You, I suppose, are that man?"

"I am," said Cahal. "Come with me now, I will free you; but what are we to do with White Beard?"

"Leave him as he is. There is no knowing what he would do should we rouse him."

The two went with the henwife to her cottage. Cahal lighted the torch a second time, mounted the mare, put Bloom of Youth in front, rode first to Hathony, and then home to Erin.

King Conor made a great feast of welcome for Cahal and his bride. There were seven hundred guests at the short table, eight hundred at the long table, nine hundred at the round table, and a thousand in the grand hall. I was there and heard the whole story, but got no present except shoes of paper and stockings of buttermilk, and these a herder stole from me in crossing the mountains.

COLDFEET AND THE QUEEN OF LONESOME ISLAND.

ONCE upon a time, and a long time ago it was, there lived an old woman in Erin. This old woman's house was at the northeast corner of Mount Brandon. Of all the friends and relatives that ever she had in the world there was but one left, her only son, Sean,[1] nicknamed Fuarcosa (Coldfeet).

The reason that people called the boy Coldfeet was this: When a child he was growing always; what of him did not grow one hour grew another; what did not grow in the day grew in the night; what did not grow in the night grew in the day; and he grew that fast that when seven years old he could not find room enough in his mother's house. When night came and he was sleeping, whatever corner of the house his head was in, it was out of doors that his feet were, and, of course, they were cold, especially in winter.

[1] Pronounce Shawn, — John.

It was not long till his legs as well as his feet were out of the house, first to the knees, and then to the body. When fifteen years old it was all that he could do to put his head in, and he lived outdoors entirely. What the mother could gather in a year would not support the son for a day, he was that large and had such an appetite.

Coldfeet had to find his own food, and he had no means of living but to bring home sheep and bullocks from whatever place he met them.

He was going on in this way, faring rather ill than well, when one day above another he said, "I think I must go into the great world, mother. I am half starving in this place. I can do little good for myself as I am, and no good at all for you."

He rose early next morning, washed his face and hands, asked assistance and protection of God, and if he did not, may we. He left good, health with his mother at parting, and away he went, crossing high hills, passing low dales, and kept on his way without halt or rest, the clear day going and the dark night coming, taking lodgings each evening wherever he found them, till at last he came to a high roomy castle.

He entered the castle without delaying outside, and when he went in, the owner asked was he a servant in search of a master.

"I am in search of a master," said Coldfeet.

He engaged to herd cows for small hire and his keeping, and the time of his service was a day and a year.

Next morning, when Coldfeet was driving the cattle to pasture, his master was outside in the field before him, and said, "You must take good care of yourself, for of all the herders who took service with me never a man but was killed by one or another of four giants who live next to my pastures. One of these giants has four, the next six, the third eight, and the fourth twelve heads on him."

"By my hand!" said Coldfeet, "I did not come here to be killed by the like of them. They will not hurt me, never fear."

Coldfeet went on with the cattle, and when he came to the boundary he put them on the land of the giants. The cows were not long grazing when one of the giants at his castle caught the odor of the strange herder and rushed out. When coming at a distance he shouted, "I smell the blood of a man from Erin; his liver and lights for my supper to-night, his blood for my morning dram, his jawbones for stepping-stones, his shins for hurleys!"

When the giant came up he cried, "Ah, that is you, Coldfeet, and was n't it the impudence in you to come here from the butt of Brandon Mountain and put cattle on my land to annoy me?"

"It isn't to give satisfaction to you that I am here, but to knock satisfaction out of your bones," said Coldfeet.

With that the giant faced the herder, and the two went at each other and fought till near evening. They broke old trees and bent young ones; they made hard places soft and soft places hard; they made high places low and low places high; they made spring wells dry, and brought water through hard, gray rocks till near sunset, when Coldfeet took the heads off the giant and put the four skulls in muddy gaps to make a dry, solid road for the cows.

Coldfeet drove out his master's cattle on a second, third, and fourth morning; each day he killed a giant, each day the battle was fiercer, but on the fourth evening the fourth giant was dead.

On the fifth day Coldfeet was not long on the land of the dead giants when a dreadful enchanted old hag came out against him, and she raging with anger. She had nails of steel on her fingers and toes, each nail of them weighing seven pounds.

"Oh, you insolent, bloodthirsty villain,"

screamed she, "to come all the way from Brandon Mountain to kill my young sons, and, poor boys, only that timber is dear in this country it 's in their cradles they 'd be to-day instead of being murdered by you."

"It is n't to give satisfaction to you that I 'm here, you old witch, but to knock it out of your wicked old bones," said Coldfeet.

"Glad would I be to tear you to pieces," said the hag; "but 't is better to get some good of you first. I put you under spells of heavy enchantment that you cannot escape, not to eat two meals off the one table nor to sleep two nights in the one house till you go to the Queen of Lonesome Island, and bring the sword of light that never fails, the loaf of bread that is never eaten, and the bottle of water that is never drained."

"Where is Lonesome Island?" asked Coldfeet.

"Follow your nose, and make out the place with your own wit," said the hag.

Coldfeet drove the cows home in the evening, and said to his master, "The giants will never harm you again; all their heads are in the muddy gaps from this to the end of the pasture, and there are good roads now for your cattle. I have been with you only five days, but another would not do my work in a day and a year; pay me my wages. You'll never have trouble again in finding men to mind cattle."

The man paid Coldfeet his wages, gave him a good suit of clothes for the journey, and his blessing.

Away went Coldfeet now on the long road, and by my word it was a strange road to him. He went across high hills and low dales, passing each night where he found it, till the evening of the third day, when he came to a house where a little old man was living. The old man had lived in that house without leaving it for seven hundred years, and had not seen a living soul in that time.

Coldfeet gave good health to the old man, and received a hundred thousand welcomes in return.

"Will you give me a night's lodging?" asked Coldfeet.

"I will indeed," said the old man, "and is it any harm to ask, where are you going?"

"What harm in a plain question? I am going to Lonesome Island if I can find it."

"You will travel to-morrow, and if you are loose and lively on the road you'll come at night to a house, and inside in it an old man like myself, only older. He will give you lodgings, and tell where to go the day after."

Coldfeet rose very early next morning, ate his

breakfast, asked aid of God, and if he did n't he let it alone. He left good health with the old man, and received his blessing. Away with him then over high hills and low dales, and if any one wished to see a great walker Coldfeet was the man to look at. He overtook the hare in the wind that was before him, and the hare in the wind behind could not overtake him; he went at that gait without halt or rest till he came in the heel of the evening to a small house, and went in. Inside in the house was a little old man sitting by the fire.

Coldfeet gave good health to the old man, and got a hundred thousand welcomes with a night's lodging.

"Why did you come, and where are you going?" asked the old man. "Fourteen hundred years am I in this house alone, and not a living soul came in to see me till yourself came this evening."

"I am going to Lonesome Island, if I can find it."

"I have no knowledge of that place, but if you are a swift walker you will come to-morrow evening to an old man like myself, only older; he will tell you all that you need, and show you the way to the island."

Next morning early Coldfeet went away after

breakfast, leaving good health behind him and taking good wishes for the road. He travelled this day as on the other two days, only more swiftly, and at nightfall gave a greeting to the third old man.

"A hundred thousand welcomes," said the old man. "I am living alone in this house twenty-one hundred years, and not a living soul walked the way in that time. You are the first man I see in this house. Is it to stay with me that you are here?"

"It is not," said Coldfeet, "for I must be moving. I cannot spend two nights in the one house till I go to Lonesome Island, and I have no knowledge of where that place is."

"Oh, then, it 's the long road between this and Lonesome Island, but I 'll tell where the place is, and how you are to go, if you go there. The road lies straight from my door to the sea. From the shore to the island no man has gone unless the queen brought him, but you may go if the strength and the courage are in you. I will give you this staff; it may help you. When you reach the sea throw the staff in the water, and you 'll have a boat that will take you without sail or oar straight to the island. When you touch shore pull up the boat on the strand; it will turn into a staff and be again what it now is.

The queen's castle goes whirling around always. It has only one door, and that on the roof of it. If you lean on the staff you can rise with one spring to the roof, go in at the door, and to the queen's chamber.

"The queen sleeps but one day in each year, and she will be sleeping to-morrow. The sword of light will be hanging at the head of her bed, the loaf and the bottle of water on the table near by. Seize the sword with the loaf and the bottle, and away with you, for the journey must be made in a day, and you must be on this side of those hills before nightfall. Do you think you can do that?"

"I will do it, or die in the trial," said Coldfeet.

"If you make that journey you will do what no man has done yet," said the old man. "Before I came to live in this house champions and hundreds of king's sons tried to go to Lonesome Island, but not a man of them had the strength and the swiftness to go as far as the seashore, and that is but one part of the journey. All perished, and if their skulls are not crumbled, you'll see them to-morrow. The country is open and safe in the daytime, but when night falls the Queen of Lonesome Island sends her wild beasts to destroy every man they can find until daybreak. You must be in Lonesome Island to-morrow before noon, leave the place very soon after mid-day, and be on this side of those hills before nightfall, or perish."

Next morning Coldfeet rose early, ate his breakfast, and started at daybreak. Away he went swiftly over hills, dales, and level places, through a land where the wind never blows and the cock never crows, and though he went quickly the day before, he went five times more quickly that day, for the staff added speed to whatever man had it.

Coldfeet came to the sea, threw the staff into the water, and a boat was before him. Away he went in the boat, and before noon was in the chamber of the Queen of Lonesome Island. He found everything there as the old man had told him. Seizing the sword of light quickly and taking the bottle and loaf, he went toward the door; but there he halted, turned back, stopped a while with the queen. It was very near he was then to forgetting himself; but he sprang up, took one of the queen's golden garters, and away with him.

If Coldfeet strove to move swiftly when coming, he strove more in going back. On he raced over hills, dales, and flat places where the wind never blows and the cock never crows; he never stopped nor halted. When the sun was near setting he saw the last line of hills, and remembering that death was behind and not far from him, he used his last strength and was over the hilltops at nightfall.

The whole country behind him was filled with wild beasts.

"Oh," said the old man, "but you are the hero, and I was in dread that you'd lose your life on the journey, and by my hand you had no time to spare."

"I had not, indeed," answered Coldfeet. "Here is your staff, and many thanks for it."

The two spent a pleasant evening together. Next morning Coldfeet left his blessing with the old man and went on, spent a night with each of the other old men, and never stopped after that till he reached the hag's castle. She was outside before him with the steel nails on her toes and fingers.

"Have you the sword, the bottle, and the loaf?" asked she.

"I have," said Coldfeet; "here they are."

"Give them to me," said the hag.

"If I was bound to bring the three things," said Coldfeet, "I was not bound to give them to you; I will keep them."

"Give them here!" screamed the hag, raising her nails to rush at him.

With that Coldfeet drew the sword of light, and sent her head spinning through the sky in the way that 't is not known in what part of the world it fell or did it fall in any place. He burned her body then, scattered the ashes, and went his way farther.

"I will go to my mother first of all," thought he, and he travelled till evening. When his feet struck small stones on the road, the stones never stopped till they knocked wool off the spinning-wheels of old hags in the Eastern World. In the evening he came to a house and asked lodgings.

"I will give you lodgings, and welcome," said the man of the house; "but I have no food for you."

"I have enough for us both," said Coldfeet, "and for twenty more if they were in it;" and he put the loaf on the table.

The man called his whole family. All had their fill, and left the loaf as large as it was before supper. The woman of the house made a loaf in the night like the one they had eaten from, and while Coldfeet was sleeping took his bread and left her own in the place of it. Away went Coldfeet next morning with the wrong loaf, and if he travelled differently from the day before it was because he travelled faster. In the evening he came to a house, and asked would they give him a night's lodging.

"We will, indeed," said the woman, "but we have no water to cook supper for you; the water is far away entirely, and no one to go for it."

"I have water here in plenty," said Coldfeet, putting his bottle on the table.

The woman took the bottle, poured water from it, filled one pot and then another, filled every vessel in the kitchen, and not a drop less in the bottle. What wonder, when no man or woman ever born could drain the bottle in a lifetime.

Said the woman to her husband that night, "If we had the bottle, we need n't be killing ourselves running for water."

"We need not," said the man.

What did the woman do in the night, when Coldfeet was asleep, but take a bottle, fill it with water from one of the pots, and put that false bottle in place of the true one. Away went Coldfeet next morning, without knowledge of the harm done, and that day he travelled in the way that when he fell in running he had not time to rise, but rolled on till the speed that was under him brought him to his feet again. At sunset he was in sight of a house, and at dusk he was in it.

Coldfeet found welcome in the house, with food and lodgings.

"It is great darkness we are in," said the man to Coldfeet; "we have neither oil nor rushes."

"I can give you light," said Coldfeet, and he unsheathed the sword from Lonesome Island; it was clear inside the house as on a hilltop in sunlight.

When the people had gone to bed Coldfeet put the sword into its sheath, and all was dark again.

"Oh," said the woman to her husband that night, "if we had the sword we'd have light in the house always. You have an old sword above on the loft. Rise out of the bed now and put it in the place of that bright one."

The man rose, took the two swords out doors, put the old blade in Coldfeet's sheath, and hid away Coldfeet's sword in the loft. Next morning Coldfeet went away, and never stopped till he came to his mother's cabin at the foot of Mount Brandon. The poor old woman was crying and lamenting every day. She felt sure that it was killed her son was, for she had never got tale or tidings of him. Many is the welcome she had for him, but if she had welcomes she had little to eat.

"Oh, then, mother, you need n't be complaining," said Coldfeet, "we have as much bread now as will do us a lifetime;" with that he put the loaf on the table, cut a slice for the mother, and began to eat himself. He was hungry, and the next thing he knew the loaf was gone.

"There is a little meal in the house," said the mother. "I'll go for water and make stirabout."

"I have water here in plenty," said Coldfeet. "Bring a pot."

The bottle was empty in a breath, and they had n't what water would make stirabout nor half of it.

"Oh, then," said Coldfeet, "the old hag enchanted the three things before I killed her and knocked the strength out of every one of them." With that he drew the sword, and it had no more light than any rusty old blade.

The mother and son had to live in the old way again; but as Coldfeet was far stronger than the first time, he did n't go hungry himself, and the mother had plenty. There were cattle in the country, and all the men in it could n't keep them from Coldfeet or stop him. The old woman and the son had beef and mutton, and lived on for themselves at the foot of Brandon Mountain.

In three-quarters of a year the Queen of Lonesome Island had a son, the finest child that sun or moon could shine on, and he grew in the way that what of him did n't grow in the day grew in the night following, and what did n't grow that night grew the next day, and when he was two years old he was very large entirely.

The queen was grieving always for the loaf
and the bottle, and there was no light in her
chamber from the day the sword was gone. All
at once she thought, "The father of the boy took
the three things. I will never sleep two nights
in the one house till I find him."

Away she went then with the boy, — went over
the sea, went through the land where wind never
blows and where cock never crows, came to the
house of the oldest old man, stopped one night
there, then stopped with the middle and the
youngest old man. Where should she go next
night but to the woman who stole the loaf from
Coldfeet. When the queen sat down to supper
the woman brought the loaf, cut slice after slice;
the loaf was no smaller.

"Where did you get that loaf?" asked the
queen.

"I baked it myself."

"That is my loaf," thought the queen.

The following evening she came to a house and
found lodgings. At supper the woman poured
water from a bottle, but the bottle was full
always.

"Where did you get that bottle?"

"It was left to us," said the woman; "my
grandfather had it."

"That is my bottle," thought the queen.

The next night she stopped at a house where a sword filled the whole place with light.

"Where did you find that beautiful sword?" asked the queen.

"My grandfather left it to me," said the man. "We have it hanging here always."

"That is my sword," said the queen to herself.

Next day the queen set out early, travelled quickly, and never stopped till she came near Brandon Mountain. At a distance she saw a man coming down hill with a fat bullock under each arm. He was carrying the beasts as easily as another would carry two geese. The man put the bullocks in a pen near a house at the foot of the mountain, came out toward the queen, and never stopped till he saluted her. When the man stopped, the boy broke away from the mother and ran to the stranger.

"How is this?" asked the queen; "the child knows you." She tried to take the boy, but he would not go to her.

"Have you lived always in this place?" asked the queen.

"I was born in that house beyond, and reared at the foot of that mountain before you. I went away from home once and killed four giants, the first with four, the second with six, the third with eight, and the fourth with twelve heads on him. When I had the giants killed, their mother came out against me, and she raging with vengeance. She wanted to kill me at first, but she did not. She put me under bonds of enchantment to go to the castle of the Queen of Lonesome Island, and bring the sword of light that can never fail to cut or give light, the loaf of bread that can never be eaten, and the bottle of water that can never be drained."

"Did you go?" asked the queen.

"I did."

"How could you go to Lonesome Island?"

"I journeyed and travelled, inquiring for the island, stopping one night at one place, and the next night at another, till I came to the house of a little man seven hundred years old. He sent me to a second man twice as old as himself, and the second to a third three times as old as the first man.

"The third old man showed me the road to Lonesome Island, and gave me a staff to assist me. When I reached the sea I made a boat of the staff, and it took me to the island. On the island the boat was a staff again.

"I sprang to the top of the queen's turning castle, went down and entered the chamber where she was sleeping, took the sword of light, with the loaf and the bottle, and was coming away again. I looked at the queen. The heart softened within me at sight of her beauty. I turned back and came near forgetting my life with her. I brought her gold garter with me, took the three things, sprang down from the castle, ran to the water, made a boat of the staff again, came quickly to mainland, and from that hour till darkness I ran with what strength I could draw from each bit of my body. Hardly had I crossed the hilltop and was before the door of the oldest old man when the country behind me was covered with wild beasts. I escaped death by one moment. I brought the three things to the hag who had sent me, but I did not give them. I struck the head from her, but before dying she destroyed them, for when I came home they were useless."

"Have you the golden garter?"

"Here it is," said the young man.

"What is your name?" asked the queen.

"Coldfeet," said the stranger.

"You are the man," said the queen. "Long ago it was prophesied that a hero named Coldfeet would come to Lonesome Island without my request or assistance, and that our son would cover the whole world with his power. Come with me now to Lonesome Island."

The queen gave Coldfeet's old mother good clothing, and said, "You will live in my castle."

They all left Brandon Mountain and journeyed on toward Lonesome Island till they reached the house where the sword of light was. It was night when they came and dark outside, but bright as day in the house from the sword, which was hanging on the wall.

"Where did you find this blade?" asked Coldfeet, catching the hilt of the sword.

"My grandfather had it," said the woman.

"He had not," said Coldfeet, "and I ought to take the head off your husband for stealing it when I was here last."

Coldfeet put the sword in his scabbard and kept it. Next day they reached the house where the bottle was, and Coldfeet took that. The following night he found the loaf and recovered it. All the old men were glad to see Coldfeet, especially the oldest, who loved him.

The queen with her son and Coldfeet with his mother arrived safely in Lonesome Island. They lived on in happiness; there is no account of their death, and they may be in it yet for aught we know.

LAWN DYARRIG, SON OF THE KING OF ERIN, AND THE KNIGHT OF TERRIBLE VALLEY.

THERE was a king in his own time in Erin, and he went hunting one day. The king met a man whose head was out through his cap, whose elbows and knees were out through his clothing, and whose toes were out through his shoes.

The man went up to the king, gave him a blow on the face, and drove three teeth from his mouth. The same blow put the king's head in the dirt. When he rose from the earth the king went back to his castle, and lay down sick and sorrowful.

The king had three sons, and their names were Ur, Arthur, and Lawn Dyarrig. The three were at school that day and came home in the evening. The father sighed when the sons were coming in.

"What is wrong with our father?" asked the eldest.

"Your father is sick on his bed," said the mother.

The three sons went to their father and asked what was on him.

"A strong man that I met to-day gave me a blow in the face, put my head in the dirt, and knocked three teeth from my mouth. What would you do to him if you met him?" asked the father of the eldest son.

"If I met that man," replied Ur, "I would make four parts of him between four horses."

"You are my son," said the king. "What would you do if you met him?" asked he then, as he turned to the second son.

"If I had a grip on that man I would burn him between four fires."

"You, too, are my son. What would you do?" asked the king of Lawn Dyarrig.

"If I met that man I would do my best against him, and he might not stand long before me."

"You are not my son. I would not lose lands or property on you," said the father. "You must go from me, and leave this to-morrow."

On the following morning the three brothers rose with the dawn; the order was given Lawn Dyarrig to leave the castle, and make his own way for himself. The other two brothers were going to travel the world to know could they find the man who had injured their father. Lawn Dyarrig lingered outside till he saw the two, and they going off by themselves.

"It is a strange thing," said he, "for two men of high degree to go travelling without a servant."

"We need no one," said Ur.

"Company would n't harm us," said Arthur.

The two let Lawn Dyarrig go with them then as a serving-boy, and set out to find the man who had struck down their father. They spent all that day walking, and came late to a house where one woman was living. She shook hands with Ur and Arthur, and greeted them. Lawn Dyarrig she kissed and welcomed, called him son of the King of Erin.

"'T is a strange thing to shake hands with the elder and kiss the younger," said Ur.

"This is a story to tell," said the woman; "the same as if your death were in it."

They made three parts of that night. The first part they spent in conversation, the second in telling tales, the third in eating and drinking, with sound sleep and sweet slumber. As early as the day dawned next morning, the old woman was up and had food for the young men. When the three had eaten she spoke to Ur, and this is what she asked of him, "What was it that drove you from home, and what brought you to this place?"

"A champion met my father, took three teeth

from him, and put his head in the dirt. I am looking for that man to find him alive or dead."

"That was the Green Knight from Terrible Valley. He is the man who took the three teeth from your father. I am three hundred years living in this place, and there is not a year of the three hundred in which three hundred heroes fresh, young, and noble have not passed on the way to Terrible Valley, and never have I seen one coming back, and each of them had the look of a man better than you. And now, where are you going, Arthur?"

"I am on the same journey with my brother."

"Where are you going, Lawn Dyarrig?"

"I am going with these as a servant," said Lawn Dyarrig.

"God's help to you, it's bad clothing that's on your body," said the woman; "and now I will speak to Ur. A day and a year since a champion passed this way; he wore a suit as good as was ever above ground. I had a daughter sewing there in the open window. He came outside, put a finger under her girdle, and took her with him. Her father followed straightway to save her, but I have never seen daughter or father from that day to this. That man was the Green Knight of Terrible Valley. He is better than all the men that could stand on a field a mile in length and a mile in breadth. If you take my advice you 'll turn back and go home to your father."

'T is how she vexed Ur with this talk, and he made a vow to himself to go on. When Ur did not agree to turn home, the woman said to Lawn Dyarrig, " Go back to my chamber, you 'll find in it the apparel of a hero."

He went back, and there was not a bit of the apparel that he did not go into with a spring.

"You may be able to do something now," said the woman, when Lawn Dyarrig came to the front. "Go back to my chamber and search through all the old swords. You will find one at the bottom; take that."

He found the old sword, and at the first shake that he gave he knocked seven barrels of rust out of it; after the second shake, it was as bright as when made.

"You may be able to do well with that," said the woman. "Go out now to that stable abroad, and take the slim white steed that is in it. That one will never stop nor halt in any place till he brings you to the Eastern World. If you like, take these two men behind you; if not, let them walk. But I think it is useless for you to have them at all with you."

Lawn Dyarrig went out to the stable, took the

slim white steed, mounted, rode to the front, and catching the two brothers, planted them on the horse behind him.

"Now, Lawn Dyarrig," said the woman, "this horse will never stop till he stands on the little white meadow in the Eastern World. When he stops, you 'll come down and cut the turf under his beautiful right front foot."

The horse started from the door, and at every leap he crossed seven hills and valleys, seven castles with villages, acres, roods, and odd perches. He could overtake the whirlwind before him seven hundred times before the whirlwind behind could overtake him once. Early in the afternoon of the next day he was in the Eastern World. When he dismounted, Lawn Dyarrig cut the sod from under the foot of the slim white steed in the name of the Father, Son, and Holy Ghost, and Terrible Valley was down under him there. What he did next was to tighten the reins on the neck of the steed and let him go home.

" Now," said Lawn Dyarrig to the brothers, "which would ye rather be doing, making a basket or twisting gads (withes)? "

"We would rather be making a basket; our help is among ourselves," answered they.

Ur and Arthur went at the basket and Lawn

Dyarrig at twisting the gads. When Lawn Dyarrig came to the opening with the gads, all twisted and made into one, they had n't the ribs of the basket in the ground yet.

"Oh, then, have n't ye anything done but that?"

"Stop your mouth," said Ur, "or we 'll make a mortar of your head on the next stone."

"To be kind to one another is the best for us," said Lawn Dyarrig. "I 'll make the basket."

While they 'd be putting one rod in the basket he had the basket finished.

"Oh, brother," said they, "you are a quick workman."

They had not called him brother since they left home till that moment.

"Who will go in the basket now?" asked Lawn Dyarrig, when it was finished, and the gad tied to it.

"Who but me?" said Ur. "I am sure, brothers, if I see anything to frighten me ye 'll draw me up."

"We will," said the other two.

He went in, but had not gone far when he cried to pull him up again.

"By my father and the tooth of my father, and by all that is in Erin dead or alive, I would not give one other sight on Terrible Valley!" cried he, when he stepped out of the basket.

"Who will go now?" asked Lawn Dyarrig.

"Who will go but me?" answered Arthur.

Whatever length Ur went, Arthur did n't go the half of it.

"By my father and the tooth of my father, I would n't give another look at Terrible Valley for all that 's in Erin dead or alive!"

"I will go now," said Lawn Dyarrig, "and as I put no foul play on you, I hope ye 'll not put foul play on me."

"We will not, indeed," said they.

Whatever length the other two went, Lawn Dyarrig did n't go the half of it till he stepped out of the basket and went down on his own feet. It was not far he had travelled in Terrible Valley when he met seven hundred heroes guarding the country.

"In what place here has the Green Knight his castle?" asked he of the seven hundred.

"What sort of a sprìsawn goat or sheep from Erin are you?" asked they.

"If we had a hold of you, that 's a question you would not put the second time; but if we have n't you, we 'll not be so long."

They faced Lawn Dyarrig then and attacked him; but he went through them like a hawk or a raven through small birds. He made a heap of their feet, a heap of their heads, and a castle of their arms.

After that he went his way walking, and had not gone far when he came to a spring. "I'll have a drink before I go farther," thought he. With that he stooped down and took a drink of the water. When he had drunk he lay on the ground and fell asleep.

Now there was n't a morning that the lady in the Green Knight's castle did n't wash in the water of that spring, and she sent a maid for the water each time. Whatever part of the day it was when Lawn Dyarrig fell asleep, he was sleeping in the morning when the girl came. She thought it was dead the man was, and she was so in dread of him that she would not come near the spring for a long time. At last she saw he was asleep, and then she took the water. Her mistress was complaining of her for being so long.

"Do not blame me," said the maid. "I am sure that if it was yourself that was in my place you 'd not come back so soon."

"How so?" asked the lady.

"The finest hero that a woman ever laid eyes on is sleeping at the spring."

"That 's a thing that cannot be till Lawn Dyarrig comes to the age of a hero. When that time comes he 'll be sleeping at the spring."

"He is in it now," said the girl.

The lady did not stay to get any drop of the water on herself, but ran quickly from the castle. When she came to the spring she roused Lawn Dyarrig. If she found him lying, she left him standing. She smothered him with kisses, drowned him with tears, dried him with garments of fine silk, and with her own hair. Herself and himself locked arms and walked into the castle of the Green Knight. After that they were inviting each other with the best food and entertainment till the middle of the following day. Then the lady said, —

"When the Green Knight bore me away from my father and mother, he brought me straight to this castle, but I put him under bonds not to marry me for seven years and a day, and he cannot; still I must serve him. When he goes fowling he spends three days away, and the next three days at home. This is the day for him to come back, and for me to prepare his dinner. There is no stir that you or I have made here to-day but that brass head beyond there will tell of it."

"It is equal to you what it tells," said Lawn Dyarrig, "only make ready a clean, long chamber for me."

She did so, and he went back into it. Herself

rose up then to prepare dinner for the Green Knight. When he came she welcomed him as every day. She left down his food before him, and he sat to take his dinner. He was sitting with knife and fork in hand when the brass head spoke. "I thought when I saw you taking food and drink with your wife that you had the blood of a man in you. If you could see that sprisawn of a goat or sheep out of Erin taking meat and drink with her all day, what would you do?"

"Oh, my suffering and sorrow!" cried the knight. "I 'll never take another bite or sup till I eat some of his liver and heart. Let three hundred heroes fresh and young go back and bring his heart to me, with the liver and lights, till I eat them."

The three hundred heroes went, and hardly were they behind in the chamber when Lawn Dyarrig had them all dead in one heap.

"He must have some exercise to delay my men, they are so long away," said the knight. "Let three hundred more heroes go for his heart, with the liver and lights, and bring them here to me."

The second three hundred went, and as they were entering the chamber, Lawn Dyarrig was making a heap of them, till the last one was inside, where there were two heaps.

"He has some way of coaxing my men to delay," said the knight. "Do you go now, three hundred of my savage hirelings, and bring him."

The three hundred savage hirelings went, and Lawn Dyarrig let every man of them enter before he raised a hand, then he caught the bulkiest of them all by the two ankles and began to wallop the others with him, and he walloped them till he drove the life out of the two hundred and ninety-nine. The bulkiest one was worn to the shin bones that Lawn Dyarrig held in his two hands. The Green Knight, who thought Lawn Dyarrig was coaxing the men, called out then, "Come down, my men, and take dinner!"

"I'll be with you," said Lawn Dyarrig, "and have the best food in the house, and I'll have the best bed in the house. God not be good to you for it, either."

He went down to the Green Knight and took the food from before him and put it before himself. Then he took the lady, set her on his own knee, and he and she went on eating. After dinner he put his finger under her girdle, took her to the best chamber in the castle, and remained there till morning. Before dawn the lady said to Lawn Dyarrig, —

"If the Green Knight strikes the pole of combat first, he 'll win the day; if you strike first, you 'll win, if you do what I tell you. The Green Knight has so much enchantment that if he sees it is going against him the battle is, he 'll rise like a fog in the air, come down in the same form, strike you, and make a green stone of you. When yourself and himself are going out to fight in the morning, cut a sod a perch long in the name of the Father, Son, and Holy Ghost; you 'll leave the sod on the next little hillock you meet. When the Green Knight is coming down and is ready to strike, give him a blow with the sod; you 'll make a green stone of him."

As early as the dawn Lawn Dyarrig rose and struck the pole of combat. The blow that he gave did not leave calf, foal, lamb, kid, or child waiting for birth, without turning them five times to the left and five times to the right.

"What do you want?" asked the knight.

"All that 's in your kingdom to be against me the first quarter of the day, and yourself the second quarter."

"You have not left in the kingdom now but myself, and it is early enough for you that I 'll be at you."

The knight faced him, and they went at each other and fought till late in the day. The battle was strong against Lawn Dyarrig when the lady stood in the door of the castle.

"Increase on your blows and increase on your courage," cried she. "There is no woman here but myself to wail over you, or to stretch you before burial."

When the knight heard the voice, he rose in the air like a lump of fog. As he was coming down, Lawn Dyarrig struck him with the sod on the right side of his breast, and made a green stone of him.

The lady rushed out then, and whatever welcome she had for Lawn Dyarrig the first time, she had twice as much now. Herself and himself went into the castle and spent that night very comfortably. In the morning they rose early, and collected all the gold, utensils, and treasures. Lawn Dyarrig found the three teeth of his father in a pocket of the Green Knight, and took them. He and the lady brought all the riches to where the basket was. "If I send up this beautiful lady," thought Lawn Dyarrig, "she may be taken from me by my brothers; if I remain below with her, she may be taken from me by people here." He put her in the basket, and she gave him a ring so that they might know each other if they met. He shook the gad, and she rose in the basket.

When Ur saw the basket he thought, "What's above let it be above, and what's below let it stay where it is."

"I'll have you as wife forever for myself," said he to the lady.

"I put you under bonds," said she, "not to lay a hand on me for a day and three years."

"That itself would not be long even if twice the time," said Ur.

The two brothers started home with the lady; on the way Ur found the head of an old horse with teeth in it and took them, saying, "These will be my father's three teeth."

They travelled on, and reached home at last. Ur would not have left a tooth in his father's mouth, trying to put in the three that he had brought; but the father stopped him.

Lawn Dyarrig, left in Terrible Valley, began to walk around for himself. He had been walking but one day when whom should he meet but the lad Shortclothes, and he saluted him. "By what way can I leave Terrible Valley?" asked Lawn Dyarrig.

"If I had a grip on you that's what you wouldn't ask of me a second time," said Short-clothes.

"If you have not touched me you will before you are much older."

"If I do, you will not treat me as you did all my people and my master."

"I'll do worse to you than I did to them," said Lawn Dyarrig.

They caught each other then, one grip under the arm and one grip on the shoulder. 'T is not long they were wrestling when Lawn Dyarrig had Shortclothes on the earth, and he gave him the five thin tyings dear and tight.

"You are the best hero I have ever met," said Shortclothes; "give me quarter for my soul, — spare me. When I did not tell you of my own will, I must tell in spite of myself."

"It is as easy for me to loosen you as to tie you," said Lawn Dyarrig, and he freed him. The moment he was free, Shortclothes said, —

"I put you under bonds, and the misfortune of the year to be walking and going always till you go to the northeast point of the world, and get the heart and liver of the serpent which is seven years asleep and seven years awake."

Lawn Dyarrig went away then, and never stopped till he was in the northeast of the world, where he found the serpent asleep.

"I will not go unawares on you while you are asleep," said Lawn Dyarrig, and he turned to go. When he was going, the serpent drew him down her throat with one breath.

Inside he found three men playing cards in her belly. Each laughed when he looked at Lawn Dyarrig.

"What reason have you for laughing?" asked he.

"We are laughing with glee to have another partner to fill out our number."

Lawn Dyarrig did not sit down to play. He drew his sword, and was searching and looking till he found the heart and liver of the serpent. He took a part of each, and cut out a way for himself between two ribs. The three card-players followed when they saw the chance of escape.

Lawn Dyarrig, free of the serpent, never stopped till he came to Shortclothes, and he was a day and three years on the journey, and doing the work.

"Since you are not dead now," said Shortclothes, "there is no death allotted to you. I'll find a way for you to leave Terrible Valley. Go and take that old bridle hanging there beyond and shake it; whatever beast comes and puts its head into the bridle will carry you."

Lawn Dyarrig shook the bridle, and a dirty, shaggy little foal came and put head in the bridle. Lawn Dyarrig mounted, dropped the reins on the foal's neck, and let him take his own choice of roads. The foal brought Lawn Dyarrig

out by another way to the upper world, and took
him to Erin. Lawn Dyarrig stopped some distance from his father's castle, and knocked at the
house of an old weaver.

"Who are you?" asked the old man.

"I am a weaver," said Lawn Dyarrig.

"What can you do?"

"I can spin for twelve and twist for twelve."

"This is a very good man," said the old weaver
to his sons. "Let us try him."

The work they would be doing for a year he
had done in one hour. When dinner was over
the old man began to wash and shave, and his
two sons began to do the same.

"Why is this?" asked Lawn Dyarrig.

"Haven't you heard that Ur, son of the king,
is to marry to-night the woman that he took
from the Green Knight of Terrible Valley?"

"I have not," said Lawn Dyarrig; "but as all
are going to the wedding, I suppose I may go
without offence."

"Oh, you may," said the weaver. "There will
be a hundred thousand welcomes before you."

"Are there any linen sheets within?"

"There are," said the weaver.

"It is well to have bags ready for yourself and
two sons."

The weaver made bags for the three very

quickly They went to the wedding. Lawn
Dyarrig put what dinner was on the first table
into the weaver's bag, and sent the old man
home with it. The food of the second table he
put in the eldest son's bag, filled the second
son's bag from the third table, and sent the two
home.

The complaint went to Ur that an impudent
stranger was taking all the food.

"It is not right to turn any man away," said
the bridegroom; "but if that stranger does not
mind he will be thrown out of the castle."

"Let me look at the face of the disturber,"
said the bride.

"Go and bring the fellow who is troubling the
guests," said Ur, to the servants.

Lawn Dyarrig was brought right away, and
stood before the bride, who filled a glass with
wine and gave it to him. Lawn Dyarrig drank
half the wine, and dropped in the ring which the
lady had given him in Terrible Valley.

When the bride took the glass again the ring
went of itself with one leap to her finger. She
knew then who was standing before her.

"This is the man who conquered the Green
Knight, and saved me from Terrible Valley,"
said she to the King of Erin; "this is Lawn
Dyarrig, your son."

Lawn Dyarrig took out the three teeth, and put them in his father's mouth. They fitted there perfectly, and grew into their old place. The king was satisfied; and as the lady would marry no man but Lawn Dyarrig he was the bridegroom.

"I must give you a present," said the bride to the queen. "Here is a beautiful scarf which you are to wear as a girdle this evening."

The queen put the scarf around her waist.

"Tell me now," said the bride to the queen, "who was Ur's father?"

"What father could he have but his own father, the King of Erin?"

"Tighten, scarf," said the bride.

That moment the queen thought that her head was in the sky, and the lower half of her body down deep in the earth.

"Oh, my grief and my woe!" cried the queen.

"Answer my question in truth, and the scarf will stop squeezing you. Who was Ur's father?"

"The gardener," said the queen.

"Whose son is Arthur?"

"The king's son."

"Tighten, scarf," said the bride.

If the queen suffered before, she suffered twice as much this time, and screamed for help.

"Answer me truly, and you'll be without pain;

if not, death will be on you this minute.   Whose
son is Arthur?"

"The swineherd's."

"Who is the king's son?"

"The king has no son but Lawn Dyarrig."

"Tighten, scarf."

The scarf did not tighten, and if the bride had
been commanding it for a day and a year it
would not have tightened, for the queen told the
truth that time.   When the wedding was over,
the king gave Lawn Dyarrig half his kingdom,
and made Ur and Arthur his servants.

BALOR ON TORY ISLAND.

LONG ago Ri Balor lived on Tory Island, and he lived there because it was prophesied that he was never to die unless he'd be killed by the son of his only daughter.

Balor, to put the daughter in the way that she'd never have a son, went to live on Tory, and built a castle on Tor Mor, a cliff jutting into the ocean. He put twelve women to guard the daughter, and all around the castle he had cords fixed, and every one of them tied to bells, so that no man could come in secret. If any man touched a cord all the bells would ring and give notice, and Balor would seize him.

Balor lived that way, well satisfied. He was full sure that his life was out of danger.

Opposite on the mainland, at Druim na Teine (hill of fire), lived a smith, Gavidin, who had his forge there. The smith owned a cow called Glas Gavlen, and she was his enchanted step-sister.

This cow was called Gavlen because she was giving milk, and she the fifth year without a calf. Glas Gavlen was very choice of food;

she would eat no grass but the best.   But if the cow ate much good grass there was no measuring the milk she gave; she filled every vessel, and the milk was sweet and rich.

The smith set great value on Glas Gavlen, and no wonder, for she was the first cow that came to Erin, and at that time the only one.

The smith took care of the cow himself, and never let her out of his sight except when working in his forge, and then he had a careful man minding her.

Balor had an eye on Glas Gavlen, and wanted to bring her to Tory for his own use, so he told two agents of his, Maol and Mullag, who were living near Druim na Teine, to get the cow for him.   The smith would not part with Glas Gavlen for any price, so there was no way left but to steal her.   There was no chance for stealing till one time when three brothers, named Duv, Donn, and Fin, sons of Ceanfaeligh (Kinealy), went to the forge to have three swords made.

"Each man of you is to mind the cow while I am working," said the smith, "and if he loses her I 'll take the head off him."

"We will agree to that," said the brothers.

Duv and Donn went with Glas Gavlen on the first day and the second, and brought her back to the smith safely. When his turn came Fin took the cow out on the third day, but when some distance from the forge he bethought himself and ran back to tell the smith not to make his sword so heavy as those of his brothers. The moment he was inside in the forge Maol and Mullag, Balor's men, stole the cow, and away they went quickly, driving her toward Baile Nass. When they came to the brow of the slope, where the sand begins, they drew her down to the water's edge by the tail, and put her into a boat which they had there prepared and ready.

They sailed toward Tory, but stopped at Inis Bofin (island of the white cow) and put the cow out on land. She drank from a well there, which is called since that time Tobar na Glaise (well of the gray cow). After that they sailed on, and landed the same day at Port na Glaise, on Tory Island.

When Fin came out of the forge he saw nothing of Glas Gavlen, — neither trace nor sign of her. He ran back then with the evil tidings to the smith.

"If you fail to bring her back to me within three days," said Gavidin, "I'll take the head off you, according to our bargain. I made the sword to oblige you, and you promised to bring the cow or give your head."

Away with Fin then, travelling and lamenting, looking for Glas Gavlen. He went toward Baile Nass and came to a place on the strand where a party of men were playing ball. He inquired of them about the cow, but they began to make game of him, he looked so queer in himself, and was so sad. At last one of the players, whose name was Gial Duv (Black Jaw), came up to Fin and spoke to him: "Stand aside till the game is over, and I'll talk to you. This is a party of players that you should not interfere with; they are lucht sidhe [people of the mounds, fairies]. I know what your trouble is. I will go with you, and do my best to bring the cow. I know where she is, and if I cannot bring her, no one can."

They searched down as far as Maheroerty, and went then to Minlara, where a boat was found. They sailed away in the boat, and reached Tory that night a few hours after Maol and Mullag.

"Go now," said Gial Duv to Fin, "and ask Balor what would release the cow, and what can you do to earn her. I'll stay here till you come back to me."

Fin went to Balor and asked the question.

"To get the cow," said Balor, "you must eat seven green hides while one inch of a rush-light is burning, and I'll light it myself."

Fin returned and told Gial Duv. "Go," said Gial, "and tell him you will try to do that. He will put you in a room apart with the hides and take the rush himself. Cut the hides quickly, and if you can cut them I'll make away with them. I'll be there with you, invisible."

All this was done. Fin cut the hides and Gial Duv put them away. The moment the rush-light was burned Balor came in, and there wasn't a hand's breadth of the hides left.

"I have the seven hides eaten," said Fin.

"Come to me to-morrow. My daughter will throw the cow's halter. If she throws it to you the cow will be yours."

Fin was let out of the room then.

"Now," said Gial Duv, "I'll take you to Balor's daughter. There is a wall between the castle and the rest of the island, and I'll take you over it. There are cords along the wall everywhere, and whoever tries to pass over will touch them and sound all the bells in the place. I will raise you above them all and take you in without noise. You will go first to Balor's daughter; she will be pleased with you and like you. After that you will see all the other women, and do you be as intimate with them as with Balor's daughter, so that they will not tell that you were in it, and be sure to tell the daughter to throw you the cow's halter to-morrow."

Fin was taken into the castle by Gial Duv without noise, and he did all that Gial directed.   Next day Fin went to Balor and asked for the cow.

"Well, come with me.   Let my daughter throw the halter.   If she throws it to you the cow will be yours."

They went.   She threw the halter at Fin, and Balor was very angry.   "Oh, daughter," cried he, "what have you done?"

"Don't you know," said she, "that there is a false cast in every woman's hand?   There is a crooked vein in my arm, and I could not help it; that's what gave the halter to Fin."

Balor had to give the cow and forgive the daughter.   Fin took Glas Gavlen to the mainland that day and gave her to the smith.

Before the year was out Gial Duv went to Fin and said, "Make ready and come with me to Tory; if you don't Balor will find out what happened when you were on the island, and kill his own daughter, with the twelve women and all the children."

The two went to Tory that evening, and when the children were born the women gave twelve of them to Fin in a blanket, and one, Balor's grandson, by himself in a separate cloth.   Fin took his place in the boat with the twelve on his back, and one at his breast.   The blanket was fastened at his throat with a dealg (thorn); the thorn broke (there was a great stress on it, for the weather was rough), and the twelve children fell in the water at Sruth Deilg and became seals.

"Oh!" cried Gial, "the children are lost. Have you Balor's grandson?"

"I have," answered Fin.

"That is well. We don't care for the others while we have him."

They brought the child to the mainland, where a nurse was found, but the child was not thriving with her.

"Let us return to Tory with the boy," said Gial Duv. "There is nothing that Balor wishes for so much as trees. He has tried often to make trees grow on the island, but it was no use for him. Do you promise that you'll make a grand forest on Tory if he'll let some of the women nurse the child. Tell him that your wife died not long ago. Balor will say, How could we find a nurse here when there is no woman on the island who has a child of her own?' You will say that 't is a power this child has that whatever woman touches him has her breast full of milk. I will put you in with the women in the evening, and do you tell them what is wanted. The mother is to take the child first when you go in to-morrow, and she will hand him quickly to another and that one to a third, and so on before any can be stopped."

Fin gave the child to Balor's daughter before her father could come near her; she gave him to one of the women, and he was passed on till all twelve had had him. It was found that all had milk, and Balor consented to let the child be nursed.

Gial Duv made a large fine forest of various trees. For two years Balor was delighted; he was the gladdest man, for all he wanted was trees and shelter on Tory Island.

The child was in good hands now with his mother and the twelve women, and when able to walk, Fin used to bring him out in the daytime. Once he kept him and went to the mainland. The next day a terrible wind rose, and it did n't leave a tree standing on Tory. Balor knew now that the forest was all enchantment and deceit, and said that he would destroy Fin and all his clan for playing such a trick on him. Balor sent his agents and servants to watch Fin and kill him.

Fin was warned by Gial Duv, and took care of himself for a long time, but at last they caught him. It was his custom to hunt in Glen Ath, for there were many deer and much game there in those days, and Fin was very fond of hunting; but he shunned all their ambushes, till one evening when they were lying in wait for him in the bushes by a path which he was travelling for the first time. They leaped up when he was near, caught him, and bound him.

"Take the head off me at one blow," said he, "and be done with it."

They put his head on a stone and cut it off with one blow. In this way died Fin Mac-Kinealy, the father of Balor's grandson. This grandson was a strong youth now. He was a young man, in fact, and his name was Lui Lavada (Lui Longhand). He was called Lavada because his arms were so long that he could tie his shoes without stooping. Lui did not know that he was Balor's grandson. He knew that his father had been killed by Balor's men, and he was waiting to avenge him.

A couple of years later there was a wedding on the mainland, and it was the custom that no one was to begin to eat at a wedding till Maol and Mullag should carve the first slices. They did not come this time in season, and all the guests were impatient.

"I'll carve the meat for you," said Balor's grandson. With that he carved some slices, and all present began to eat and drink.

After a while Maol and Mullag came, and they
were in a great rage because the people were
eating, drinking, and enjoying the wedding feast
without themselves.

When all had finished eating and drinking, and
were ready to go home, Maol said, "The bride
will go with me."

The bride began to cry when she heard that,
and was in great distress. Lui Lavada asked
what trouble was on her, and the people told
him, that since Balor's two deputies were ruling
on the mainland it was their custom at weddings
that Maol, the first in authority, should keep
company with the bride the first evening, and
Mullag the second evening.

"It's time to put a stop to that," said Lui
Lavada, Balor's grandson. With that he walked
up to the two and said, "Ye'll go home out of
this as ye are."

Maol answered with insult, and made an offer
to strike him. Lui caught Maol then and split
his tongue; he cut a hole in each of his cheeks,
and putting one half of the tongue through the
left cheek, and the other through the right, he
thrust a sliver of wood through the tips of each
half. He took Mullag then and treated him in
like manner.

The people led the two down to the seashore

after that. Lui put Maol in one boat and
Mullag in another, and let them go with the
wind, which carried them out in the ocean, and
there is no account that any man saved them.

Balor swore vengeance on the people for
destroying his men, and especially on Lui
Lavada. He had an eye in the middle of his
forehead which he kept covered always with
nine shields of thick leather, so that he might
not open his eye and turn it on anything, for
no matter what Balor looked at with the naked
eye he burned it to ashes. He set out in a rage
then from Tory, and never stopped till he landed
at Baile Nass and went toward Gavidin's forge.
The grandson was there before him, and had a
spear ready and red hot.

When Balor had eight shields raised from the
evil eye, and was just raising the ninth, Lui
Lavada sent the red spear into it. Balor pursued his grandson, who retreated before him,
going south, and never stopped till he reached
Dun Lui, near Errigal Mountain. There he sat
on a rock, wearied and exhausted. While he
was sitting there, everything came to his mind
that he did since the time that his men stole
Glas Gavlen from Gavidin Gow. "I see it all
now," said he. "This is my grandson who has
given the mortal blow to me. He is the son of

my daughter and Fin MacKinealy.   No one else
could have given that spear cast but him."
With that Balor called to the grandson and
said, "Come near now.   Take the head off me
and place it above on your own a few moments.
You will know everything in the world, and no
one will be able to conquer you."

Lui took the head off his grandfather, and,
instead of putting it on his own head, he put it
on a rock.   The next moment a drop came out
of the head, made a thousand pieces of the rock,
and dug a hole in the earth three times deeper
than Loch Foyle, — the deepest lake in the
world up to that time, — and so long that in that
hole are the waters of Gweedore Loch, they
have been there from that day to this.

The above tale I wrote down on the mainland,
where I found also another version, but inferior
to this.   On Tory itself I found two versions,
both incomplete.   Though differing in particu-
lars, the argument is the same in all.   Balor is
represented as living on Tory to escape the doom
which threatens him through a coming grandson;
he covets the cow Glas Gavlen, and finally gains
her through his agents.

The theft of the cow is the first act in a series
which ends with the death of Balor at Gweedore,

and brings about the fulfilment of the prophecy. In all the variants of the tale Balor is the same unrepentant, unconquerable character, — the man whom nothing can bend, who tries to avenge his own fate after his death by the destruction of his grandson. The grandson does not know whom he is about to kill. He slays Balor to avenge his father, Fin MacKinealy, according to the vendetta of the time.

BALOR OF THE EVIL EYE AND LUI
LAVADA HIS GRANDSON.

LONG ago there were people in Erin called
Firbolgs; and they lived undisturbed many
years, till a king called Balor Beiman came from
Lochlin with great forces, made war on the
Firbolgs, killed their king, and drove themselves
out of Erin.

The Firbolgs went to Spain; and there they
were looking for means of support, but could
find none, unless what they got for work in
carrying mortar.

They carried mortar, and lived that way till at
long last the Spaniards said, "These people are
too many in number; let us drive them out of
the country." So the Spaniards drove out the
Firbolgs, and they came back to Erin. In Erin
they attacked Balor and his Lochlin men, but
were defeated with loss a second time. When
they left Erin again, the Firbolgs went to the
lands of Gallowna, and there they lived undisturbed and unharmed.

When the Firbolgs were driven out of Erin the second time, Balor Beiman summoned his chief men, and said to them, "I will go back to Lochlin now and live there in quiet. I am too old to fight with new enemies. I will leave my sons here with you to rule in place of myself; and do ye obey them, and be as brave under them as ye were under me."

With that Balor left Erin, sailed away, and never stopped till he reached home in Lochlin.

At that time there was a smith in Erin named Gaivnin Gow, and he had a cow called Glas Gownach. The smith had a magic halter with which he used to tie the cow every night.

Glas Gownach travelled three provinces of Erin every day, and came home in the evening; the halter had power over her, and she went always to the halter in the evening if left to herself.

The cow gave milk to every one on her journey each day, — no matter how large the vessels were that people brought, or how many, she filled them; there was no lack of milk in Erin while that cow was in it. She was sent to give food and comfort to all, and she gave it, but especially to poor people.

Balor Beiman had his eye on the cow, and, when going back to Lochlin from Erin, he watched his chance and stole the halter. Gaivnin

Gow saw the theft, but too late to prevent it. Balor escaped with the halter, and made off to Lochlin.

Gaivnin Gow ran quickly to Glas Gownach, caught her by the tail, and held her that way till evening, when he drove her home carefully, and shut her up in the forge behind the bellows, where he milked her.

Gaivnin Gow stopped work in his forge now, and did nothing but mind the cow. He went out in the morning, followed her through every place, and brought her back in the evening. He held her tail all the day, and never let go his hold of her till he had her fastened behind the bellows.

The people got milk as before from Glas Gownach wherever she went through the country; but the smith got no milk till he had the cow enclosed in the forge.

The widow of the king of the Firbolgs took a new husband in the land of Gallowna, and had seven sons there. When the eldest, Geali Dianvir, had grown up, she said to him, " I will give you ships now, and go you to Erin with warriors and good champions to know can we get satisfaction of those people who hunted us out of our country like hares or foxes."

The son took the ships, and sailed away with

champions and heroes, and never stopped till he sailed into Caola Beag (Killybegs, in Donegal). He landed in that place, left his ships safely fastened, and went forward travelling. He never stopped on his way nor halted till he came to a place called Blan Ri. He halted in that place, for before him were three armies fighting.

When they saw the new forces coming, the armies stopped fighting.

"Why are ye fighting here with three armies?" asked Dianvir; "what is the cause of your struggle?"

The leader of one army said, "We are brothers; our father died not long since; he was king of three provinces, and I think it my right to be king in his place."

The leader of the second army, the middle brother, said, "I have as much right to be king after my father as he has."

The third brother said, "I have as much right to be king as either of them."

Neither of the three was willing to yield his claim, or obey one of the others; but they were all ready to fight while their strength lasted.

"Your trouble can be settled easily," said Dianvir; "if ye are willing."

"Settle it, and do us a service," said the eldest brother.

"I will; but ye must take my judgment and obey it."

"We will," said all the brothers. "We will accept your decision, and do what you tell us."

"Listen, then," said Dianvir: "you, the eldest, will be king for this year. You, the second, will be king in his place the second year; and you, the youngest brother, will be king the third year. The fourth year, you, the eldest brother, will be king again for a year; and so it will go on, and you and your two brothers will be spending time happily all your lives."

The three brothers agreed, and were glad. The eldest was king that first year. Dianvir went his way; but he had hardly gone out of their sight when the youngest of the three brothers said, "That man will make trouble for us yet; my advice is to follow him, and put an end to himself and his men before they can harm us."

"Oh," said the eldest, "sure ye would not kill the man who gave us good counsel and settled our difficulty?"

"No matter what he did," said the youngest; "he will give you trouble yet if ye let him go. Follow him, put an end to him, or he will put an end to us."

They sent men after Dianvir. As Dianvir was a stranger in Erin he had no knowledge of the roads: when a lake was before him he was long going around it; when he came to a deep river he was long finding a ford.

Dianvir's men were cut off, most of them fell, and he himself fell with others. A small number escaped to the ships, took one of them, and sailed to the land of Gallowna. They told the queen the whole story, told how they had been treated with treachery.

"I will have satisfaction for my son," said the mother. "I will have it without waiting long." With that she had ships and boats prepared, and went herself with her other sons, and strong forces, to take vengeance on the brothers. The queen and her forces were six weeks sailing hither and over, driven by strong winds, when one morning a sailor at the topmast cried, "I see land!"

"Is it more or less of it that you see?" asked the queen.

"I see land, the size of a pig's back," said the sailor, "and a black back it is."

They sailed three days and nights longer, and on the fourth morning they were near shore, and landed in Bantry (White Strand). The queen fixed her house at Ardneevy, and prepared for action; but instead of the three brothers it was the sons of Balor she had against her.

War began, and the Lochlin men were getting the upper hand the first days.   At some distance from their camp was a well of venom, and into this well they dipped their swords and spears before going to battle, and the man of the enemy who was barely grazed by a weapon dipped in the well was as badly off as the man whose head was taken from him.   There was no chance now for the queen's forces, so she called her sons and said to them, "We 'll be destroyed to the last one unless we find help against this venom.   Go to the Old Blind Sage, and ask advice of him."

The sons went to the sage, and the advice they got was this, —

"There is a well of venom not far from the camp of the Lochlin men.   Before going to battle they dip their swords and spears in that water, and the enemy who is touched by those weapons that day is killed as surely as if the head had been swept from him.   Ye are to get twenty measures of the milk of Glas Gownach, and pour it into that well in the night-time; the milk will be going down in the well and the poison will be rising and going out till it flows away and is lost altogether.   Take, then, a hundred swords and spears to Gaivnin Gow, the smith, to put temper on their points and edges. He will do this if ye follow the cow all day for him and bring her home safely in the evening."

The queen's sons did what the sage advised. The venom went from the well when the cow's milk was poured into it. From that night out the weapons of the Lochlin men were common swords and spears.

When the queen's sons went with the swords and spears to Gaivnin Gow, he said, "I cannot work for you. I am minding this cow, Glas Gownach, that travels three provinces of Erin every day; I must go with her wherever she goes, bring her home, and put her behind the bellows in the forge every night. If the cow goes from me I am lost, with my wife and children. We have no means of support but her milk."

"I am as good a man as you," said the best of the brothers; "I will mind the cow, and bring her back in the evening."

The smith let the cow go with him at last, and went to work at the swords and spears. The young man followed the cow faithfully, all day, brought her back in the evening, left her outside the forge, and went in himself. The smith had the swords and spears tempered.

"Where is the cow Glas Gownach?" asked Gaivnin Gow.

"Outside at the door."

"Bad luck to you, she is gone from me now, gone forever!"

They went out. Not a trace of Glas Gownach. She had gone to Balor Beiman in Lochlin, for he had the halter.

There was a great battle on the following day, the queen fell and her sons, except two. Balor's sons were all killed, and the Lochlin men driven away.

Balor rose up in anger when the news came to Lochlin. "I'll have satisfaction for my sons," said he. "I will burn all Erin!"

Besides his two eyes Balor had a third one, an evil eye, in the middle of his forehead, with the power to burn everything in the world that it looked upon. Over this eye he kept seven steel shields, and a lock on each one of them.

"I will destroy Erin, and no man can stop me," said Balor; "for no man can kill me but the son of my daughter. She has no son, and if she had itself, he could kill me only with the red spear made by Gaivnin Gow, and it cast into my eye the moment I raise the last shield from it, when I am standing on Muin Duv [1] [Black Back] to burn Erin."

One day the two brothers were talking, and

---

[1] This is the high point, " the size of a pig's back," which the sailor saw from the topmast.

Cian, the youngest son of the queen of the Firbolgs, said to his only living brother, "We have done great harm to Gaivnin Gow. It is by us that the cow went from him, and we should bring her back."

"That is more than we can do," said the second brother, "unless we get help from Bark an Tra, the druid."

The two brothers went to Bark an Tra, and Cian told their story.

"The work is a hard one; I don't know can you do it," said the druid; "but you can try; I will help you. The cow is with Balor Beiman, in Lochlin. He stole her halter when he went from Erin; and she followed it the day your brother left her outside the forge. No man can bring the cow with him unless he has the halter, and it is hard to get that.

"Balor Beiman can be killed only by the son of his daughter; he has her behind seven locked doors. No living person sees the daughter but himself. He sees her every day, takes food and drink to her. To bring back the cow you must make the acquaintance of Balor's daughter. I will give you a cloak of darkness; put it over you, and make your way to Lochlin. When Balor goes to see his daughter, you go with him. He opens one door, goes in and locks it, opens the second, goes in and locks that, and so on. When he is inside in his daughter's chamber the seven doors are locked behind him."

Cian put on the cloak of darkness, and no man could see him; he went to Lochlin then, and followed Balor to his daughter's chamber. He waited till the night when she was sleeping, went then to her bedside, and put his hand on her heavily.

She screamed, saying, "Some one is in the chamber."

Balor came, very angry and with an evil face, to see who was in it. He searched the chamber through, searched many times, found no one. Failing to find any one, he returned to his own place and went to bed. Cian came again and put a heavier hand on Balor's daughter. She roared out that some one was in the chamber. Balor came, searched, and looked several times, and went away. The third time the young man put a still heavier hand on the maiden, and she screamed louder. Balor searched this time more carefully, found no man, and said, "Oh, you are a torment; it 's dreaming you are. You are hoping for some one to be in the world to destroy me, but that is what never will be. If I hear another scream here I will take the head off you surely."

No sooner was Balor gone this time, and the seven doors locked, than the young man came again, and put a heavier hand than ever on the maiden. She did not scream then; she was in dread of her father, but said slowly, "Are you a living man or a ghost?"

"I am so and so," said Cian, "the best champion in the world, and I have come here to win you." He talked on till he pleased her, they agreed then. He spent three days in her company. On the fourth day he followed Balor out of the chamber, and away with him back to Erin. He went to Bark an Tra, the druid.

"Were you in Lochlin with Balor?"

"I was."

"How did you behave?"

"So and so," said Cian.

"You must be there again at the right time."

Cian was back in Lochlin at the right time, unseen in his cloak of darkness, and brought away a child with him to Erin. The child was not thriving for three years, hardly lived, and was puny.

"The child is not doing well," said Cian to the druid.

"The child will do well yet," answered Bark an Tra. "Take him now to Lochlin as far as Balor; the child will not thrive till his grandfather calls him by name."

Cian went to Balor. "Well," said Balor, "who are you and what journey are you on?"

"I am a poor man looking for service."

"What child is that you have with you?"

"My own child," said Cian; "my wife is dead."

"What can you do?" asked Balor.

"I am the best gardener in the world."

"I have a better gardener than you," said Balor.

"You have not. What can your gardener do?"

"The tree that he plants on Monday morning has the finest ripe apples in the world on Saturday night."

"That's nothing. The tree that I plant in the morning I'll pluck from it in the evening the finest ripe apples you have ever set eyes on."

"I do not like to have any child near my castle," said Balor; "but I will keep you for a time, even with the child, if your wages are not too great for me."

"I will work a day and a year for the cow."

Balor agreed to the terms, and took Cian. Balor spoke no word to the child, good or bad, and the boy was not thriving. One day Cian was bringing to Balor a lot of fine apples from one of his trees; he stumbled on the threshold, and the apples fell to the floor. All the people present ran to gather the apples, the child better than others. He worked so nimbly that he picked up two-thirds of all that had fallen, though a whole crowd was picking as well as himself.

"Tog leat Lui Lavada [Take away with you Little Long Hand]," cried Balor.

"Oh, he has the name now," said Cian.

Cian worked his time out then, and said, "I will take my pay another day."

"You may take it when you like," said Balor.

Cian took his son to Erin; the child grew wonderfully after that, and was soon of full strength.

Cian went to the druid.

"The time is near," said the druid, "when Balor will stand on Muin Duv. He 'll raise his eye-shields; and if the red spear is not put in his eye when the last shield is raised, all Erin will be burned in one flash. Go now and ask Balor Beiman for your wages; say that you want the cow Glas Gownach, for we want her and must have her. He will refuse, dispute, and quarrel, give bad names. You will say that he must pay you, must give the cow or go to judgment. He will go to judgment rather than give the cow; and do you choose his daughter as judge; she will give the cow to you."

"I will go to judgment," said Balor, when Cian insisted on getting the cow. "What judgment will you have?"

"My case is a true one," said Cian. "I ask no judge but the one yourself will take. I ask no judge but your own daughter."

"Let her be the judge," said Balor.

Cian put on his cloak of darkness, and, going to the daughter, explained his case to her. Next day Balor went in and told her all the story of the cow Glas Gownach.

"I must have nine days to think the matter over," said Balor's daughter.

She got the time, then she asked three days more. On the thirteenth morning Balor went to her and said, "The judgment must be made to-day."

"Well," said the daughter, "go out now and stand before the window, you and the gardener, and to whomever the halter comes from me he 'll have the cow."

When they stood in front of the window, she threw the halter to Cian.

"How could you do that?" cried out Balor.

"Oh, father, they say there is always a crooked cast in a woman's hand. I threw toward you; but it 's to the gardener the halter went."

Balor let the cow go. He was very angry,

but could not help himself. "You have Glas Gownach; but I 'll have satisfaction in my own time," cried he, as Cian went away.

"We have troubled you greatly with our work," said Cian to Gaivnin Gow; "but here is the cow for you, and with her the halter. You can stay at home now and rest; you need follow her no longer."

Cian went that night to the druid, and said, "I have the cow back in Erin."

"It is well that you have," answered the druid. "In five days from this Balor will be here to burn up Erin. He will stand on Muin Duv at daybreak. He will raise all the shields from his eye; and unless a spear made by Gaivnin Gow is hurled into his eye by his grandson that instant, he will have all Erin in flames. You must bring Gaivnin Gow and the forge with you to Muin Duv, have the spear made, and all things prepared there; and your son must be ready to throw the red spear at the right moment."

Gaivnin Gow came. They brought the forge, the spear, and all that was needed, put them behind a rock on the side of Muin Duv. On the fifth morning, at daylight, Balor was on the top of Muin Duv; and the instant the last shield reached his upper eyelid Lui Lavada struck him with the spear, and Balor fell dead.

ART, THE KING'S SON, AND BALOR BEI-MENACH, TWO SONS-IN-LAW OF KING UNDER THE WAVE.

THE King of Leinster was at war for twenty years, and conquered all before him. He had a son named Art; and, when the wars were over, this son was troubled because he could find no right bride for himself. No princess could suit him or his father; for they wanted an only daughter. In this trouble they went to the old druid.

"Wait," said the druid, "till I read my book of enchantment; and then I will tell you where to find such a woman."

He read his book, but could find no account of an only daughter of the right age and station. At last the druid said to the king, "Proclaim over all Erin that if any man knows of such a princess he is to come to this castle and tell you."

The king did as the druid advised. At long last a sailor walked the way, and went to the king. "I know," said he, "of the woman you wish."

"Who is she?" asked the king.

"The only daughter of the King of Greece, and she is beautiful. But it is better to keep your son at home than to send him abroad; for there is no man who could not find a good wife in Erin."

Art would not listen to this advice, but said, "I will go and get that one."

Next morning he made ready, took farewell of his father, and away he went on his journey. He rode a fine steed to the seashore; there he took a ship, and nothing more is told of him till he touched land in Greece. The King of Greece received Art with great welcome, gave a feast of seven days in his honor, and sent heralds through the city declaring that any man who would fall asleep till the end of the seven days would have the head swept off his body.

Silk and satin were spread under Art's feet, and respect of every kind shown him. He was entertained seven days, and at last, when the king did n't ask him what journey he was on, he said, "It is a wonder to me that you do not ask what brought me, and why I am travelling."

"I am not surprised at all," said the king. "A good father's son like you, and a man of such beauty, ought to travel all nations, and see every people."

"I am not travelling to show myself nor to see people. Men told me that you have an only daughter. I want her in marriage, and 't is for her sake that I am here."

"I have never heard news I liked better," said the king; "and if my daughter is willing, and her mother is satisfied, you have my blessing."

Art went to the queen and told her the cause of his coming.

"If the king and my daughter are satisfied," replied she, "that is the best tale that man could bring me."

Art went to the princess, and she said, "If my father and mother are willing, your words are most welcome to me; but there is one obstacle between us, — I can marry no man but the man who will bring me the head of the Gruagach of Bungling Leaps."

"Where is he to be found?" asked Art.

"If 't was in the east he was, I would direct you to the west; and if 't was in the west he was, I would send you to the east : but not to harm you would I do this, for thousands of men have gone toward that gruagach, and not a man of them has ever come back."

"Your opinion of me is not very high. I must follow my nose and find the road."

Next morning Art took farewell of the king,

and went his way travelling to know could he find the gruagach. At that time gruagachs and heroes lived in old castles. Art inquired and inquired till he heard where the gruagach lived.

At last he came to the castle, and shouted outside; but if he did it was no use for him, he got no answer. Art walked in, found the gruagach on the flat of his back, fast asleep and snoring. The gruagach had a sword in his hand. Art caught the sword, but could not stir it from the grasp of the gruagach.

" 'T is hard to say," thought he, "that I could master you awake, if I can do nothing to you in your slumber; but it would be a shame to strike a sleeping man."

He hit the gruagach with the flat of his sword below the knee, and woke him. The gruagach opened his eyes, sat up, and said, "It would be fitter for you to be herding cows and horses than to be coming to this place to vex me."

"I am not here to give excuse or satisfaction to you," said Art, "but to knock satisfaction out of your flesh, bones, and legs, and I'll take the head off you if I can."

"It seems, young man, that it is a princess you want; and she will not marry you without my head."

"That is the truth."

"What is your name?" asked the gruagach; "and from what country do you come?"

"My name is Art, and I am son of the King of Leinster, in Erin."

"Your name is great, and there is loud talk of you, but your size is not much; and if the princess were in question between us, I would think as little of putting that small hill there on the top of the big one beyond it as of killing you. For your father's sake, I would not harm you; your father is as good a man for a stranger to walk to as there is in the world; and for that reason go home and don't mind me or the princess, for your father and mother waited long for you, and would be sorry to lose you."

"Very thankful am I," said Art, "for your kind speech; but as I came so far from home, and want the princess, I'll knock a trial out of you before I leave this place."

Next morning the two faced each other, and fought like wild bulls, wild geese, or wolves, fought all day with spears and swords. Art was growing weak, and was not injuring the gruagach till evening, when he thought, "Far away am I from father, mother, home, and country." With that he got the strength of a hundred men, gave one blow to the gruagach under the chin, and sent his head spinning through the air. That moment the body went down through the earth.

When the body disappeared, Art thought the head would come down like any other thing; but the earth opened, and the head flew into the earth and vanished.

"I will go back to the castle of the King of Greece," thought Art, "and tell him the whole story."

On the way to the castle, and while passing a cabin, a big old man came out of the cabin, and cried, "Welcome, Art, son of the King of Leinster. It is too far you are going to-night. Stay with me, if you like my entertainment."

"Very thankful am I," said Art, "and glad to stay with you. It is weak and tired I am."

When he went in, the old man stripped him, put him first into a caldron of venom, and then into a caldron of cure, and he was as well as ever.

"Would go against the gruagach to-morrow?" asked the old man.

"I would if I knew where to find him."

"You will find him where he was to-day; but he will be twice as strong to-morrow, since you vexed him to-day."

After breakfast Art went to the castle, and found the gruagach asleep, as the first time, struck him with the flat of his sword, but so hard that he saw stars.

"Art, son of the King of Leinster, you are not satisfied yet; but you will suffer."

"I am not satisfied," said Art. "I'll have your head or you will have mine."

"Go home to your father and mother; don't trouble me: that is my advice."

"I am thankful to you," said Art, jestingly; "but I'll take a trial of you."

They fought as before. The gruagach had twice the strength of the first day; and Art was knocking no quarters out of him, but suffering from every blow, his flesh falling and his blood flowing.

"I am not to last long," thought Art, "unless I can do something." He remembered his father and mother then, and how far he was from home; that moment the strength of two hundred men came to him. With one blow he swept off the gruagach's head and sent it twice as far into the sky as on the first day; the body sank through the earth. Art stood at the place where the body had vanished.

When the head was coming down, and was near, he caught it and held it firmly by the hair; then, cutting a withe, he thrust it through the ears and, throwing the head over his shoulder, started for the castle of the King of Greece; but before reaching the old man's cabin, he met three men and with them a headless body.

"Where are ye going?" asked Art.

"This body lost its head in the eastern world, and we are travelling the earth to know can we find a head to match it."

"Do you think this one would do?" asked Art of one of the men.

"I don't know," said he; "it is only for us to try."

The moment the head was put on the body, men, head, and body went down through the earth.

Art went to the old man, and told him of all that had happened.

"You were very foolish," said the old man, "to do what you did. Why did you not keep the head and bring it to me? I would tell you what to do." The old man cured Art's wounds, and after supper he asked, "Will you fight the gruagach again?"

"I will."

"Well, if you have the luck to knock the head off him a third time, never part with it till you come to me."

Art went a third time to the gruagach, struck him with the flat of his sword, and knocked ferns out of his eyes.

"Oh, ho! Art, son of the King of Leinster, you are not satisfied yet, it seems. To-day will tell all. You'll fall here."

They went at each other with venom; and each sought the head of the other so fiercely that each hair on him would hold an iron apple. The gruagach had the upper hand till evening. Art thought of home then, of the young princess, and of the mean opinion that she had of him, and gave such a blow that the gruagach's head vanished in the sky. The body went through the earth, and Art stood as before at the place where it sank till he saw the head coming; he seized it, cut two withes, passed them through the ears, threw the head over his shoulder, and went toward the old man's cabin. He was within one mile of the house, when he saw, flying from the southeast, three ravens, and each bird seemed the size of a horse. At that time a terrible thirst came on him; he put the gruagach's head on the ground, and stooped to drink from a spring near the wayside; that moment one of the ravens swept down and carried off the head.

"I am in a worse state now than ever," said Art, lamenting.

He went to the cabin of the old man, who received him well, and cured him, and said, "You may go home now, since you did not keep the head when you had it; or you may go into a forest where there is a boar, and that boar is far stronger and fiercer than the gruagach: but if you can kill the boar, you will win yet, if you do what I tell you. When the boar is dead, open the body and hide in it. The three ravens will come after awhile to eat; you can catch one of them, and hold it till the others bring the head."

Art went away to the forest. He was not long in it when the boar caught the scent of him, and ran at him, snapped at his body, and took pieces out of it. Art defended himself till evening, and was more losing than gaining, when he remembered home and that princess who thought so little of his valor. He got the strength of four hundred men then, and made two even halves of the boar. When Art tried to draw his sword, it was broken at the hilt; and he let three screeches out of him that were heard all over the kingdom. He could not prepare the carcass, so he went to the old man with the sword hilt.

"A hundred thousand welcomes to you," said the old man; "and you deserve them. You are the best man I have seen in life."

"I do not deserve the welcomes," said Art; "'t is badly the day has gone with me: my sword is broken."

"I will give you a better one," said the old man, taking him to a room where there was nothing but swords. "Here are swords in plenty; take your choice of them."

Art tried many but broke one after another. At last he caught an old rusty blade, and shook it. The sword screeched so fiercely that it was heard in seven kingdoms, and his father and mother heard it in Erin.

"This blade will do," said Art.

"Come, now, and we'll prepare the boar," said the old man.

The two went and dressed the boar in the way to give Art room within the body, and a place to seize the raven. The old man went to a hilltop, at a distance, and sat there till he heard the three ravens coming, and they cawing as before. "Oh, it is ye that are coming!" thought he. The birds came to the ground, and walked about, till at last one of them began to peck at the carcass. Art caught that one quickly by the neck; the bird struggled and struggled.

"You might as well stop," said Art; "you'll not go from me. This fellow's head, or the head ye took yesterday," said Art to the other two.

"Kill not our brother," cried they; "we'll bring the head quickly."

"He has but two hours to live, unless ye bring here the head ye took from me."

The ravens were not gone one hour when the gruagach's head was in Art's hands, and the raven was free.

"Come home with me now," said the old man. Art went with him. "Show this head to the princess," said the old man; "but do not give it to her; bring it back here to me."

Art went to the king's castle, and, showing the head to the princess, said, "Here is the head which you wanted; but I will not marry you." He turned away then, went to the old man, and gave him the head. The old man threw the head on a body which was lying in the cabin; the head and the body became one, and just like the old man.

"Now, Art, king's son from Erin, the gruagach was my brother, and for the last three hundred years he was under the enchantment of that princess, the only daughter of the King of Greece. The princess is old, although young in appearance; my brother would have killed me as quickly as he would you; and he was to be enchanted till you should come and cut the head off him, and show it to the princess, and not marry her, and I should do as I have done. My brother and I will stay here, take care of our forests, and be friends to you. Go you back to Erin : a man can find a good wife near home, and need not look after foreign women."

Art went to Erin, and lived with his father and mother. One morning he saw a ship coming in, and only one man on board, the Red Gruagach, and he having a golden apple on the end of a silver spindle, and throwing the apple up in the air and catching it on the spindle.

The Red Gruagach came to Art, and asked, "Will you play a game with me?"

"I have never refused to play," said Art; "but I have no dice."

The gruagach took out dice; they played. Art won. "What is your wish?" asked the gruagach.

"Get for me in one moment the finest woman on earth, with twelve attendant maidens and thirteen horses."

The Red Gruagach ran to his ship, and brought the woman with her maidens; the horses came bridled and saddled. When Art saw the woman, he fell in love, took her by the hand, and went to the castle. They were married that day. The Red Gruagach would not sail away; he stayed near the castle and watched. Art's young wife knew this, and would not let her husband leave the castle without her.

Two or three months later she fell ill, and sent for the old king. "You must guard Art, and keep him safe," said she, "till I recover."

Next morning the king was called aside for some reason, and Art went out of the castle that moment. At the gate he met the gruagach, who asked him to play. They played with the gruagach's dice, and Art lost.

"Give your sentence," said he to the gruagach.

"You will hear it too soon for your comfort. You are to bring me the sword of light, and the story of the man who has it."

Art's wife saw the king coming back. "Where is Art?" asked she.

"Outside at the gate."

She sprang through the door, though sick, but too late.

"You are not a husband for me now, you must go from me," said she to Art. "The man who has the sword of light is my sister's husband; he has the strength of thousands in him, and can run with the speed of wild beasts. You did not know me, did not know that I was not that gruagach's daughter; you did not ask me who I was. Now you are in trouble, you must go. Sit on the horse that I rode, and that the gruagach gave you, take the bridle in your right hand, and let the horse go where he pleases; he will face the ocean, but a road will open before him, and he will never stop till he comes to my father's castle. My father is King Under the Wave. The horse will stop at steps in front of the castle; you will dismount then. My father will ask where you got that steed, and you will say you got him when you won him and the daughter of King Under the Wave from the Red Gruagach."

Next morning Art took farewell of his wife and his father and mother, started, and never stopped nor dismounted till he came to the steps outside the castle-yard where horsemen used to mount and dismount. He came down then.

"Where did you get that horse?" asked King Under the Wave; "and where is the rider who left my castle on his back?"

"I won him and the daughter of King Under the Wave from the Red Gruagach."

"Ah, 't is easily known to me that it was the Foxy Gruagach who stole my child. Now, who are you, and where are you going?"

"I am Art, son of the King of Leinster, in Erin."

King Under the Wave gave a hundred thousand welcomes to Art then, and said, "You are the best king's son that has ever lived; and if my daughter was to go from me, I am glad that it is to you she went. It is for the fortune that you are here, I suppose?"

"I am not here for a fortune; but I am in heavy trouble. I am in search of the sword of light."

"If you are going for that sword, I fear that you will not be a son-in-law of mine long. It is the husband of another daughter of mine who has the sword of light now; and while he has it, he could kill the whole world. But I like you better, and will send servants to the stable to get you the worst horse for to-night; you will need the best afterward. Balor Beimenach, this son-in-law of mine, will grow stronger each time you go to his castle. One of my men will ride with you, and show you where Balor lives, and show you the window of the room where he sleeps. You will turn your horse's back to the window, and call out, 'Are you asleep, Balor Beimenach?' He will reply, and call out, 'What do you want?' You will answer, ' The sword of light and the story of Balor Beimenach.' Put spurs to your horse that instant, and ride away, with what breath the horse has. I will have the twelve gates of this castle open before you, to know will you bring the life with you. Balor is bound not to cross a gate or a wall of this castle without my request, or to follow any man through a gate or over a wall of mine. He must stop outside."

On the following day, Art and a serving-man rode away; the man pointed out Balor's castle, and the window of his bedchamber. In the evening, Art rode up to the window, and shouted, " Are you asleep, Balor Beimenach? "

"Not very soundly. What do you want?"

"The sword of light and the story of Balor Beimenach."

"Wait, and you will get them!"

Art put spurs to his horse, and shot away. Balor Beimenach was after him in a flash. Art's horse was the worst in the stables of King Under the Wave, though better than the best horse in another kingdom. Still Balor was gaining on him, and when he came near the castle, he had not time to reach the gate. He spurred over the wall; but if he did, Balor cut his horse in two behind the saddle, and Art fell in over the wall with the front half.

Balor was raging; he went to his castle, but slept not a wink, — walked his chamber till morning to know would Art come again.

Next evening, Art rode to the window on a better horse, and called out, "Balor Beimenach, are you asleep?" and raced away. Balor followed, and followed faster. Art could not reach the gate before him, so he spurred his horse over the wall. Balor cut this one in two just at the saddle. Art tumbled down from the wall with his life.

This enraged Balor more than the first escape; he slept not a wink that night, but was walking around the whole castle and cursing till morning.

King Under the Wave gave Art the best horse in his stable, for the third night, and said, "This is your last chance with horses. I hope you will escape; but I'm greatly in dread that Balor will catch you. Now put this horse to full speed before you shout, and you will have some chance if your horse runs with what speed there is in him."

Art obeyed the king. But Balor killed that horse as he had the other two, and came nearer killing Art; for he cut a piece of the saddle behind him, and Art came very near falling outside the wall; but he fell in, and escaped with his life.

"Well," said King Under the Wave, on the fourth day, "no horse that ever lived could escape him the fourth time. Every vein in his body is wide open from thirst for blood; he would use every power that is in him before he would let you escape. But here is where your chance is. Balor has not slept for three nights; he will be sound asleep this time; the sword of light will be hanging above his head near his grasp. Do you slip into the room, and walk without noise; if you can touch the sword, you will have all Balor's strength, and then he will give you the story."

Art did as the king directed. He slipped into

the room, saw the sword of light hanging just above Balor's head. He went up without noise till he caught the hilt of the sword; and that moment it let out a screech that was heard throughout the dominions of King Under the Wave, and through all Erin.

Balor woke, and was very weak when he saw Art. The moment Art touched the hilt of the sword, he had all the strength that Balor had before. The screech that the sword gave put Balor in such fear that he fell to the floor, struck his face against the bed-post, and got a great lump on his forehead.

"Be quiet," said Art; "the sword is mine, and now I want the story."

"Who are you?" asked Balor, "and what land are you from? It seems that you are a friend of my father-in-law; for he is shielding and aiding you these four nights."

"I am a friend of his, and also his son-in-law. I wish to be your friend as well."

"What is your name?" asked Balor.

"Art, son of the King of Leinster, in Erin."

"I would rather you had the sword than any other man save myself."

Balor rose, and went to his wife, and said, "Come with me to your father's castle."

King Under the Wave gave a great feast, and

when the feast was over Balor Beimenach took Art aside, and told him this story: "I was married to my wife but a short time, and living in that castle beyond, when I wanted to go to a fair. When not far from the castle, I found I had left my whip behind, and went back for it. For years there had lived in my castle a cripple. On returning I found that my wife had disappeared with this cripple. I went after them in a rage. When I reached her, she struck me with a rod of enchantment, and made a white horse of me. She gave me then to a servant, who was to take grain to a mill with me. I had no saddle on my back, only a chain to cut and gall me. Though a horse, I had my own knowledge. I wanted freedom. The boy who drove me misused me, and beat me. I broke his leg with a kick, and ran away among wild hills to pasture. I had the best grass, and lived for a time at my ease; but my wife heard of me, and had me brought home. She struck me again with her rod of enchantment, made a wolf of me. I ran away to rocky places. The wolves of the mountains bit and tore me; but at last they grew friendly. I took twelve of these with me, and we killed my wife's cattle, day and night. She collected hunters and hounds, who killed six of the wolves. The other six and I were more harmful than ever. A second party killed the other six, and I was alone. They surrounded me; there was no escape then. I saw among the hunters my own father-in-law. I ran to King Under the Wave, fell down before him, looked into his face; he pitied and saved me, took me home with him.

"My wife was at her father's that day, and knew me. She begged the king to kill me; but he would not; he kept me. I served him well, and he loved me. I slept in the castle. One night a great serpent came down the chimney, and began to crawl toward the king's little son, sleeping there in the cradle. I saw the serpent, and killed it. My wife was at her father's castle that night, and rose first on the following morning. She saw the child sleeping, and the serpent lying dead. She took the child to her own chamber, rubbed me with blood from the serpent, and told the king that I had eaten the child. ' I begged you long ago to kill that wolf,' said she to her father; ' if you had followed my advice you would not be without your son now.' She turned and went out.

"Right there on a table was the rod of enchantment, which my wife had forgotten. I sprang toward the king; he was startled, and struck me with the rod, without knowing its power. I became a man, was myself again, and told the king my whole story. We went to my wife's chamber; there the king found his son living and well. King Under the Wave gave command then to bring seven loads of turf with seven barrels of pitch, make one pile of them, and burn his daughter and the cripple on the top of the pile.

"'Grant me one favor,' cried I. 'I will,' said the king. 'Spare your daughter; she may live better now.' 'I will,' said the king; 'but they will burn the cripple.'

"That is my story for you. Go now, and tell it to the Red Gruagach; keep the sword in your hand while telling the story; and when you have finished, throw the sword into the air, and say, 'Go to Balor Beimenach!' It will come to me. When you need the sword, send me word; I will throw it to you; and we'll have the strength of thousands between us."

Art gave a blessing to all, and mounted his wife's steed; the road through the sea opened before him. The wife received him with a hundred thousand welcomes. After that he went to the Red Gruagach, and, holding the sword of light in his hand, told the story. When the story was finished, he threw the sword in the air, and said, "Go to Balor Beimenach."

"Why did you not give me the sword?" cried the Red Gruagach, in a rage.

"If I was bound to bring the sword, I was not bound to give it to you," answered Art. "And now leave this place forever."

Art lived happily with his wife, and succeeded his father.

SHAWN MACBREOGAN AND THE
KING OF THE WHITE NATION.

THERE was a very rich man once who lived near Brandon Bay, and his name was Breogan.

This Breogan had a deal of fine land, and was well liked by all people who knew him. One morning as he was walking on the strand for himself, he found, above the highest tide, a little colt, barely the size of a goat; and a very nice colt he was.

"Oh, what a beautiful little beast!" said Breogan; "he does n't belong to any one in this country. He is not mine; but still and all I 'll take him. If an owner comes the way, sure he can prove his claim, if he is able."

Breogan carried the colt to the stable, and fed him as well as any beast that he had. The colt was thriving well; and when twelve months were passed, it was a pleasure to look at him. Breogan put him in a stable by himself after that, and kept him three years. At the end of the third year, it is n't a little colt he was, but a grand, fiery steed. Breogan invited all his friends and neighbors to a feast and a great merrymaking. "This will be a good time," thought he, "to find a man to ride the strange colt."

There was a splendid race-course on the seashore. The appointed day came, and all the people were assembled. The horse was brought out, bridled and saddled, and led to the strand. The place was so crowded that a pin falling from the sky would not fall on any place but the head of some person old or young, some man, woman, or child that was there at the festival.

For three days the women of the village were cooking food for all that would come; there was enough ready, and to spare. Breogan strove to come at a man who would ride the horse; but not a man could he find. The horse was so fiery that all were in dread of him.

Not to spoil sport for the people, Breogan made up his mind to ride himself. As soon as the man mounted, and was firm in the saddle, the horse stood on his hind-legs, rose with a leap in the air, and away with him faster than any wind, first over the land, and then over the sea. The horse never stopped till he came down on his fore-feet in Breasil, which is a part of Tir nan Og (the Land of the Young).

Breogan found himself now in the finest country man could set eyes on. He rode forward, looking on all sides with delight and pleasure, till out before him he saw a grand castle, and a beautiful gate in front of it, and the gate partly open.

"Well," thought he, "I'll go in here for a bit, to know are there people living inside." With that he tied the bridle to one of the bars of the gate, and left the horse, thinking to come back in a short time. He went to the door of the castle, and knocked on it. A woman came and opened the door to him.

"Oh, then, a hundred thousand welcomes to you, Breogan from Brandon," said she.

He thanked her, and was greatly surprised when he heard her calling him by name. She brought him then to a parlor; and, though he had fine rooms in his own house, he hardly knew at first how to sit in this parlor, it was that grand and splendid. He wasn't long sitting, when who should come in but a young woman, a beauty; the like of her he had never seen before in his life. She was first in every way, in good looks as well as in manners. She sat down at his side, and welcomed him.

Breogan remained in the castle a few hours, eating, drinking, talking, and enjoying himself.

At long last he thought, "I must be going;" and then he said so.

The first woman laughed. "Well, now, my good friend," said she, "of all the men that ever came to this place, — and it's many a man that came here in my time, — there never was a worse man to care for his horse than what you are. Your poor beast is tied to a bar of the gate outside since you came, and you have never as much as thought that he was dry or hungry; and if I had not thought of him, it's in a bad state he'd be now. How long do you think you are in this castle?"

"Oh, then, I am about seven hours in it."

"You are in this country just seven years," said the woman. "The beauty and comfort of this Land of the Young is so great that the life of twelve months seems the length of one hour in another place."

"If I am here that long, I must be going this minute," said Breogan.

"Well," said the woman, "if you are going, I must ask you one question. There will be a child in this castle; and as you are the father, 't is you that should name it. Now what will the name be?"

"If 't is a son, you 'll call him Shawn, the son of Breogan, from Brandon in Erin. You 'll rear

him for seven years. At the end of that time
give him your blessing and the means of making
a journey to Erin. Tell him who I am; and if
he is anything of a hero, he 'll not fail to make
me out."

Breogan left his blessing with the women,
went to the gate, and found his horse standing
there, tied in the same way that he left him.
He untied the beast, mounted, and away through
the air with him, leaving Breasil behind, and
never stopped nor halted till he came down about
a mile from his own house, near Brandon, exactly
seven years from the day that he left it. Seeing
on the strand a great number of people, he wondered why they were in it, and what brought
them together. A large, fine-looking man was
passing the way, and Breogan called out to him:
"What are these people all doing that I see on
the strand?" asked he.

"You must be a stranger," said the man, "not
to know what these people are here for."

"I am no stranger," said Breogan; "but I
went out of the country a few years before this,
and while I was gone there were changes."

"If a man leaves his own country for a short
time itself," said the other, "he will find things
changed when he comes again to it. I will tell
you why these people are here. We had in this

place a fine master, and it's good and kind he was
to us. He went out to the strand one day, walking,
and found a little colt above the high tide. He
took the colt home, reared and fed him three
years. Then this man gathered the people to give
them a feast, and to know could he find some one
to ride the horse. When no one would venture,
he mounted himself; and all saw how the horse
rose in the air, made a leap over the harbor, and
then away out of sight. We think that he fell,
and was drowned in the sea; for neither Breogan
nor the horse was seen ever after. We are sorry
for the man, because he was kind to us; but 't is
equal what became of the horse. After waiting
seven years, Breogan's wife is to be married this
evening to some great man from the North. We
don't know what kind is he. He may destroy us,
or drive us out of our houses."

Breogan thanked the man for his words, and
hurried on toward his own house. The servants
saw him coming, knew him, and cried, "Here
comes the master!" and there was a great stir
up and down in the house. Next minute the
wife heard the news; and out she ran to meet her
husband. Any man would think she was glad to
see Breogan. "Why are all the people here to-
day?" asked he of the wife.

"And was not it this day seven years that you

put the country behind you, wherever you went?
You left dinner here ready; and the dinner is in
the same state it was the day you went away
from me. I thought it better to send for the
people again, and eat the dinner in memory of
you that prepared it."

The husband said nothing. The people ate
the dinner; and every man, woman, and child
went home satisfied.

At the end of another seven years, Breogan
made a great dinner again. All was ready; a
great crowd of people were present. The day
being fine, you could see far in every direction.

"Look, now," said Breogan, to one of his men
who had very good eyesight. "Look out toward
the water, to know can you see any one coming.
Seven years ago to-day, I came home from
Breasil, in the Land of the Young; and my son,
if I have one, is to be here to-day. He ought to
be coming by this time."

The man looked out as well as he could. "I
see a boat with one mast coming toward us,"
said he; "and it's sailing faster than any boat I
have ever set eyes on. In the boat I can see
only one young man; and very young he is
too."

"Oh, that is he," said Breogan.

The boat came in at full sail; and it was n't

long till the youth was standing before his father. "Who are you?" asked Breogan.

"My name is Shawn MacBreogan."

"If that is your name, sit down here at dinner; for you are my son."

When the feast was over, the people went home. When Breogan's wife found out who the boy was, she would n't give the breadth of a ha'penny piece of his body for a fortune, she was that fond of him.

Things went on well till one day when Breogan and his son were out hunting. The day being warm, they sat down to rest; and the son said to the father, "Since I came to you in Erin, you seem vexed in yourself. I have not asked what trouble is on you, or is there anything amiss with you."

"All things are well with me but one thing," said Breogan. "There is some understanding between my wife and a man in the north of Erin. I 'm in dread of my life; for while I was in Breasil she saw this man, and the day I came home they were going to be married. Since then I have not slept soundly in bed; for messages are passing between them."

"Very well, father, I 'll put an end to that soon," said Shawn. He rose on the following morning, caught his hurley in his right hand, and his ball in the left. He threw up the ball, then struck it with the hurley, and was driving it that way before him till he reached the north of Erin,. and never let his ball touch the ground even one time. He inquired for his father's opponent. When he found out the house, he knocked at the door. "Is your master inside?" asked he.

"He is," said the servant.

"Go," said Shawn, "and tell him that I want him, and not to delay, as I must be at dinner in Brandon this evening."

The master of the house came out, and, seeing a boy there before him, thought it strange that he should speak rudely to a man like himself. "If you don't beg my pardon this minute, I'll take the head off you," said the man.

"Well," said Shawn, "I am not here to beg pardon of you nor of any man; but I came to have satisfaction for the trouble you put on my father, and I far away from him."

"Who is your father?"

"My father is Breogan of Brandon."

Out the man went; and the two stood on a fine green plain, and began to fight with swords, cutting each other's flesh. They were not long at the swords when Shawn said, "It is getting late, and I must be at home before dinner to-day, as I promised; there is no use in delaying." With that he rose out of his body, and gave the man a blow between the head and shoulders that put the head a mile from the body. Shawn caught the head before it touched earth; then, grasping it by the hair, he left the body where it fell, took his hurley in his right hand, threw his ball in the air, and drove it far to the south with the hurley; and he drove it across Erin in that way, the ball never touching ground from the far north of Erin to Brandon. Holding the ball and hurley in his hand, he went into the house, and laid the head at his father's feet.

"Now, my dear father," said he, "here is the head of your enemy; he'll trouble you no more from this out."

When Breogan's wife saw the head, she was cut to the heart and troubled; though she would not let any man know it. One day when the father and son came home from killing ducks, she was groaning, and said she was ready to die.

"Is there any cure for you here or there in the world?" asked Shawn.

"There is no getting the cure that would heal me; there is no cure but three apples from the white orchard in the White Nation."

"Well," said the boy, "I promise you not to eat the third meal at the one table, nor sleep the second night in the one bed, till I get three apples from the White Nation."

The father was very angry when they came out of the bed-room. "Sure," said he, "it would be enough for you to risk your life for your own mother."

"Well, I must go now," said Shawn; "the promise is given; I'll not break my word." So away with him on the following morning; and on that day's journey he came to a glen, and in it a house. In the house there was no living creature but a white mare with nine eyes.

"A hundred thousand welcomes to you, Shawn MacBreogan from Brandon. You must be tired and hungry after the day's journey," cried the mare. "Go in now to the next room, and take supper, and strengthen yourself."

He went to the next room, and inside in it was a table, and on the table was everything that the best king could wish for. He ate, drank, and went then and gave a hundred thousand thanks for the supper. He stood near the fire for a while; then the mare said, "Come here, and lie under my head; wonder at nothing you see, and let no word out of you."

He did as the mare said. About dusk three

seals came in, and went to the supper-room. They threw off their sealskins, and became three as fine young men as one could look at.

"I wish Shawn MacBreogan from Brandon were here to-night.. I 'd be glad to see him, and give him a present, and have his good company," said one of the three.

"I 'd be glad to see him, too," said the second; "and I 'd give him a present."

"So would I," said the third.

"Go to them now," said the mare; "enjoy their company. In the morning you 'll ask for the presents."

He went out among them.

"A hundred thousand welcomes to you, Shawn MacBreogan," cried the young men; "and 't is glad we are to see you."

They drank wine then, sang songs, and told tales, and never slept a wink all the night. Before sunrise they went as seals; and when going Shawn said, "I hope you will not forget the presents you promised last evening."

"We will not," said the eldest. "Here is a cloak for you. While it is on you, you 'll be the finest man in the world to look at."

"Here is a ball," said the second. "If you throw it in the air, and wish for anything you like, you will have it before the ball comes to the ground."

The third gave a whistle: "When you blow this," said he, "every enemy that hears it will lie down asleep, and be powerless; and, besides, you 're to have the white mare to ride."

He took the gifts.

"Give me a feed of grain before we start," said the mare. "No man has sat on me without being turned into froth and blown away, or else thrown and killed. This will not happen to you; still I must throw you three times: but I 'll take you to a soft place where you 'll not be killed."

Shawn mounted her then, and she tossed him. She threw him very far the first time. He was badly shocked, but recovered. The second and third times it was easier. The fourth time he mounted for the journey. It was not long till he came to the seashore. On the third day he was in sight of land in the White Nation. The mare ran over the water and swiftly, without trouble; no bird ever went with such speed.

When Shawn came near the castle, he stopped before a house at the edge of the town, and asked a lodging of the owner, an old man.

"I 'll give you that," said the old man, "and welcome, and a place for your horse." After supper Shawn told his errand.

"I pity you," said the man. "I am in dread you 'll lose your life; but I 'll do what I can for you. No man has ever been able to get one of those apples; and if a stranger is caught making up to them, the king takes his head without mercy or pardon. There is no kind of savage beast in the world but is guarding the apples; and there is not a minute in the night or the day when some of the beasts are not watching."

"Do you know what virtue is in the apples?" asked Shawn.

"I do well," said the old man; "and it's I that would like to have one of them. If a man is sick, and eats even one bite of an apple, he'll be well; if old, he'll grow young again, and never know grief from that out; he will always be happy and healthy. I'll give you a pigeon to let loose in the orchard; she will go flying from one tree to another till she goes to the last one. All the beasts will follow her; and while they are hunting the pigeon, you will take what you can of the apples : but I hope you will not think it too much to give one to me."

"Never fear," said Shawn, "if I get one apple, you'll have the half of it; if two, you'll have one of them."

The old man was glad. Next morning at daybreak Shawn took the pigeon, mounted the mare, and away with him then to the orchard. When the pigeon flew in, and was going from tree to tree with a flutter, the beasts started after her. Shawn sprang in on the back of the mare, left her, and went to climb the first tree that he met for the apples; but the king's men were at him before he could touch a single apple, or go back to the mare. They caught him, and took him to the king. The mare sprang over the wall, and ran to the house of the old man. Shawn told the king his whole story, said that his father was Breogan of Brandon, and his mother the Prin- cess of Breasil in the Land of the Young.

"Oh," said the king, "you are the hero that I am waiting for this long time. A fine part of my kingdom is that island beyond; but 't is taken by a giant who holds it with an army of hire- lings. Clear that island of the giant and his men, bring me his head, and you 'll have the apples."

Shawn went to the old man, then to the mare, and told her.

"You can do that without trouble," said she; "you have the power needed to do it."

Shawn took his breakfast, then sat on the mare, and rode toward the island. Just before the mare touched the land, Shawn sounded the whistle; and every one who heard it was asleep the next instant. Shawn took his sword then, swept the head off the giant, and before evening there

was n't a man alive on the island except Shawn
himself. He tied the giant's head to the saddle-
bow, mounted the mare, and was ready to start,
when she spoke to him: "Be careful not to look
back toward the island till you come down from
my back." With that she swept on, and soon
they were nearing the castle. While crossing
the yard, Shawn thought, "I have the island
cleared; the head is safe on me; and the apples
are mine." With that he forgot the mare's
words, and turned to look back at the island; but
as he did, he fell from the saddle, and where
should he fall but down on a dust-heap. A son
of the comb woman, a youth who fed dogs and
small animals, was lying there at the time, and
he sickly and full of sores. Shawn's cloak
slipped from his shoulders, and fell on this dirty,
foul fellow; that moment he sprang up the finest-
looking man in the kingdom. He fastened the
cloak on his shoulders, mounted the white mare,
and rode to the castle. The king was that glad
when he looked at the head of the giant that he
did n't know where to put the counterfeit hero
who brought it.

"How did you clear the island?" asked the
king; "and was it a hard task to take the head
off the giant?"

"Oh, then," said the dog-feeder, "there was

never such a battle in the world as the battle to-day on that island between myself and the giant with his forces; and 't is well I earned what will come to me."

"You 'll get good pay," said the king; "I promised you apples from my white orchard; but I 'll give you more, I 'll give you my youngest daughter in marriage, and that island for her portion. My daughter will not be of age to marry for a year and a day. Till that time is out, you 'll live with me here in the castle."

Believe me, the dog-feeder was a great man in his own mind that evening.

There was one woman in the yard who saw the deception, and that was the henwife. She knew well what the dog-feeder was, and 't is often she said, "He 's the greatest liar on earth, and kind mother for him." She drew Shawn into her own house, and he sick and full of sores, just like the dog-feeder, not a man in the world would have known him. She nursed and tended Shawn. On the sixth day he was able to speak; but he lay in great weakness, and covered with sores.

"How am I to be cured?" asked he of the henwife.

"I know," answered she; "I spoke to a wise woman to-day, and got the right cure for you." With that the henwife went down to a spring that belonged to the king's youngest daughter, and pulled up nine rushes growing near it. Three of these she threw away, and kept six of them. She cut the white from the green parts, crushed them in water, gave Shawn some of the water to drink, and rubbed the rest on his body. A week was not gone, when he was as sound and well as ever.

Shawn heard now the whole story of the dog-feeder's lies and prosperity. He took service himself in the castle; and a few days after that the king gave a hunt, and invited all the guests in the castle to go with him. Shawn had to go as a basket-boy, and carry provisions like any servant. Toward evening, when the company were on a wild moor twenty miles from the castle, a thick mist fell, and all were afraid that their lives would be gone from them.

"I can take you to a castle," said Shawn.

"Take us," said the king.

"I will if you will give me your daughter to marry."

"She is promised to another," said the king.

"I have the best right to her," said Shawn. " It was I cleared the island."

"I don't believe you," said the king.

"We 'll be lost, every man of us," said the chief hunter; "give him the promise, he may be dead before the day of the wedding."

The king gave his promise. The basket-boy stepped behind a great rock, threw up the ball, and wished for the finest castle on earth. Before the ball touched the ground the king, the guests, and attendants were in a castle far finer than any they had looked on in daylight or seen in a dream. The best food and drink of all kinds were in it, shining chambers and beds of silk and gold. When all had eaten and drunk their fill, they fell asleep to sweet music, and slept soundly till morning. At daybreak each man woke up, and found himself lying on the wild moor, a tuft of rushes under his head, and the gray sky above him. Glad to see light, they rose and went home.

Now the henwife told the king's daughter the story of Shawn, who had cleared out the island, and the comb-woman's son, the deceiver. When the year was ended, and the day came for the marriage, the king's daughter said she would marry no man but the man who would ride the white mare with nine eyes (the mare could either kill or make froth of a man). The comb-woman's son was the first man to mount; but the cloak fell from him, and he vanished in froth blown away by the wind, and no one saw sight of him from that day to this. Sixteen king's sons tried to ride the white mare, and were killed every man of them; but their bodies were found. Shawn, who had taken the cloak, sat on the mare, and rode three times past the castle. At the door the mare knelt for him to come down.

The king's daughter would have jumped through her window, and killed herself, if her maids had not held her. She rushed down the stairs, kissed Shawn, and embraced him. The wedding began then. It lasted for a day and a year, and the last was the best day of all.

When the wedding was over, Shawn remembered the mare, and went to the stable. She had not been fed, and a white skin was all that was left of her. When Shawn came to the mare's place, three young men and two women were playing chess in it.

"Oh, I forgot the mare from the first day of the wedding till this moment," said Shawn; and he began to cry.

"Why are you crying?" asked the elder of the two women.

He told the reason.

"You needn't cry," said the woman; "I can revive her." With that she took the skin, put it on herself; and that minute she was the white mare. "Would you rather see me a white mare as I am now, or the woman that I was a minute ago?"

"The woman," said Shawn.

She took off the skin, and was a woman again. She told him then how the king, her father, made three seals of her brothers and a white mare of herself, to be in those forms till a hero should come who could clear out the island. "You cleared the island," said she; "and we are all free again."

The king gave the island to his son-in-law, and as many apples from the orchard as he wished. The first thing that Shawn did was to take an apple to the old man who gave him lodgings when he came to the White Nation. At the first bite he swallowed, the old man was twenty-one years of age, young and hearty, and so happy that it would do any man good to have one look at him.

Shawn and his young wife lived another day and a year with her father, and then they went to visit his father in Brandon. From pretending to be sick, Breogan's wife became sick in earnest, and died. Breogan himself was now old and dissatisfied.

"The least I can do," thought Shawn, "is to give him an apple." He gave him the apple. Breogan ate it, was twenty-one years of age; and if ever a man was glad in Erin, 't was he was.

Shawn left the father young and happy at Brandon, and went back himself with his wife to the island.

THE COTTER'S SON AND THE HALF SLIM CHAMPION.

ONCE upon a time there was a poor cotter in Erin, and he had three sons. Whether it was well or ill that he reared them, he reared them, and then died. When their father was dead and buried, the three sons lived with their mother for a day and a year; and at the end of that time the eldest brother said, "I will go to seek my fortune in the world."

He took his mother's blessing with him, and went away on the following morning.

The two sons and the mother lived on together for another day and a year, when the second son said, "I will go out to seek my fortune."

He went away like the first brother.

The mother and the youngest son lived on together for a day and a year, and then the mother died. When she was buried, the youngest of the three brothers, whose name was Arthur, went out in the world to seek his fortune. He travelled, and was walking always for a day and a year without finding a master, till on the afternoon of the last day of the year he took service with a hill.

On the last day of Arthur's service with the hill, the Half Slim Champion came in the afternoon, and asked would he play a game of cards.

"If you win," said the champion, "you will have a castle with lands and cattle of all kinds; if you lose, you will do me a service."

"I will play," answered Arthur.

With that they sat down to play; and Arthur won. Now, Arthur had lands and a castle, cattle of all kinds, and wealth in abundance.

The Half Slim Champion went his way; and Arthur lived for a day and a year on his lands. On the last day of the year, the champion came in the afternoon, and with him was the most beautiful lady that man could set eyes on. "Will you play a second game?" asked the champion. "If you lose, you will do me a service; if you win, I give you this lady as wife."

"I will play with you," said Arthur.

They played, and Arthur won.

Arthur lived with his wife in the castle for a day and a year; and on the last afternoon, the champion came the way leading a hound.

They played the third time, and Arthur won the hound. The champion went his way; and again Arthur lived for a day and a year with his wife in the castle in ease, in plenty, and in great delight.

On the afternoon of the last day, the champion came the fourth time. Arthur's wife saw him at a distance, and said to her husband, "My advice is to play no more with that champion. Remain as you are, and keep out of harm's way."

But Arthur would not listen to the wife, nor be said by her. He went out to play with the champion, and lost.

"I put you under bonds," said the champion, "not to sleep two nights in the same bed, nor eat two meals off the same table; but to be walking through the world, and searching always till you find the birth that has never been born, and that never will be."

The champion turned, walked away, and disappeared. Arthur went home in grief; and when he sat down the chair that was under him broke into pieces.

"I told you," said the wife, "not to play with him. What has he put on you?"

"To be walking and searching, ever and always, through the world till I find the birth that has never been born, and never will be."

"Take the hound with you," said the wife, "and go first to the castle of the son of the King of Lochlin. Take service with him; you may learn something there."

Away went Arthur next morning, and the hound with him. They were long on the road, lodging one time at a house, and another time where the night found them, till at last a great castle was in sight. When the hound saw the castle, he grew so wild with delight that he broke his chain, and rushed away. But if he did, Arthur followed; and when the hound sprang into the castle, Arthur was at his side.

"It was lucky for you," cried the son of the King of Lochlin, "to come in with the hound. Without that you 'd have been done for. Who are you, and where are you going?"

"I am a man in search of a master."

"I am seeking a man," said the king's son. "Will you take service with me?"

"I will," answered Arthur.

He hired for a day and a year, and wages according to service.

Arthur went to work on the following morning, and his first task was to bring fagots from the forest. When he went to the forest, he found half of it green, and the other half dry. Nothing was growing in the dry part; all was withered and dead. Arthur collected dry fagots, and brought them to the castle. In the evening he spoke to the king's son, and this is what he asked of him, "Why is half of your forest green, and the other half withered and dry?"

"A day and seven years ago," said the king's son, "a terrible serpent came the way, and took half of my forest for herself. In that part she is living till this time, — that is the green part. She knocked the life out of my half, — that is the dry part."

"Why do you not take wood from the green part?" asked Arthur.

"Neither you nor all who ever came before you could do that," said the son of the king. Next morning Arthur went out for fagots the second time. He stopped before the largest green tree to be found in the forest, and was cutting away at it. The moment the serpent saw this, she came out, and called, "Why are you cutting my timber?"

"I am cutting it because I am sorry to see you as you are," said Arthur, "without a roof over you or a shelter of any kind. I wish to build a house to protect you."

When the serpent heard this, she was glad and thankful to Arthur. When he had two wedges in the tree, and it partly cut, he said, "If yourself would only come over now, and put your tail in the cut and help me, we could throw down this tree."

She went to him then, and put her tail in the cut. Arthur knocked out the wedges, and left her tail in the tree. She begged and cried, screaming, "The tree is killing me; the tree is killing me! Let me free! Let me out of this!"

"It was n't to let you out that I put you in," replied Arthur.

What he did then was to jump behind her, and vex her until he got her in the way that, out of rage and great strength, she tore up the tree with its roots, and seven acres and seven ridges of land with it. Arthur was vexing the serpent until she rushed into the dry part of the forest, and was fastened among the trees; then he cut down dry trees, and piled them on the serpent and on the green tree till they were the size of a hill. In the evening he drove her to the castle before him, with all the hill of dry wood on her. When a maid was going from the castle for water, and saw this, she ran in with the story that Arthur was coming home with the serpent, and all the dry wood of the forest above on her back.

When the people inside heard this, they were in dread that she 'd kill them all, and they rushed out to run away. There was one girl in the castle who heard the tidings too late, or was slow in preparing, for when she was ready, the serpent was at the door.

"Where are the people of the castle?" asked Arthur.

"All made away, and took their lives with them," said she.

"Run now and call them back," said Arthur.

"I'm in dread to go out. I will not go unless you take the head off the serpent."

Arthur swept the head off the serpent. The girl ran after the people, and brought them back. Arthur piled all the wood near the castle. The king's son was delighted to have so much fuel, and was so glad that he took Arthur to his bed to sleep that night with him.

"It's a wonder," said Arthur, "such a good king's son as you to be without a wife."

"I had a wife," said the king's son; "but the giant with five heads, five necks, and five lumps on his heads, came and took her to the Eastern World."

"Why did you not take her from him?"

"Neither I, nor you, nor all that ever came before us could do that."

On the following morning Arthur rose, washed his face, rubbed his eyes, and said to the king's son, "I am going to the Eastern World to bring back your wife." Away he went; but the king's son would not believe that any man living could bring back the wife.

When Arthur came to the castle of the giant in the Eastern World, the giant himself was not in it, only the wife of the King of Lochlin's son, who said, "There is no use in your delaying in this place; you 'll be killed, if you stay till the giant comes home."

"I 'll never leave this castle till I see the giant; and when I go home you 'll go with me."

It was n't long till Arthur heard the great voice of the giant. As he came toward the castle the bottom of the forest was rising to the top, and the top of the forest was going to the bottom. In front of the giant went a shaggy goat, and another behind him. In his hand was a club with a yellow flea on the end of it; on one shoulder he carried a dead hag, and on the other a great hog of a wild boar.

"Fu fa my beard!" cried the giant. "I catch the smell of a lying rogue from Erin, too big for one bite and too small for two. I don't know whether to blow him away through the air, or put him under my feet."

"You filthy giant, 't is not to give satisfaction to you, or the like of you, that I came, but to knock satisfaction out of you."

"I want only time till morning to give you what you came for," said the giant.

It was day-break when Arthur was up and

struck the pole of combat.   There was n't a calf, kid, lamb, foal, or child awaiting birth that did n't turn five times to the right and five times to the left from the strength of the blow.

"What do you want?" asked the answering man.

"Seven hundred against me, and then seven hundred to every hundred of these, till I find the man who can put me down."

"You fool of the world, it would be better for you to hide under a leaf than to stand before the giant."

The giant came out to Arthur; and the two went at each other like two lions of the desert, or two bulls of great growth, and fought with rage.   They made the softest places hardest, and the hardest places softest; they brought spring wells up through dry slate rocks, and great tufts of green rushes through their own shoe-strings. The wounds that they made on each other were so great that little birds flew through them, and men of small growth could crawl through on their hands and knees.

It was dark and the end of the day, when Arthur cried out, "It is a bad thing for me, filthy giant, to have a fine day spent on you!"

With that he gave him one blow on the five

necks, and sent the five heads flying through the
air.   After a while the heads were coming down,
croning (singing the coronach), Arthur caught
them, and struck the giant's breast with them;
the body and heads fell dead on the ground.
The wife of the son of the King of Lochlin ran
out now, smothered Arthur with kisses, washed
him with tears, and dried him with a cloak of
fine silk; she put her hand under his arm, and
they went to the castle of the giant.   The two
had good entertainment, plenty to eat, and no
bit dry.   They made three parts of that night, —
one part for conversation, one for tales, and one
for soft sleep.

When they rose in the morning, the woman
said, "It is a poor thing for us to go and leave
here behind all the gold the giant had."

"Let us not be in so great a hurry; we 'll find
a cure for that," said Arthur.

They went out, found three ships belonging to
the giant, and filled them with gold.   When the
three ships were laden, Arthur took hawsers and
lashed the first ship to the second, the second to
the third, raised the anchors, and sailed away.
When he was in sight of Lochlin, a messenger
was walking toward the water, and saw the ships
coming.   He ran to the castle, and cried to the
king's son, "The servant-boy is coming, and
bringing your wife with him."

"That I will never believe," said the king's son, "till she puts her hand in my hand"

The king's son had kept his head by the fire, without rising from the hearth, all the time that Arthur was away. When the wife came in, and put her hand on his hand, he rose up, and shook seven tons of ashes from himself, with seven barrels of rust.

There was great gladness in the castle; and the king's son was ready to do anything for Arthur, he was so thankful to him. Arthur's time was out on the following day. The king's son spoke to him, and asked, "What am I to give you now for the service? What wages do you expect?"

"No more than is just. I hope that you will find out for me who is the birth that has never been born, and that never will be."

"That is no great thing for me to discover," said the king's son.

There was a hollow place in the wall of the castle near the fireplace, and in that hollow the king's son kept his own father, and gave him food. He opened a secret door, and brought out the old king.

"Now tell me, father," said he, "who is it that has never been born, and never will be?"

"That's a thing of which no tidings have been given, or ever will be," replied the king.

When the father was n't giving him the answer

he wanted, the son put the old king, standing, on a red-hot iron griddle.

"It's fried and roasted you'll be till you answer my question, and tell who is the birth that has never been born, and that never will be," said the son.

The old king stood on the griddle till the marrow was melting in the bones of his feet. They took him off then; and the son asked him a second time.

"That's a question not to be answered by me," said the king.

He was put, standing, again on the red-hot griddle, and kept on it, till the marrow was melting in the bones to his knees.

"Release me out of this now," cried the king; "and I will tell where that birth is."

They took him from the griddle. He sat down then, and told this story to his son, in presence of Arthur: —

"I was walking out beyond there in the garden one day, when I came on a beautiful rod, which I cut and took with me. I discovered soon after that that was a rod of enchantment, and never let it go from me. When I went walking or riding in the day, I took the rod with me. In the night, I slept with it under my pillow. Misfortune came on me at last; for I left the rod in my chamber one time that I started away to go fowling. After I had gone a good piece of road, I remembered the rod, and hurried home then to get it.

"When I came to the castle I found a dark tall man inside in my chamber with the queen. They saw me, and I turned from the door to let them slip out, and think that I had not seen them. I went to the door not long after, and opened it. Your mother was standing inside, not two feet from the threshold. She struck me right there with the rod, and made a wild deer of me.

"When she had me a deer, she let out a great pack of hounds; for every hand's breadth of my body there was a savage dog to tear me, and hunt me to death. The hounds chased me, and followed till I ran to the far away mountains. There I escaped. So great was my swiftness and strength that I brought my life with me.

"After that I went back to injure the queen; and I did every harm in my power to her grain, and her crops, and her gardens.

"One day she sprang up from behind a stone wall, when I thought no one near, struck me with the rod, and made a wolf of me. She called a hunt then. Hounds and men chased me fiercely till evening. At nightfall I escaped to an island in a lake where no man was living. Next day

I went around each perch of that island. I searched every place, and found only a she-wolf.

"But the wolf was a woman enchanted years before, — enchanted when she was within one week of her time to give birth to a hero. There she was; but the hero could not be born unless she received her own form again.

"There was little to eat on the island for the she-wolf, and still less after I came. What I suffered from hunger in that place no man can know; for I had a wolf's craving, and only scant food to stop it. One day above another, I was lying half asleep, half famished, and dreaming. I thought that a kid was there near me. I snapped at it, and awoke. I had torn open the side of the she-wolf. Before me was an infant, which grew to the size of a man in one moment. That man is the birth that has never been born, and never will be; that man is the Half Slim Champion.

"When I snapped at the she-wolf, I bit her so deeply that I took a piece from behind the ear of the child, and killed the mother. When you go back to the Half Slim Champion, and he asks who is the man that has never been born, and never will be, you will say: Try behind your own ear, you will find the mark on him.

"The infant, grown to a man before my eyes,

attacked me, to kill me.   I ran, and he followed.
He hunted me through every part of that island.
At last I had no escape but to swim to the
country-side opposite.   I sprang to the water,
though I had not the strength of the time when
I went from the hunters; but on the way were
two rocks.   On these I drew breath, and then
came to land.   I could not have swum five
perches farther.

"I lived after that in close hiding, and met
with no danger till I was going through a small
lane one evening, and, looking behind, saw the
hero whose mother I killed on the island.   I
started; he rushed along after me.   I came to
a turn, and was thinking to go over the wall, and
escape by the fields, when I met my false queen.
She struck me with the rod in her fright, and I
got back my own form again.   I snatched the
rod quickly, and struck her.   ' You 'll be a wolf
now,' said I; ' you 'll have your own share of
misfortune.'   With that she sprang over the wall,
a gray wolf, and ran off through the pastures.

"The dark tall man was a little behind and
saw everything.   He turned to escape; but I
struck him with the rod, and made a sheep of
the traitor, in hopes that the gray wolf might
eat him.   The hero saw all, saw the wolf that
I was, turned into a man.   I entered the castle;
he followed me.   I took you at once with me,

showed you this hollow place near the chimney, and hid in it. The hero searched every foot of the castle, but found no trace of me. He had no knowledge of who I was; and when you denied that I was here, he waited one day, a second day, and then went away, taking your sister and the best hound at the castle.

"That hero of the island, whose mother I killed, is the Half Slim Champion. There is nothing he wishes so much as my death; and when he hears who it was that has never been born, and never will be, he will know that I am alive yet, and he 'll kill half the people in Lochlin, unless he kills me first of all, or this champion kills him."

When Arthur heard this story, he went away quickly from the castle of the King of Lochlin, and never stopped till he came to the hill where he played cards the first time. The Half Slim Champion was before him there, standing.

"Have you found the answer, and can you tell who has never been born, and never will be?"

"Try behind your own ear, and you 'll find the mark on him."

"That 's true," said the champion, "and the man who killed my mother is alive yet; but if he is, he will not be so long, and you 'll not leave this till you and I have a trial."

The two went at each other then; and it was early enough in the day when Arthur had the head off the champion. He put a gad through his ears, took the head on his shoulder, hurried back to the King of Lochlin, and threw it on the floor, saying, "Here is the head of the Half Slim Champion."

When the old king heard these words in his place of concealment, he burst out the wall, and went through the end of the castle, so great was his joy. As soon as he was in the open air, free from confinement and dread, he became the best man in Lochlin.

They made three parts of that night, which they passed in great enjoyment, and discovered that Arthur's wife was the sister of the son of the King of Lochlin, the lady who was carried away by the Half Slim Champion, and lost in a game of cards.

When the old king got the head of the Half Slim Champion, he gave the three ships full of gold to Arthur, and would have given six ships, if he had had them, he was so glad to be free. Arthur took farewell of the old king and his son, and sailed away with his three ships full of gold to Erin, where his wife was.

BLAIMAN, SON OF APPLE, IN THE KINGDOM OF THE WHITE STRAND.

THERE was a king in Erin long ago who had two sons and one daughter. On a day of days, the daughter walked into her father's garden, in which she saw an apple-tree with only one apple on it; she took the apple, and ate it.

There was an old druid in the castle, who saw the king's daughter going out, and met her coming in.

"Well," said he, "you had the look of a maiden when you were going out, and you have the look of a married woman coming in."

Those who were near heard the saying of the druid, and it was going the rounds till it came to the king. The king went at once to the druid, and asked, "What is this that you say about my daughter?"

"I say nothing," answered the druid.

"You must tell me your words," said the king, "and prove them, or lose your head."

"Oh, as you are going that far you must give me time, and if a few months do not prove my words true, you may cut the head off me."

The princess was then taken to the top of the king's castle, where no one could see her but her maid. There she remained till she gave birth to a son with a golden spot on his poll, and a silver spot on his forehead. He was so beautiful that if sunshine and breeze ever rested on a child, they would rest on him; and what of him did not grow in the day grew at night. He grew so quickly that soon he was as large as the king's sons, his uncles, and rose out to be a great champion.

One day when the two sons of the king were hunting, there was snow on the ground, and they killed a hare. Some of the hare's blood fell on the snow, and they said that that was a beautiful meeting of colors. They were wondering could any woman be found with such colors on her face, white shining through the red. When they came home in the evening, they asked the old druid could a woman of that sort be found. He answered that if she could itself, little good would it do them; they could find wives good enough for them near home. They said that that was no matter, but to tell them where was the woman they had asked for.

"That woman," said the druid, "is the daugh-

ter of the King of the kingdom of the White
Strand. Hundreds of champions have lost their
heads for her; and if you go, you will lose your
heads too."

The elder son said, "We do not mind that; we
will go."

The brothers had no vessel to take them to the
kingdom of the White Strand; and the elder said
he would build one. He took tools one morning,
and started for the seashore. When just outside
the castle, he heard a voice, asking, "Where are
you going, king's son?"

"I am going to make a turkey-pen," answered
the young man. "May you prosper in justice and
truth," said the voice.

The king's son began to build the ship that
day; and in the evening what had he built but
a turkey-pen? When he came home, they asked
what had he made.

"Nothing; I made only a turkey-pen."

"Oh," said the second son, "you are a fool.
I knew that you could do nothing good."

On the following morning, the second son
started for the seashore; and the voice spoke to
him, and asked, "Where are you going, king's
son?"

"To build a pig-sty," answered he. "May you
prosper in justice and truth," said the voice.

He worked all day; and in the evening it was a pig-sty that he had. He came home; and now the brothers were doleful because they had not a ship in which to sail to the princess.

The following morning, the king's grandson said, "Give me the tools, to see can I myself do anything."

"What can you do, you fool?" asked the uncles.

"That matters not," replied he. He left the castle; and at the place where the voice spoke to his uncles, it spoke to him also, and asked, "What are you going to do, Blaiman, son of Apple?" (He did not know his origin till then.)

"I am going to build a ship," said Blaiman.

"That it may thrive with you in justice and truth," said the voice.

He went off to the edge of a wood that was growing at the seashore, gave one blow to a tree, and it went to its own proper place in the vessel. In the evening Blaiman had the nicest ship that ever moved on the deep sea. When finished, the ship was at the edge of the shore; he gave it one blow of a sledge, and sent it out to deep water. Blaiman went home full of gladness.

"What have you made?" asked the uncles.

"Go out and see for yourselves," answered Blaiman.

The two went, and saw the ship in the harbor. They were delighted to see the fine vessel, as they themselves could not build it. The voice had built it with Blaiman in return for his truth.

Next morning provisions for a day and a year were placed in the vessel. The two sons of the king went on board, raised the sails, and were moving out toward the great ocean. Blaiman saw the ship leaving, and began to cry; he was sorry that, after building the ship, it was not he who had the first trial of his own work. When his mother heard him, she grew sorry too, and asked what trouble was on him; and he told her that after he had built the ship, he wanted to have the first trial of it.

"You are foolish," said she. "You are only a boy yet; your bones are not hard. You must not think of going to strange countries."

He answered, that nothing would do him but to go. The old king, the grandfather, wanted Blaiman to stay; but he would not.

"Well," said the king, "what I have not done for another I will do now for you. I will give you my sword; and you will never be put back by any man while you keep that blade."

Blaiman left the house then; the vessel was outside the harbor already. He ran to the mouth of the harbor, and, placing the point of his sword on the brink of the shore, gave one leap out on board. The two uncles were amazed when they saw what their nephew had done, and were full of joy at having him with them. They turned the ship's prow to the sea, and the stern to land. They raised to the tops of the hard, tough, stained masts the great sweeping sails, and took their capacious, smoothly-polished vessel past harbors with gently sloping shores, and there the ship left behind it pale-green wavelets. Then, with a mighty wind, they went through great flashing, stern-dashing waves with such force that not a nail in the ship was unheated, or a finger on a man inactive; and so did the ship hurry forward that its stern rubbed its prow, and it raised before it, by dint of sailing, a proud, haughty ridge through the middle of the fair, red sea.

When the wind failed, they sat down with the oars of fragrant beech or white ash, and with every stroke they sent the ship forward three leagues on the sea, where fishes, seals, and monsters rose around them, making music and sport, and giving courage to the men; and the three never stopped nor cooled until they sailed into the kindgom of the White Strand. Then they drew their vessel to a place where no wave was striking, nor wind rocking it, nor the sun splitting it, nor even a crow of the air dropping upon it; but a clean strand before it, and coarse sand on which wavelets were breaking. They cast two anchors toward the sea, and one toward land, and gave the vessel the fixing of a day and a full year, though they might not be absent more than one hour.

On the following day they saw one wide forest as far as the eye could reach; they knew not what manner of land was it.

"Would you go and inquire," said Blaiman to the elder uncle, "what sort of a country that is inside?" The uncle went in, very slowly, among the trees, and at last, seeing flashes of light through the forest, rushed back in terror, the eyes starting out of his head.

"What news have you?" asked Blaiman.

"I saw flashes of fire, and could not go farther," said the elder king's son.

"Go you," said Blaiman to the other, "and bring some account of the country."

He did not go much farther than the elder brother, then came back, and said, "We may as well sail home again."

"Well," said Blaiman, "ye have provisions for a day and a year in this vessel. I will go now, and do ye remain here; if I am not back before the end of the day and the year, wait no longer." He gave them good by, then went on, and entered the forest. It was not long till he met with the flashes. He did not mind them, but went forward; and when he had gone a good distance, he found the trees farther apart and scattered. Leaving the trees, he came out on a broad, open plain; in the middle of the plain was a castle; in front of the castle twelve champions practising at feats of arms; and it was the flashes from the blows of their swords that he and his uncles had seen in the forest. So skilled were the champions that not one of them could draw a drop of blood from another.

Blaiman was making toward them. By the side of the path there was a small hut, and as he was passing the door, an old woman came out, and hailed him. He turned, and she said, "A hundred thousand welcomes to you, Blaiman, son of Apple, from Erin."

"Well, good woman," said Blaiman, "you have the advantage. You know me; but I have no knowledge of you."

"I know you well," said she; "and it's sorry I am that you are here. Do you see those twelve men out there opposite? You are going to make for them now; but rest on your legs, and let the beginning of another day come to you."

"Your advice may be good," said Blaiman, and he went in. The old woman prepared his supper as well as it was ever prepared at his grandfather's house at home, and prepared a bed for him as good as ever he had. He slept enough, and he wanted it. When day overtook him on the morrow, he rose, and washed his face and hands, and asked mercy and help from God, and if he did not he let it alone; and the old woman prepared breakfast in the best way she could, and it was not the wrong way. He went off then in good courage to the castle of the king; and there was a pole of combat in front of the castle which a man wanting combat would strike with his sword. He struck the pole a blow that was heard throughout the whole kingdom.

"Good, good!" said the king; "the like of that blow was not struck while I am in this castle."

He put his head through a window above, and saw Blaiman outside.

Around the rear of the castle was a high wall set with iron spikes. Few were the spikes without heads on them; some heads were fresh, some with part of the flesh on them, and some were only bare skulls. It was a dreadful sight to see; and strong was the man that it would not put fright on.

"What do you want?" asked the king of Blaiman.

"Your daughter to marry, or combat."

"'T is combat you will get," said the king; and the twelve champions of valor were let out at him together. It was pitiful to see him; each one of the twelve aiming a blow at him, he trying to defend himself, and he all wounded and hacked by them. When the day was growing late, he began to be angry; the noble blood swelled in his breast to be uppermost; and he rose, with the activity of his limbs, out of the joints of his bones over them, and with three sweeping blows took the twelve heads off the champions. He left the place then, deeply wounded, and went back to the old woman's cabin; and if he did, it was a pleasure for the old woman to see him. She put him into a caldron of venom, and then into a caldron of cure. When he came out, he was perfectly healed; and the old woman said, —

"Victory and prosperity to you, my boy. I think you will do something good; for the twelve were the strongest and ablest of all the king's forces. You have done more than any man that ever walked this way before."

They made three parts of the night: the first part, they spent in eating and drinking; the second, in telling tales and singing ballads; the third, in rest and sound sleep.

He had a good sleep, and he needed it. Being anxious, he rose early; and as early as he rose, breakfast was ready before him, prepared by the old woman. He ate his breakfast, went to the king's castle, and struck the pole.

"What do you want?" asked the king, thrusting his head through the window.

"Seven hundred men at my right hand, seven hundred at my left, seven hundred behind me, and as many as on the three sides out before me."

They were sent to him four deep through four gates. He went through them as a hawk through a flock of small birds on a March day, or as a blackbird or a small boy from Iraghti Conor between two thickets. He made lanes and roads through them, and slew them all. He made then a heap of their heads, a heap of their bodies, and a heap of their weapons. Trembling fear came on the king, and Blaiman went to the old woman's cabin.

"Victory and prosperity to you, my boy; you have all his forces stretched now, unless he comes out against you himself; and I'm full sure that he will not. He'll give you the daughter."

She had a good dinner before him. He had

fought so well that there was neither spot nor scar on his skin; for he had not let a man of the forty-two hundred come within sword's length of his body.   He passed the night as the previous night.

Next morning after breakfast, he went to the castle, and with one blow made wood lice of the king's pole of combat.   The king went down to Blaiman, took him under the arm, and, leading him up to the high chamber where the daughter was, put her hand in his.

The king's daughter kissed Blaiman, and embraced him, and gave him a ring with her name and surname written inside on it.   This was their marriage.

Next day Blaiman, thinking that his uncles had waited long enough, and might go back to Erin, said to the king, "I will visit my uncles, and then return hither."

His wife, an only child, was heir to the king-dom, and he was to reign with her.

"Oh," said the king, "something else is troub-ling me now.   There are three giants, neighbors of mine, and they are great robbers.   All my forces are killed; and before one day passes the giants will be at me, and throw me out of the kingdom."

"Well," said Blaiman, "I will not leave you

till I settle the giants; but now tell where they are to be found."

"I will," said the king; and he gave him all needful instruction. Blaiman went first to the house of the youngest giant, where he struck the pole of combat, and the sound was heard over ·all that giant's kingdom.

"Good, good!" said the giant; "the like of that blow has never been struck on that pole of combat before," and out he came.

"A nerve burning of the heart to you, you miserable wretch!" said the giant to Blaiman; "and great was your impudence to come to my castle at all."

"It is not caring to give you pleasure that I am," said Blaiman, "but to knock a tormenting satisfaction out of your ribs."

"Is it hard, thorny wrestling that you want, or fighting with sharp gray swords in the lower and upper ribs?" asked the giant.

"I will fight with sharp gray swords," said Blaiman.

The giant went in, and fitted on his wide, roomy vest, his strong, unbreakable helmet, his cross-worked coat-of-mail; then he took his bossy, pale-red shield and his spear. Every hair on his head and in his beard was so stiffly erect from anger and rage that a small apple or a sloe, an iron apple or a smith's anvil, might stand on each hair of them.

Blaiman fitted on his smooth, flowery stockings, and his two dry warm boots of the hide of a small cow, that was the first calf of another cow that never lay on any one of her sides. He fitted on his single-threaded silken girdle which three craftsmen had made, underneath his broad-pointed, sharp sword that would not leave a remnant uncut, or, if it did, what it left at the first blow it took at the second. This sword was to be unsheathed with the right hand, and sheathed with the left. He gave the first blood of battle as a terrible oath that he himself was, the choice champion of the Fenians, the feather of greatness, the slayer of a champion of bravery; a man to compel justice and right, but not give either justice or right; a man who had earned what he owned in the gap of every danger, in the path of every hardship, who was sure to get what belonged to him, or to know who de- tained it.

They rushed at each then like two bulls of the wilderness, or two wild echoes of the cliff; they made soft ground of the hard, and hard ground of the soft; they made low ground of high, and high ground of low. They made whirling circles of the earth, and mill-wheels of the sky; and if any one were to come from the lower to the upper world, it was to see those two that he should come. They were this way at each other to the height of the evening. Blaiman was growing hungry; and through dint of anger he rose with the activity of his limbs, and with one stroke of his sword cut off the giant's head. There was a tree growing near. Blaiman knocked off a tough, slender branch, put one end of it in through the left ear and out through the right, then putting the head on the sword, and the sword on his shoulder, went home to the king. Coming near the castle with the giant's head, he met a man tied in a tree whose name was Hung Up Naked.

"Victory and prosperity to you, young champion," said the man; "you have done well hitherto; now loose me from this."

"Are you long there?" asked Blaiman.

"I am seven years here," answered the other.

"Many a man passed this way during that time. As no man of them loosed you, I will not loose you."

He went home then, and threw down the head by the side of the castle. The head was so weighty that the castle shook to its deepest foundations. The king came to the hall-door, shook Blamian's hand, and kissed him. They spent that night as the previous night; and on the next day he went to meet the second giant, came to his house, and struck the pole of combat. The giant put out his head, and said, "You rascal, I lay a wager it was you who killed my young brother yesterday; you 'll pay for it now, for I think it is a sufficient length of life to get a glimpse of you, and I know not what manner of death I should give you."

"It is not to offer satisfaction that I am here," said Blaiman, "but to give you the same as your brother."

"Is it any courage you have to fight me?" asked the giant.

"It is indeed," said Blaiman; "'t is for that I am here."

"What will you have?" asked the gaint; "hard, thorny wrestling, or fighting with sharp gray swords?"

"I prefer hard, thorny wrestling," said Blaiman; "as I have practised it on the lawns with noble children."

They seized each other, and made soft places hard, and hard places soft; they drew wells of spring water through the hard, stony ground in such fashion that the place under them was a soft quagmire, in which the giant, who was weighty, was sinking. He sank to his knees. Blaiman then caught hold of him firmly, and forced him down to his hips.

"Am I to cut off your head now?" asked Blaiman.

"Do not do that," said the giant. "Spare me, and I will give you my treasure-room, and all that I have of gold and silver."

"I will give you your own award," said Blaiman. "If I were in your place, and you in mine, would you let me go free?"

"I would not," said the giant.

Blaiman drew his broad, shadowy sword made in Erin. It had edge, temper, and endurance; and with one blow he took the two heads off the giant, and carried the heads to the castle. He passed by Hung Up Naked, who asked him to loose him; but he refused. When Blaiman threw the heads down, much as the castle shook the first day, it shook more the second.

The king and his daughter were greatly rejoiced. They stifled him with kisses, drowned him with tears, and dried him with stuffs of silk and satin; they gave him the taste of every food and the odor of every drink, — Greek honey and Lochlin beer in dry, warm cups, and the taste of honey in every drop of the beer. I bailing it out, it would be a wonder if I myself was not thirsty.

They passed that night as the night before. Next morning Blaiman was very tired and weary after his two days' fight, and the third giant's land was far distant.

"Have you a horse of any kind for me to ride?" asked he of the king.

"Be not troubled," said the king. "There is a stallion in my stable that has not been out for seven years, but fed on red wheat and pure spring water; if you think you can ride that horse, you may take him."

Blaiman went to the stable. When the horse saw the stranger, he bared his teeth back to the ears, and made a drive at him to tear him asunder; but Blaiman struck the horse with his fist on the ear, and stretched him. The horse rose, but was quiet. Blaiman bridled and saddled him, then drove out that slender, low-sided, bare-shouldered, long flanked, tame, meek-mannered steed, in which were twelve qualities combined: three of a bull, three of a woman, three of a fox, and three of a hare. Three of a bull, — a full eye, a thick neck, and a bold forehead; three of a woman, — full hips, slender waist, and a mind for a burden; three of a hare, — a swift run against a hill, a sharp turn about, and a high leap; three of a fox, — a light, treacherous, proud gait, to take in the two sides of the road by dint of study and acuteness, and to look only ahead. He now went on, and could overtake the wind that was before him; and the wind that was behind, carrying rough hailstones, could not overtake him.

Blaiman never stopped nor stayed till he arrived at the giant's castle; and this giant had three heads. He dismounted, and struck the pole a blow that was heard throughout the kingdom. The giant looked out, and said, "Oh, you villain! I 'll wager it was you that killed my two brothers. I think it sufficient life to see you; and I don't know yet what manner of death will I put on you."

"It is not to give satisfaction to you that I am here, you vile worm!" said Blaiman. "Ugly is the smile of your laugh; and it must be that your crying will be uglier still."

"Is it hard, thorny wrestling that you want, or fighting with sharp gray swords?" asked the giant.

"I will fight with sharp gray swords," said Blaiman.

They rushed at each other then like two bulls of the wilderness. Toward the end of the afternoon, the heavier blows were falling on Blaiman. Just then a robin came on a bush in front of him, and said, "Oh, Blaiman, son of Apple, from Erin, far away are you from the women who would lay you out and weep over you! There would be no one to care for you unless I were to put two green leaves on your eyes to protect them from the crows of the air. Stand between the sun and the giant, and remember where men draw blood from sheep in Erin."

Blaiman followed the advice of the robin. The two combatants kept at each other; but the giant was blinded by the sun, for he had to bend himself often to look at his foe. One time, when he stretched forward, his helmet was lifted a little, Blaiman got a glimpse of his neck, near the ear. That instant he stabbed him. The giant was bleeding till he lost the last of his blood. Then Blaiman cut the three heads off him, and carried them home on the pommel of his saddle. When he was passing, Hung Up Naked begged for release; but Blaiman refused and went on. Hung Up Naked praised him for his deeds, and continued to praise. On second thought, Blaiman turned back, and began to release Hung Up Naked; but if he did, as fast as he loosened one bond, two squeezed on himself, in such fashion that when he had Hung Up Naked unbound, he was himself doubly bound; he had the binding of five men hard and tough on his body. Hung Up Naked was free now; he mounted Blaiman's steed, and rode to the king's castle. He threw down the giant's heads, and never stopped nor stayed till he went to where the king's daughter was, put a finger under her girdle, bore her out of the castle, and rode away swiftly.

Blaiman remained bound for two days to the tree. The king's swine-herd came the way, and saw Blaiman bound in the tree. "Ah, my boy," said he, "you are bound there, and Hung Up Naked is freed by you; and if you had passed him as you did twice before, you need not be where you are now."

"It cannot be helped," said Blaiman; "I must suffer."

"Oh, then," said the swine-herd, "it is a pity to have you there and me here; I will never leave you till I free you."

Up went the swine-herd, and began to loosen Blaiman; and it happened to him as to Blaiman himself: the bonds that had been on Blaiman were now on the swine-herd.

"I have heard always that strength is more powerful than magic," said Blaiman. He went at the tree, and pulled it up by the roots; then, taking his sword, he made small pieces of the tree, and freed the swine-herd.

Blaiman and the swine-herd then went to the castle. They found the king sitting by the table, with his head on his hand, and a stream of tears flowing from his eyes to the table, and from the table to the floor.

"What is your trouble?" asked Blaiman.

"Hung Up Naked came, and said that it was himself who killed the giant; and he took my daughter."

When he found that his wife was taken, and that he knew not where to look for her, Blaiman was raging.

"Stay here to-night," said the king.

Next morning the king brought a table-cloth, and said, "You may often need food, and not know where to find it. Wherever you spread this, what food you require will be on it."

Although Blaiman, because of his troubles, had no care for anything, he took the cloth with him. He was travelling all day, and at night-fall came to a break in the mountain, a sheltered spot, and he saw remains of a fire.

"I will go no farther to-night," said he. After a time he pulled out the table-cloth, and food for a king or a champion appeared on it quickly. He was not long eating, when a little hound from the break in the mountain came toward him, and stood at some distance, being afraid to come near.

"Oh," said the hound, "have you crumbs or burned bread-crusts that you would give me to take to my children, now dying of hunger? For three days I have not been able to hunt food for them."

"I have, of course," said Blaiman. "Come, eat enough of what you like best, and carry away what you can."

"You have my dear love forever," said the hound. "You are not like the thief that was here three nights ago. When I asked him for help, he threw a log of wood at me, and broke my shoulder-blade; and I have not been able to find food for my little children since that night. Doleful and sad was the lady who was with him; she ate no bite and drank no sup the whole night, but was shedding tears. If ever you are in hardship, and need my assistance, call for the Little Hound of Tranamee, and you will have me to help you."

"Stay with me," said Blaiman, "a part of the night; I am lonely, and you may take with you what food you can carry."

The hound remained till he thought it time to go home; Blaiman gave him what he could carry, and he was thankful.

Blaiman stayed there till day-break, spread his cloth again, and ate what he wanted. He was in very good courage from the tidings concerning his wife. He journeyed swiftly all day, thinking he would reach the castle of Hung Up Naked in the evening; but it was still far away.

He came in the evening to a place like that

in which he had been the night previous, and thought to himself, I will stay here to-night. He spread his cloth, and had food for a king or a champion. He was not long eating, when there came opposite him out a hawk, and asked, "Have you crumbs or burned crusts to give me for my little children?"

"Oh," said Blaiman, "come and eat your fill, and take away what you are able to carry."

The hawk ate his fill. "My love to you forever," said the hawk; "this is not how I was treated by the thief who was here three nights ago. When I asked him for food, he flung a log of wood at me, and almost broke my wing."

"Give me your company a part of the night; I am lonely," said Blaiman.

The hawk remained with him, and later on added, "The lady who went with the thief was doleful and careworn; she ate nothing, but shed tears all the time." When going, and Blaiman had given him all the food he could carry, the hawk said, "If ever you need my assistance, you have only to call for the Hawk of Cold Cliff, and I will be with you."

The hawk went away, very thankful; and Blaiman was glad that he had tidings again of his wife. Not much of next day overtook him asleep. He rose, ate his breakfast, and hastened forward.

He was in such courage that he passed a mountain at a leap, a valley at a step, and a broad untilled field at a hop. He journeyed all day till he came to a break in the mountain; there he stopped, and was not long eating from his cloth, when an otter came down through the glen, stood before him, and asked, "Will you give me crumbs or burned crusts for my little children?"

Blaiman gave him plenty to eat, and all he could carry home. "My love to you forever," said the otter. "When you need aid, call on the Otter of Frothy Pool, and I will be with you. You are not like the thief who was here three nights ago, having your wife with him. She was melting all night with tears, and neither ate nor drank. You will reach the castle of Hung Up Naked to-morrow at midday. It whirls around like a mill-stone, continually, and no one can enter but himself; for the castle is enchanted."

The otter went home. Blaiman reached the castle at midday, and knew the place well, from the words of the otter. He stood looking at the castle; and when the window at which his wife was sitting came before him, she saw him, and, opening the window, made a sign with her hand, and told him to go. She thought that no one could get the upper hand of Hung Up Naked; for the report had gone through the world that no man could kill him.

"I will not go," said Blaiman. "I will not leave you where you are; and now keep the window open."

He stepped back some paces, and went in with one bound through the window, when it came around the second time.

While Hung Up Naked was tied to the tree, the tributes of his kingdom remained uncollected; and when he had the woman he wanted safe in his castle, he went to collect the tributes. She had laid an injunction on him to leave her in freedom for a day and a year. She knew when he would be returning; and when that time was near she hid Blaiman.

"Good, good!" cried Hung Up Naked, when he came. "I smell on this little sod of truth that a man from Erin is here."

"How could a man from Erin be here?" asked Blaiman's wife. "The only person from Erin in this place is a robin. I threw a fork at him. There is a drop of blood on the fork now; that is what you smell on the little sod."

"That may be," said Hung Up Naked.

Blaiman and the wife were planning to destroy Hung Up Naked; but no one had knowledge how to kill him. At last they made a plan to come at the knowledge.

"It is a wonder," said the woman to Hung Up

Naked, "that a great man like yourself should go travelling alone; my father always takes guards with him."

"I need no guards; no one can kill me."

"How is that?"

"Oh, my life is in that block of wood there."

"If it is there, 't is in a strange place; and it is little trouble you take for it. You should put it in some secure spot in the castle."

"The place is good enough," said he.

When Hung Up Naked went off next day, the wife told Blaiman all she had heard.

"His life is not there," answered Blaiman; "try him again to-night."

She searched the whole castle, and what silk or satin or jewels she found, she dressed with them the block of wood. When Hung Up Naked came home in the evening, and saw the block so richly decked, he laughed heartily.

"Why do you laugh?" asked the woman.

"Out of pity for you. It is not there that my life is at all."

On hearing these words, she fainted, was stiff and cold for some time, till he began to fear she was dead.

"What is the matter?" asked Hung Up Naked.

"I did not think you would make sport of me.

You know that I love you, and why did you deceive me?"

Hung Up Naked was wonderfully glad. He took her to the window, and, pointing to a large tree growing opposite, asked, "Do you see that tree?"

"I do."

"Do you see that axe under my bed-post?" He showed the axe. "I cannot be killed till a champion with one blow of that axe splits the tree from the top to the roots of it. Out of the tree a ram will rush forth, and nothing on earth can come up with the ram but the Hound of Tranamee. If the ram is caught, he will drop a duck; the duck will fly out on the sea, and nothing on earth can catch that duck but the Hawk of Cold Cliff. If the duck is caught, she will drop an egg into the sea, and nothing on earth can find that egg but the Otter of Frothy Pool. If the egg is found, the champion must strike with one cast of it this dark spot here under my left breast, and strike me through the heart. If the tree were touched, I should feel it, wherever I might be."

He went away next morning. Blaiman took the axe, and with one blow split the tree from top to roots; out rushed the ram. Blaiman rushed after him through the fields. Blaiman hunted the ram till he was dropping from weariness. Only then did he think of the hound, and cry, "Where are you now, Little Hound of Tranamee?"

"I am here," said the hound; "but I could not come till you called me."

The hound seized the ram in one moment; but, if he did, out sprang a duck, and away she flew over the sea. Blaiman called for the Hawk of Cold Cliff. The hawk caught the duck; the duck dropped an egg. He called the Otter of Frothy Pool; the otter brought the egg in his mouth. Blaiman took the egg, and ran to the castle, which was whirling no longer; the enchantment left the place when the tree was split. He opened the door, and stood inside, but was not long there when he saw Hung Up Naked coming in haste. When the tree was split, he felt it, and hurried home. When nearing the castle, his breast open and bare, and he sweating and sweltering, Blaiman aimed at the black spot, and killed Hung Up Naked.

They were all very glad then. The hawk, hound, and otter were delighted; they were three sons of the king of that kingdom which Hung Up Naked had seized; they received their own forms again, and all rejoiced.

Blaiman did not stay long. He left the three

brothers in their own castle and kingdom. "If ever you need my assistance," said Blaiman to the brothers, "send for me at my father-in-law's." On his return, he spent a night at each place where he had stopped in going.

When the king saw his daughter and Blaiman, he almost dropped dead from joy. They all spent some days very happily. Blaiman now thought of his uncles; and for three days servants were drawing every choice thing to his vessel. His wife went also to the ship. When all was ready, Blaiman remembered a present that he had set aside for his mother, and hurried back to the castle, leaving his wife on the ship with his uncles. The uncles sailed at once for Erin. When Blaiman came back with the present, he found neither wife, ship, nor uncles before him. He ran away like one mad, would not return to his father-in-law, but went wild in the woods, and began to live like the beasts of the wilderness. One time he came out on an edge of the forest, which was on a headland running into the sea, and saw a vessel near land; he was coming that time to his senses, and signalled. The captain saw him, and said, "That must be a wild beast of some kind; hair is growing all over his body. Will some of you go to see what is there? If a man, bring him on board."

Five men rowed to land, and hailed Blaiman. He answered, "I am from Erin, and I am perishing here from hunger and cold." They took him on board. The captain treated him kindly, had his hair cut, and gave him good clothing. Where should the captain be sailing to but the very same port of his grandfather's kingdom from which Blaiman had sailed. There was a high tide when the ship neared, and they never stopped till she was in at the quay. Blaiman went on shore, walked to the chief street, and stood with his back to a house. Soon he saw men and horses carrying and drawing many kinds of provisions, and all going one way.

"Why are these people all going one way?" inquired Blaiman of a man in the crowd.

"You must be a stranger," answered the man, "since you do not know that they are going to the castle. The king's elder son will be married this evening. The bride is the only daughter of the King of the kingdom of the White Strand; they brought her to this place twelve months ago."

"I am a stranger," said Blaiman, "and have only come now from sea."

"All are invited to the wedding, high and low, rich and poor."

"I will go as well as another," said Blaiman;

and he went toward the castle.　He met a sturdy old beggar in a long gray coat.　"Will you sell me the coat?" inquired Blaiman.

"Take your joke to some other man," answered the beggar.

"I am not joking," said Blaiman.　"I 'll buy your coat."

The beggar asked more for the coat than he thought would be given by any one.

"Here is your money," said Blaiman.

The beggar gave up the coat, and started to go in another direction.

"Come back here," said Blaiman.　"I will do you more good, and I need your company."

They went toward the castle together.　There was a broad space in front of the kitchen filled with poor people, for the greater part beggars, and these were all fighting for places.　When Blaiman came, he commanded the crowd to be quiet, and threatened.　He soon controlled all, and was himself neither eating nor drinking, but seeing justice done those who were eating and drinking.　The servants, astonished that the great, threatening beggar was neither eating nor drinking, gave a great cup of wine to him.　He took a good draught of the wine, but left still a fair share in the cup.　In this he dropped the ring that he got from his wife in her own father's castle, and said to a servant, "Put this cup in the hand of the bride, and say, ' 'T is the big beggar that sends back this much of his wine, and asks you to drink to your own health.' "

She was astonished, and, taking the cup to the window, saw a ring at the bottom. She took the ring, knew it, and ran out wild with delight through the people. All thought 't was enchantment the beggar had used; but she embraced him and kissed him. The servants surrounded the beggar to seize him. The king's daughter ordered them off, and brought him into the castle; and Blaiman locked the doors. The bride then put a girdle around the queen's waist, and this was a girdle of truth. If any one having it on did not tell the truth, the girdle would shrink and tighten, and squeeze the life out of that person.

"Tell me now," said the bride, "who your elder son's father is."

"Who is he," said the queen, "but the king?"

The girdle grew tighter and tighter till the queen screamed, "The coachman."

"Who is the second son's father?"

"The butler."

"Who is your daughter's father?"

"The king."

"I knew," said the bride, "that there was no

kingly blood in the veins of the two, from the way that they treated my husband." She told them all present how the two had taken her away, and left her husband behind. When Blaiman's mother saw her son, she dropped almost dead from delight.

The king now commanded his subjects to bring poles and branches and all dry wood, and put down a great fire. The heads and heels of the queen's two sons were tied together, and they were flung in and burned to ashes.

Blaiman remained awhile with his grandfather, and then took his wife back to her father's kingdom, where they lived many years.

FIN MACCOOL AND THE DAUGHTER OF THE KING OF THE WHITE NATION.

ONE day Fin MacCool and the Fenians of Erin set out on a hunt from the Castle of Rahonain, and never stopped till they came near Brandon Creek, and started a hornless deer in a field called Parcnagri.

Over hills and through valleys they chased the deer till they came to Aun na Vian (the river of the Fenians). The deer sprang from one side of this river toward the other, but before reaching the bank was taken on a spear by Dyeermud.

When the hunt was over, Fin and the Fenians went back to the place where the deer had been started at Parcnagri, for they always returned to the spot where they roused the first game, and there they feasted.

The feast was nearly ready when Fin saw a boat sailing in toward the harbor of Ard na Conye (Smerwick Harbor), and no one on board but a woman.

"'T is a wonder to me," said Fin, "that one woman should manage a boat under sail on the sea. I have a great wish to know who that woman is."

"'T is not long I would be in bringing you tidings," said Dyeermud.

Fin laughed; for Dyeermud was fond of the women. "I would not refuse you permission to go, but that I myself will go, and be here before our feast is ready."

Fin went down from Parcnagri, and stood at the strand of Ard na Conye. Though great was his speed, the woman was there before him, and her boat anchored safely four miles from shore.

Fin saluted the woman with friendly greeting; and she returned the salute in like manner.

"Will you tell me, kind man, where I am now?" asked the woman.

"In the harbor of Ard na Conye."

"Thanks to you for that answer," said the woman. "Can you tell where is Fin MacCool's dwelling-place?"

"Wherever Fin MacCool's dwelling-place is, I am that man myself."

"Thanks to you a second time," said the woman; "and would you play a game of chess for a sentence?"

"I would," replied Fin, "if I had my own board and chessmen."

"I will give you as good as your own," said the woman.

"I have never refused, and never asked another to play," said Fin. "I will play with you."

They sat down, and Fin won the first game.

"What is your sentence, Fin MacCool?" asked the woman.

"I put you under bonds of heavy enchantment," said Fin, "not to eat twice at the one table, nor to sleep two nights in the one bed, till you bring a white steed with red bridle and saddle to me, and the same to each man of the Fenians of Erin."

"You are very severe, O Fin," said the woman. "I beg you to soften the sentence."

"No," answered Fin, "you must give what is asked; I will not soften the sentence."

"Look behind," said the woman.

Fin turned, and saw a white steed for himself, and the like for each man of the Fenians of Erin, all with red bridles and saddles.

"Play a second game, now," said the woman.

They played, and she won.

"Hasten, kind woman," said Fin, "and tell me the sentence."

"Too soon for you to hear it," said she.

"The sooner I hear it, the better," said Fin.

"I put you, O Fin, under bonds of heavy

enchantment to be my husband till a shovel puts seven of its fulls of earth on your head."

"Soften the sentence, good woman," said Fin; "for this cannot be."

"The gad may tighten on my throat if I do," said the woman; "for you did not soften your sentence on me."

"Do you stop here," said Fin to the woman, "till I give my men the steeds, tell them how I am, and return. But where are the steeds?"

"If I was bound by sentence to bring you the steeds, I was not bound to keep them."

Fin went his way to Parcnagri, where the Fenians were waiting, and though dinner was ready, no man tasted it from that day to this.

Fin posted his men on watch at various harbors, left Dyeermud on Beann Dyeermud (Dyeermud's peak), just above the harbor of Ard na Conye, and went to the woman. She took his hand; they sprang together, and came down in the woman's boat, which was four miles from land.

The woman weighed anchor, raised sails, and never stopped ploughing the weighty sea till she came to the White Nation in the Eastern World, where her father was king. She entered the harbor, cast anchor, and landed.

"When you were at home," said the woman to Fin, "you were Chief of the Fenians of Erin, and held in great honor; I will not that men in this kingdom belittle you, and I am the king's only daughter. From the place where we are standing to my father's castle there is a narrow and a short path. I 'll hasten forward on that. There is another way, a broad and long one; do you choose that. I fear that for you there will not be suitable seat and a place in the castle, unless I am there to prepare it before you."

Fin went the long way, and the woman took the short path. It was many a day since the woman had seen her own father. For twenty-one years she had travelled the world, learning witchcraft and every enchantment. She hurried, and was soon at the door of the castle. Great was the welcome before her, and loud was the joy of her father. Servants came running, one after another, with food, and one thing better than the other.

"Father," said she, "I will taste neither food nor drink till you tell me the one thing to please your mind most."

"My child," said the king, "you have but small chance of coming at that. The one thing on earth to delight my mind most is the head of Fin MacCool of Erin. If there was a poor man of my name, he would not be myself if I had that head."

"Many a year do I know your desire, my father; and it was not for me to come back after twenty-one years without bringing Fin's head. You have it now, without losing one drop of your blood or a single night's rest. Fin is coming hither over the broad road; and do you put men out over against him with music to meet him, and when he comes between your two store-houses, let the men dash him against one corner and the other, and give every reason worse than another to bring him to death."

The king obeyed his daughter, and sent out guards and musicians.

Fin, going over the broad road, saw men coming with music, and said to himself, "Great is my joy, or may be my sorrow, for I fear that my life will be ended in trouble."

The men received Fin with shouts, and, running up, pushed him from side to side till he was bruised and bleeding; then they brought him into the castle.

Glad was the king, and far was the laugh heard that he let out of himself at sight of Fin MacCool.

The king gave command then to bind the captive, putting seven knots of cord on every joint of his body, to throw him into a deep vault, and give him one ounce of black bread with a pint of cold water each day.

Fin was put in the vault, and a very old little woman brought his daily allowance of food.

On his eighth day in prison, Fin said to the old little woman, "Go now to the king, and say that I have a petition. I ask not my head, as I would not get it; but say that my right arm is rotting. I ask to be free in the garden for one hour; let him send with me men, if he chooses."

The old woman told the request; and the king said, "I will grant that with willingness; for it will not take his head from me."

Thirty armed men were sent, and Fin was set free in the garden. While walking, he asked the chief of the thirty, "Have you musical instruments?"

"We have not," said the chief; "we forgot them. If they were here, we would give music; for I pity you, Fin MacCool."

"When I was at home," said Fin, "having the care and charge over men, we had music; and, if it please you, I will play some of the music of Erin."

"I would be more than glad if you would do that," said the chief.

The Fenians of Erin had a horn called the

borabu; and when one of them went wandering
he took the borabu with him, as Fin had done
this time.   It was the only instrument on which
he could play.   Fin blew the horn, and the sound
of it came to Beann Dyeermud from the Eastern
World.   Dyeermud himself was in deep sleep at
the moment; but the sound entered his right ear
and came out through the left.   The spring that
he made then took him across seven ridges of
land before he was firm on his feet.   Dyeermud,
wiping his eyes, said, "Great is the trouble that
is on you, Fin; for the sound of the borabu has
never yet entered my right ear unless you were
in peril."

Then, going at a spring to Cuas a Wudig, he
found the remains of an old currachan, and, drawing out a chisel, knife, and axe, made a fine boat
of the old one.   With one kick of his right foot,
he sent the boat seven leagues from land, and, following with a bound, dropped into it.   He hoisted
sails, not knowing whither to go, north, south,
east, or west, but held on his way, and ploughed
the mighty ocean before him, till, as good luck
would have it, he reached the same harbor to
which the woman had come with Fin MacCool.

Dyeermud saw the boat which had brought
them, and said, laughing heartily, "I have tidings of Fin; he's in this kingdom in some place,

for this is the boat that brought him from
Erin."

Dyeermud cast anchor, and, landing, drew his
sword; and a man seeing his look at that moment
would have wished to be twenty miles distant.
On he went, walking, till he had passed through
a broad tract of country. On the high-road, he
saw men, women, and children all going one
way, and none any other. High and low, they
were hurrying and hastening; the man behind
outstripping the man in front.

Dyeermud sat on a ditch to rest, and soon a
wayfarer halted in front of him. "Where are
these people all hastening?" asked Dyeermud.

"From what country or place are you," asked
the man, "not to know whither all these people
are going?"

"Surely I am not of this place or your country," said Dyeermud; "and I care not to know
whither you or these people are going, since
you cannot give a civil answer to an honest
question."

"Be patient, good man," said the wayfarer.
"From what country or place are you?"

"From Erin," said Dyeermud.

"I suppose, then, you have known Fin Mac-
Cool, or have heard of him?"

"I have, indeed," said Dyeermud.

"If you take my advice," said the wayfaring man, "you'll go out on the same road by which you came in, or else not acknowledge Fin Mac-Cool of Erin, for that man will be hanged this day before the king's castle; the gallows is ready and built for him. When the life is gone out of him, his head will be struck off, and left as a plaything to please the king's mind forever. The body is to be dragged between four wild horses; and the same will be done to you, if you acknowledge Fin MacCool of Erin."

"I thank you for your answer," said Dyeermud; "and only because I don't like to lay a weighty hand on you, you would never again give advice like that to a man of the Fenians of Erin. But show me the way to the castle."

"If you were on the top of that mountain," said the wayfarer, pointing northward, "you would see the king's castle."

Dyeermud went on in strong haste, and from the mountain-top saw the king's castle. On the green field in front of it so many people had gathered to see Fin MacCool's death, that if a pin were to drop from the middle of the sky it could not fall without striking the head of man, woman, or child. When Dyeermud came down to the field, it was useless to ask for room or for passage, since each wished himself to be nearest the place of Fin's death. Dyeermud drew his sword; and as a mower goes through the grass of a meadow on a harvest day, or a hawk through a flock of starlings on a chilly March morning, so did Dyeermud cut his way through the crowd till he came to the gallows. He turned then toward the castle, struck the pole of combat, and far was the sound of his blow heard. The king put his head through the window.

"Who struck that blow?" asked the king. "He must be an enemy!"

"You could not expect a friend to do the like of that," replied Dyeermud. "I struck the blow."

"Who are you?" cried the king.

"My name when in Erin is Dyeermud."

"What brought you hither?" asked the king.

"I came," replied Dyeermud, "to succor my chief, Fin MacCool."

The king let a laugh out of him, and asked, "Have any more men come besides you?"

"When you finish with me, you may be looking for others," said Dyeermud.

"What do you want to-day?" asked the king.

"I want to see Fin MacCool, or to fight for him."

"Fight you may," said the king; "but see him you will not."

"Well," said Dyeermud, "it is too early in the evening for me to rest without having the blood of enemies on my sword, so send out against me seven hundred of your best-armed men on my right hand, seven hundred on my left, seven hundred behind me, and twenty one hundred before my eyesight."

Fin's death was delayed; and the men that he asked for put out against Dyeermud. Coming sunset, he had the last head cut from the last body, and, going through his day's work, made heaps of the bodies, and piles of the heads.

"Will you give me shelter from the night air?" asked Dyeermud, then turning to the castle.

"I will, and welcome," said the king, pointing to a long house at a distance.

Dyeermud went to the long house, and to his wonder saw there a troop of wild small men without faith, but no food, fire, or bed. These men were the agents of the king, who put to death all people who went against his law. Though a small race of people, they were strong through their numbers.

When Dyeermud entered, they rose, and began to fill every cranny and crack they could find in the building.

"Why are you doing that?" inquired Dyeermud.

"For fear that you might escape; for it 's our duty to eat you."

Dyeermud then seized by the ankles the one who gave him this answer, and flailed the others with this man, till he wore him down to the two shin-bones; all the others were killed saving one, who was chief. The small chief untouched by Dyeermud fell on his knees, and cried out, "Spare my head! O Dyeermud, there is not a place where you will put one foot, in which I will not put my two feet, nor a place on which you 'll put one hand, in which I will not put my two hands; and I can be a good servant to you."

"No man ever asked his head of me with peace, but I gave it to him," said Dyeermud.

Sitting down then, Dyeermud asked, "Have you any food?"

"I have not," said the small chief. "We have nothing to eat but men sent here from one time to another. If you go to the king's bakery, you may find loaves of bread."

Dyeermud went to the baker, and asked, "Will you give me two loaves of bread?"

"Hardened ruffian," said the baker, "how dare you come to this place for bread, or any other thing, you who killed so many of our friends and near neighbors? Go out of this, or I 'll burn you in the oven."

"I am thankful," said Dyeermud; "but before you can do to me what you threaten, I will do the same to you."

With that he opened the oven-door, threw in the baker, and burned him to death. Then he caught up as much bread as he could carry, and went to the long house; but, being used to good food, could not eat bread alone, and asked the small chief, "Where can I find drink and meat to go with the bread?"

"There is a slaughter-house behind us, not far from here," said the chief, "and the head butcher might give you a piece to roast or boil."

Dyeermud went then to the butcher. "Will you give me meat for supper?" asked he.

"You scoundrel from Erin, if you don't leave this place I 'll cut off your head on the block here, and separate it from the body."

"Never have I met better people to oblige a stranger; but before you can do to me what you promise, I will do the like to you."

So Dyeermud caught the butcher, stretched him across the block, and with the butcher's own cleaver struck the head off him.

Turning around, Dyeermud saw two fine stalled bullocks dressed for the king's table. Taking one under each arm, he brought them to the long house, and cut them up with his sword;

then the small chief cooked nicely what was needed. The two ate a hearty supper.

Next morning Dyeermud rose up refreshed, and went to the castle, where he struck the pole of combat.

"What is your wish?" asked the king.

"To see Fin MacCool, or get battle."

"How many men do you wish for?"

"One thousand of your best armed men on my right hand, as many on my left, as many behind me, and twice three thousand in front of my eyesight."

The champions were sent out to Dyeermud. They went at him, and he at them; they were that way all day, and when the sun was setting there was not a man of the nine thousand that had his head on him.

In the evening he made piles of the bodies and heaps of the heads.

Then he went back to the long house, and it was better there than the first night; the small chief had food and drink ready in plenty.

The combats continued for seven days in succession as on this day. On the eighth morning, when Dyeermud appeared, the king asked for a truce.

"I will grant it," said Dyeermud, "if you give me a sight of Fin MacCool."

"A sight of Fin MacCool you are not to have," said the king, "till you bring the hound-whelp with the golden chain."

"Where can I find that whelp?" inquired Dyeermud.

"The world is wide," said the king. "Follow your nose. It will lead you. If I were to say 't is in the west the whelp is, maybe 't is in the east he'd be; or in the north, maybe he'd be in the south. So here and now you cannot blame me if I say not where he is."

"Well," said Dyeermud, "as I am going for the whelp, I ask you to loose Fin MacCool from what bonds he is in, to place him in the best chamber of your castle, to give him the best food and drink, the best bed to lie on, and, besides, the amusements most pleasing to his mind."

"What you ask shall be granted," said the king, who thought to himself, "Your head and Fin's will be mine in the end."

Dyeermud went home to the long house, sat down in his chair, and gloomy was his face.

"O Dyeermud," said the small chief, "you are not coming in with such looks, nor so bright in the face, as when you left here this morning. I'll lay my head as a wager that you are sent to bring the hound-whelp with the golden chain."

"True," said Dyeermud, "and where to find him I know not."

"Eat your supper, then sleep, and to-morrow I'll show you where that whelp is. Indeed, it is the task you have on you; for many a good champion lost his head in striving to come at that whelp."

Next morning Dyeermud and the small chief set out, and toward evening they came within sight of a grand, splendid castle.

"Now," said the small chief, "this castle was built by the Red Gruagach Blind-on-One-Side; within is the hound-whelp with the golden chain; and now let me see what you'll do."

Dyeermud entered the castle, where he found a great chamber, and in it the gruagach asleep. The hound was tied to the gruagach's bed with a golden chain. Untying the chain from the bed, Dyeermud carried whelp and chain with him under his arm, and hurried on homeward. When he had gone three miles of road, he turned to the small chief and said, "That was a mean act I did to the gruagach."

"What's on you now?" asked the small chief.

"It would be hard for a man to call me anything higher than a thief; for I have only stolen the man's whelp and golden chain." So Dyeermud went back to the gruagach, and put the hound-whelp and chain where he had found them. As the gruagach was sleeping, Dyeermud struck a slight blow on his face to rouse him.

"Oh," said the gruagach, "I catch the foul smell of a man from Erin. He must be Dyeermud, who has destroyed the champions of our country."

"I am the man that you mention," said Dyeermud; "and I am not here to ask satisfaction of you or thanks, but to wear out my anger on your body and flesh, if you refuse what I want of you."

"And what is it that you want of me?" asked the gruagach.

"The hound-whelp with the golden chain."

"You will not get him from me, nor will another."

"Be on your feet, then," said Dyeermud. "The whelp is mine, or your head in place of him; if not, you'll have my head."

One champion put his back to the front wall, and the other to the rear wall; then the two went at each other wrestling, and were that way till the roof of the house was ready to fly from the walls, such was the strength in the hands of the combatants.

"Shame on you both!" cried the gruagach's wife, running out. "Shame on two men like you to be tumbling the house on my children."

"True," said Dyeermud. And the two, without letting go the hold that they had, went through the roof with one bound, and came down on the field outside. The first wheel that Dyeermud knocked out of the gruagach, he put him in the hard ground to his ankles, the second to his hips, and the third to his neck.

"Suffer your head to be cut off, O gruagach."

"Spare me, Dyeermud, and you'll get the hound-whelp with the golden chain, and my good wish and desire."

"If you had said that at first, you would not have gone through this hardship or kindled my anger," said Dyeermud. With that he pulled out the gruagach, and spared his head.

The two spent that night as two brothers, eating and drinking of the best, and in the morning the gruagach gave Dyeermud the whelp with the golden chain.

Dyeermud went home with the small chief, and went to the castle next morning.

"Have you brought the hound-whelp with the golden chain?" asked the king.

"I have," answered Dyeermud; "and I had no trouble in bringing them. Here they are before you."

"Well, am I to have them now?" asked the king.

"You are not," answered Dyeermud. "If I was bound to bring them, I was not bound to give them to you. The man who reared this whelp has a better right to him than you or I."

Then Dyeermud went home to the long house, followed by the small chief; and the next morning he asked battle of the king.

"I am not ready for battle to-day," said the king.

"Am I to get sight of Fin MacCool?" inquired Dyeermud.

"You are not," said the king, "till you bring me an account of how the Rueful Knight Without-Laughter lost his eye and his laugh."

"Where can I find that knight?" asked Dyeermud.

"The world is wide," said the king; "and it is for you alone to make out where that man is."

Dyeermud went home to the long house, sat in his chair, dropped his head, and was gloomy.

"O Dyeermud," said the small chief, "something has gone wrong to-day, and I'll lay my head that you are sent to get knowledge of the Rueful Knight Without-Laughter; but sit down and take supper, then sleep, and to-morrow you'll not go astray; I'll lead you to where that man lives."

Next morning the two set out together, and
that evening reached the gruagach's castle, where
there was many a welcome before them, and not
like the first time. The whelp was returned to
his owner; and that night was spent in pleasure
by the gruagach, Dyeermud, and the small
chief.

The next morning Dyeermud went forward
attended by his two friends, and toward evening
came in sight of a large splendid castle. Dyeermud approached it, and when he went in, saw
that he had never before set foot in a grander
building.

The Rueful Knight Without-Laughter was
sitting alone in his parlor at a great heavy table.
His face, resting on the palm of one hand, was
worn by it; his elbow, placed on the table, had
worn a deep trench in the table; and there he
sat, trusting to the one eye that was left him.

Dyeermud shook the sleeping man gently; and
when he woke, the knight welcomed Dyeermud
as one of the Fenians of Erin. Dinner was made
ready for all; and when they sat down at the
table, Dyeermud thrust his fork in the meat as a
sign of request. "Is there something you wish
to know?" asked the knight.

"There is," answered Dyeermud.

"All in my power or possession is for you,

except one thing," said the knight, "and ask not for that."

"It is that thing that brought me," said Dyeermud. "I 'll take no refusal. I 'll have your head or that knowledge."

"Well, Dyeermud, eat your dinner, and then I will tell you; though I have never told any one yet, not even my own lawful wife."

When the dinner was over, the knight told his story to Dyeermud, as follows, —

"I was living once in this place here, both happy and well. I had twelve sons of my own and my own wife. Each of my twelve sons had his pack of hounds. I and my wife had one pack between us. On a May morning after breakfast, I and my sons set out to hunt. We started a deer without horns, and, rushing forward in chase of her, followed on swiftly all day. Toward evening the deer disappeared in a cave. In we raced after her, and found ourselves soon in the land of small men, but saw not a trace of the deer.

"Going to a great lofty castle, we entered, and found many people inside. The king of the small men bade us welcome, and asked had I men to prepare us a dinner. I said that I had my own twelve sons. The small men then brought in from a forest twelve wild boars. I put down twelve kettles with water to scald and dress the

game. When the water was boiling, it was of
no use to us; and we could not have softened
with it one bristle on the wild boars from that
day to this. Then a small man, putting the
twelve boars in a row with the head of one near
the tail of the other, took from the hall-door a
whistle, and, blowing first on one side of the
row and then on the other, made all the twelve
white and clean; then he dressed, cut, and cooked
them, and we all ate to our own satisfaction.

"In the course of the evening, the king of the
small men asked had I any one who could shorten
the night by showing action. I said that I had
my own twelve sons. Twelve small men now
rose, and drew out a long weighty chain, holding
one end in their hands. My sons caught the
other end, pulled against the twelve small men,
and the small men against them; but the small
men soon threw a loop of the chain around the
necks of my twelve sons, and swept the heads off
them; one of the small men came then with a
long knife, and, opening the breasts of my sons,
took out their twelve hearts, and put them all on
a dish; then they pushed me to a bench, and I had
to sit with my twelve sons stretched dead there
before me. Now they brought the dish to make
me eat the twelve hearts for my supper. When
I would not, they drove them down my throat,

and gave me a blow of a fist that knocked one eye out of me. They left me that way in torment till morning; then they opened the door, and threw me out of the castle.

"From that day to this I have not seen my children, nor a trace of them; and 't is just twenty-one years, coming May-day, since I lost my twelve sons and my eye. There is not a May-day but the deer comes to this castle and shouts, ' Here is the deer; but where are the hunters to follow?   Now you have the knowledge, Dyeermud, of how I lost my eye and my laugh."

"Well," asked Dyeermud, "will May-day come soon in this country? "

" To-morrow, as early as you will rise."

"Is there any chance that the deer will come in the morning? "

"There is," said the knight; "and you 'll not have much of the morning behind you when she 'll give a call."

Next morning the deer shouted, "Here is the deer; but where are the hunters to follow?" and made away swiftly.

Dyeermud, the small chief, the gruagach, and the knight hurried on in pursuit.   Coming evening, the knight saw the cave, and called out to Dyeermud, "Have a care of that place; for 't is there she will enter."

When the deer reached the cave, Dyeermud gave a kick with his right foot, and struck off one half her hind-quarter.

Barely was this done, when out rushed a dreadful and ugly old hag, with every tooth in her upper jaw a yard long, and she screaming, "You hungry, scorched scoundrel from Erin, how dared you ruin the sport of the small men?"

The words were hardly out of her mouth, when Dyeermud made at her with his fist, and sent jaws and teeth down her throat. What the old hag did not swallow, went half a mile into the country behind her.

The hag raced on through the land of the small men, and Dyeermud with his forces made after her. When they came to the castle, the king let a loud laugh out of him.

"Why do you give such a laugh?" inquired Dyeermud.

"I thought that the knight had enough the first time he came to this castle."

"This proves to you that he had not," said Dyeermud; "or he would not be in it the second time."

"Well," asked the king of the knight, "have you any man now to cook dinner?"

"He has," said Dyeermud; "and it's long

since you or he had the like of him.   I 'll cook
your dinner, and we 'll find the food."

Out they went to a forest, and brought in
twelve wild boars.   Dyeermud skinned the game
with his sword, dressed, cut, and cooked it.   All
ate to satisfaction.

Later on in the evening, the king asked the
knight, "Have you any man to show action?"

"He has," said Dyeermud, "if you will put
out the same twelve men as you did the first
evening."

The king put them out; and Dyeermud took
the end of the chain to pull against them.   He
pulled till he sank in the floor to his ankles; then
he made a whirl of the chain, and swept their
twelve heads off the small men.   He opened the
twelve, put their hearts on a plate, and made the
king eat them.   "You forced the knight to swallow the hearts of his own sons," said Dyeermud.

"Walk out of the castle, and punish us no
more," cried the king.   "I 'll let out to the
knight his sons, with their horses and hounds,
and his own horse and hounds, if you will not
come to this kingdom again."

"We will go if you do that," said Dyeermud;
"but you are not to offend the knight or his
people; if you do, I am a better guide to find you
a second time than I was the first."

The king took his rod of enchantment, went out to twelve stones, struck the first, out came the first son on horseback, and a pack of hounds after him. The king struck stone after stone till he put the twelve sons in front of the castle, with their horses and hounds; then he struck the thirteenth stone, and the horse and hounds of the knight appeared.

The knight looked around, and saw his eye in the hole of the chimney, and as much soot on it as would manure land under two stone of seed-potatoes.

"Look at my eye," said the knight.

Dyeermud looked. Then the king put the eye in the head of the knight, who could see with it better than when he had it before.

Out they went now from the king, safe and sound, and never stopped till they reached the knight's castle for dinner. When dinner was over, Dyeermud, the gruagach, and the small chief hastened on to the gruagach's castle, and slept there.

Next day Dyeermud and the small chief went home. On the following morning, Dyeermud went to the king, told him the Rueful Knight's story, and said, "Now I must have battle, or a sight of Fin MacCool."

"Battle I'll not give you," said the king; "and

a sight of Fin MacCool you 'll not have till you tell me what happened to the Lad of True Tales."

"I am sorry," said Dyeermud, "that this was not said by you sooner. It is late for me now to be tearing my shoes on strange roads, and tiring my feet in a foreign land." With that he sprang at the king, brought him down by the throat from the window to the ground, and there broke every bone in his body. Then he put the castle foundation upward, looking for Fin, and destroying all that he met, but could not find Fin till he met the old little woman.

"O Dyeermud," said she, "spare my head. I am more than a hundred years old. I have been faithful to Fin since he came here. I have never refused to do what he asked of me."

"Your head shall be spared," replied Dyeermud, "though old life is as dear to you as it is to young people; and take me now to where Fin is."

Dyeermud went with the old little woman to the door of Fin's chamber, and knocked. Fin knew the knock, and cried out, "Reach me your sword."

"Take it," said Dyeermud.

Fin's strength was trebled at sight of Dyeermud; and when he grasped the sword, he swore by it, saying, "I will cut off your head if you come a foot nearer."

"You are not in your mind to speak thus to the man who has gone through so much for you."

"I am in my mind," said Fin; "but if we were to close our arms embracing each other in friendship, we could not open them for seven days and nights. Now, the woman who brought me from Ard na Conye, the bay which we love most in Erin, save Fintra, will be here soon. Though there was nothing on earth to please the King of the White Nation more than my head, there is another good man in the world, and the king wishes his head as greatly as mine. The daughter has gone, and is using her highest endeavor to bring that head to her father; so hasten on to the boat, Dyeermud, I will follow. If you find food, take it with you."

Dyeermud hurried off. In passing through the king's meadow he saw two fat bullocks grazing. He caught them, and, clapping one under each arm, ran off to the boat. When Fin came, he found both bullocks skinned and dressed there before him.

They weighed anchor now. and raised sails for Erin, ploughing the weighty sea before them night and day. Once Fin said to Dyeermud, "Look behind." Dyeermud looked, but saw nothing.

Three hours later, Fin said, "Look behind, and look keenly."

Dyeermud looked, and cried, "I see behind us in the sky some bird like an eagle, and flashes of fire blazing out from her beak."

"Oh, we are caught at last, and it 's a bad place we are in on the sea; we cannot fight here."

The bird was coming nearer, and gaining; but the wind favored, filled every sail, and sent them bounding along till they were within five leagues of land; then they made one spring, and came down in Ferriter's Cove.

No sooner had they landed, than the bird perched on the boat, turned it over, stood on the bottom, and from that saw Fin and Dyeermud on land. She made for them; and the moment she touched shore became a woman.

She rushed to Fin, caught him in her arms most lovingly, and said, turning to Dyeermud, "You are the wicked man who put words between me and my husband and parted us."

Then, turning to Fin, she said, "Now, my darling, come home with me. You will be King of the White Nation, and I, your loving wife."

"Right and true for you," said Dyeermud. "It 's the good wife and friend you were to this man; and now I ask how long must he be your husband?"

"Till a shovel puts seven of its fulls of earth on his head."

Dyeermud drew his sword, and struck a champion's blow on a ridge of land that was near him; he was so enraged that he made a deep glen with that blow; then he caught Fin, and, stretching him in the glen, thrust his sword in the earth, and, throwing it as with a shovel on Fin, counted one, two, three, four, five, six, seven. "Your time is up with Fin," said he to the king's daughter; "he is in his own country, and you are a stranger. Take him a second time if you can, and I pledge you the faith of a champion that I will not put words between you."

The woman stooped down to put away the seven shovels of earth, and said to Fin while she was working, "We'll both be happy this time."

With that Dyeermud gave her one blow of his fist on the left ear, and sent her spinning through the air. She never stopped till she fell at the edge of the ocean, and became Fail Mahisht; and not another cliff in Erin has so many limpets and periwinkles on it as that one.

So the daughter of the King of the White Nation gives much food to people in Erin from that day to this.

FIN MACCOOL, THE THREE GIANTS, AND THE SMALL MEN.

ON a day of the days when Fin MacCool was living at Rahin, he went out to walk near Fintra. He had many cows and sheep at that time, and was going among his cattle, when all at once he saw a big man coming in from the sea.

At first he saw the man's head and shoulders, then half his body, and at last his whole body. When the big man stood on the strand, he saluted Fin. Fin returned the salute, and asked, "Who are you, and what brought you to Erin?"

"I have come from the King of the Big Men; and I want to see Fin MacCool."

"Fin MacCool is not at home now," said Fin. "Are you here with a message?"

"I am," said the big man.

"I will give the message to Fin MacCool when he comes home; there is no one he trusts more than me."

"My master, the King of the Big Men, has heard much of Fin MacCool, and invites him to come to his castle. The king lost two children. Some one came in the night and stole them. Though guarded with wonderful strictness, the children were carried away. The king fears to lose a third child soon, unless Fin MacCool comes to advise and assist him."

"I will give that message to Fin MacCool," said Fin.

The big man left good health with Fin, then turned and went forward, going deeper till his head disappeared under water.

A few days later Fin was walking in the same place where he had met the messenger from the King of the Big Men, and he saw some very small men playing hurley on the strand. He went to them, and spoke. They answered, and called him King of the Fenians.

"You seem to know me," said Fin.

"We do indeed, and we know you very well," said the small men.

"Who are you?" asked Fin, "or what can you do?"

"Oh, we have many virtues," replied they.

"What virtue have you?" asked Fin, turning to the biggest of the small men.

"Well, whenever I sit down in any place I stay in it as long as I like; no man can lift me; no power can take me out of it."

"What is your name?" asked Fin.

"Lazy Back," said the little fellow. "No man can stir me when I sit down."

"How am I to know that you have that virtue?" asked Fin.

"You are a strong man yourself," answered Lazy Back; "give me a trial."

The little man sat down. Fin caught him with one hand, and tried to raise him; but not a stir could he take out of Lazy Back.

"Try with both hands now," said Lazy Back.

Fin tried with both hands, tried with all the strength that was in him, but could not move the little man.

"What is your virtue?" asked Fin, turning to the second man; "and who are you?"

"My name is Hearing Ear."

"What can you hear?"

"I can hear a whisper in the Eastern World, and I sitting in this place."

"What is your name?" asked Fin of the third player.

"My name is Far Feeler."

"What can you feel?" asked Fin.

"I can feel an ivy-leaf falling at the Eastern World, and I playing here at Fintra."

"What is your name?" asked Fin, turning to the fourth player.

"My name is Knowing Man."

"What do you know?"

"I know all that will happen in every part of the world."

"What power have you, and who are you?" asked Fin of the fifth man.

"I am called Always Taking; I steal."

"What can you steal?"

"Whatever I set my mind on. I can steal the eggs from a snipe, and she sitting on them; and the snipe is the wariest bird in existence."

"What can you do?" asked Fin, looking at the sixth man.

"My name is Climber. I can climb the highest castle in the world, though its sides were as slippery as glass."

"Who are you?" asked he of the seventh stranger.

"I am called Bowman."

"What can you do?"

"I can hit any midge out of a cloud of midges dancing in the air."

"You have good eyesight," said Fin, "and good aim as well.

"Who are you?" asked Fin of the eighth.

"I am called Three Sticks. I understand woodwork."

"What can you do?" asked Fin.

"I can make anything I please out of wood."

"Can you make a ship?"

"I can."

"How long would it take you to make one?"

"While you would be turning on your heel."

He took a chip of wood then from the shore, and asked Fin to turn on his heel. While Fin was turning, Three Sticks flung the piece of wood out on the sea, and there it became a beautiful ship.

"Well, have you the ship made?" ased Fin, looking on the strand.

"There it is," said Three Sticks, "floating outside."

Fin looked, and saw the finest vessel that ever sailed on the deep sea; the butt of no feather was in, nor the tip of one out, except one brown-backed red feather that stood at the top of the mast, and that making music and sport to encourage whatever champion would come on board.

"Will you all take service with me?" asked Fin, looking at the eight small strangers. "I wish to go to the kingdom of the Big Men. Will you guide me on the journey, and help me?"

"We are willing to serve you," answered they. "There is no part of the world to which we cannot guide you."

"What are your wages?" asked Fin.

"Five gold-pieces to each man of us for a day and a year."

"How much time do we need for the journey to the kingdom of the Big Men?"

"Not many days," said Knowing Man.

Stores and provisions were put on the ship. Fin and the small men went on board, and set sail; before many days they arrived at the kingdom of the Big Men, and drew up their ship high and dry. They set out then for the castle of the king; and no greater wonder was ever seen in that place than Fin and his eight little men.

The king invited Fin and his company to a great feast. At the end of the feast, the king said, "My third son was born to-day. My first son was taken away on the night after his birth, and so was my second. I am full sure that this one will be taken from me to-night."

"I will guard the child," said Fin; "and if I let your son go with any one, I will give you my head."

The king was satisfied. Fin asked for a strong chamber and two nurses. The strongest chamber in the castle was made ready; then Fin and his men, with the child and two nurses, took their places inside.

"Do you know what will happen to-night?" asked Knowing Man.

"I do not," replied Fin; "and I do not like to chew my thumb.[1] You can tell me."

"You gave your head in pledge," said Knowing Man, "for the safety of the child; and you were a strange man to do so, for the child will be taken from this to-night."

"Do you say that?" asked Fin.

" I do. And do you know who will do it? "

" I do not."

"I will tell you. In the Eastern World lives a sister of this king, a savage hag and a terrible witch. This hag went to the Eastern World because she had a dispute with her brother. She is ungrateful, and full of malice; she comes now and steals away her brother's children to leave him without heirs to his kingdom. When she finds this room closed on every side, and sees no other way of reaching the child, she will climb to the roof, and stretch her arm down to catch the king's little son, and take him away with her."

Lazy Back sat down near the hearth, and swore a great oath that if the hag thrust her hand down, he would hold her or keep the hand.

---

[1] Fin's wisdom came in each case from chewing his thumb, which he pressed once on the Salmon of Knowledge. An account of this is given in a tale in my "Myths and Folk-Lore of Ireland," p. 211.

A little after midnight, Hearing Ear said, "I hear the hag; she is making ready to leave her castle in the Eastern World, and giving strict orders to guard the two children while she is gone."

"Well," said Far Feeler, "now I feel her going up through her own castle; now I feel her going out through the door on the roof. Her castle has no entrance except an opening in the roof, and the walls of it are as slippery as glass."

"You will warn me when she is coming," said Fin to Hearing Ear.

"Oh, I will," said Hearing Ear; "I will not forget that."

In a little while the hag was at the castle, and going around it trying to enter. Although the castle was surrounded by sentries, not one of them saw her; for she was invisible, through power of enchantment.

"She has come," said Hearing Ear; "she is walking around the castle. Now is the time to watch her well."

A few moments later, she thrust her arm down the chimney; and no sooner was it down than Lazy Back caught her hand. When she felt her hand caught, she struggled greatly; but Lazy Back kept the hold that he had, and nothing could stir him. At last the arm left the shoulder of the hag. Lazy Back drew the arm down the chimney. All looked at it with amazement; and while the nurses were wondering at the arm, and Fin measuring its length and its thickness, they forgot the child. The hag thrust her other arm down then, caught the child, and hurried away home with it. When the nurses saw that the child was gone, they screamed; and Fin said, —

"It would be better for us to hurry to our vessel, and leave the country before the king is up in the morning; he will destroy us all for losing his son."

"We will not do that," said the little men. "Late as it is, we will follow the hag, and bring back the child."

They set out that moment; and since Fin could not keep up with the little men, Lazy Back took him on his shoulder: and, in the twinkle of an eye, they reached the ship, and set sail for the Eastern World.

Indeed, they were not long on the journey; for they were enchanted. When they came to land near the hag's castle, Fin, Bowman, and two others remained on the vessel. Climber, Thief, and the rest went for the child.

"Where are you, Climber?" asked Thief, when they were at the wall.

"Here," said Climber.

"Take me to the top of the castle."

Climber took Thief on his back, and climbed like a butterfly to the top of the building; then Thief crept down into the castle, and returned quickly with the youngest of the children.

"Take this one down to our comrades, and hurry back to me."

Climber went down, and hastened up again. Thief had another of the children at the top of the castle before him. Climber took that down, with orders from Thief to carry the two children to the vessel. Then he returned a third time, and Thief had the third child.

"Take this one, and come for me," said Thief.

The little men at the foot of the castle ran off to the ship with the last child. Nimble as Thief was, he could not have taken the children at another time. All the servants were busied with the hag, who was suffering terribly from the loss of her arm. They forgot the children for a short time.

Climber took Thief to the ground, and they started at full speed toward the ship. When they came, Fin set sail for the kingdom of the Big Men.

"We shall be pursued right away," said Knowing Man. "If the hag comes up with the ship, she will destroy every man of us."

"She will not," said Bowman. "If I get one glimpse of that hag, I will put an end to her life; and do you listen, Hearing Ear, to know is she coming, and tell me when you hear her."

"I hear her now," said Hearing Ear. "She is raging, and she is cursing those who were minding the children, and let them be taken. Now she is leaving the castle; now she is racing on after us."

"Tell us, Far Feeler, when she is coming near," said Fin.

"She is making a terrible uproar," said Hearing Ear.

"She is coming toward us. She is very near," said Far Feeler.

Bowman saw her, rested his bow on the shoulder of another, aimed, and sent an arrow through the one eye in the middle of the hag's forehead. She fell flat on the sea, and lay dead there. Fin and his small men moved forward swiftly to the castle. They arrived one hour before the end of night, and from that time till day-break there was joy in the chamber. The small men and the two children of the king were playing together and enjoying themselves. Just before day, the king sent a servant to know what had happened in the chamber where his son was. The man could not enter, for they would not let him; but he looked through the keyhole. He went back then, and said to the king, —

"They seem to be very merry inside; and there are two lads in the room bigger than any of the small men."

The king knew they would not be merry unless the child was there. What he did was to throw on his mantle, and go himself to see. He knocked at the door.

"Who is there?" asked Fin.

"I, — the king."

The door was thrown open, and in walked the king. He saw the child in the cradle; but what was his wonder when he saw the other two. Without saying a word, he seized Fin's hand and shook it; and then he thanked him.

"There are your other two children," said Fin; "and do you know who stole them?"

"I do not."

"I will tell you," said Fin. "Have you a sister?"

"I had," answered the king, "but we became enemies; and I know not where she is at this moment."

Then Fin told everything that had happened in the night. "And now you have your three sons," said he to the king.

The king made a feast, which lasted seven days

and seven nights. Never had there been such a feast in the kingdom of the Big Men as that; and sure why not, for was n't it a great thing for the king to have his three sons home with him? When the feast was over, the king sent his men to carry all kinds of riches and treasures to Fin's ship; and for three days they were carrying them. At parting, the king said to Fin, "If ever you need my assistance, you have only to send for it."

Fin and his men sailed homeward then swiftly; and it was not long till they reached Fintra. The ship was unloaded; and Fin was glad, looking at his treasures, and thinking of his adventures in the land of the Big Men.

Some time after Fin had come from the land of the Big Men, he sent warriors to the chief ports of Erin to guard against enemies. One day his face was anxious and gloomy.

"You seem to be grieving," said Dyeermud; "you would better tell us what trouble is on you."

"Some trouble is near me," said Fin.

"By my hand," said Oscar, "if you do not tell me your trouble, I will not eat one morsel to-day."

"Trouble is near me; but I know not yet what it is."

"Chew your thumb then," said Oscar.

Fin chewed his thumb from the flesh to the bone, from the bone to the marrow, from the marrow to the quick, and found out that there were three giants in the Eastern World who were coming to attack himself and his forces, drive them into the sea like sheep, and leave not a man of them living.

Fin knew not what to do; and he was in great grief that there should be three men who could invade all Erin, and destroy its defenders.

"Chew your thumb a second time," said Oscar, "to know is there any way to conquer them. We have travelled the world, and no people have the upper hand of us so far. There must be arms against these three."

Fin chewed his thumb the second time; and the knowledge he got was this, that fire would not burn, water would not drown, swords would not cut either of the three giants. There was nothing to kill them but three things which their father had at home in the Eastern World; and if they saw those three things, they would fall dead, and dissolve into three heaps of jelly. What the three things were, was not told. "Go now," said Fin to Dyeermud, "and find the forces, and I will watch myself for the enemy."

Next morning Fin took his sword under his

arm, went to Fintra, and began to herd bullocks. He did this for some time, till one day above another he saw three giants coming in toward him, the water not past their hips. He was n't long waiting when they came near the cliff where he was; and he saw their hearts, their mouths were stretched open so widely, laughing at the boy herding the cattle.

"Where is Fin MacCool and his forces?" asked one of the giants.

"Well," said Fin, "it is not for me to tell you where Fin MacCool is; I am only his herder. But is there anything in the world to kill you? It must be there is not, and ye to have the courage to face Fin MacCool and his forces; for no people in the world have ever yet beaten them in battle."

"We have come to Erin," said the giants, "to find Fin MacCool; and we will drive him and his forces into the sea, like sheep from the side of a mountain. Fire cannot burn us; swords do not cut us; and water will not drown us. Nothing in the world can cause our death but our own three caps; and where they are, neither you nor Fin will ever know."

"How am I to know," asked the herdsman, "that fire will not burn you, or water drown you, or swords cut you? Let me give you a blow; and I 'll know will swords cut you."

"Oh, little man," said one of the giants, "how could you reach us with a sword?"

"I will show you a place," said Fin, "where I may be strong enough to give a blow ye would remember."

He led the giants to a narrow place between two cliffs, and stood himself on the top of one cliff. He gave then a terrible blow of his sword to the head of one giant, but left not a sign of blood on him.

"By my hand!" said the giant, "if every warrior in Fin MacCool's forces is as good at the sword as you, he need not be in dread of any men but us."

Fin gave the second giant a terrible blow, and staggered him.

"Oh!" said the giant, "no man ever gave me the like of that."

He struck the third giant a blow, and knocked him to his knees; but not a drop of blood came.

"Such a blow as that," said the giant, "I never got from any man before. Now, how are you to know that water will not drown us?"

"There is a place which I will show you," said Fin. "If ye sleep in it to night, and rise up in the morning before me, I shall know that water does not drown you."

Fin showed a place where the water was twenty

fathoms deep. The three lay down together under the water to stay till next morning. Fin hurried home then, gathered the Fenians together, and said, —

"I am in dread that these are the right giants. I knocked one trial out of them; swords will not cut them. They are sleeping to-night under twenty fathoms of water; but I am full sure that they will rise from it healthy and sound in the morning. Now, be ready, all of you, to scatter and go here and there throughout Erin. To-morrow, I am to try will fire burn them; when I know that, I will tell you what to do."

The following morning, Fin went to where the giants had spent the night, and whistled. The three rose up to him at once, and came to land.

"Now," said the eldest, as he looked around and saw the cattle, "a bite to eat would not harm us."

With that he faced one of the bullocks, and caught the beast by one horn.

"Leave him," said Fin; "you have no call to that bullock."

Fin caught the bullock by the other horn. The giant pulled, and Fin held his own. One pulled, the other pulled, till between them they split the bullock from his muzzle to the tip of his tail, and made two equal parts of him.

" 'T is a deal for me to have this much itself," said Fin. "I have saved half of my master's property. If ye want food, ye will get it at Fin's house. I will show the way; but first let me see will fire burn you."

"Very well; we will make a great fire, and go into it; we 'll stay in the fire till the wood is burned down, and then rise out of it as well as ever."

There were many trees in the country at that time. The giants and Fin were not long making a great pile of dry limbs and logs. When the pile was finished, the giants sat on the top of it, and Fin brought fire. The flames rose as high as the tree-tops.

" 'T is too hot here for me," said Fin.

"This is pleasant for us," said the giants; and they laughed as Fin went from the heat.

Fin could not come within ten perches of the fire. It burned all day, and the blaze of it was seen all the following night. In the afternoon of the next day, the pile had burned down, and the three giants were sitting at their ease on the hot coals.

"Fire does not harm us; you see that," said the giants.

"I do, indeed," said Fin; "and now ye may go to Fin's house for refreshment."

Fin showed them a long road, hurried home

himself by a short one, and gave command to the Fenians to scatter through Erin, and escape. Then, turning to his mother, he said, "Make three cakes for the gaints, put iron griddles in the middle of them, and bake them a little in the ashes. You will give these to the giants to eat. You will say that they are soft, not well baked; that we complain when the bread is not hard. I will lie down in the dark corner, in that big box there. Do you bind my head and face with a cloth, and say, when the giants are eating, 'This poor child is sick; I think his teeth are coming.'"

The old woman put three cakes in the ashes, and the griddles inside in them. When the giants came, the cakes were ready, and the old woman was sitting near the cradle.

"Is this Fin MacCool's house?" asked the giants.

"It is," said the old woman.

"And is Fin himself in the house?"

"He is not then," said the old woman; "and it is seldom he is in it."

"Have you any food to give us?"

"I have nothing but three loaves of bread; ye may have these, and welcome."

"Give us the bread," said the giants.

The old woman put the cakes on the table.

One took a bite, another took a bite, then the third took a bite; and they all looked at one another.

"I know ye think the bread too soft," said Fin's mother. "The Fenians always blame me for making it too soft; and these cakes are not baked very well. They are softer than the usual bread of the Fenians."

From shame, the giants ate the cakes, griddles and all. "Well," muttered they, "to say that men would eat the like of that bread, and call it too soft! It is no wonder that they walked the world without finding their equals."

"What exercise do the Fenians have after meals?" asked the giants.

"There is a stone outside," said the old woman, "which they throw over the house. They throw the stone, run in one door, run out the door opposite, and catch the stone before it comes to the earth."

One giant caught the stone, but did not throw it. "What is that?" said the other, running up and lifting the stone. To show his power, he threw it over the house, ran through both doors, and caught it coming down. The same giant threw the stone back again, and left it in its old place. Each of the others then did the same as the first. The life came near leaving Fin when he heard the giants throwing the stone, and racing to catch it. He was in dread they'd make bits of the house, and kill his old mother and himself.

"Oh, then," said the giants, when they left the stone, "it is no wonder that other people get no hand of the Fenians."

"Well, old woman," said the eldest giant, "what is that you have there in the dark corner?"

"My grandson, and it is sick and peevish he is."

"I suppose the child is getting his teeth?" said the giant.

"Indeed, then, I don't know," said the old woman; "but maybe it is the teeth that are troubling him."

With that the eldest giant walked up to the cradle, and put his finger in the child's mouth; but if he did, Fin took two joints off his finger with a bite.

"Oh!" said the giant, "if the child grows like that till he is a man, he will be the greatest champion in the world. To say that a child could take the finger off me, and he in the cradle!"

Away went the giants; and when they were gone, Fin called his eight small men, and hurried to the ship. They hoisted sails, and away they went. They raised gravel from the bottom of the sea, and put the foam of the waves in the place of the gravel; and with every bound the ship made, she went forward ten leagues. Never before did a ship cross the water so swiftly; and Fin never stopped till he anchored in the Eastern World. He put the fastenings of a day and a year on the ship, though he might not be absent one hour, and went away with his men. They were going on and travelling, and where did they come at last but to the castle of the old King of the Eastern World, the father of the three giants. The old king laughed when he saw Fin and the eight small men with him.

"In what part of the world do such people live, and where are you going?" asked the king. "You would better stay with me till my three sons come home."

"Where are your sons?" asked Fin.

"They are in Erin. They went to that country to bring me the head of Fin MacCool, and to drown all his forces in the deep ocean."

"They must be great men," said Fin, "to go against Fin MacCool, and to think of drowning his forces, and bringing Fin's head to you. Do you know that no man ever got the better of Fin, or made any hand of the Fenians of Erin?"

"My sons are not like others," said the king; "but will you stay with me?"

"I will," said Fin, "and why not?"

The old king was very fond of amusement; and after a while Fin told what a wonderful archer one of his little boys was. The king appointed a day for a trial of skill in archery. All the greatest marksmen in the Eastern World were invited.

"Where does the king keep his sons' three caps?" asked Fin of Knowing Man.

"There is a secret chamber in the castle; no one here but the king knows where it is. In that chamber are the caps. The king always keeps the key of that chamber in his pocket."

"You must show the chamber to Thief, to-morrow," said Fin.

Next day, while the king was looking at the archery, and wondering at the skill of Bowman, who sent an arrow through the two eyes of a bird on the wing, Thief stole the key, and Knowing Man showed the secret chamber.

Thief stole the three caps, and gave them to Fin. Lazy Back ran for Bowman; and all were soon on the ship sailing for Erin as swiftly as they had come.

When the ship was near land in Erin, what should Fin see but all the Fenians coming down from the hill-tops, and the three giants behind, driving them toward the water? He went to the top of the mast then, and raised the three caps on three sticks.

The giants looked at the vessel sailing in, and saw their own caps. That moment there was neither strength nor life left in them. They fell to the ground, and turned into three heaps of jelly. Fin had come just in season to rescue his forces; in another half hour, he would not have found a man of the Fenians alive in Erin.

"Oh, but you are here in time!" said Oscar.

"I am," said Fin; "and it is well for you that I was able to come."

Fin and the Fenians had a great feast in Rahin, and a joyful night of it; and no wonder, for life is sweet.

Next day the time of the small men was out; and Fin went to the strand with them.

"I will pay you your wages to day," said Fin. "To each man five gold-pieces. I am willing and glad to give more; for ye were the good servants to me."

"We want nothing but our wages," said the small men.

Fin paid each five gold-pieces. He wanted the ship in which he had sailed to the Eastern World, and kept his eye on it.

"Oh," said Three Sticks, "don't mind that ship; look at the one beyond."

Fin turned in the other direction, and saw nothing but water.

"There is no ship there," said he, turning to Three Sticks.

But Three Sticks and all his comrades were gone. Fin looked out on the water; the ship was gone too. He was sorry for the ship, and sorry for the small men; he would rather have them than all the Fenians of Erin.

FIN MACCOOL, CEADACH OG, AND THE FISH-HAG.

ON a time Fin MacCool and the Fenians were living at Rahonain, a mile distant from Fintra. While Fin and his men were near Fintra, a champion called Ceadach Og, son of the King of Sorach, came to them to learn feats of skill. They received Ceadach with gladness; and after a time he learned all their feats, and departed. Fin and the Fenians were pleased with his company; and Ceadach was grateful to Fin and the Fenians.

At some distance from Fintra, there lived at that time a famed champion, who taught feats of valor and arms, and was surnamed the Knight of Instruction. With this man Ceadach engaged to gain still more knowledge.

The Knight of Instruction had a daughter; and there was with him a second man learning, whose nickname was Red Face.

When the champions had learned all the feats from the knight, the two were in love with his daughter. Not wishing that one of his pupils should envy the other, the knight could not settle which man to choose. He called then his druid, and laid the whole question before him.

"My advice," said the druid, "is this: Open two opposite doors in your castle; place your daughter half-way between them; and let the two champions pass out, one through one door, and one through the other. Whomever your daughter will follow, let her be the wife of that man."

The champions had their own compact, that the man whom the young woman would follow should let the other have three casts of a spear at him, and he without right of defence; but if another would defend, he might let him.

The knight brought his daughter to the middle of the chamber, and opened the doors. The young woman went out after Ceadach.

Ceadach and his wife went their way then together; and he feared to stop at any place till he came to a great lonesome forest. He went to the middle of the forest, built a house there, and lived with his wife for a season.

One day as Fin was walking near the water at Fintra, he met a strange creature, — a woman to the waist, from the waist a fish. The human half was like an old hag. When Fin stopped before her, he greeted the hag. She returned the greeting, and asked him to play chess for a sentence.

"I would," answered Fin, "if I had my own board and chessmen."

"I have a good board," said the fish-hag.

"If you have," said Fin, "we will play; but if you win the first game, I must go for my own board, and you will play the second on that."

The hag consented. They played on her chess-board, and the hag won that game.

"Well," said Fin, "I must go for my own board, and do you wait till I bring it."

"I will," said the fish-hag.

Fin brought his own board; and they played, and he won.

"Now," said Fin, "pass your sentence on me, since you won the first game."

"I will," said the hag; "and I place you under sentence of weighty druidic spells not to eat two meals off the one table, nor to sleep two nights in the one bed, nor to pass out by the door through which you came in, till you bring me the head of the Red Ox, and an account of what took the eye from the Doleful Knight of the Island, and how he lost speech and laughter. Now pass sentence on me."

"You will think it too soon when you hear it," said Fin, "but here it is for you. I place you under bonds of weighty druidic spells to stand on the top of that gable above there, to have a sheaf of oats fixed on the gable beyond you, and to have no earthly food while I'm gone, except what the wind will blow through the eye of a needle fixed in front of you."

"Hard is your sentence, O Fin," said the fish-hag. "Forgive me, and I'll take from your head my sentence."

"Never," said Fin. "Go to your place without waiting."

Before Fin departed, the fish-hag had mounted the gable.

The fame of the Red Ox had spread through all lands in the world, and no man could go near him without losing life. The Fenians were greatly unwilling to face the Red Ox, and thought that no man could match him, unless, perhaps, Ceadach.

Though they knew not where Ceadach was living, nor where they were likely to find him, they started in search of that champion. They played with a ball, as they travelled, driving it forward before them, knowing that if Ceadach saw the ball he would give it a blow.

While passing the forest where Ceadach and his wife, the knight's daughter, were hiding, one of the Fenians gave the ball a great blow;

but as he aimed badly, the ball flew to one side, went far away, and fell into the forest.

Ceadach was walking away from his house when the ball fell, and he saw it. He pulled down a tree-branch, and, giving a strong, direct blow, drove the ball high in the air, and out of the forest.

"No one struck that blow," said the Fenians, "but Ceadach, and he is here surely." They went then toward the point from which they had seen the ball coming, and there they found Ceadach.

"A thousand welcomes, Fin MacCool," said Ceadach. "Where are you going?"

"I am under sentence to bring the head of the Red Ox; and 't is for it that I am going: but I never can bring it unless you assist me. Without you, I cannot lift from my head the sentence that is on it."

"If it lay with me, I would go with you gladly; but I know that my wife will not let me leave her. But do as I tell you now. When you come to us to eat dinner, taste nothing, and when my wife asks you to eat, say that you will not eat till she grants a request: if she will not grant it, leave the house, and let all the Fenians follow; if she grants you a request, you are to ask that I go with you. I know that she will grant you any request, except to take me in your company; for she is in dread that I may meet Red Face."

They went to the house; the wife welcomed Fin with the others, and prepared dinner. When meat was placed before Fin, he would not taste it.

"Why not eat, O King of the Fenians?"

"I have a request to make. If you grant it, I will eat; if not, neither I nor my men will taste food."

"Any request in my power, I will grant," said she, "except one."

"What is that?" inquired Fin.

"If you want Ceadach to go with you, I'll not grant that."

"'T is he that I want," answered Fin.

"You'll not get him."

"Well, you may keep him," said Fin, rising from the table; and all the men followed. Conan Maol, who was with them, thought it hard to leave the dinner untasted, so he took a joint of meat with him.

When Fin and the Fenians had gone, Ceadach said to his wife, "It is a great shame to us that Fin and the Fenians have left our house without tasting food, and this their first visit. Never can I face a man of the Fenians after what has happened this day." And he talked till the wife consented to let him go with them.

Ceadach then whistled after Fin, who came back with his men; and they raised three shouts of joy when they heard that Ceadach would go with them. They entered the house then; all sat down to dinner, and they needed it badly.

After dinner, all set out together, and went to Ceadach's father, the King of Sorach, who was very powerful, and had many ships (Fin and the Fenians had no ships at that time). Ceadach's father had received no account of his son from the time that he left him at first, and was rejoiced at his coming.

Said Fin to the King of Sorach, " I need a ship to bear me to the land where the Red Ox is kept."

"You may take the best ship I have," said the king.

Fin chose the best ship, and was going on board with his men when Ceadach's wife said to him, "When coming back, you are to raise black sails if Ceadach is killed, but white sails if he is living."

Fin commanded, and the men turned the prow to the sea, and the stern to land; they raised the great sweeping sails, and took their smoothly-polished ship past harbors with gently-sloping shores, and there the ship left behind it pale-green wavelets. Then a mighty wind swept

through great flashing waves with such force that
not a nail in the ship was left unheated, nor the
finger of a man inactive; and the ship raised
with its sailing a proud, haughty ridge in the
sea. When the wind failed, they sat down with
their oars of fragrant beech or white ash, and
with every stroke they sent the ship forward
three leagues through the water, where fishes,
seals, and monsters rose around them, making
music and sport, and giving courage to the men;
and they never stopped nor cooled till they
entered the chief port of the land where the Red
Ox was kept.

When all had landed; Ceadach said, "I need
the fleetest man of the Fenians to help me against
the Red Ox; and now tell me what each of you
can do, and how fast he can run."

"Let out," said one man, "twelve hares in a
field with twelve gaps in it, and I will not let a
hare out through any gap of the twelve."

"Take a sieve full of chaff," said a second man,
"to the top of a mountain; let the chaff go out
with the wind; and I will gather all in again
before as much as one bit of it comes to the
ground."

"When I run at full speed," said a third man,
"my tread is so light that the dry, withered grass
is not crushed underneath me."

"Now, Dyeermud," said Ceadach, "I think that you were the swiftest of all when I was the guest of Fin MacCool and the Fenians of Erin; tell me, how swift are you now?"

"I am swifter," said Dyeermud, "than the thought of a woman when she is thinking of two men."

"Oh, you will do," said Ceadach; "you are the fleetest of the Fenians; come with me."

Fin and the Fenians remained near the ship, while Ceadach and Dyeermud went off to face the Red Ox.

The Red Ox's resting-place was enclosed by a wall and a hedge; outside was a lofty stone pillar; on this pillar the Red Ox used to rub his two sides. The Ox had but one horn, and that in the middle of his forehead. With that horn, which was four feet in length, he let neither fly, wasp, gnat, nor biting insect come near, and whatever creature came toward him, he sniffed from a distance.

When he sniffed the two champions, he rushed at them. Ceadach bounded toward the pillar.

Dyeermud took shelter at the hedge, and waited to see what would happen.

Ceadach ran round the pillar, and the Red Ox ran after him. Three days and three nights did they run; such was the speed of the two that

Dyeermud never caught sight of them during that time, nor did they have sight of each other: the Red Ox followed by scent. Near the close of the third day, when both were growing tired, the Ox, seeing Ceadach, stopped for an instant to run across and pierce him with his horn. Dyeermud got a glimpse of the Ox, then rose in the air like a bird, split the forehead of the Ox with one blow, and stretched him.

"My love on your blow," said Ceadach; "and it was time for you to give it."

"Purblindness and blindness to me," replied Dyeermud, "if I saw the Ox till that instant."

Both were now joyful; for they had the head to take with them.

"If Fin and his men had this carcass," said Dyeermud, "it would give them beef for many a day."

"Well, Dyeermud," asked Ceadach, "how much of the Ox can you carry?"

"I think I can take one quarter, with the head."

"If you can do that," said Ceadach, "I'll take the rest of the carcass myself."

Cutting off one quarter, he thrust through it the point of the horn, put the horn on Dyeermud's shoulder, with the head and quarter before and behind him. Ceadach took the other three quarters himself. Before they had gone half the way to the vessel, Dyeermud was tired, and Ceadach had to take that quarter as well as his own three; the head was as much as Dyeermud could carry.

When the two men appeared at the ship, all rejoiced greatly, and welcomed them. Fin took the borabu then, and sounded it from joy; this sound could be heard through the world. As the report had gone to all regions that Fin was under sentence to kill the Red Ox, when Red Face heard the borabu, he said to himself, "That is Fin; the Red Ox is killed; no one could kill him but Ceadach, and Ceadach is where the borabu is." Red Face had the power of druidic spells; so he rose in the air, and soon dropped down near the Fenians, and was unseen till he stood there before them.

Said Red Face to Ceadach, " 'T is many a day that I am following you; you must stand your ground now."

"What you ask is but fair," answered Ceadach.

Red Face went to the distance of a spear's cast, and hurled his spear at Ceadach; but Dyeermud sprang up and caught it on his heel. Red Face made a second cast. Goll MacMorna raised his hand to stop the spear; but it went through his hand, and, going farther, pierced Ceadach, and killed him.

Red Face then vanished; and no man knew when he vanished, or to what place he went.

When Ceadach fell, the Fenians raised seven loud cries of grief that drove the badgers from the glens in which they were sleeping.

Said Dyeermud to Fin, "Chew your thumb to know how we can bring Ceadach to life."

Fin chewed his thumb from the skin to the flesh, from the flesh to the bone, from the bone to the marrow, from the marrow to the juice, and then he knew that there was a sow with three pigs in the Eastern World, and if blood from one of these pigs were put on Ceadach's wound, he would rise up well and healthy.

Fin took some men, and, leaving others to watch over Ceadach, set sail for the Eastern World, and never stopped till he anchored in a port near the place where the sow and her pigs were.

Fin knew all paths to the lair of the sow; and they went to it straightway. When they came, she was away hunting food; so they took the three pigs, hurried back to the vessel, set sail in all haste, and were soon out at sea. When the sow came back to her lair, it was empty. Then she found the scent of the men, followed it to the sea, and swam after the ship.

When the ship had made one-third of the voyage, the sow came in sight, and was soon near the stern. Fin ordered his men to throw out one pig of the three. The sow took the pig in her mouth, turned back, swam home, and left it in her lair. She turned a second time, followed the ship, and such was her speed and her venom, that little more than one-half of the voyage was over when the sow was in sight again. When near the ship, they threw her the second pig. The mother went back to her lair with the second pig, left it with the first, and rushed after the ship a third time. Land was in sight when they saw the sow raging on after them.

"Oh, we are lost!" cried the Fenians.

Dyeermud then took a bow with an arrow, and, resting the bow on another man's shoulder, aimed so truly at the widely-opened mouth of the sow, that the arrow, going in through her mouth, pierced her blood veins, and in no long time she turned her back downward and died.

They landed in safety, bled the pig; and when they let some of the blood into Ceadach's spear-wound, he sprang up alive.

When Ceadach was restored, Fin blew the borabu, and the Fenians raised seven shouts of joy that were heard throughout the whole kingdom. Then they set sail for Sorach.

Ceadach's wife thought her husband long in coming, and was watching and waiting every day for him.   At last she saw the ship with white sails, and was glad.

Fin and his men landed, but left Ceadach on board.

"Where is Ceadach?" asked the wife, running out to meet Fin.

"He is dead on the vessel," said Fin.

"Why did you not raise black sails as you promised?"

"We were so troubled that we forgot it."

"It was well for you to forget; for if you had raised black sails, I should have drowned every man of you."

"Ceadach is living and well; have no fear," said Fin, and he sounded the borabu.

Ceadach landed.   His father and wife were so glad to see him that they feasted Fin and the Fenians for seven days and seven nights.

Fin told Ceadach's wife of all their adventures, and what struggles they had in bringing her husband to life.   She was glad; for the trouble with Red Face was ended.

Ceadach went now with Fin to visit the Doleful Knight of the Island; and they never halted nor stopped till they came to his castle.

Fin found the knight sitting at a great heavy table, his head on his hand, his elbow on the table, into which it had worn a deep hole; a stream of tears was flowing from his eye to the table, and from the table to the floor.

"A hundred thousand welcomes to you, Fin MacCool," said the knight; and he began to weep more than ever. "I was once in prosperity, and at that time this was a pleasant place for a good man to visit; but now it is different. I have food in plenty, but no one to cook it."

"If that's all your trouble," said Fin, "we can cure it."

Fin's men were not slow in preparing a dinner. When the dinner was eaten, the knight turned to Fin and inquired, "Why have you come to my castle, Chief of the Fenians of Erin?"

"I will tell you," said Fin. Then he related his story, and all his adventures with Ceadach.

"Well," said the knight, "it will shorten my life by seven years to give the tale of my sufferings; for they will be as fresh to me now, as when first I went through them. But as you are under bonds to know them, I will tell you.

"I was here in wealth and prosperity, myself and my three sons. We used to hunt beasts and birds with our dogs when it pleased us. On a May morning a hare came, and frisked before my hall-door. Myself and my three sons then followed her with dogs, and followed all day till the height of the evening. Then we saw the hare enter an old fairy fort. The opening was wide; we were able to follow. In we rushed, all of us, and the next thing we saw was a fine roomy building. We went in, looked around for the hare, but saw not a sight of her. There was no one within but an old man and woman. We were not long inside till three gruagachs came, each with a wild boar on his shoulders. They threw the wild boars on the floor, and told me to clean them, and cook them for dinner. One of my sons fell to cleaning a boar; but for every hair that he took from him, ten new ones came out, so the sooner he stopped work the better.

"Then one of the old gruagach's sons placed the boars in a row, the head of the one near the tail of the other, and, taking a reed, blew once, the hair was gone from all three; twice, the three boars were dressed; a third time, all were swept into one caldron.

"When the meal was cooked and ready, a gruagach brought two spits to me, one of dull wood, the other formed of sharp iron. The old man asked, ' Which will you choose?'

"I chose the sharp iron spit, went to the caldron, and thrust in the spit; but if I did, I raised only a poor, small bit of meat, mostly bone. That was what I and my three sons had for dinner.

"After dinner, the old man said, 'Your sons may perform now a feat for amusement.'

"In three rooms were three cross-beams, as high from the floor as a man's throat. In the middle of each beam was a hole. Through this hole passed a chain, with a loop at each end of it. In front of the hole on each side of the beam was a knife, broad and sharp. One loop of each chain was put on the neck of a son of mine, and one on the neck of a gruagach. Then each of the six was striving to save his own throat, and to cut off the head of the other man; but the gruagachs pulled my three sons to the cross-beams, and took the three heads off them.

"Then they dressed them, and boiled them for supper. When that supper was ready, they struggled to force me to eat some, but could not. Next they threw me across the broad table, plucked out one eye from my head, thrust a light in the socket, and made me lie there, and serve as a candlestick. In the morning, I was flung out through the door, while the gruagach cried after me, 'You'll not come to this castle a second time!'"

"Have you seen that hare since?" inquired Ceadach.

"I have, for she comes each May morning, and that renews and gives strength to my sorrow."

"To-morrow will be May day; come with me, and we 'll hunt her," said Ceadach.

"I will not," said the Knight of the Island.

The hare came after breakfast next morning, and halted in front of the castle. The knight was unwilling to hunt, but still yielded to Ceadach, and followed with the others.

Time after time, they came close to the hare, but never could catch her. At last, in the height of the evening, when nearing the same fairy fort, the hound Bran snapped at the haunch of the hare, and took a full bite from her. All passed through the entrance, found the house, and no person inside but an old man and wo- man. The old woman was lying in bed, and she groaning.

"Have you seen a hare in this house?" inquired Ceadach.

"I have not," said the old man.

Ceadach saw traces of blood on the bed, and went toward the old woman, who was covered up closely; raising the clothes, he said, "Maybe 't is here that the hare is."

The old woman was covered with blood, and wounded in the very same way as the hare. They knew then who was the cause of misfortune to the Knight of the Island, and who made the visits each year on May morning.

They were not long in the house when the gruagachs, the sons of the old man, came in, each with a wild boar on his shoulders. Seeing the Knight of the Island, they laughed, and said, "We thought you had enough of this place the first time that you came here."

"I saw more than I wished to see," said the Knight of the Island; "but I had to come this time."

"Have you any man to cook dinner for us?" asked the old gruagach of Fin.

"I'll do that myself," put in Ceadach, who turned to one of the brothers, and asked, "Where is your reed; I must use it."

The reed was brought. Ceadach blew once, the boars were clean; twice, they were dressed, and ready; thrice, they were in the caldron.

When the spits were brought, Ceadach took the dull wooden spit, thrust it into the pot, and took up all that was in there.

Fin, Ceadach, and the knight ate to their own satisfaction; then they invited the old gruagach and his three sons to dinner.

"What amusement have you in this place?" asked Fin, later in the evening.

"We have nothing," said the old gruagach and his sons.

"Where are your chains?" asked Ceadach.

"We make no use of them now," said the young gruagachs.

"You must bring them," said Ceadach.

The chains were brought, drawn through the cross-beams, and three loops of them put on the necks of the gruagachs. No matter what strength was in the three brothers, nor how they struggled, Ceadach brought their throats to the knives, and took the three heads off them. Next they were boiled in the caldron, as the knight's three sons had been boiled the first time. Then Ceadach seized the old gruagach, flung him across the broad table, plucked out one eye from his head, and fixed a light in the empty socket.

At sight of what the gruagachs passed through, the Doleful Knight of the Island let one roaring laugh out of him, his first laugh in seven years.

Next morning Ceadach, pointing to the Knight of the Island, said to the old gruagach, "Unless you bring this man's three sons to life, I will take your own head from you."

The bones of the three sons were in three heaps of dust outside the door. The gruagach took a rod of enchantment, and struck the bones. The three sons of the knight rose up as well and strong as ever, and went home. The Knight of the Island gave a feast to Fin and Ceadach. After that Fin, with his men and Ceadach, sailed

back to the King of Sorach. Ceadach remained
with his wife and father. Fin went to the harbor of Fintra, taking with him the head of the
Red Ox, and the story of the Doleful Knight, to
the fish-hag.

"Have you the head of the Red Ox?" asked
the hag.

"I have," answered Fin.

"You will give it to me," said the hag.

"I will not," answered Fin. "If I was bound
to bring it, I was not bound to give it."

When she heard that, the hag dropped to the
earth, and became a few bones.

FIN MACCOOL, FAOLAN, AND THE
MOUNTAIN OF HAPPINESS.

WHEN Fin MacCool and the Fenians of Erin were at Fintra, they went hunting one day; and the man who killed the first deer was Dyeermud. When the hunt was over, they returned to the place where the first deer was started, and began, as was usual, to prepare the day's feast. While preparing the feast, they saw a ship sailing into the harbor, with only one woman on board. The Fenians were greatly surprised at the speed of the vessel; and Dyeermud said to Fin, "I will go and see who is the woman coming in that vessel."

"You killed the first deer," replied Fin, "and the honors of the feast on this day are yours. I myself will go down and see who the woman is."

The woman cast anchor, sprang ashore, and saluted Fin, when he came to the strand. Fin returned the salute, and, after a while, she asked, "Will you play a game of chess for a sentence?"

"I will," answered Fin.

They played, and she won.

"What is your sentence on me?" inquired Fin.

"I sentence you, under bonds of heavy enchantment," said she, "to take me for your wife."

Fin had to marry the woman. After a time, she said, "I must leave you now for a season."

Fin drove his sword then, with one mighty blow, into a tree-stump, and said, "Call your son Faolan [little wolf], and never send him to me until he is able to draw the sword from this stump."

She took the stump with her, and sailed away homeward. She nursed her son for only three days, and preserved the rest of the milk for a different use. The boy was called Faolan, was trained well in the use of all arms, and when ten years of age, he was skilled beyond any master. One day there was a game of hurley, and Faolan played alone, against twenty one others. The rule of that game was that whoever won was to get three blows of his club on each one who played against him. Faolan gave three blows to each of the twenty-one men; among them was one who was very much hurt by the blows, and he began to say harsh words to Faolan, and added, "You don't know your own father."

Faolan was greatly offended at this. He went home to his mother, in tears, and asked, "Who is my father? I will never stop nor stay till I find him."

"What caused your vexation?" asked the mother. "Why do you ask such a question at this time?"

Faolan told her the words of the player. At last she said, "Your father is Fin MacCool, Chief of the Fenians of Erin; but you are not to be sent to him till you can draw his sword from the tree-stump into which he drove it with one blow."

"Show me the sword and the tree-stump," said Faolan.

She took him then to the stump. With one pull, he drew out the sword.

"Prepare me food for the road," said Faolan. "I will go to my father."

The mother made ready three loaves of bread, kneaded them with the milk which she had saved, and baked them.

"My son," said she, "do not refuse bread on the journey to any one whom you meet; give it from these loaves, even should you meet your worst enemy."

She took down a sword then, gave it to him, and said, "This was your grandfather's sword; keep it, and use it till a better one comes to you."

Faolan took a blessing of his mother, set out on his journey, and was walking always, till he came to a harbor where he found a ship bound for Erin. He went on board, and was not sailing long, when a venomous hound rose up in the sea, and cast such high waves at the vessel as to throw it back a long distance.

Remembering his mother's advice about sharing the bread, Faolan threw one loaf to the hound. This seemed to appease him. He had not sailed much further, when the hound rose again. Faolan threw out the second loaf; and the beast disappeared for a while, but rose the third time, and drove back the vessel. Faolan threw the third loaf; and, after disappearing the third time, the hound rose the fourth time. Having nothing to give, Faolan seized a brazen ball which his mother had given him, and, hurling it at the hound with good aim, killed him on the spot. As soon as the hound fell, there rose up a splendid youth, who came on board, and, shaking Faolan's hand, said, —

"I thank you; you delivered me from enchantment. I am your mother's brother; and there was nothing to free me till I ate three loaves kneaded with your mother's milk, and was then killed by you with that brazen ball. You are near Ventry Strand now; among the first men you meet will be your own father. You will know him by his dress; and when you meet him, kneel down and ask for his blessing. As I have nothing else to give, here is a ring to wear on your finger, and whenever you look at it you will feel neither cold, thirst, nor hunger."

When they landed, the uncle went his own way and vanished. Faolan saw champions playing on the strand, throwing a great weighty sledge.

Knowing Fin from his mother's description, he knelt down at his feet, and asked for his blessing.

"If you are a son of mine," said Fin, "you are able to hurl this sledge."

"He is too young," said Dyeermud, "to throw such a weight; and it is a shame for you to ask him to throw it."

The youth then, growing angry, caught the sledge, and hurled it seven paces beyond the best man of the Fenians.

Fin shook hands with the youth; and his heart grew big at having such a son. Dyeermud shook his hand also, and swore that as long as he lived he would be to him a true comrade.

When dinner-time came, Fin bade Faolan sit down at his right hand, where Conan Maol, son of Morna, sat usually. Fin gave this place to Conan to keep him in humor. Conan grew enraged now, and said, "It is great impudence for a stripling to sit in my place."

"I know not who you are," said Faolan, "but from what I hear you must be Conan Maol, who has never a good word for any man; and I would break your head on the wall, but I don't wish to annoy people present."

It was a custom of the Fenians in eating to set aside every bone that had marrow for Oscar, and as Faolan had a thick marrow-bone in his hand, he began to pick out the marrow, and eat it. This enraged Oscar, and he said, "You must put that bone aside as the others put their bones; that is my due, and I will have it."

"As the meat is mine," said Faolan, "so is the marrow."

Oscar snatched at the youth, and caught the bone by one end. Faolan held the other end. Both pulled till they broke the bone, then, seizing each other, they went outside for a struggle. As the two were so nearly related, the other men stopped them. Fin took Oscar aside then, and asked, "How long could you live if we let the youth keep his grip on you?"

"If he kept his grip with the same strength, I could not live five minutes longer."

Fin took Faolan aside then, and asked the same question.

"I could live for twelve months, if he squeezed me no tighter."

The two then kept peace with each other. All were very fond of Faolan, especially Dyeermud, who was a good, loyal comrade; and he warned Faolan to distrust and avoid Grainne, Fin's wife, as much as he could. The youth was learning, meanwhile, to practise feats of activity and bravery. At the end of twelve months, the Fenians were setting out on a distant hunt, for which they had long been preparing. On the eve of the hunt, Grainne dropped on her knees before Fin, and begged him to leave Faolan with her for company, until he and the rest would return. Fin consented, and Faolan stayed with Grainne.

When all the others had gone to the great hunt, Faolan and Grainne went also to hunt in the neighborhood. They did not go far, and returned. After dinner, Grainne asked Faolan would he play a game of chess for a small sentence. He said that he would. They played, and he won.

"What is your sentence on me?" asked Grainne.

"I have no sentence at this time," replied Faolan.

They played again, and she won.

"Now put your sentence on me," said the youth.

"You will think it soon enough when you hear it. You are not to eat two meals off the same table, nor sleep two nights on the same bed, till you bring me the tallow of the three oxen on Sliav Sein [Mountain of Happiness]."

When he heard this sentence, he went off, threw himself face downward on his bed, and remained there without eating or drinking till the Fenians came back from the hunt. Fin and Dyeermud, not seeing Faolan when they came, went in search of him.

"Have you found Foalan?" asked Dyeermud of Fin, when he met him soon after.

"I have not," answered Fin.

Dyeermud then went to see if he could find Faolan in bed. As the door of his chamber was fastened, and no one gave answer, Dyeermud forced it, and found Faolan on his face in the bed. After they had greeted each other, Faolan told of the trouble that was on him.

"I gave you warning against Grainne," said Dyeermud; "but did you win any game of her?"

"I did; but have put no sentence on her yet."

"I am glad," answered Dyeermud; "and let me frame the sentence. I swear by my sword to be loyal to you; and where you fall, I will fall also. But be cheerful, and come to the feast."

They went together, and Fin, seeing them, was glad. He knew, however, that something had happened to Faolan. Dyeermud went to Fin, and told him of the mishap to the youth. Fin was troubled at what had come on his son.

"I have sworn," said Dyeermud, "to follow Faolan wherever he may be."

"I will send with him," said Fin, "the best man of the Fenians."

Dyeermud, Oscar, and Goll, son of Morna, were summoned.

"What is your greatest feat?" inquired Fin of Goll.

"If I were to stand in the middle of a field with my sword in my hand on the rainiest day that ever rose, I could keep my head dry with my sword, not for that day alone, but for a day and a year," answered Goll.

"That is a good feat," said Fin. "What is your greatest feat, Oscar?"

"If I open a bag filled with feathers on a mountain-top of a stormy day, and let the feathers fly with the wind, the last feather will barely be out of the bag, when I will have every feather of them back into the bag again."

"That is a very good feat," answered Fin,

"but it is not enough yet. Now, Dyeermud, what is your feat of swiftness?"

"If I were put on a space of seven hundred acres, and each acre with a hedge around it, and there were seven hundred gaps in the hedge of each acre, and seven hundred hares were put on each acre of the seven hundred, I would not let one hare out of the seven hundred acres for a day and a year."

"That is a great feat," remarked Fin; "that will do."

"Chew your thumb, O Fin," said Dyeermud, "and tell me if it is fated to us to come back from the journey?"

Fin chewed his thumb. "You will come back; but the journey will be a hard and a long one: you will be ankle deep in your own blood."

Dyeermud went to Faolan, and told him what sentence to put upon Grainne.

On the following day, Fin led Grainne forth for her sentence; and Faolan said, "You are to stand on the top of Sliav Iolar [Mount Eagle], till I come back to Fintra; you are to hold in your hand a fine needle; you are to have no drink saving what rain you can suck through the eye of that needle, no food except what oats will be blown through the eye of that very needle from a sheaf on Sliav Varhin; and Dyeermud will give three blows of a flail to the sheaf to loosen the grain."

Faolan and Dyeermud set out on their journey. They travelled three days, and saw no house in which they could rest for the night.

"When we find a house," said Dyeermud, "we will have from the people a lodging, either with their good will, or in spite of them."

"I will help you in that," said Faolan.

On the evening of the fourth day, a large white-fronted castle appeared in the distance. They went toward it, and knocked at the door. A fine young woman welcomed them kindly, and kissed Faolan. "You and I," said she, "were born at the same hour, and betrothed at our birth. Your mother married Fin to rescue her brothers, your uncles, from the bonds of enchantment."

They sat down to eat and drink, the young woman, Dyeermud, and Faolan; they were not long eating when in came four champions, all torn, cut, and bleeding. When Dyeermud saw these, he started up, and seized his sword.

"Have no fear," said the young woman to Dyeermud.

"We are returning from battle with a wild hag in the neighborhood," said the four champions. "She is trying to take our land from us; and this is the seventh year that we are battling with the hag. All of her warriors that we kill in the daytime, she raises at night; and we have to fight them again the next day."

"No man killed by my sword revives; and these will not, if I kill them," said Dyeermud.

"They would revive after your sword," said the four champions.

"Do you stay at home to-morrow," said Dyeermud; "Faolan and I will give battle to the hag and her forces; no one whom we slay will trouble you hereafter."

The four champions agreed, and gave every direction how to find the wild hag and her army. Faolan and Dyeermud went to the field; one began at one end, and one at the other, and fought till they met in the middle at sunset, and slew all the hag's warriors.

"Go back to the castle," said Faolan to Dyeermud; "I will rest here to night, and see what gives life to the corpses."

"I will stay," replied Dyeermud, "and you may return."

"No, I will stay here," said Faolan; "if I want help, I will run to the castle."

Dyeermud went back to the castle. About midnight, Faolan heard the voice of a man in the air just above him. "Is there any one living?" asked the voice. Faolan, with a bound, grasped the man, and, drawing him down with one hand, pierced him through with a sword in his other hand. The man fell dead; and then, instead of

the old man that he seemed at first, he rose up
a fresh young man of twenty two years. The
young man embraced and thanked Faolan. "I am
your uncle," said he, "brother of the poisonous
hound that you freed from enchantment at sea.
I was fourteen years in the power of the wild
hag, and could not be freed till my father's sword
pierced me. Give me that sword which belonged
to my father. It was to deliver me that your mother
gave you that blade. I will give you a better one
still, since you are a greater champion than I. I
will give you my grandfather's sword; here it is.
When the wild hag grows uneasy at my delay,
she herself will hasten hither. She knew that
you were to come and release me, and she is preparing this long time to meet you. For seven
years, she has been making steel nails to tear
you to pieces; and she has sweet music which
she will play when she sees you: that music
makes every man sleep when he hears it. When
you feel the sleep coming, stab your leg with
your sword; that will keep you awake. She
will then give you battle; and if you chance to
cut off her head, let not the head come to the
body: for if it comes on the body, all the world
could not take it away. When you cut off her
head, grasp it in one hand, and hold it till all the
blood flows out; make two halves of the head,

holding it in your hand all the while; and I will remove the stone cover from a very deep well here at hand; and do you throw the split head into that well, and put the cover on again."

The uncle went aside then; and soon the hag came through the air. Seeing Faolan, she began to play strains of beautiful music, which were putting him to sleep; but he thrust his new sword in the calf of his leg, and kept away sleep. The wild hag, outwitted, attacked the youth fiercely, and he went at her in earnest. Every time that she caught him with her nails, she scraped skin and flesh from his head to his heels; and then, remembering his mother, and being aroused by his uncle, he collected his strength, and with one blow cut the head off the hag; but he was so spent from the struggle that it took him some time to seize the head, and so weak was he that he could not raise his hand to split it.

"Lay your sword on the head; the blade alone will split it!" cried the uncle.

Faolan did this. The sword cut the head; and then Faolan threw the head into the well. Just as he was going to cover the well, the head spoke, and said, "I put you under bonds of heavy enchantment not to eat two meals off the same table, nor sleep two nights on the same bed, till you tell the Cat of Gray Fort that you destroyed the wild hag out of her kingdom."

The uncle embraced Faolan then, and said, "Now I will go to my sister, your mother; but first I will guide you to this hag's enchanted well: if you bathe in its water, you will be as sound and well as ever."

Faolan went, bathed in the well, and, when fully recovered, returned to the castle. Thinking Gray Fort must be near by, he did not rouse Dyeermud, but went alone in search of the cat. He travelled all day, and at last saw a great fort with the tail of a cat sticking out of it. "This may be the cat," thought he, and he went around the whole fort to find the head. He found it thrust out just beyond the tail.

"Are you the Cat of Gray Fort?" inquired Faolan.

"I am," said the cat.

"If you are," said Faolan, "I destroyed the wild hag out of her kingdom."

"If you did," said the cat, "you will kill no one else; for the hag was my sister."

The cat rushed at Faolan then; and, bad as the hag had been, the cat was far worse. The two fought that night furiously, till the following morning, when Faolan cut the cat in two halves across the middle. The half that the head was on ran around trying to meet the other half; but before it could do so, Faolan cut the head off the front half. Then the head spoke, and said, —

"I put you under bonds of enchantment not to eat two meals off the one table, nor sleep two nights on the one bed, till you tell the Kitten of Cul MacKip that you killed the Cat of Gray Fort and destroyed the wild hag out of her kingdom."

Faolan then hurried forward to find the kitten. Thinking that her place was near, he did not go back to the castle for Dyeermud, but held on the whole day, walking always. Toward evening, he saw a castle, went toward it, and entered it. When inside he saw half a loaf of barley-bread and a quart of ale placed on the window. "Whoever owns these, I will use them," said the youth.

When he had eaten and drunk, he put down a fire for the night, and saw a kitten lying near the ashes. "This may be the Kitten of Cul Mac-Kip," thought he; and, shaking it, he asked, "Are you the Kitten of Cul MacKip?"

"I am," said the kitten.

"If you are," said Faolan, "then I tell you that I killed the Cat of Gray Fort and destroyed the wild hag out of her kingdom."

"If you did," said the kitten, "you will never

kill any one else," and, starting up, the kitten stretched, and was as big as a horse in a moment. She sprang at Faolan, and he at her. They fought fiercely that night, and the following day, but Faolan, toward evening, swept the head off the kitten; but as he did, the head spoke, and said, "I put you under bonds of heavy enchantment not to eat two meals off the same table, nor sleep two nights on the same bed, till you tell the Dun Ox that you slew the Kitten of Cul Mac-Kip, killed the Cat of Gray Fort, and destroyed the wild hag out of her kingdom."

Before setting out, Faolan saw a brass ball on the window, and, taking it, said to himself, "I may kill some game with this on the road."

Away he went then, and walked on till he came to where the road lay through a wood; near the road was a forester's cabin. Out came the forester with a hundred thousand welcomes.

"Glad am I to see you; gladder still would I be if your comrade, Dyeermud, were with you," said the forester.

"Can you tell me where the Dun Ox is?" asked Faolan.

"In this wood," said the forester; "but do you bring your comrade to help you against the Dun Ox; by no chance can you slay him alone. The Dun Ox has only one eye, and that in the middle of his forehead; over that eye is a shield of white metal; from that shield two bars of iron run back to the tail of the ox.   Behind him, two champions are on guard always; and when any one nears him, the ox sniffs the stranger, and roars; the champions lean on the bars then, and raise up the shield.   When the one eye of the ox sees the person approaching, that moment the person falls dead.   What are your chances of slaying that ox?   Go back for your comrade."

"I will not," said Faolan; "the ox will fall by me, or I by the ox."

"It is you that will fall," said the forester.

Faolan entered the cabin, where the forester treated him well.   Next morning the forester showed the path that lay toward the place where the ox was.   Faolan had not gone far when the ox roared, and, looking in the direction of the roar, he saw the two champions just seizing the bars to raise up the shield, so, failing other means, he sent the ball, with a well-aimed cast, and crushed in the forehead of the ox through the shield.   The ox fell dead, but, before falling, his eye turned on Faolan, who dropped dead also.

Dyeermud slept a hero's sleep of seven days and seven nights.   When he woke, and found no tidings of Faolan, he was furious; but the four champions calmed him; and the young woman said, "The wild hag may have killed him; but if as much as one bone of his body can be found, I will bring him to life again."

Dyeermud, Faolan's betrothed, and her four brothers set out, and, coming to the battle-field, found the army of the wild hag slain, but no trace of Faolan. They went to the well then, and saw the split head there.

The six went to Gray Fort, and found the cat dead, the hind-part in one place, the fore-part in a second, and the head in a third.

"The head must have sent him to the Kitten of Cul MacKip," said the young woman; "that kitten has twice as much witch power as the cat and the old hag; all three are sisters."

They went farther, and, finding the kitten dead, went to find the Dun Ox; "for Faolan must be dead near him," said the young woman. When they came to his cabin, the forester greeted them, and gave a hundred thousand welcomes to Dyeermud, who was surprised, and inquired, "How do you know me? I have never been in this country before."

"I know you well; for I saw you two years ago in combat with the Champion of the Eastern World on Ventry Strand. Many persons were looking at that combat, but you did not see them. I was there with the others."

"Have you seen a young champion pass this way?" asked Dyeermud.

"I have," said the forester; "but he must have perished by the Dun Ox, for I have not heard the ox bellow this long time."

The six spent that night at the forester's cabin; and, setting out next morning early, they soon found Faolan. The young woman bathed him with some fluid from a vial, and, opening his mouth, poured the rest down his throat. He rose up at once, as sound and healthy as ever. All went to the ox, which they found lying dead, and the two champions also; and, searching about, they found the brazen ball sunk in the earth some distance away. Faolan took it up carefully. They went back to the forester's cabin, and enjoyed themselves well.

"Do you know where the Mountain of Happiness is?" inquired Dyeermud of the forester, during the night.

"I do not," said the forester; "but I know where the Black-Blue Giant lives, and he knows every place in the world. That giant has never given a meal or a night's lodging to any man. He has an only daughter, who is in love with you, since she saw you two years ago in combat with the Champion of the Eastern World on Ventry Strand, although you did not see her. This daughter is closely confined by the giant, fearing she may escape to you; and if you succeed in reaching her, she is likely to know, if her father knows, where the Mountain of Happiness is."

"How did you get tidings of the giant's daughter?" asked Dyeermud.

"I will not tell you now," said the forester, "but I will go with you to guide you to the giant, and I may give you assistance. Here are three keys, — the keys of the castles of the Dun Ox, of the Kitten of Cul MacKip, and of the Cat of Gray Fort; they are yours now."

"Those keys are not mine," said Dyeermud; "they belong to Faolan, who slew the three owners."

"If Faolan slew them," said the forester, "he had assistance, which caused you to come to him."

"Keep the keys till we come back," said Dyeermud.

The seven travelled on then, and were going ten days when they saw the giant's castle. Now this castle stood on one leg, and whirled around always.

"I will use my strength on that castle, to know can I stop it," said Dyeermud.

"You cannot stop it," said the forester. "I will stop it myself. Do you watch the door of the castle, which is on the top of the roof, and, when the castle stops, spring in through the door, and seize the giant, if he is inside, and compel him to give a night's lodging."

The forester then made for the castle, and, placing his shoulder against one of the corners, kept it standing still; and Dyeermud, leaping in by the roof, came down before the giant, who had started up, knowing something was wrong when the castle stood still.

Dyeermud and the giant grappled each other so fiercely, and fought with such fury, that the castle was shivering. The giant's wife begged them to go out of the castle, and fight on the open, and not frighten the life out of herself and the child in her arms.

Out went the Black-Blue Giant and Dyeermud, and fought until Dyeermud brought down the giant and sprained his back. The giant let a roar out of him, and begged there for quarter.

"Your head is mine," answered Dyeermud.

"It is," said the giant; "but spare me, and I will give you whatever you ask for."

"I want lodging for myself and my company."

"You will get that," said the giant.

All then went into the giant's castle; and when they were sitting at dinner, Dyeermud ate nothing.

"Why is this?" asked the giant.

"It is the custom of the Fenians of Erin," said he, "not to eat at a table where all the members of the house are not present."

"All my people are here," said the giant.

"They are not," answered Dyeermud; "you have one daughter not present."

The giant had to bring the daughter. They ate then. The forester talked after dinner with Dyeermud, and said, "The giant's daughter has a maid; you must bribe her to give you the key of her mistress's chamber; and if you come by the young woman's secrets, she may tell you where the Mountain of Happiness is, if she knows."

Dyeermud went to the maid. "You will not be here always," said he; "your mistress will marry me, and leave this castle; then you 'll have no business here. I will take you with us if you give me the key of the chamber."

"The giant himself keeps that key under his pillow at night; he sleeps only one nap, like a bird, but sleeps heavily that time. If you promise to take me with my mistress, I 'll strive to bring the key hither."

"I promise," said Dyeermud.

The maid brought the key, and gave it on condition that she was to have it again within an hour. Dyeermud went then to the giant's daughter, and when her first wonder was over, he asked, "Do you know where the Mountain of Happiness is?"

"I do not. My father knows well, but for some reason he has never told me, so he must have fared very badly there; but if you lay his head on a block, and threaten to cut it off with your sword, he will tell you, if you ask him; but otherwise he will not tell."

"I will do that; and I will take you to Erin when I go," answered Dyeermud.

"Where is the Mountain of Happiness?" asked Dyeermud of the giant, next morning.

He would not tell. Dyeermud caught the giant, who could not resist him on account of his sprained back; he drew him out, placed his head on a block, and said, "I will cut the head off you now, unless you tell me what you know of the Mountain of Happiness. The Fenians of Erin have but the one word, and it is useless for you to resist me; you must go with us, and show us the way to the mountain."

The giant, finding no escape possible, promised to go. They set out soon, taking all the arms needed. As the mountain was not far distant, they reached the place without great delay. The giant showed them the lair of the oxen, but after a promise that he should be free to escape should danger threaten.

"I know all the rest now," said the forester. "Do you," said he to Dyeermud, "stand straight in front of the lair, and I, with Faolan, will stand with drawn swords, one on each side of the entrance; and do you," said he to the four brothers, "knock down the entrance, and open the place for the oxen to rush out. If the head of each ox is not cut off when he stands in the entrance, the world would not kill him from that out "

All was done at the forester's word. The entrance was not long open, when out rushed an ox; but his head was knocked off by the forester. Faolan slew the second ox; but the third ox followed the second so quickly that he broke away, took Dyeermud on his horns, and went like a flash to the top of the Mountain of Happiness. This mountain stood straight in front of the lair, but was far away. On the mountain, the ox attacked Dyeermud; and they fought for seven days and nights in a savage encounter. At the end of seven days, Dyeermud remembered that there was no help for him there, that he was far from his mother and sister, who were all he had living, and that if he himself did not slay the fierce ox, he would never see home again; so, with one final effort, he drove his sword through the heart of the ox. He himself was so spent from the struggle and blood-loss that he fainted, and would have died on the mountain, but for his companions, who came now. They were seven days on the road over which the ox passed in a very few minutes.

The forester rubbed Dyeermud with ointment, and all his strength came to him. They opened the ox, took out all the tallow, and, going back to the other two oxen, did in like manner, saving the tallow of each of them separately. They went next to the castle of the Black-Blue Giant.

"Will you set out for home to-morrow?" asked the forester, turning to Dyeermud.

"We will," answered Dyeermud.

"Oh, foolish people!" said the forester. "Those three oxen were brothers of Grainne, and were living in enchantment; should she get the tallow of each ox by itself and entire, she would bring back the three brothers to life, and they would destroy all the Fenians of Erin. We will hang up the tallow in the smoke of the Black-Blue Giant's chimney; it will lose some of itself there. When she gets it, it will not have full weight. We will change your beds and your tables while you are waiting, so as to observe the injunction. You must do this; for if you do not make an end of Grainne, Grainne will make an end of you."

All was done as the forester said.   At the end
of a week, when Faolan and his friend were setting out for Erin, the giant and his wife fell to
weeping and wailing after their daughter, who
was going with Dyeermud.

"We will come back again soon," said Dyeermud, "and then will have a great feast for this
marriage."

"It is here that I will have my marriage feast,
too," said Faolan.

The forester, who was an old man, said perhaps he might have a marriage feast at that time
as well as the others.   At this they all laughed.

The giant and his wife were then satisfied; and
the company set out for the forester's cabin.
When they reached the cabin, the forester said
to Dyeermud, "As I served you, I hope that you
will do me a good turn."

"I will do you a good turn," said Dyeermud,
"if I lose my life in doing it."

"Cut off my head," said the forester.

"I will not," replied Dyeermud.

"Well," said the old man, "if you do not, you
will leave me in great distress; for I, too, am
under enchantment, and there is no power to save
me unless you, Dyeermud, cut off my head with
the sword that killed the oldest of the oxen."

When Dyeermud saw how he could serve the

forester, he cut off his head with one blow, and there rose up before him a young man of twenty-one years.

"My name is Arthur, son of Deara," said the young man to Dyeermud; "I was enchanted by my stepmother, and I am in love with your sister since I saw her two years ago on Ventry Strand, when you were in combat with the Champion of the Eastern World. Will you let your sister marry me?"

"I will," replied Dyeermud; "and she will not marry any man but the one that I will choose for her."

"I helped Faolan," said Arthur, "in all his struggles, except that against the Dun Ox."

Next day all went to the castle of the four champions and their sister, and, leaving the women in that place, they set out for Erin.

When the Fenians of Erin saw them sailing in toward Ventry Strand, they raised three shouts of joyous welcome. Whoever was glad, or was not glad, Grainne was glad, because there was an end, as she thought, to her suffering. Indeed, she would not have lived at all had she kept the injunctions, but she did not; she received meat and eggs on Sliav Iolar from all the women who took pity on her and went to visit her. So when she got the tallow, she weighed it, and finding it some ounces short, gave out three piercing wails of distress, and when Dyeermud, who was of fiery temper, saw that Faolan was not willing to punish the woman, ·he raised his own sword, and swept the head off her.

Fin embraced Faolan and welcomed him. Dyeermud went to his mother and sister.

"Will you marry a young champion whom I have brought with me?" asked he of the sister.

"I will marry no one," said she, "but the man you will choose for me."

"Very well," said Dyeermud, "there is such a man outside." He led her out, and she and Arthur were well pleased with each other.

Dyeermud, with his sister and Arthur and Faolan, set out on the following day, and never stopped nor stayed till they reached the castle of the four champions and their sister; and, taking Faolan's betrothed and Dyeermud along with them, they travelled on till they stopped at the castle of the Black-Blue Giant. Faolan's mother was there before him; and glad was she, and rejoiced, to see her own son.

There were three weddings in one at the castle of the giant: Arthur and Dyeermud's sister; Faolan and the sister of the four champions; Dyeermud and the daughter of the Black-Blue Giant.

When the feasting was over, Faolan's mother called him, and asked, "Will you go to my kingdom, which is yours by inheritance, the country of the Dark Men, and rule there?"

"I will," said Faolan, "on condition that I am to be sent for if ever the Fenians should need my assistance." He then gave his share in the land of the wild hag, and his claim to the castles of the Cat of Gray Fort, the Kitten of Cul MacKip, and the Dun Ox, to Arthur and Dyeermud, and these two shared those places between them. They attended Faolan and his wife to the country of the Dark Men, and then returned. Faolan's mother went to Fintra, and lived with Fin MacCool.

FIN MACCOOL, THE HARD GILLA, AND THE HIGH KING.

ON a day when the Fenians were living at Fintra, Fin MacCool called them together, held a council, complained of remissness, and warned the men to be cautious, to keep a better watch on the harbors, and to take good care of their arms. They promised to do better in future, and asked Fin to forgive them for that time. Fin forgave them, and sent men to keep watch on Cruach Varhin.

When on the mountain awhile, the chief sentry saw, in the distance, a man leading a horse toward Fintra. He thought to run down with word to Fin, but did not; he waited to see what kind of person was coming. The man leading the horse was far from being tidy : his shoes were untied, and the strings hanging down; on his shoulders was a mantle, flapping around in the wind. The horse had a broad, surly face; his neck was thick at the throat, and thin toward the body : the beast was scrawny, long-legged, lean, thin-maned, and ugly to look at. The only bridle on the horse was a long, heavy chain; the whip in the hand of the man was a strong iron staff. Each blow that the man gave his steed was heard through the glens and the mountains, and knocked echoes out of every cliff in that region. Each pull that the man gave the bridle was that strong, that you would think he'd tear the head off the ugly beast's body. Every clump of earth that the horse rooted up with his feet, in striving to hold back, was three times the size of a sod of turf ready for burning.

"It is time for me now," said the watchman, at last, "to hurry from this, and tell Fin," and with that he rushed down from Cruach Varhin.

Fin saw him coming, and was ready for his story; and not too soon was it told; for just then the horseman came up to the King of the Fenians at Fintra.

"Who are you?" inquired Fin.

"I do not know who my father was," said the stranger. "I am of one place as well as another. Men call me the Hard Gilla; and it is a good name: for no matter how well people treat me I forget all they do. I have heard, though, that you give most wages, and best treatment of any man."

"I will give you good wages," said Fin, "and fair treatment; but how much do you want of me?"

"I want whatever I ask."

"I will give you that and more, if I promise," said Fin.

"I am your man," said the Gilla. "Now that we have agreed, I may let my horse out to graze, I suppose?"

"You may," answered Fin.

The Gilla untied the chain bridle from his horse, and struck him with the chain. The beast went to the other horses; but if he did, he fell to eating the mane, legs, ears, and tail of each one of them, and ate all till he came to a steed grazing apart, and this steed belonged to Conan Maol. Conan ran, caught the ugly old horse by the skull, and pulled him up to his owner.

Mind your wicked old cripple!" cried Conan, in anger.

"If any man does not like how my horse feeds, he may herd the good steed himself."

When Conan heard this insolence, he went to the adviser for counsel. The adviser told him to go upon the back of the horse, and to ride till he broke him. Conan mounted the horse; but not a stir could he get from the stubborn beast.

"He is used to heavy loads," said the adviser. "Let others mount with you."

The Fenians were mounting the horse till twenty-eight men of them went up with Conan.

The twenty-nine began then to wallop the horse, but could not raise a stir out of him. The old horse only cocked one ear. When the Gilla saw the twenty-nine on his horse, he called out, "It seems that we do not agree; and the sooner I go from this place the better."

He tightened his cloak, flapping loose on his body, tied his shoes, and said, "In place of praising, I will dispraise you." Then he went in front of the horse. The horse raised his tail and his head, and between his tail and his neck he held the men firmly. Some tried to jump off, but were as secure on the horse as his own skin. Conan was the first to speak. When he saw that he could not spring from the horse, he turned to Fin, and cried out, "I bind you, O Fin, not to eat two meals off the one table, or sleep two nights on the one bed, till you have me freed from this serpent."

When Fin and the Fenians heard this, they looked at one another. The adviser spoke then, and said, "There is no time for delay. We have here a man to follow, and he is Leeagawn of Lúachar Garv."

Fin called Leeagawn, and he went after the steed quickly, caught him at the edge of the strand, and seized him by the tail; but if he did, he grew fast to the tail of the horse, and was

pulled forward to the strand.   He tried to loose
himself from the tail, but no use for him to try.
The horse drew him into the water.   The sea
opened before the strange steed, and closed
behind.   The Gilla ran in front.   Twenty-nine
men were on the back of the horse, and one fixed
to his tail.

Fin and the Fenians were greatly distressed at
the sight, but could give no assistance.   They
held council; and the druid said, "There is an
old ship in Ben Eadan; put that ship in repair,
and sail after the steed."

"Let us go," said the Fenians, "for the ship."

As they were making ready to start, two young
champions hurried up to Fin, and saluted him.

"Who are ye?" asked Fin, returning the
salute; "and whither are ye going?"

"We are the two sons of a king," replied they;
"each has a gift, and we have come to you to
know which is the better gift to live by.   The
two gifts are two powers left us by our father."

"What is your power?" asked Fin of the elder
brother.

"Do you see this branch?" said he.   "If I
strike the water of the harbor with this branch,
the harbor will be filled with ships till they are
crushing one another.   When you choose the
one you like, I will make the others disappear
as quickly as you can bow your head."

"What can you do?" asked Fin of the younger brother.

"If a wild duck were to dart forth from her nest, I could keep in sight of the bird, and she going straight or crooked, high or low, I could catch her before she could fly back to the nest from which she came."

When they had done speaking, Fin said, "I have never been in more need of your help than I am at this moment." He told them then of the Gilla, and of all that had happened. The elder brother struck the harbor with his branch; the harbor was filled with ships in one minute. Fin chose the ship he liked best, and said, "I'll take that one." In a twinkle the other ships vanished.

When the men were all ready to go on the ship, Fin called Oisin, and said to him, "I leave the ruling of Erin with you, till I come back to this harbor." He bade farewell then to Oisin and the Fenians. The younger of the two champions stood at the prow, the elder at the stern. The younger followed the horse in crooked and straight paths through the sea, told his brother how to steer on the voyage. They kept on till, at length, and at last, they came to a haven with a steep, rugged shore, and no ship could enter.

"This is where the steed went in," said the younger brother.

When the Fenians saw the haven, they looked at one another. It was a very steep place; and all said, "We cannot land here."

"There will be an evil report for the Fenians of Erin, or for men trained by Fin, if no one can spring to land," said the druid.

"Well," said Dyeermud, "there was never a man at Fintra who could make such a spring, if I cannot make it."

He buckled his belt firmly, and went to the stern of the ship to find space for a run; then he rushed to the prow, and rose with one bound to the top of the cliff. When he looked back, and saw his comrades below, he was frightened.

Dyeermud left the ship and the Fenians, and walked forward alone. Toward evening, he saw a herd of deer; he pursued them, and caught a doe, which he killed; he made a fire, roasted the carcass, ate of it, and drank pure spring-water. He made a hut then of limbs, and slept quietly till morning. After breakfast, a gruagach came the way, and called out to him, "Is not Erin wide enough for you to live in, instead of coming hither to steal my herds from me?"

"Though I might have been willing to go when you came," replied Dyeermud, "I will not go now since you speak so unmannerly."

"You must fight with me then," said the gruagach.

"I will indeed," said Dyeermud.

They took their spears and swords, and fought all that day until evening, when the gruagach saw that Dyeermud was getting the upper hand. He leaped into the spring from which Dyeermud had drunk the cool water. Dyeermud ran quickly, and thrust his sword into the water, but no sign of the gruagach.

"I will watch for you to-morrow," said Dyeermud to himself; so he waited near the spring until morning.

The gruagach stood before him next day more threatening to look at than ever, and said, "It seems you had n't fighting enough from me yesterday."

"I told you that I would not go," answered Dyeermud, "till I had knocked satisfaction out of you for your ugly speech."

They went at each other then, and fought fiercely till very near evening. Dyeermud watched the spring closely, and when the gruagach leaped in, he was with him. In the side of the spring was a passage; the two walked through that passage, and came out in a kingdom where there was a grand castle, and seven men at each side of the door. When Dyeermud went toward the castle, the fourteen rushed against him. He slew these, and all others who faced him till nightfall. He would not enter the castle, but stretched himself on the ground, and fell fast asleep. Soon a champion came, tapped him lightly with a sword, and said, "Rise now, and speak to me."

Dyeermud sprang up, and grasped his sword.

"I am not an enemy, but a friend," said the champion. "It is not proper for you to be sleeping in the midst of your enemies. Come to my castle; I will entertain you, and give you good keeping."

Dyeermud went with the stranger; and they became faithful friends. "The king of this country, which is called Tir Fohin [Land Under the Wave], is my brother," said the champion. "The kingdom is rightfully mine, and 't is I that should be King of Tir Fohin; but my brother corrupted my warriors with promises, so that all except thirty men of them left me."

This champion was called the Knight of Valor. Dyeermud told this knight his whole story, — told of the Hard Gilla, and his long-legged, scrawny, thin-maned, ugly old horse.

"I am the man," said the knight, "that will find out the Hard Gilla for you. That Gilla is the best swordsman and champion in this land, and the greatest enchanter. Your men, brought away by him, are as safe and as sound as when they left Erin. He is a good friend of mine."

"Now," said Dyeermud, "for your kindness (you might have killed me when I was asleep), and for your entertainment, I give my word to fight against your brother, and win back your kingdom."

Dyeermud sent a challenge to the King of Tir Fohin. The knight and Dyeermud, with the knight's thirty men, fought against the king's forces, fought all that day until evening; then the king withdrew to the castle to keep his hold firm on the chief place, but Dyeermud rushed in, brought him out to the green, threw him on the flat of his back, and shouted, "Are you not satisfied yet?"

"I am if the men are," said the king.

"Will you obey the Knight of Valor?" asked Dyeermud of the men.

"We will," answered they.

The men gave their word to obey with all faithfulness. Dyeermud gave the false king thirty men then; and the Knight of Valor became king in his own land. On the morrow, Dyeermud and the king went with forces to the Gilla's castle; and when they entered the gates, the Gilla came out, received them with welcome and hand-shaking. There was great rejoicing, and good cheer at the Gilla's castle.

When Dyeermud did not return to the vessel,

Fin and the two young champions thought to find an easier landing in some place; they put their ship around, and sailed forward, sailed and sailed; and where should they come at last but to the castle of the King of Sorách (Light), who received them with welcome, and entertained them with the best that he had in his castle.

But they were hardly seated at table, when the chief messenger of the King of Sorách came hurrying in and said, that there was a fleet sailing toward them, which was as numerous as the sands on the seashore, that it was coming for tribute, which had not been collected for many a year.

The king had a grieved and sorrowful face. "That is the High King of the World coming against me," said he.

"Never fear," said Fin MacCool. "Cheer up, and have courage. I and my men will stand up for you. We will fight to the death to defend you."

On the following day, the High King sent forces to land, to attack the King of Sorách in his castle. These forces were under command of Borb Sinnsior na Gah, son of the High King. The greatest delight of the High King was his daughter, a beautiful maiden called Teasa Taov Geal; and the thought came to her that day to see the battle. "I will go," said she, "with my brother, and see him take the king's castle."

On Fin's side, the two young champions his guides were eager to be in the struggle; but Fin would not hear of that. "You must stay with the ship," said he, "and take us to Erin, when the time comes."

As soon as Fin saw the attack was led by the son of the High King, he said, "I will take command in the battle, and lead the men in action to-day. We will show the invaders what the Fenians do in battle."

Oscar went with Fin, and so did Goll Mac-Morna. The battle raged grandly; the men of the High King fell in crowds until evening, what was left of them then went to the ships, and sailed back in haste to their master.

When the news reached the High King, he called his druid for advice.

"This is not the time to make war on the King of Sorách," said the druid; "for Fin MacCool and his men are living in friendship at his castle; they will help him to the end of this struggle. Go home for the present, and come again when Fin has gone back to Erin."

The king was inclined to do this; but his daughter had seen Fin MacCool in the battle, and fallen in love with him. She sent him a message, saying, "I will go with you. I will leave my father for your sake. I love you."

The answer that Fin sent, was to come to him; he would take her with gladness to Erin.

The king was grieved at the loss of his daughter. "I might go home now," said he, "and come back at another time; but how can I go, and leave my daughter behind me?"

There was a champion called Lavran MacSuain, who could steal anything while men were asleep, and make them sleep all the more, but could not do harm to them. Lavran volunteered to bring back the daughter.

"If I find them asleep," said he, "I will bring her back; if you give me a reward."

"I will pay you well," said the king. "I will not spare rewards on you, if you bring me my daughter."

When Lavran came to where Fin was, he found him and the Fenians asleep, and put them in a still deeper sleep. He brought Teasa Taov Geal to her father's ship then. The fleet sailed away in the night; and at day-break there was not a trace of it.

Next morning when Fin woke, and found that the king's daughter was gone, he sprang up, and was raging with anger. He sent men to look for the fleet; but not a boat nor a ship was in sight.

Oscar and Goll, seeing Fin in such passion, said, "We will go, if a druid goes with us. He will find out the castle by his knowledge; and we will bring the woman back, or die while striving to bring her."

Next morning, Goll and Oscar took a ready ship from the fleet of the King of Sorách, set sail, and never stopped till they touched land near the castle of the High King.

"The best way for us," said the druid, on landing, "is to say that we are bards, till we learn where the strength of the king is."

"We will not do that," said Oscar. "We will go straight forward, and bring the woman back with the strength of our arms."

They went straight from the strand toward the castle. At the wayside was a rath where the daughter of the king was at that time, and no great number of men there to guard her. Goll and Oscar attacked the guards, cut them down, and took Taov Geal.

"The king is coming home from a hunt," said the druid; "it is better to hurry back to our ship."

"We will sharpen our weapons," said Oscar, "and strike the king's men, if they come toward us; but do you take the woman, and go in all haste to the ship. We will stay behind to protect you."

The druid took Taov Geal, who was willing and glad, when she heard who had come for her.

They reached the ship safely. Goll and Oscar came soon after, sprang into the ship, set sail, and never stopped till they brought Teasa Taov Geal to Fin at the castle of the King of Sorách. There was a feast then far greater than the one which the High King had interrupted the first day.

"I will take you to Erin," said Fin to Taov Geal.

"I will go with you," said she.

"I know the Hard Gilla well," said the King of Sorách to Fin MacCool. "I will go with you to him; he is a great champion, and a mighty enchanter."

The king and his men, with Fin and the Fenians, went to the lands of the Gilla; and when he saw them all, he brought them into his castle, and treated them well. Dyeermud and the King of Tir Fohin were there also; they had been enjoying themselves, and feasting with the Gilla, while Fin and the others were fighting with the High King, and stealing his daughter.

Conan and the twenty-nine Fenians were all in good health; and Fin had the daughter of the High King in the castle, intending to take her to Erin.

Said Fin to the Gilla one day, "It was you and Conan who had the first quarrel, he and you are the men who began these adventures. I will leave him and you to end the whole story. Conan is not easy to talk with, and you are a hard man to conquer."

Conan was called up.

"What have you to say of our host," inquired Fin; "and what would you do for him?"

"I was treated here as well as you have ever treated me in Fintra, or as any man treated me in another place," said Conan. "My sentence is this, Let him come to Erin with us in our ship, feast with us in Fintra, and ride home on his own horse."

"I will do that," said the Gilla.

Conan and the Gilla, with all the Fenians, went to the ship. Fin brought the daughter of the High King on board, and all sailed away to Erin.

The Gilla was entertained to his heart's content, till one day he said, "I must leave you now, and go to my own place."

Conan and a number of Fenians went to the seashore to see him ride away. "Where is your horse?" asked Conan.

"Here," said the Gilla.

Conan turned to see the ugly long-legged beast, but saw nothing. He turned then to look at the Gilla, but saw only mist stretching out toward the water.

THE BATTLE OF VENTRY.

IT was predicted seven years before the battle of Ventry, that Daire Donn, High King of the Great World, would invade Erin to conquer it. Fin MacCool, for this reason, placed sentries at the chief ports of Erin. At Ventry, Conn Crithir was stationed on the top of Cruach Varhin to give warning; but he overslept when the fleet came: and the first news he had of its coming was from the cries of people attacked by the invaders. Conn Crithir sprang up, and said, —

"Great is the misery that has come by my sleep; but Fin and the Fenians will not see me alive after this. I will rush into the midst of the foreigners; and they will fall by me, till I fall by them."

So he ran down toward the strand. On the way, he saw three strange women running before him. He increased his speed; but, unable to overtake them, he caught his spear to hurl it at the one nearest him.

The women stopped that moment, and cried, "Stay your hand, and do not kill innocent women who have come not to harm but to help you."

"Who are ye?" asked Conn Crithir.

"We are three sisters who have come from Tirnanog. We are all three in love with you; but no one of us is jealous of the other. We will hide you with an enchanted cloud, so that you can attack the foreign forces unseen. We have a well of healing at the foot of Sliav Iolar; and its waters will cure every wound made in battle. After bathing in it, you will be as sound as the day you were born."

Conn Crithir was grateful, and hurried to the strand, where he slew four hundred men of the enemy on the first day. He was covered with wounds himself; but the three sisters took him to the well. He bathed in it, and was as sound as on the day he was born.

Conn Crithir was this way in struggle and combat, till Teastalach Treunmhar, the chief courier of Fin MacCool, came to Ventry.

"Have you tidings of Fin and the Fenians?" asked Conn.

"I have. They are at the River Lee," said Teastalach.

"Go to them quickly," said Conn, "and tell

how we are here.   Let them come hither to save us."

"It would ill become me to go till I had moistened my sword in the blood of the enemy," said Teastalach; and he sent a challenge for single combat to the High King.

"I am the man to meet that warrior," said Colahan MacDochar, the king's champion; and he went on shore without waiting.

Colahan was thirty feet in height, and fifteen around the waist.   When he landed, he went at Teastalach.   They fought one hour, and fought with such fury, the two of them, that their swords and spears went to pieces.   The sword of Colahan was broken at the hilt; but of Teastalach's blade there remained a piece as long as the breadth of a man's palm.

Colahan, who was enraged that any champion could stand against him for the space of even one hour, seized Teastalach in his arms, to carry him living to the ship of the High King, twist off his head there, and raise it on a stake before the forces of the world.   When he came to deep water, he raised Teastalach on his shoulder; but Teastalach, the swift courier of Fin MacCool, turned quickly, cut the head off his enemy, brought that head to the strand, and made boast of his deed.

Now Teastalach went to where Fin and his forces were, and told him of all that happened. Fin marched straightway, and never stopped nor rested till he came to Maminch, within twenty miles of Ventry. Fin rested there for the night; but Oscar, son of Oisin, with Conn Ceadach and one other, went forward. Before going, Oscar turned to Fin, and said, " Chew your thumb, and tell us what will be the end of our struggle."

Fin chewed his thumb from the skin to the flesh, from the flesh to the bone, from the bone to the marrow, from the marrow to the juice, and said, " The victory will be on our side, but little else will be with us. The battle will last for a day and a year, and every day will be a day of fierce struggle. No man of the foreigners will escape; and on our side few will be left living, and none without wounds."

Oscar went his way then till he reached Ventry. Fin came on the second day, and stopped with all his forces at Rahonáin. Next morning, he asked, " Who will command the battle to-day? "

" We will go with two hundred," said Oisin and Oscar.

They went toward the harbor; and a great troop landed to meet them. The two parties faced each other then, and fought till near evening;

when all were killed on the side of the foreigners except three smiths, and of Fin's men there remained only Oisin, Oscar, and Goll, son of Morna.

On the following morning, Oisin and Oscar went with two hundred more, but without Goll. The foreign troop came in numbers as before: and at midday there was no man left living of Fin's men but Oisin and Oscar; on the foreign side all had fallen except the three smiths, who were mighty champions. Oscar and Oisin faced the smiths. Oscar had two men against him; and Oisin's enemy was forcing him backward toward the water. Fin, seeing this, feared for his son, and sent a poet to praise and encourage him.

"Now is the time to prove your valor and greatness, Oisin", said the poet. "You never went to any place but a king's daughter, or a high beauty, fell in love with you. Many are looking this day at you; and now is your time to show bravery."

Oisin was greatly encouraged; so he grew in fury and increased on his blows, till at last he swept the head off his enemy. About the same time, Oscar killed the two other smiths; but, being faint from open wounds and blood-loss, he fell senseless on the strand. Oisin, his father, rushed to him, and held him till aid came.   They carried him to Rahonáin, where, after a long time, he revived.

The smiths had one brother in the fleet of the High King, and his name was Dealv Dura.   This man, who was the first champion in the armies of the High King, fell into great grief, and swore to have vengeance for his brothers.   He went to the High King, and said, "I will go alone to the strand, and will slay two hundred men every day till I have slain all the forces of Erin; and if any man of your troops interfere, I will kill him."

Next morning, Fin asked who would conduct the battle on that day.

"I will," said Duvan, son of Donn, "with two hundred men."

"Go not," said Fin.   "Let another go."

But Duvan went to the strand with two hundred; and there was no one before him but Dealv Dura, who demanded two hundred men in combat.   A shout of derision went up from Duvan's men; but Dealv rushed at them, and he slew the two hundred without a man of them being able to put a sword-cut on him.   Then, taking a hurley and ball, Dealv Dura threw up the ball, and kept it in the air with the hurley from the western to the eastern end of the strand, without letting it touch the ground even one time. Then, he put the ball on his right foot, and kicked it high in the air; when it was near the earth, he sent it up with the left foot, and kept the ball in the air with his two feet, and never let it touch the earth once, while he was rushing from one end of the strand to the other. Next, he put the ball on his right knee, sent it up with that, caught it on the left knee, and kept the ball in the air with his two knees while he was running from one end of the strand to the other. Last, he put the ball on one shoulder, threw it up with that shoulder, caught it on the other, and kept the ball in the air with his two shoulders while he was rushing like a blast of March wind from one end of the strand to the other.

When he had finished, he walked back and forth on the strand vauntingly, and challenged the men of Erin to do the like of those feats.

Next day, Fin sent out two hundred men. Dealv Dura was down on the strand before them, and not a man of the two hundred returned.

Day after day, two hundred went out, and all fell before Dealv Dura. A report ran now through all Erin that Fin's troops were perishing daily from one man; and this report reached at last the castle of the King of Ulster. The king had one son, and he only thirteen years of age. This son, who was the fairest and shape-liest youth in Erin, said to his father, "Let me go to help Fin MacCool and his men."

"You are not old enough, nor strong enough, my son; your bones are too soft."

When the youth insisted, his father confined him, and set twelve youths, his own foster-brothers, to guard him, lest he might escape to Ventry Strand.

The king's son was enraged at being confined, and said to his foster-brothers, "It is through valor and daring that my father gained glory in his young years; and why should I not win a name as well as he? Help me, and I will be a friend to you forever."

He talked and persuaded, till they agreed to go with him to Fin MacCool. They took arms then, hurried across Erin, and, when they came to Ventry, Dealv Dura was on the strand reviling the Fenians.

"O Fenians of Erin," said Oisin, "many have fallen by Dealv Dura; and I would rather die in combat against him, than see the ruin he brings every day!"

A great cry was raised by all at these words.

Now the son of the King of Ulster stood before Fin, and saluted him.

"Who are you?" asked Fin.

"I am Goll, son of the King of Ulster, and these twelve are my foster-brothers. We have come to give you what assistance we can."

"My welcome to you," said Fin.

The reviling of Dealv Dura was heard now again.

"Who is that?" asked the king's son from Ulster.

"An enemy asking for two hundred warriors of mine to meet him," said Fin.

Here the twelve foster-brothers went to the strand, unknown to the king's son.

"You are not a man," said Conan Maol, "and none of these twelve could face any warrior."

"I have never seen the Fenians till this day," said the king's son, "still I know that you are Conan Maol, who never speaks well of any man; but you will see that I am not in dread of Dealv Dura, or any champion on earth. I will go down now, and meet the warrior single-handed."

Fin and the Fenians stopped the young hero, and detained him, and talked to him. Then, Conan began again, and said, "In six days that champion has slain twelve hundred men; and there was not a man of the twelve hundred who could not have killed twelve hundred like you every day."

These words enraged the king's son. He

sprang up, and then heard the shouting of Dealv Dura on the strand. "What does he want now?" asked the king's son.

"More men for combat," said Conan. "He has just slain your twelve body-guards."

With that the king's son seized his weapons, and no man could stop or delay him. He rushed to the strand, and went toward Dealv Dura. When the champion saw the youth coming, he sneered, and the hosts of the High King sent up a roar of laughter; for they thought Fin's men were all killed, since he had sent a stripling to meet Dealv Dura. The courage of the boy was all the greater from the derision; and he rushed on Dealv Dura, who got many wounds from the youth before he knew it.

They fought a sharp, bloody combat; and no matter how the champion, Dealv Dura, used his strength, swiftness, and skill, he was met by the king's son: and if the world could be searched, from its eastern edge to its western border, no braver battle would be found than was that one.

The two fought through the day, the hosts of the Great World and the Fenians cheering and urging them on. Toward evening their shields were hacked to pieces, and their weapons all shivered, but they did not stop the battle; they grappled and caught each other, and fought so that the sand on the beach was boiling like water beneath them. They wrestled that way, seeing nothing in the world but each other, till the tide of the sea went over them, and drowned the two there before the eyes of the Fenians and the hosts of the High King.

A great cry of wailing and sorrow was raised on both sides, when the water closed over the champions. Next morning, after the tide-ebb, the two bodies were found stiff and cold, each one in the grasp of the other; but Dealv Dura was under the king's son, so it was known that the youth was a better man than the other.

The king's son was buried with great honor by the Fenians; and never before did they mourn for a hero as on that day.

"Who will command the battle this time?" asked Fin, on the following morning.

"I and my son Oscar," said Oisin.

They went to the strand with two hundred men; and against them came the King of France with his forces. The two sides fought with such venom that at midday there was no one alive on either side but Oscar, Oisin, and the King of France. The king and Oisin were fighting at the eastern end of Ventry; and the king gave such a blow that he knocked a groan from Oisin. Oscar, who was at the western end of

the strand then, — Oscar, of noble deeds, the man
with a heart that never knew fear, and a foot that
never stepped back before many or few, — rushed
to see who had injured his father; and the noise
that he made was like the noise of fifty horses
while racing.

The king looked toward the point where the
thundering sound was, and saw Oscar coming.
He knew then that unless he escaped he had not
long to live; his beauty and bravery left him,
and his terror was like that of a hundred horses
at the sound of a thunderbolt. Lightness of mind
and body came on him; he stretched himself,
sprang up, flew through the air, and never
stopped till he came down in Glean nan Allt, —
a place to which, since that time, insane persons go, and every madman in Erin would go
there in twenty four hours, if people would let
him.

In the battle of the next day, the King of Norway was chief; and there was never such destruction of men in Erin before as on that day. This
king had a venomous shield with red flames, and
if it were put under the sea not one of its flames
would stop blazing, and the king himself was not
hotter from any of them. When he had the shield
on his arm no man could come near him; and
he went against the Fenians with only a sword.
Not to use weapon had he come, but to let the

poison of his shield fly among them. The balls of fire that he sent from the shield went through the bodies of men, so that each blazed up like a splinter of oak which had hung a whole year in the smoke of a chimney, and whoever touched the burning man, blazed up as well as he; and small was every evil that came into Erin before, when compared with that evil.

"Lift up your hands," said Fin, "and give three shouts of blessing to the man who will put some delay on that foreigner."

A smile came on the king's face when he heard the shouts that Fin's men were giving. It was then that the Chief of the Fenians of Ulster came near; and he had a venomous spear, the Crodearg. He looked at the King of Norway, and saw nothing of him without armor, save his mouth, and that open wide in laughter at the Fenians. He made a cast of his venomous spear, which entered the king's mouth, and went out through his neck. The shield fell, and its blazing was quenched with the life of its master. The chief cut the head off the king, and made boast of the deed; and his help was the best that the Fenians received from any man of their own men. Many were the deeds of that day; and but few of the forces of the High King went back to their ships in the evening.

On the following day, the foreigners came in thousands; for the High King had resolved to put an and to the struggle. Conan Maol, who never spoke well of any man, had a power which he knew not himself, and which no one in Erin knew except Fin. When Conan looked through his fingers at any man, that man fell dead the next instant.

Fin never told Conan of this, and never told any one; for he knew that Conan would kill all the Fenians when he got vexed if he knew his own power. When the foreigners landed, Fin sent a party of men with Conan to a suitable place, so that when the enemy were attacking, these men would look with Conan through their fingers at the enemy, and pray for assistance against them.

When Conan and his men looked through their fingers, the enemy fell dead in great numbers, and no one knew that it was Conan's look alone, without prayers or assistance from others, that slew them.

Conan and his company stood there all day, looking through their fingers and praying, whenever a new face made its way from the harbor.

The struggle lasted day after day, till his men spoke to the High King and said to him, "We can never conquer unless you meet Fin in single combat."

The king challenged Fin to meet him on the third day. Fin accepted, though he was greatly

in dread; for he knew that the trunk of the High
King's body was formed of one bone, and that no
sword in the world could cut it but the king's own
sword, which was kept in the Eastern World by
his grandsire, the King of the Land of the White
Men. That old king had seven chambers in a
part of his castle, one inside the other. On the
door of the outer chamber was one lock, on the
second two, and so on to the door of the seventh
and innermost chamber, which had seven locks,
and in that chamber the sword and shield of the
High King were kept. In the service of Daire
Donn was a champion, a great wizard, who wished
ill to the High King. This man went to Fin,
and said, " I will bring you the sword and shield
from the Eastern World."

"Good will be my reward to you," said Fin,
" if you bring them in time."

Away went the man in a cloud of enchantment,
and soon stood before the old king. "Your
grandson," said he, " is to fight with Fin Mac-
Cool, and has sent me for his weapons."

The old king had the sword and shield brought
quickly, and gave them. The man hurried back
to Erin, and gave the weapons to Fin on the eve
of the battle.

Next morning, the High King came to the
strand full of confidence. Believing himself safe,
he thought he could kill Fin MacCool easily;

but when he stood in front of the chief of the Fenians, and saw his own venomous sword unsheathed in the hand of his enemy, and knew that death was fated him from that blade, his face left him for a moment, and his fingers were unsteady.

He rallied, and thinking to win by surprise, rushed suddenly, fiercely and mightily, to combat. One of Fin's men sprang out, and dealt a great blow with a broadaxe; it laid open the helmet, cut some of the hair of the High King, but touched not the skin of his body. The High King with one blow made two parts of the Fenian, and, rushing at Fin, cut a slice from his shield, and a strip of flesh from his thigh. Fin gave one blow then in answer, which made two equal parts of the king, so that one eye, one ear, one arm, and one leg of him dropped on one side, and the other eye, ear, arm, and leg went to the other side.

Now, the hosts of the High King, and the Fenians of Erin, fought till there was no man standing in the field except one. He raised the body of the High King, and said, "It was bad for us, O Fenians of Erin, but worse for you; I go home in health, and ye have fallen side by side. I will come again soon, and take all Erin."

"Sad am I," said Fin, as he lay on the field, "that I did not find death before I heard these words from the mouth of a foreigner, and he going into the Great World with tidings. Is there any man alive near me?"

"I am," said Fergus Finbel; "and there is no warrior who is not lying in his blood save the chief man of the High King and your own foster-son, Caol."

"Go to seek my foster-son," said Fin.

Fergus went to Caol, and asked him how his health was. "If my battle-harness were loosened, my body would fall asunder from wounds; but more grieved am I at the escape of the foreigner with tidings than at my own woful state. Take me to the sea, Fergus, that I may swim after the foreigner; perhaps he will fall by this hand before the life leaves me."

Fergus took him to the sea; and he swam to the ship. The foreigner thought him one of his own men, and reached down to raise him to the ship-board; but Caol grasped the man firmly and drew him to the water. Both sank in the clear, cold sea, and were drowned.

No man saw the foreigner afterward; but Caol's body was carried by the waves, borne northward, and past the islands, till it came to land, at the port which is now called Caoil Cuan (Caol's Harbor).

NOTES.

NOTES.

THE tales in this volume were told me by the following persons : —

Nos. 1, 5, 18, 21. Maurice Lynch, Mount Eagle, West of Dingle, Kerry.

Nos. 2, 11, 24. John Malone, Rahonain, West of Dingle.

Nos. 3, 15. Shea, Kil Vicadowny, West of Dingle.

No. 4. Thomas Brady, Teelin, County Donegal.

No. 6. Maurice Fitzgerald, Emilich Slat, West of Dingle.

Nos. 7, 9, 12, 17. John O'Brien, Connemara.

No. 8. James Byrne, Glen Columkil, County Donegal.

Nos. 10, 14. Colman Gorm, Connemara.

No. 13. Michael Curran, Gortahork, County Donegal.

No. 16. Michael O'Conor, six miles north of Newcastle West, County Limerick.

Nos. 19, 20. Michael Sullivan, Dingle.

No. 22. Dyeermud Duvane, Milltown, County Kerry.

No. 23. Daniel Sheehy, Dunquin, Kerry, a man over a hundred years old.

Elin Gow, the Swordsmith from Erin, and the Cow Glas Gainach.

Glas Gainach. In this name of the celebrated cow *glas* means gray; *gainach* is a corruption of *gaunach*, written *gamhnach*, which means a cow whose calf is a

year old, that is, a cow without a calf that year, a farrow
cow. *Gamhnach* is an adjective from *gamhan,* a year-
ling calf.

In Donegal, *gavlen* is used instead of *gaunach ;* and the
best story-teller informed me that *gavlen* means a cow
that has not had a calf for five years. He gave the terms
for cows that have not had calves for one, two, three,
four, and five years. These terms I wrote down ; but
unfortunately they are not accessible at present. The
first in the series is *gaunach,* the last *gavlen ;* the inter-
vening ones I cannot recall.

King Under the Wave is a personage met with frequently in Gaelic ; his name is descriptive enough, and
his character more or less clear in other tales.

Cluainte is a place in the parish of Bally Ferriter, the
westernmost district in Ireland. The site of Elin Gow's
house and forge was pointed out by the man who told
the story, also the stone pillars between which the cow
used to stand and scratch her two sides at once when
coming home from pasture in the evening. The pillars
are thirteen feet and a half apart, so that Glas Gainach
had a bulky body.

Glas Gainach went away finally through the bay called
Ferriter's Cove. In Gaelic, this bay is Caoil Cuan
(Caol's harbor), so called because the body of Caol,
foster-son of Fin MacCool, was washed in there after the
Battle of Ventry. (See last paragraph of the Battle of
Ventry.)

Saudan Og and the Daughter of the King of Spain, &c.

Saudan Og means young Sultan. This is a curious
naturalization of the son of the Sultan in Ireland, a very

striking example of the substitution of new heroes in old tales.

Conal Gulban was the great grandfather of Columbkil, founder of Iona and apostle of Scotland ; hence, he lived a good many years before any King of the Turks could be in any place. In a certain tale of three brothers which I have heard, the narrator made " two halves " of Mark Antony, the three heroes being Mark, Antony, and Lepidus.

Laian, written *Laighean* in Gaelic, means Leinster; the King of Laian is King of Leinster.

The Black Thief.

There are many variants of this tale, both in the north and south of Ireland. It seems to have been a great favorite, and is mentioned often, though few know it well.

There are versions connected with Killarney and the O'Donohue.

The adventures in the present tale are very striking. It would be difficult indeed to have narrower escapes than those of the Black Thief.

The racing of the cats through all underground Erin is paralleléd in Indian tales, especially those of the Modocs, in which immense journeys are made underground.

The King's Son from Erin, the Sprisawn, and the Dark King.

Lochlinn is used to mean Denmark, though there is no connection whatever between the names. Lochlinn is doubtless one of the old names in Gaelic tales, and referred to some kind of water region. Instead of put-

ting the name " Denmark " in place of the name " Lochlinn," it was said in this case that Lochlinn was Denmark.
Other regions or kingdoms in the old tales lost their
names: Spain, Sicily, Greece, France were put in place
of them ; we have lost the clew to what they were. Lochlinn has a look that invites investigation. Were all the
people of Lochlinn, creatures of the water, turned by
Gaelic tale-tellers into Scandinavians? Very likely.

In the stealing of Manus, we have a case similar to
that of Tobit in the Apocrypha.

I know of no parallel to the scene in the three chambers with the chains and the cross-beams. It is terribly
grim and merciless. There was no chance for the weak
in those chambers.

The work of the serpent in drying the lake by lashing
it, and sending the water in showers over the country, is
equalled in an Indian tale by ducks which rise from a
lake suddenly, and in such incredible numbers that they
take all the water away, carry off the lake with them.

Amadan Mor.

The boyhood of the Amadan Mor has some resem-
blance to that of the Russian hero, Ilyá Múromets, who
sat so many years in the ashes without power to rise.

The fear of stopping in unknown places finds expres-
sion frequently in Indian tales, and arises from the fact
that the visitor does not know what spirits inhabit them,
and therefore does not know how to avoid offending
those spirits. Eilin Og seems to have a similar idea in
the dark glen.

Cud, Cad, and Micad.

Urhu is called *Nurhu* sometimes, and appears to be the same as the old English Norroway, Norway. *Hadone* is said to be Sicily.

Cahal, Son of King Conor.

In this tale we have a number of elemental heroes, such as Striker and Wet Mantle. Against Striker, the great blower, no one can do anything at sea. This is the kind of hero who can walk on the water, or at least who never sinks in it much beyond his ankles. This Striker appears in another story as a giant out in the ocean, which he is beating with a club.

In Wet Mantle, whose virtue is in his cloak, which is rain itself, we have an excellent friend for a rain-maker.

Coldfeet.

This is a good hero, an excellent herdsman and cattle-thief. What a splendid cowboy he would be in the Indian Territory or Wyoming. He has a good strain of simplicity and heroism in him. The bottle of water that is never drained, is like the basket of trout's blood (also water) in the Indian tale of Walokit and Tumukit.

Lawn Dyarrig, Son of the King of Erin, and the Knight of Terrible Valley.

The serpent that sleeps seven years can be matched by monsters in American tales. The hearts of these creatures are sliced away by heroes who go down their throats and find other people before them, alive, but unable to escape. Sometimes the monster is killed; sometimes it is weakened and rendered comparatively harmless. There was an Indian monster of this kind in the Columbia River, near the Dalles, and one in the Klamath River, near its mouth.

Balor and Glas Gavlen.

This was a great tale in the old time; but it is badly broken up now. If we could discover who Balor and his daughter were really, we might, perhaps, be able to understand why his grandson was fated to kill him. The theft of Glas Gavlen is the first act in a series which ends with the death of Balor. No doubt the whole story is as natural as that of Wimaloimis, the grisly-bear cloud-woman (Introduction) who tries to eat her own sons, lightning and thunder, and is killed by them afterward.

Art, the King's Son.

This is a striking tale, the head following the body of the gruagach into the earth is peculiar. The pursuit of Art by Balor is as vigorous as it could be. Shall we say that the blade of the screeching sword is lightning, and the screech itself thunder?

In Balor's account of how his wife maltreated him, we have the incident of the infant saved by the faithful animal. Balor, however, when a wolf, saved himself by prompt action from the fate of Llewelyn's dog and that of the ichneumen in the Sanscrit tale.

There is no more interesting fact than this in myth

tales, that no matter how good the hero, he must have the right weapon. Often there is only one spear or sword, or one kind of spear or sword, in the world with which a certain deed can be done. The hero must have that weapon or fail.

Shawn Mac Breogan.

In Gaelic, we meet more frequently the cloak of darkness, a cloak of effacement. In this tale we have a cloak or mantle of power, one that makes the wearer the finest person in the world. This is like the mantle of the prophet, which, if it falls on a successor to the office, gives him power equal to that of his predecessor. Of a similar character is the garment of the Wet Mantle Hero, in Cahal, son of King Conor, whose power is in his mantle, which is rain itself.

In a certain Indian tale, two skins are described, — one the skin of a black rain cloud, the other the skin of a gray snow cloud ; whenever rain is wanted, the black skin is shaken out in the air, when snow is desired, the gray one is shaken. This shaking is done by two deities in the sky (stones at present), who thus produce rain and snow *ad libitum*. The mantles of power were skins originally. When people had forgotten the special virtue of the skins, and mantles were of cloth or skin indifferently, or later on of cloth exclusively, the virtue connected with mantles by tradition remained to them without reference to material.

In Hungarian tales the food of the steed, very often a mare, is glowing coals. There are Hungarian tales in which little if any doubt is left that the steed is lightning.

It was a steed of this character that carried Cahal, son of King Conor, to Striker's castle, a place to which no ship could go.

The skin of the white mare is like the skin of Klakherrit or Pitis in the Indian tale. When the young woman puts on the skin, she becomes the white mare ; when she takes it off, she is herself again.

The Cotter's Son and the Half Slim Champion.

Instead of a king's son, the more usual substitute for an earlier hero, we have in this tale a cotter's son. The scene of shaking ashes from his person by a mourner who has sat by the fire for a long time, finds a parallel in Indian stories. The Gaelic heroes, however, manage to get vastly more ashes onto themselves than the Indians. The son of the King of Lochlin in this case shakes off seven tons. In one Irish tale that I know, the hero goes out into the field after mourning long at the hearth, and shakes from his person an amount of ashes that covers seven acres in front of him, seven acres behind him, seven acres on his right hand, and seven acres on his left.

The old King of Lochlin, who has the same kind of story to tell as Balor, is a tremendously stubborn old fellow ; there is a savage cruelty in the torture which his son inflicts on him that is without parallel, even in myth tales. The old man goes through the roasting with a strength which no stoic or martyr could equal. When he yields at last, he does so serenely, and tells a tale which solves the conundrum completely.

Fin MacCool, the three Giants, and the Small Men.

The theft of the children of the King of the Big Men has an interesting parallel in an Indian tale from California, a part of which is as follows : —

There was a man named Kuril (which means rib). He did n't seem to know much ; but he could walk right through rocks, in at one side and out at the other. He walked across gullies, through thickets, and over precipices, as easily as on a smooth road. One evening people saw him coming from the west toward the village. When he had come near, the sun went down, and Kuril disappeared right before their eyes. They saw this several times afterwards. He came always just before sunset, never came quite to the village. The children used to play in the evening ; and he would stop and look at them, and at sunset he would be gone, turned into something.

One evening a very poor man saw Kuril pass his thumbnail along the top of his head, and split himself, the left half of him became a woman, and the right half remained a man. That night the new pair appeared to the poor man who had seen the splitting, they said that each of them was to be called Kukupiwit now (crooked breast), and talked with him. After that the poor man had great luck, killed many deer ; what he wanted, he had. The male Kukupiwit came home late every evening. His other half watched the village children playing ; if one stepped aside, or left the others, she thrust it into a basket, and ran home. People looked for their children, but never found them. She would listen, climb a house where she heard a child cry, and look down the smoke-hole. One evening a little boy was crying; his mother could not stop him. At last she said, " Cry away; I 'll go to sleep." The woman fell asleep; the boy sat crying by the hearth. Soon he saw a piece of roast venison hanging by a string over the fire. He took a piece, ate it, stopped crying, took another; the string was drawn up a little. He reached after it; the string was drawn farther. He reached higher; Kukupiwit the woman caught his hand, pulled him up, put him in her basket, and ran home.

The mother woke now; the boy was gone. She roused her husband; they looked everywhere, found no trace of their son. Next night all in the village were watching. In one house a baby cried, and soon the men who were there heard creeping on the house. One man took the baby, held it high over the fire, and said, " Take this baby ! " Kukupiwit reached down; the man lowered the child a little. She reached farther; that moment five or six men caught her arm, and tried to pull her down; but all who were in the house could not do that. One man chopped her arm right off with a flint knife, and threw it out; she fell to the ground where her arm was, she picked it up, and ran home.

The Hard Gilla.

This tale has a special interest, in that it gives the cause of the Battle of Ventry, described in the next tale. The cause, like that of the Trojan war, was a woman. The daughter of the High King of the World goes to Fin at first, and is then stolen away by him afterwards.

THE END.

A CATALOG OF SELECTED
DOVER BOOKS
IN ALL FIELDS OF INTEREST

A CATALOG OF SELECTED DOVER
BOOKS IN ALL FIELDS OF INTEREST

CONCERNING THE SPIRITUAL IN ART, Wassily Kandinsky. Pioneering work by father of abstract art. Thoughts on color theory, nature of art. Analysis of earlier masters. 12 illustrations. 80pp. of text. 5⅜ x 8½. 23411-8 Pa. $4.95

ANIMALS: 1,419 Copyright-Free Illustrations of Mammals, Birds, Fish, Insects, etc., Jim Harter (ed.). Clear wood engravings present, in extremely lifelike poses, over 1,000 species of animals. One of the most extensive pictorial sourcebooks of its kind. Captions. Index. 284pp. 9 x 12. 23766-4 Pa. $14.95

CELTIC ART: The Methods of Construction, George Bain. Simple geometric techniques for making Celtic interlacements, spirals, Kells-type initials, animals, humans, etc. Over 500 illustrations. 160pp. 9 x 12. (USO) 22923-8 Pa. $9.95

AN ATLAS OF ANATOMY FOR ARTISTS, Fritz Schider. Most thorough reference work on art anatomy in the world. Hundreds of illustrations, including selections from works by Vesalius, Leonardo, Goya, Ingres, Michelangelo, others. 593 illustrations. 192pp. 7⅛ x 10¼. 20241-0 Pa. $9.95

CELTIC HAND STROKE-BY-STROKE (Irish Half-Uncial from "The Book of Kells"): An Arthur Baker Calligraphy Manual, Arthur Baker. Complete guide to creating each letter of the alphabet in distinctive Celtic manner. Covers hand position, strokes, pens, inks, paper, more. Illustrated. 48pp. 8¼ x 11. 24336-2 Pa. $3.95

EASY ORIGAMI, John Montroll. Charming collection of 32 projects (hat, cup, pelican, piano, swan, many more) specially designed for the novice origami hobbyist. Clearly illustrated easy-to-follow instructions insure that even beginning papercrafters will achieve successful results. 48pp. 8¼ x 11. 27298-2 Pa. $3.50

THE COMPLETE BOOK OF BIRDHOUSE CONSTRUCTION FOR WOODWORKERS, Scott D. Campbell. Detailed instructions, illustrations, tables. Also data on bird habitat and instinct patterns. Bibliography. 3 tables. 63 illustrations in 15 figures. 48pp. 5¼ x 8½. 24407-5 Pa. $2.50

BLOOMINGDALE'S ILLUSTRATED 1886 CATALOG: Fashions, Dry Goods and Housewares, Bloomingdale Brothers. Famed merchants' extremely rare catalog depicting about 1,700 products: clothing, housewares, firearms, dry goods, jewelry, more. Invaluable for dating, identifying vintage items. Also, copyright-free graphics for artists, designers. Co-published with Henry Ford Museum & Greenfield Village. 160pp. 8¼ x 11. 25780-0 Pa. $10.95

HISTORIC COSTUME IN PICTURES, Braun & Schneider. Over 1,450 costumed figures in clearly detailed engravings–from dawn of civilization to end of 19th century. Captions. Many folk costumes. 256pp. 8⅜ x 11¾. 23150-X Pa. $12.95

STICKLEY CRAFTSMAN FURNITURE CATALOGS, Gustav Stickley and L. & J. G. Stickley. Beautiful, functional furniture in two authentic catalogs from 1910. 594 illustrations, including 277 photos, show settles, rockers, armchairs, reclining chairs, bookcases, desks, tables. 183pp. 6½ x 9¼. 23838-5 Pa. $11.95

AMERICAN LOCOMOTIVES IN HISTORIC PHOTOGRAPHS: 1858 to 1949, Ron Ziel (ed.). A rare collection of 126 meticulously detailed official photographs, called "builder portraits," of American locomotives that majestically chronicle the rise of steam locomotive power in America. Introduction. Detailed captions. xi + 129pp. 9 x 12. 27393-8 Pa. $13.95

AMERICA'S LIGHTHOUSES: An Illustrated History, Francis Ross Holland, Jr. Delightfully written, profusely illustrated fact-filled survey of over 200 American lighthouses since 1716. History, anecdotes, technological advances, more. 240pp. 8 x 10¾. 25576-X Pa. $12.95

TOWARDS A NEW ARCHITECTURE, Le Corbusier. Pioneering manifesto by founder of "International School." Technical and aesthetic theories, views of industry, economics, relation of form to function, "mass-production split" and much more. Profusely illustrated. 320pp. 6⅛ x 9¼. (USO) 25023-7 Pa. $9.95

HOW THE OTHER HALF LIVES, Jacob Riis. Famous journalistic record, exposing poverty and degradation of New York slums around 1900, by major social reformer. 100 striking and influential photographs. 233pp. 10 x 7⅞. 22012-5 Pa. $11.95

FRUIT KEY AND TWIG KEY TO TREES AND SHRUBS, William M. Harlow. One of the handiest and most widely used identification aids. Fruit key covers 120 deciduous and evergreen species; twig key 160 deciduous species. Easily used. Over 300 photographs. 126pp. 5⅜ x 8½. 20511-8 Pa. $3.95

COMMON BIRD SONGS, Dr. Donald J. Borror. Songs of 60 most common U.S. birds: robins, sparrows, cardinals, bluejays, finches, more—arranged in order of increasing complexity. Up to 9 variations of songs of each species.
Cassette and manual 99911-4 $8.95

ORCHIDS AS HOUSE PLANTS, Rebecca Tyson Northen. Grow cattleyas and many other kinds of orchids—in a window, in a case, or under artificial light. 63 illustrations. 148pp. 5⅜ x 8½. 23261-1 Pa. $5.95

MONSTER MAZES, Dave Phillips. Masterful mazes at four levels of difficulty. Avoid deadly perils and evil creatures to find magical treasures. Solutions for all 32 exciting illustrated puzzles. 48pp. 8¼ x 11. 26005-4 Pa. $2.95

MOZART'S DON GIOVANNI (DOVER OPERA LIBRETTO SERIES), Wolfgang Amadeus Mozart. Introduced and translated by Ellen H. Bleiler. Standard Italian libretto, with complete English translation. Convenient and thoroughly portable—an ideal companion for reading along with a recording or the performance itself. Introduction. List of characters. Plot summary. 121pp. 5¼ x 8½. 24944-1 Pa. $3.95

TECHNICAL MANUAL AND DICTIONARY OF CLASSICAL BALLET, Gail Grant. Defines, explains, comments on steps, movements, poses and concepts. 15-page pictorial section. Basic book for student, viewer. 127pp. 5⅜ x 8½. 21843-0 Pa. $4.95

BRASS INSTRUMENTS: Their History and Development, Anthony Baines. Authoritative, updated survey of the evolution of trumpets, trombones, bugles, cornets, French horns, tubas and other brass wind instruments. Over 140 illustrations and 48 music examples. Corrected and updated by author. New preface. Bibliography. 320pp. 5⅜ x 8½.   27574-4 Pa. $9.95

HOLLYWOOD GLAMOR PORTRAITS, John Kobal (ed.). 145 photos from 1926-49. Harlow, Gable, Bogart, Bacall; 94 stars in all. Full background on photographers, technical aspects. 160pp. 8⅜ x 11¼.   23352-9 Pa. $12.95

MAX AND MORITZ, Wilhelm Busch. Great humor classic in both German and English. Also 10 other works: "Cat and Mouse," "Plisch and Plumm," etc. 216pp. 5⅜ x 8½.
                                                                  20181-3 Pa. $6.95

THE RAVEN AND OTHER FAVORITE POEMS, Edgar Allan Poe. Over 40 of the author's most memorable poems: "The Bells," "Ulalume," "Israfel," "To Helen," "The Conqueror Worm," "Eldorado," "Annabel Lee," many more. Alphabetic lists of titles and first lines. 64pp. 5³⁄₁₆ x 8¼.   26685-0 Pa. $1.00

PERSONAL MEMOIRS OF U. S. GRANT, Ulysses Simpson Grant. Intelligent, deeply moving firsthand account of Civil War campaigns, considered by many the finest military memoirs ever written. Includes letters, historic photographs, maps and more. 528pp. 6⅛ x 9¼.   28587-1 Pa. $12.95

AMULETS AND SUPERSTITIONS, E. A. Wallis Budge. Comprehensive discourse on origin, powers of amulets in many ancient cultures: Arab, Persian Babylonian, Assyrian, Egyptian, Gnostic, Hebrew, Phoenician, Syriac, etc. Covers cross, swastika, crucifix, seals, rings, stones, etc. 584pp. 5⅜ x 8½. 23573-4 Pa. $15.95

RUSSIAN STORIES/PYCCKNE PACCKA3bl: A Dual-Language Book, edited by Gleb Struve. Twelve tales by such masters as Chekhov, Tolstoy, Dostoevsky, Pushkin, others. Excellent word-for-word English translations on facing pages, plus teaching and study aids, Russian/English vocabulary, biographical/critical introductions, more. 416pp. 5⅜ x 8½.   26244-8 Pa. $9.95

PHILADELPHIA THEN AND NOW: 60 Sites Photographed in the Past and Present, Kenneth Finkel and Susan Oyama. Rare photographs of City Hall, Logan Square, Independence Hall, Betsy Ross House, other landmarks juxtaposed with contemporary views. Captures changing face of historic city. Introduction. Captions. 128pp. 8¼ x 11.   25790-8 Pa. $9.95

AIA ARCHITECTURAL GUIDE TO NASSAU AND SUFFOLK COUNTIES, LONG ISLAND, The American Institute of Architects, Long Island Chapter, and the Society for the Preservation of Long Island Antiquities. Comprehensive, well-researched and generously illustrated volume brings to life over three centuries of Long Island's great architectural heritage. More than 240 photographs with authoritative, extensively detailed captions. 176pp. 8¼ x 11.   26946-9 Pa. $14.95

NORTH AMERICAN INDIAN LIFE: Customs and Traditions of 23 Tribes, Elsie Clews Parsons (ed.). 27 fictionalized essays by noted anthropologists examine religion, customs, government, additional facets of life among the Winnebago, Crow, Zuni, Eskimo, other tribes. 480pp. 6⅛ x 9¼.   27377-6 Pa. $10.95

FRANK LLOYD WRIGHT'S HOLLYHOCK HOUSE, Donald Hoffmann. Lavishly illustrated, carefully documented study of one of Wright's most controversial residential designs. Over 120 photographs, floor plans, elevations, etc. Detailed perceptive text by noted Wright scholar. Index. 128pp. 9¼ x 10¾. 27133-1 Pa. $11.95

THE MALE AND FEMALE FIGURE IN MOTION: 60 Classic Photographic Sequences, Eadweard Muybridge. 60 true-action photographs of men and women walking, running, climbing, bending, turning, etc., reproduced from rare 19th-century masterpiece. vi + 121pp. 9 x 12. 24745-7 Pa. $10.95

1001 QUESTIONS ANSWERED ABOUT THE SEASHORE, N. J. Berrill and Jacquelyn Berrill. Queries answered about dolphins, sea snails, sponges, starfish, fishes, shore birds, many others. Covers appearance, breeding, growth, feeding, much more. 305pp. 5¼ x 8¼. 23366-9 Pa. $9.95

GUIDE TO OWL WATCHING IN NORTH AMERICA, Donald S. Heintzelman. Superb guide offers complete data and descriptions of 19 species: barn owl, screech owl, snowy owl, many more. Expert coverage of owl-watching equipment, conservation, migrations and invasions, etc. Guide to observing sites. 84 illustrations. xiii + 193pp. 5⅜ x 8½. 27344-X Pa. $8.95

MEDICINAL AND OTHER USES OF NORTH AMERICAN PLANTS: A Historical Survey with Special Reference to the Eastern Indian Tribes, Charlotte Erichsen-Brown. Chronological historical citations document 500 years of usage of plants, trees, shrubs native to eastern Canada, northeastern U.S. Also complete identifying information. 343 illustrations. 544pp. 6½ x 9¼. 25951-X Pa. $12.95

STORYBOOK MAZES, Dave Phillips. 23 stories and mazes on two-page spreads: Wizard of Oz, Treasure Island, Robin Hood, etc. Solutions. 64pp. 8¼ x 11. 23628-5 Pa. $2.95

NEGRO FOLK MUSIC, U.S.A., Harold Courlander. Noted folklorist's scholarly yet readable analysis of rich and varied musical tradition. Includes authentic versions of over 40 folk songs. Valuable bibliography and discography. xi + 324pp. 5⅜ x 8½. 27350-4 Pa. $9.95

MOVIE-STAR PORTRAITS OF THE FORTIES, John Kobal (ed.). 163 glamor, studio photos of 106 stars of the 1940s: Rita Hayworth, Ava Gardner, Marlon Brando, Clark Gable, many more. 176pp. 8⅜ x 11¼. 23546-7 Pa. $14.95

BENCHLEY LOST AND FOUND, Robert Benchley. Finest humor from early 30s, about pet peeves, child psychologists, post office and others. Mostly unavailable elsewhere. 73 illustrations by Peter Arno and others. 183pp. 5⅜ x 8½. 22410-4 Pa. $6.95

YEKL and THE IMPORTED BRIDEGROOM AND OTHER STORIES OF YIDDISH NEW YORK, Abraham Cahan. Film Hester Street based on Yekl (1896). Novel, other stories among first about Jewish immigrants on N.Y.'s East Side. 240pp. 5⅜ x 8½. 22427-9 Pa. $6.95

SELECTED POEMS, Walt Whitman. Generous sampling from *Leaves of Grass*. Twenty-four poems include "I Hear America Singing," "Song of the Open Road," "I Sing the Body Electric," "When Lilacs Last in the Dooryard Bloom'd," "O Captain! My Captain!"–all reprinted from an authoritative edition. Lists of titles and first lines. 128pp. 5³⁄₁₆ x 8¼. 26878-0 Pa. $1.00

THE BEST TALES OF HOFFMANN, E. T. A. Hoffmann. 10 of Hoffmann's most important stories: "Nutcracker and the King of Mice," "The Golden Flowerpot," etc. 458pp. 5⅜ x 8½.   21793-0 Pa. $9.95

FROM FETISH TO GOD IN ANCIENT EGYPT, E. A. Wallis Budge. Rich detailed survey of Egyptian conception of "God" and gods, magic, cult of animals, Osiris, more. Also, superb English translations of hymns and legends. 240 illustrations. 545pp. 5⅜ x 8½.   25803-3 Pa. $13.95

FRENCH STORIES/CONTES FRANÇAIS: A Dual-Language Book, Wallace Fowlie. Ten stories by French masters, Voltaire to Camus: "Micromegas" by Voltaire; "The Atheist's Mass" by Balzac; "Minuet" by de Maupassant; "The Guest" by Camus, six more. Excellent English translations on facing pages. Also French-English vocabulary list, exercises, more. 352pp. 5⅜ x 8½.   26443-2 Pa. $9.95

CHICAGO AT THE TURN OF THE CENTURY IN PHOTOGRAPHS: 122 Historic Views from the Collections of the Chicago Historical Society, Larry A. Viskochil. Rare large-format prints offer detailed views of City Hall, State Street, the Loop, Hull House, Union Station, many other landmarks, circa 1904-1913. Introduction. Captions. Maps. 144pp. 9⅜ x 12¼.   24656-6 Pa. $12.95

OLD BROOKLYN IN EARLY PHOTOGRAPHS, 1865-1929, William Lee Younger. Luna Park, Gravesend race track, construction of Grand Army Plaza, moving of Hotel Brighton, etc. 157 previously unpublished photographs. 165pp. 8⅞ x 11¾.
23587-4 Pa. $13.95

THE MYTHS OF THE NORTH AMERICAN INDIANS, Lewis Spence. Rich anthology of the myths and legends of the Algonquins, Iroquois, Pawnees and Sioux, prefaced by an extensive historical and ethnological commentary. 36 illustrations. 480pp. 5⅜ x 8½.   25967-6 Pa. $10.95

AN ENCYCLOPEDIA OF BATTLES: Accounts of Over 1,560 Battles from 1479 B.C. to the Present, David Eggenberger. Essential details of every major battle in recorded history from the first battle of Megiddo in 1479 B.C. to Grenada in 1984. List of Battle Maps. New Appendix covering the years 1967-1984. Index. 99 illustrations. 544pp. 6½ x 9¼.   24913-1 Pa. $16.95

SAILING ALONE AROUND THE WORLD, Captain Joshua Slocum. First man to sail around the world, alone, in small boat. One of great feats of seamanship told in delightful manner. 67 illustrations. 294pp. 5⅜ x 8½.   20326-3 Pa. $6.95

ANARCHISM AND OTHER ESSAYS, Emma Goldman. Powerful, penetrating, prophetic essays on direct action, role of minorities, prison reform, puritan hypocrisy, violence, etc. 271pp. 5⅜ x 8½.   22484-8 Pa. $7.95

MYTHS OF THE HINDUS AND BUDDHISTS, Ananda K. Coomaraswamy and Sister Nivedita. Great stories of the epics; deeds of Krishna, Shiva, taken from puranas, Vedas, folk tales; etc. 32 illustrations. 400pp. 5⅜ x 8½.   21759-0 Pa. $12.95

BEYOND PSYCHOLOGY, Otto Rank. Fear of death, desire of immortality, nature of sexuality, social organization, creativity, according to Rankian system. 291pp. 5⅜ x 8½.
20485-5 Pa. $8.95

A THEOLOGICO-POLITICAL TREATISE, Benedict Spinoza. Also contains unfinished Political Treatise. Great classic on religious liberty, theory of government on common consent. R. Elwes translation. Total of 421pp. 5⅜ x 8½. 20249-6 Pa. $9.95

ANATOMY: A Complete Guide for Artists, Joseph Sheppard. A master of figure drawing shows artists how to render human anatomy convincingly. Over 460 illustrations. 224pp. 8⅜ x 11¼. 27279-6 Pa. $11.95

MEDIEVAL CALLIGRAPHY: Its History and Technique, Marc Drogin. Spirited history, comprehensive instruction manual covers 13 styles (ca. 4th century thru 15th). Excellent photographs; directions for duplicating medieval techniques with modern tools. 224pp. 8⅜ x 11¼. 26142-5 Pa. $12.95

DRIED FLOWERS: How to Prepare Them, Sarah Whitlock and Martha Rankin. Complete instructions on how to use silica gel, meal and borax, perlite aggregate, sand and borax, glycerine and water to create attractive permanent flower arrangements. 12 illustrations. 32pp. 5⅜ x 8½. 21802-3 Pa. $1.00

EASY-TO-MAKE BIRD FEEDERS FOR WOODWORKERS, Scott D. Campbell. Detailed, simple-to-use guide for designing, constructing, caring for and using feeders. Text, illustrations for 12 classic and contemporary designs. 96pp. 5⅜ x 8½. 25847-5 Pa. $3.95

SCOTTISH WONDER TALES FROM MYTH AND LEGEND, Donald A. Mackenzie. 16 lively tales tell of giants rumbling down mountainsides, of a magic wand that turns stone pillars into warriors, of gods and goddesses, evil hags, powerful forces and more. 240pp. 5⅜ x 8½. 29677-6 Pa. $6.95

THE HISTORY OF UNDERCLOTHES, C. Willett Cunnington and Phyllis Cunnington. Fascinating, well-documented survey covering six centuries of English undergarments, enhanced with over 100 illustrations: 12th-century laced-up bodice, footed long drawers (1795), 19th-century bustles, l9th-century corsets for men, Victorian "bust improvers," much more. 272pp. 5⅜ x 8¼. 27124-2 Pa. $9.95

ARTS AND CRAFTS FURNITURE: The Complete Brooks Catalog of 1912, Brooks Manufacturing Co. Photos and detailed descriptions of more than 150 now very collectible furniture designs from the Arts and Crafts movement depict davenports, settees, buffets, desks, tables, chairs, bedsteads, dressers and more, all built of solid, quarter-sawed oak. Invaluable for students and enthusiasts of antiques, Americana and the decorative arts. 80pp. 6½ x 9¼. 27471-3 Pa. $8.95

HOW WE INVENTED THE AIRPLANE: An Illustrated History, Orville Wright. Fascinating firsthand account covers early experiments, construction of planes and motors, first flights, much more. Introduction and commentary by Fred C. Kelly. 76 photographs. 96pp. 8¼ x 11. 25662-6 Pa. $8.95

THE ARTS OF THE SAILOR: Knotting, Splicing and Ropework, Hervey Garrett Smith. Indispensable shipboard reference covers tools, basic knots and useful hitches; handsewing and canvas work, more. Over 100 illustrations. Delightful reading for sea lovers. 256pp. 5⅜ x 8½. 26440-8 Pa. $8.95

FRANK LLOYD WRIGHT'S FALLINGWATER: The House and Its History, Second, Revised Edition, Donald Hoffmann. A total revision—both in text and illustrations—of the standard document on Fallingwater, the boldest, most personal architectural statement of Wright's mature years, updated with valuable new material from the recently opened Frank Lloyd Wright Archives. "Fascinating"–*The New York Times*. 116 illustrations. 128pp. 9¼ x 10¾. 27430-6 Pa. $12.95

CATALOG OF DOVER BOOKS

PHOTOGRAPHIC SKETCHBOOK OF THE CIVIL WAR, Alexander Gardner. 100 photos taken on field during the Civil War. Famous shots of Manassas Harper's Ferry, Lincoln, Richmond, slave pens, etc. 244pp. 10⅝ x 8¼.   22731-6 Pa. $10.95

FIVE ACRES AND INDEPENDENCE, Maurice G. Kains. Great back-to-the-land classic explains basics of self-sufficient farming. The one book to get. 95 illustrations. 397pp. 5⅜ x 8½.   20974-1 Pa. $7.95

SONGS OF EASTERN BIRDS, Dr. Donald J. Borror. Songs and calls of 60 species most common to eastern U.S.: warblers, woodpeckers, flycatchers, thrushes, larks, many more in high-quality recording.   Cassette and manual 99912-2 $9.95

A MODERN HERBAL, Margaret Grieve. Much the fullest, most exact, most useful compilation of herbal material. Gigantic alphabetical encyclopedia, from aconite to zedoary, gives botanical information, medical properties, folklore, economic uses, much else. Indispensable to serious reader. 161 illustrations. 888pp. 6½ x 9¼. 2-vol. set. (USO)   Vol. I: 22798-7 Pa. $9.95
Vol. II: 22799-5 Pa. $9.95

HIDDEN TREASURE MAZE BOOK, Dave Phillips. Solve 34 challenging mazes accompanied by heroic tales of adventure. Evil dragons, people-eating plants, blood-thirsty giants, many more dangerous adversaries lurk at every twist and turn. 34 mazes, stories, solutions. 48pp. 8¼ x 11.   24566-7 Pa. $2.95

LETTERS OF W. A. MOZART, Wolfgang A. Mozart. Remarkable letters show bawdy wit, humor, imagination, musical insights, contemporary musical world; includes some letters from Leopold Mozart. 276pp. 5⅜ x 8½.   22859-2 Pa. $7.95

BASIC PRINCIPLES OF CLASSICAL BALLET, Agrippina Vaganova. Great Russian theoretician, teacher explains methods for teaching classical ballet. 118 illus-trations. 175pp. 5⅜ x 8½.   22036-2 Pa. $5.95

THE JUMPING FROG, Mark Twain. Revenge edition. The original story of The Celebrated Jumping Frog of Calaveras County, a hapless French translation, and Twain's hilarious "retranslation" from the French. 12 illustrations. 66pp. 5⅜ x 8½.
22686-7 Pa. $3.95

BEST REMEMBERED POEMS, Martin Gardner (ed.). The 126 poems in this superb collection of 19th- and 20th-century British and American verse range from Shelley's "To a Skylark" to the impassioned "Renascence" of Edna St. Vincent Millay and to Edward Lear's whimsical "The Owl and the Pussycat." 224pp. 5⅜ x 8½.
27165-X Pa. $5.95

COMPLETE SONNETS, William Shakespeare. Over 150 exquisite poems deal with love, friendship, the tyranny of time, beauty's evanescence, death and other themes in language of remarkable power, precision and beauty. Glossary of archaic terms. 80pp. 5³⁄₁₆ x 8¼.   26686-9 Pa. $1.00

BODIES IN A BOOKSHOP, R. T. Campbell. Challenging mystery of blackmail and murder with ingenious plot and superbly drawn characters. In the best tradition of British suspense fiction. 192pp. 5⅜ x 8½.   24720-1 Pa. $6.95

THE WIT AND HUMOR OF OSCAR WILDE, Alvin Redman (ed.). More than 1,000 ripostes, paradoxes, wisecracks: Work is the curse of the drinking classes; I can resist everything except temptation; etc. 258pp. 5⅜ x 8½. 20602-5 Pa. $6.95

SHAKESPEARE LEXICON AND QUOTATION DICTIONARY, Alexander Schmidt. Full definitions, locations, shades of meaning in every word in plays and poems. More than 50,000 exact quotations. 1,485pp. 6½ x 9¼. 2-vol. set.
Vol. 1: 22726-X Pa. $17.95
Vol. 2: 22727-8 Pa. $17.95

SELECTED POEMS, Emily Dickinson. Over 100 best-known, best-loved poems by one of America's foremost poets, reprinted from authoritative early editions. No comparable edition at this price. Index of first lines. 64pp. 5³⁄₁₆ x 8¼. 26466-1 Pa. $1.00

CELEBRATED CASES OF JUDGE DEE (DEE GOONG AN), translated by Robert van Gulik. Authentic 18th-century Chinese detective novel; Dee and associates solve three interlocked cases. Led to van Gulik's own stories with same characters. Extensive introduction. 9 illustrations. 237pp. 5⅜ x 8½. 23337-5 Pa. $7.95

THE MALLEUS MALEFICARUM OF KRAMER AND SPRENGER, translated by Montague Summers. Full text of most important witchhunter's "bible," used by both Catholics and Protestants. 278pp. 6⅝ x 10. 22802-9 Pa. $12.95

SPANISH STORIES/CUENTOS ESPAÑOLES: A Dual-Language Book, Angel Flores (ed.). Unique format offers 13 great stories in Spanish by Cervantes, Borges, others. Faithful English translations on facing pages. 352pp. 5⅜ x 8½. 25399-6 Pa. $8.95

THE CHICAGO WORLD'S FAIR OF 1893: A Photographic Record, Stanley Appelbaum (ed.). 128 rare photos show 200 buildings, Beaux-Arts architecture, Midway, original Ferris Wheel, Edison's kinetoscope, more. Architectural emphasis; full text. 116pp. 8¼ x 11. 23990-X Pa. $9.95

OLD QUEENS, N.Y., IN EARLY PHOTOGRAPHS, Vincent F. Seyfried and William Asadorian. Over 160 rare photographs of Maspeth, Jamaica, Jackson Heights, and other areas. Vintage views of DeWitt Clinton mansion, 1939 World's Fair and more. Captions. 192pp. 8⅞ x 11. 26358-4 Pa. $12.95

CAPTURED BY THE INDIANS: 15 Firsthand Accounts, 1750-1870, Frederick Drimmer. Astounding true historical accounts of grisly torture, bloody conflicts, relentless pursuits, miraculous escapes and more, by people who lived to tell the tale. 384pp. 5⅜ x 8½. 24901-8 Pa. $8.95

THE WORLD'S GREAT SPEECHES, Lewis Copeland and Lawrence W. Lamm (eds.). Vast collection of 278 speeches of Greeks to 1970. Powerful and effective models; unique look at history. 842pp. 5⅜ x 8½. 20468-5 Pa. $14.95

THE BOOK OF THE SWORD, Sir Richard F. Burton. Great Victorian scholar/adventurer's eloquent, erudite history of the "queen of weapons"—from prehistory to early Roman Empire. Evolution and development of early swords, variations (sabre, broadsword, cutlass, scimitar, etc.), much more. 336pp. 6⅛ x 9¼. 25434-8 Pa. $9.95

AUTOBIOGRAPHY: The Story of My Experiments with Truth, Mohandas K. Gandhi. Boyhood, legal studies, purification, the growth of the Satyagraha (nonviolent protest) movement. Critical, inspiring work of the man responsible for the freedom of India. 480pp. 5⅜ x 8½. (USO) 24593-4 Pa. $8.95

CELTIC MYTHS AND LEGENDS, T. W. Rolleston. Masterful retelling of Irish and Welsh stories and tales. Cuchulain, King Arthur, Deirdre, the Grail, many more. First paperback edition. 58 full-page illustrations. 512pp. 5⅜ x 8½. 26507-2 Pa. $9.95

THE PRINCIPLES OF PSYCHOLOGY, William James. Famous long course complete, unabridged. Stream of thought, time perception, memory, experimental methods; great work decades ahead of its time. 94 figures. 1,391pp. 5⅜ x 8½. 2-vol. set.
Vol. I: 20381-6 Pa. $13.95
Vol. II: 20382-4 Pa. $14.95

THE WORLD AS WILL AND REPRESENTATION, Arthur Schopenhauer. Definitive English translation of Schopenhauer's life work, correcting more than 1,000 errors, omissions in earlier translations. Translated by E. F. J. Payne. Total of 1,269pp. 5⅜ x 8½. 2-vol. set. Vol. 1: 21761-2 Pa. $12.95
Vol. 2: 21762-0 Pa. $12.95

MAGIC AND MYSTERY IN TIBET, Madame Alexandra David-Neel. Experiences among lamas, magicians, sages, sorcerers, Bonpa wizards. A true psychic discovery. 32 illustrations. 321pp. 5⅜ x 8½. (USO) 22682-4 Pa. $9.95

THE EGYPTIAN BOOK OF THE DEAD, E. A. Wallis Budge. Complete reproduction of Ani's papyrus, finest ever found. Full hieroglyphic text, interlinear transliteration, word-for-word translation, smooth translation. 533pp. 6½ x 9¼.
21866-X Pa. $11.95

MATHEMATICS FOR THE NONMATHEMATICIAN, Morris Kline. Detailed, college-level treatment of mathematics in cultural and historical context, with numerous exercises. Recommended Reading Lists. Tables. Numerous figures. 641pp. 5⅜ x 8½.
24823-2 Pa. $11.95

THEORY OF WING SECTIONS: Including a Summary of Airfoil Data, Ira H. Abbott and A. E. von Doenhoff. Concise compilation of subsonic aerodynamic characteristics of NACA wing sections, plus description of theory. 350pp. of tables. 693pp. 5⅜ x 8½. 60586-8 Pa. $14.95

THE RIME OF THE ANCIENT MARINER, Gustave Doré, S. T. Coleridge. Doré's finest work; 34 plates capture moods, subtleties of poem. Flawless full-size reproductions printed on facing pages with authoritative text of poem. "Beautiful. Simply beautiful."–*Publisher's Weekly.* 77pp. 9¼ x 12. 22305-1 Pa. $7.95

NORTH AMERICAN INDIAN DESIGNS FOR ARTISTS AND CRAFTSPEOPLE, Eva Wilson. Over 360 authentic copyright-free designs adapted from Navajo blankets, Hopi pottery, Sioux buffalo hides, more. Geometrics, symbolic figures, plant and animal motifs, etc. 128pp. 8⅜ x 11. (EUK) 25341-4 Pa. $8.95

SCULPTURE: Principles and Practice, Louis Slobodkin. Step-by-step approach to clay, plaster, metals, stone; classical and modern. 253 drawings, photos. 255pp. 8⅛ x 11.
22960-2 Pa. $11.95

THE INFLUENCE OF SEA POWER UPON HISTORY, 1660–1783, A. T. Mahan. Influential classic of naval history and tactics still used as text in war colleges. First paperback edition. 4 maps. 24 battle plans. 640pp. 5⅜ x 8½. 25509-3 Pa. $14.95

THE STORY OF THE TITANIC AS TOLD BY ITS SURVIVORS, Jack Winocour (ed.). What it was really like. Panic, despair, shocking inefficiency, and a little heroism. More thrilling than any fictional account. 26 illustrations. 320pp. 5⅜ x 8½. 20610-6 Pa. $8.95

FAIRY AND FOLK TALES OF THE IRISH PEASANTRY, William Butler Yeats (ed.). Treasury of 64 tales from the twilight world of Celtic myth and legend: "The Soul Cages," "The Kildare Pooka," "King O'Toole and his Goose," many more. Introduction and Notes by W. B. Yeats. 352pp. 5⅜ x 8½. 26941-8 Pa. $8.95

BUDDHIST MAHAYANA TEXTS, E. B. Cowell and Others (eds.). Superb, accurate translations of basic documents in Mahayana Buddhism, highly important in history of religions. The Buddha-karita of Asvaghosha, Larger Sukhavativyuha, more. 448pp. 5⅜ x 8½. 25552-2 Pa. $12.95

ONE TWO THREE . . . INFINITY: Facts and Speculations of Science, George Gamow. Great physicist's fascinating, readable overview of contemporary science: number theory, relativity, fourth dimension, entropy, genes, atomic structure, much more. 128 illustrations. Index. 352pp. 5⅜ x 8½. 25664-2 Pa. $8.95

ENGINEERING IN HISTORY, Richard Shelton Kirby, et al. Broad, nontechnical survey of history's major technological advances: birth of Greek science, industrial revolution, electricity and applied science, 20th-century automation, much more. 181 illustrations. ". . . excellent . . ."—*Isis*. Bibliography. vii + 530pp. 5⅜ x 8¼. 26412-2 Pa. $14.95

DALÍ ON MODERN ART: The Cuckolds of Antiquated Modern Art, Salvador Dalí. Influential painter skewers modern art and its practitioners. Outrageous evaluations of Picasso, Cézanne, Turner, more. 15 renderings of paintings discussed. 44 calligraphic decorations by Dalí. 96pp. 5⅜ x 8½. (USO) 29220-7 Pa. $4.95

ANTIQUE PLAYING CARDS: A Pictorial History, Henry René D'Allemagne. Over 900 elaborate, decorative images from rare playing cards (14th–20th centuries): Bacchus, death, dancing dogs, hunting scenes, royal coats of arms, players cheating, much more. 96pp. 9¼ x 12¼. 29265-7 Pa. $12.95

MAKING FURNITURE MASTERPIECES: 30 Projects with Measured Drawings, Franklin H. Gottshall. Step-by-step instructions, illustrations for constructing handsome, useful pieces, among them a Sheraton desk, Chippendale chair, Spanish desk, Queen Anne table and a William and Mary dressing mirror. 224pp. 8⅛ x 11¼. 29338-6 Pa. $13.95

THE FOSSIL BOOK: A Record of Prehistoric Life, Patricia V. Rich et al. Profusely illustrated definitive guide covers everything from single-celled organisms and dinosaurs to birds and mammals and the interplay between climate and man. Over 1,500 illustrations. 760pp. 7½ x 10⅛. 29371-8 Pa. $29.95